DIVINE AGENCY AND DIVINE ACTION

Divine Agency and Divine Action

VOLUME III

Systematic Theology

WILLIAM J. ABRAHAM

OXFORD

UNIVERSITY PRESS

OXFORD

UNIVERSITY PRESS

Great Clarendon Street, Oxford, OX2 6DP,
United Kingdom

Oxford University Press is a department of the University of Oxford.
It furthers the University's objective of excellence in research, scholarship,
and education by publishing worldwide. Oxford is a registered trade mark of
Oxford University Press in the UK and in certain other countries

First Edition published in 2018

Impression: 1

Published in the United States of America by Oxford University Press
198 Madison Avenue, New York, NY 10016, United States of America

British Library Cataloguing in Publication Data
Data available

Library of Congress Control Number: 2018945757

ISBN 978-0-19-878652-8

Printed and bound by
CPI Group (UK) Ltd, Croydon, CR0 4YY

To Patrick Roche

Acknowledgments

I offer heartfelt thanks for all those who have contributed to this work. I would never have begun it without the models provided by Schubert Ogden and John Deschner of Perkins School of Theology. They opened a door at a timely moment when we needed an extra hand to teach systematics; my life has never been the same, even though I retained the earlier interests that drove my research and writing. The many students that I have taught at Perkins across the years have also been instrumental in forcing me to think things through to the bottom. I will always be in debt to the network of doctoral students I have taught; I especially thank Paul Gavrilyuk for the help in sorting out the Christological developments across the ecumenical councils that I chart in Chapter 5. My colleagues at Perkins have been uniformly encouraging even when they have not known what to make of my intellectual interests and commitments. I record again the inspiration that initially came from two sabbatical years at the Center for Philosophy of Religion at the University of Notre Dame. I thank Professor Michael Rea and his team for the resources and help made available. I thank Fellipe do Vale for the invaluable help in proof-reading and David Moser for the splendid work on editing, proof-reading, and indexing. I thank the ordinary folk back in Ireland who won me to faith in Jesus Christ and set my mind on my way in love and freedom. Finally, I thank the wonderful folk in my Adult Sunday Morning classes over the years at Highland Park United Methodist Church, Dallas, for making me wrestle week in and week out with the manifold riches of Scripture. Theology lives off Scripture, even as it goes beyond its treasures; they have enacted those treasures in ways that bring joy to my heart and life.

Contents

Introduction

Orientation

I know my own poverty and both my conscience and my vice-stained mind fill me with remorse; and my many sins make this great work a difficult undertaking for me.

Simon Azar'in, cellarer of the Trinity-Saint-Sergius Monastery, 1646.

This volume represents the third in a tetralogy dealing with fundamental questions about divine agency and divine action. The first reviewed the debate about divine action that arose at Oxford in the 1950s and at Chicago in the 1960s. The basic argument there is that efforts to secure a closed concept of action and the correlative efforts to identify and solve "the problem of divine action" were a dead end. There is no closed conception of action and, even if there was, it would not help us understand—beyond a mere account of the necessary and sufficient conditions of every action—the network of specific divine actions that show up in the Christian tradition. Once we get rid of this mental cramp, we realize that when we start looking at the specific actions attributed to God then we are in fact doing theology. The whole debate over the last century has taken place in a kind of self-imposed island cut off from the mainland to which it was originally attached.

Hence, the second volume took a series of soundings in the history of the Christian tradition in order to immerse ourselves in a much richer body of material and reflection that was not handicapped by our wayward contemporary worries. So, I ran a series of field-tests from Paul to Molina in order to furnish the discussion with a sense of the diverse set of questions that actually and rightly arises in debates about divine action. For example, I looked at divine inspiration in Irenaeus and Origen, the problem of freedom and grace in Augustine, transubstantiation in Aquinas, and divine locutions in Teresa of Avila. This was a wonderfully enriching exercise, for it opened up vistas on divine action in the history of Christian theology that can operate as paradigms of salutary reflection. The focus was in part historical for I wanted to find out how past theologians thought and reasoned; however, the angle of vision was also one of doctrinal criticism, for it was clear from the start that there were at times acute problems in what was presented.

In this volume, I move entirely into my own voice and into a prescriptive mode. It has long been clear that Christian systematic theology has a very definite center of gravity; the intention is to understand what God has done in creation and redemption. So, all along I planned a volume in systematic theology that would take divine agency and divine action as its center of gravity. Nowadays, the emphasis on divine agency and divine action is often expressed by saying that Christianity operates as a story that runs from creation to final consummation in the life to come. I do not reject this theme but it too readily becomes a kind of mantra that masks more than it reveals. Thus, it evades, for example, radical questions about the truth of the story and how it is to be defended intellectually. It tends either to offer a simplistic answer to the epistemological issues that need to be addressed or it evades them entirely. Yet there are difficulties in the neighborhood for systematic theology. If the systematic theologian really takes up the full gamut of questions in the epistemology of theology, then theology proper, that is, full-bodied articulation of the central themes of systematic theology, can readily get short-changed. The solution to this challenge is to address it head-on and go to work on the epistemology of theology as a new sub-discipline in the borderlands between theology and philosophy.

The worries about the truth claims of the Christian tradition bring to light a further difficulty that needs to be identified, namely, how we should conceive systematic theology as a constructive operation in its own right. We face at this point a fascinating paradox. We live in a golden period of academic work in theological studies. The various departments in theological studies are flourishing. So, we have an abundance of work in biblical studies, the history of the church and of doctrine, practical theology, philosophy of religion, and so on. Indeed, there is so much work and so many angles of vision in play that it is easy to be completely disoriented in systematic theology. To be sure, there is plenty of lamentation about the sad state of theological studies and the disarray it displays, but this manifests much too gloomy a response.

Premodern theology was for the most part systematic theology conceived in broad terms. It was interested in the big questions about the nature of God, creation, redemption, the life to come, and so on. All this has been shattered in the modern period and the arrival of postmodernity has simply pushed us out of the frying pan into the fire. I sensed the disarray in theology right from the beginning of my academic studies when I majored in philosophy and psychology. After the rigors of experimental work in psychology and of analytical thinking in philosophy, I found much of what I encountered in contemporary systematic theology intellectually disappointing in terms of rigor and more generally in terms of substance. It took time to figure out how to read such work; and it took longer to come to terms with the rigor of work in the premodern period. My initial response to this was to stick with philosophy of religion and ethics, take up the other assignments in the study of evangelism and Methodist studies that had been added to my portfolio, and give up entirely on systematic theology. However, from the beginning I was interested in questions about God, so I could not let go of the questions that kept me awake at night and that deeply affected my life and my work in the church. Even when not working in systematic theology I was always circling back to the great themes it explored. I kept alive my interest in divine agency and divine action but kept my distance from systematic theology as best I could.

When the opportunity to take up formal work in systematic theology came more or less by accident, I was as puzzled as ever as to how to proceed. However, the curriculum into which I stepped was very clear on several fronts. First, in systematic theology it was crucial in the end to speak in one's own voice; second, there was a clear set of themes in systematic theology that ran from prolegomena to eschatology that required attention; and third, colleagues with whom I worked were very clear that the enterprise was deadly serious both in its content and in its significance for the life of faith and the life of the church. It took time to get my bearings, for I continued my work in philosophy of religion, not least on issues related to the epistemology of theology. Happily, I had long before discovered that there were issues within systematic theology that benefited from serious work in analytic philosophy.

Returning to the topic of disarray in theological studies, it is obvious that the Christian tradition has long been in crisis since it lost its place in the social and political life of the West. One can trace this in various ways; my favored narrative works through the epistemological crisis that arrived with the Reformation and then played itself out in secular and post-Christian forms, initially in Europe and then on a global scale. One can speak of this as a crisis of identity as Christians have sought to negotiate their place in a world that looks upon Christianity at best as passé and at worst as intolerant and even poisonous. My own special interest was the place that historical investigation played both in understanding and in undermining the deep faith of the church, especially as it was applied to Scripture. The narrative can easily be extended to take on board developments in science, in philosophy, and in politics. There is no need to rehearse the story of decline, as the death of Christendom is now readily acknowledged. It is much less clear how we should respond to this massive challenge. Current efforts to look again at the Reformation and its aftermath bring the challenge back on the table in fresh and interesting ways.

As I have worked through the research agenda related to the present volumes, it has become clear to me that the agenda is one effort to work through to a future that will be spiritually nourishing, intellectually defensible, and fruitful for the church. In the end the work involved cannot avoid being theologically prescriptive in nature. The challenge is to speak of God with passion and intellectual boldness. Iain Provan, in a splendid contribution to the significance of the Reformation, provides a handy map that is worth pondering at this point.[1] His focus is less on work in systematic theology and more on the challenge of a proper reading of Scripture; however, his taxonomy is well worth pondering. The focus on Scripture reflects his own effort to appropriate crucial elements that came to birth at the Reformation. His interest in both the nature of historical investigation and in the wider cultural developments after Christendom dovetail with my own; so, it will be helpful to indicate the main options he identifies in order to place my own work by way of comparison.

Provan gives us five options. First, we can follow through on developments in the historical study of Scripture and see where that takes us. Clearly, no Christian theologian can ignore the study of Scripture. Provan's worry is that much that happens in biblical studies prevents Scripture from speaking to the church; and even where it may do so, biblical scholars are not too sure that God really does speak to us today in Scripture. Second, we can opt for a postmodern reading of Scripture where Scripture is seen as an artifact and is studied with a minimum of interest in theology; in fact, God tends not to refer to a person, but to call for justice. Clearly, while making the rounds in some "emergent" church circles, this approach will bear limited fruit by way of serious content. Third, we can take what he calls the "Chicago" option and dig in for a long-haul fight with modernity and postmodernity, seeing the latter as the fundamental cause of the misfortunes that have befallen Christianity over the last three centuries. The plan is to double down on doctrines of inerrancy and opt for a continuation of a very particular rendering of the Reformation that focuses on one interpretation of its doctrine of Scripture. Provan clearly rejects this option, noting its failure to deal with a more nuanced account of the Reformation option on Scripture and its failure to recognize that many of the causes of the misfortunes of the Christian faith arise from problems within theology, not outside theology. Fourth, we can opt for a counter-Reformational Protestantism that gives a richer place for tradition, for spiritual readings of texts, and even for the adoption of Neoplatonism as the way forward. Here the difficulties begin with a much too negative reading of Protestantism and a readiness to move away from exact, "literal" readings of the biblical text. And turning the clock back to Plato repeats the perennial mistake of looking to some great philosopher to save the day.

Provan's own fifth way does not lend itself to easy description, but at its heart it involves a retrieval of the Reformers' emphasis on Scripture as the norm of Christian theology and on the perspicuity of Scripture on pertinent matters of faith and practice. He defends the former by a fresh reading of the

---

[1] Iain Provan, *The Reformation and the Right Reading of Scripture* (Waco, TX: Baylor University Press, 2017).

patristic evidence on the place of Scripture in theology and the latter by a wide-ranging discussion of hermeneutical practice. He thus paves the way for a fresh appropriation of a confessional theology that is robustly rooted in the teaching of Magisterial Protestants. Taken as a whole, it is a first-rate volume written with passion, erudition, and intellectual depth. I predict that it will have a significant impact, not least on evangelicals in the Reformed tradition; and it will provide a deep defense of crucial elements in the big story that he sees as the heart of the teaching of Scripture.

I share Provan's depiction of the current scene within Protestantism; we face afresh the crisis that arose with the loss of the Christian tradition in Western culture. I make no claim to have solved it, even as I have come to recognize my own affinities with many of his concerns. Thus, I share his positive account of the place of historical study in understanding Scripture, his claim that much of the misfortune we experience is of our own making, and that the way forward for a doctrine of Scripture is to see its primary role to be soteriological. I also agree that the other four options that he identifies are less than compelling. I see much of his work as complementing my own, even as I acknowledge that he has many irons in the fire that are not front and center in my own work. However, the journey I propose is significantly different and will help readers see where they are headed in this volume. Perhaps the following will help the reader become better oriented for what follows.

First, in order to sort through any appeal to Scripture, the real issue is how we think through the topic of divine revelation and the wider debates in the epistemology of theology. Thus, we need more than a better account of how to read Scripture. We need to tackle the nature of warrant in theology and then return afresh to Scripture and its place in theology. Provan is illuminating on the former issue: our reading of texts in their historical settings. He tends to reiterate the standard account of canon and roots it in a conventional interpretation of the patristic materials. My own account of canon is significantly different and takes much more seriously the diversity of patristic appeals to Scripture and ancillary commitments. There are watershed issues here; it is not likely that we will reach agreement; however, how we resolve them is critical for the shape and content of theology as a whole. Both of us look to continuity with the patristic era but we have very different understandings of what that means.

Second, we need a more apt way to deal with the role of the creeds in systematic theology. The classical creeds are not just handy summaries of Scripture; and they are much more important for understanding the genesis of systematic theology than is commonly recognized. So too, more generally for the place of tradition in theology. In this latter domain, much greater attention needs to be given initially to developments in the Eastern tradition; we need to transcend the typical standoff between Rome, Geneva, and Wittenberg that has come back to life in current treatments of the Reformation. Equally, far more attention needs to be given to Methodism and its offspring; the tendency of Magisterial Protestants to blame all sorts of ills on pietism and revivalism should have been abandoned a long time ago but it lingers on, in part because of an enormous lacuna in historical studies that shows no sign of repair. This is unfortunate because the demographic changes in contemporary Christianity show that there is enormous vitality in traditions that stem from what we might call the Methodist underworld.

Third, if we are to deal with the crisis in the life and work of the church, then we need to come to terms with the place of systematic theology in the training of church leaders. At the moment, many theologians come close to despising the life of the church and her clergy. They set up a bogus disjunction between "academic theology" and the training of church leaders. The systematic effort on the part of scholars in religious studies to banish theology from the university is also a critical element in the pathology involved. Not surprisingly, some church leaders return the compliment by cutting themselves off from rigorous work in theological studies. The results are disastrous. Provan notes the ruinous consequences for learning the biblical languages. However, the damage extends across the board, not least into serious work in philosophy and in philosophy of religion. The damage envisaged here is broadly academic and intellectual in nature.

Equally noteworthy is the damage done in the church at large when the vacuum is filled by mega-church pastors and other self-appointed gurus who become the real teachers of local clergy. Some of these populists are brilliant in their own way and most of them have the best intentions, even though the temptation to succumb to messianic ambitions is all too visible. Yet they tend to provide ephemeral solutions that readily assimilate some of the worst elements of contemporary culture; high-intensity piety tied to half-baked theology is not exactly what we need in the long run. The solution to our challenges is not to appoint a new set of "epistocrats" to lead the church, that is, a self-appointed academic elite who are entrusted with the public authority to lecture the church on what to do in the ongoing crises of legitimacy and fruitful practice. As Josiah Ober has noted in another context, "That solution is unrealistic. Like Plato before them, twenty-first century epistocrats lack any feasible plan for convincing an ignorant democratic majority to submit peacefully to the rule of a putative wise majority."[2] In the end the church is utterly dependent on God for her life and her survival; epistocrats in the theological arena are often more of a menace than a solution to the problems we face. At best, academics are like royalty; they should be locked away, brought out when needed, and then sent back to prepare for the next occasion when summoned to offer advice. We need local and national church leadership whose first love

---

[2] Josiah Ober, *Demopolis: Democracy before Liberalism in Theory and Practice* (Cambridge: Cambridge University Press, 2017), 179–80.

is the love of God and who have learned to teach the ways of God in a complex and often hostile world inside and outside the church. But, this is just a fancy way of saying we need the treasures of systematic theology if the church is to flourish and be faithful to the Gospel. It is not enough to hand over this work to those who have mastered the original languages of Scripture; this is but one element in the toolkit that is needed.

We can come at the problem from another angle. What is at stake is the extraordinary intellectual demands that are laid upon scholars who work in systematic theology. There are standard ways of coping that are worth noting. One is to turn theology into an exercise in confessional repetition and hermeneutics, shoring up its claims with a fresh round of biblical exegesis. Another is to reduce theology to a sub-discipline in history by returning to some great figure of the past, say, Rahner, Barth, or Aquinas, or Wesley, or Maximus, or whoever, and sheltering within his shadow. Another is to fall in line with this or that political project, or with the pursuits of some favored interest group, and move forward as best we can. Yet another is to draw on the resources of a favored secular discipline, say, philosophy or cultural studies, and use their assets to fill out a chosen theological theme or network of themes. Perhaps the most ambitious plan of all is to develop a *théologie totale* in which every possible avenue of investigation is brought to bear on the great themes of systematic theology.

All of these projects yield their own harvests of fruit for good or ill. They will be and should be pursued with flair. Yet they intentionally or unintentionally draw us away from the realistic formation of church leaders who are at the front lines in the teaching of Christian theology. This strikes me as disastrous in the end for the crisis we face. Failure at this level will guarantee failure to tackle the wider crisis of the breakdown of Christendom; we will have generals galore but no foot soldiers. Moreover, systematic theology is related to the formation of clergy just as medicine is tied to the formation of doctors. If we do not have robust formation in systematic theology, we will ensure widespread malpractice in the church. The cure of souls will become a dangerous enterprise. Thus, in this volume I have sought to practice a form of systematic theology that is fitting for this task without losing its moorings in the life of the academy.

This is not the place to offer a defense of what I have done. In the end, any practice justifies itself by its fruit; so, I am happy to let the practice speak for itself. Suffice it to say at this stage that the issue of the nature of systematic theology and its methods is taken up formally in the two chapters on prolegomena. I argue there for a conception of systematic theology that is deflationary. By deflationary I mean here a systematic theology that avoids being distracted by the host of ancillary questions, say, in exegesis, history, epistemology, metaphysics, cultural studies, and the like. I desire to speak directly and frankly about God in his amazing work of creation and redemption. And we cannot speak of God in a neutral tone of voice; we are not dealing here with a prosaic item like a cat on a mat, or a complex item, like a quark or the intricacy of constitutional law. We are dealing with our extraordinary Creator and Savior, with nothing less than the God who is named as Father, Son, and Holy Spirit and upon whom we depend for the very air we breathe. This is a daring and dangerous enterprise that we approach in fear and trembling, and with joy and adoration. Only after we have come to terms with this basic material can we speak of everything else in so far as it relates to God. To this end I argue that the heart of systematic theology has rightly been located in the standard loci or themes that show up in systematic theology, running from the doctrine of God, through Christology, pneumatology, divine creation, divine providence, human nature, ecclesiology, salvation, and eschatology. These are not a ragbag of themes cobbled together for convenience; they constitute the bricks and mortar of the trade. I do not follow slavishly the emphasis on divine agency and divine action but deploy appropriate ruminations on these where relevant; thus, there is an obvious center of gravity in the work as a whole. There is a natural flow from one topic to the next which also reflects the flow of divine action from creation to consummation in the life to come.

I have kept the footnotes to a minimum; I do not want to clutter the text with endless references that will distract the reader from entering into conversation with the text in hand. Think of taking a journey into a new world where we visit a network of distinct parks with their own flora and fauna. Or think of this work as an invitation to enter a conversation with a friend whose aim eventually is to evoke further investigation and reflection. I have no interest in writing several volumes of the kind that have been common in the past, much as I have learned from such materials. I aim at a volume that can stand alone and that will provide the reader with a rounded account of Christian teaching that is formative for their journey of faith and a platform for work across the board in theological studies.

I also want to write a volume that is genuinely helpful for the formation of church leaders. The other volumes in the tetralogy provide a prelude and postlude for the work here. The first volume sorts out the tangled debate about divine agency and divine action without which we will be severely handicapped conceptually and historically. The second volume provides a rich immersion in debates about specific divine action up to the modern period. The fourth will take up some central questions that are thrown up by systematic theology as I conceive it. However, to constantly step aside and deal with these would be a distraction. Perhaps the most important issue to tackle is my claim that God is best conceived as an Agent. For this volume, it is essentially a matter of first things first. We need a manageable treatment of the great themes of Christian theology that boldly speaks directly about God with intellectual depth and clarity. This deflationary vision of systematic theology has significant implications for curricular changes but sufficient unto the day are the troubles thereof.

1

Prolegomena

Systematic Theology as Christian Instruction

> Therefore let us go on toward perfection, leaving behind the basic teaching about Christ, and not laying again the foundation: repentance from dead works and faith toward God, instructions about baptisms, laying on of hands, resurrection from the dead, and eternal judgment. And we will do this if God permits.
>
> Hebrews 6:1–3.

Systematic theology, I propose, is formally an exercise in university-level, post-baptismal Christian instruction. Materially, systematic theology is a deep, contemporary articulation of the Christian faith in terms that focus on divine agency and divine action. Both of these claims are contentious, the first much more so than the second, so let me begin by tackling the rationale for this surprisingly deflationary vision of Christian theology. Happily, the rationale will enable me to defend very briefly and effectively the second, that is, the focus on divine agency and divine action.

Contemporary systematic theologians are faced at the outset with a dilemma at the core of their work. On the one hand, they are committed to certain essential themes that are well known: creation, redemption, the church, the last things, and so on. There is a conventional network of topics or loci that stretches from creation to eschatology. One naturally asks: Where do these come from? How come we all agree that these topics have to be covered? Why don't we leave the theologian to develop his or her own themes?

When I first started thinking seriously about systematic theology, I came up with a totally different schema for systematics.[1] It came as a shock to me that this was not allowed. Naturally, I started ruminating on how on earth we

---

[1] The schema that I liked was one that ran the following topics: background beliefs about creation, the uniqueness of human agents, a diagnosis of what has gone wrong, a prescription on how to put things right, a vision of the future, and an appropriate ethics that fitted the foregoing vision as a whole.

ended up with the themes we do have. The best answer I know to this question is historical. The answer is simple: the classical loci or topics of systematic theology clearly reflect the various articles of the Apostles' and Nicene creeds. The standard topics arise naturally once the new convert begins to inhabit the fresh new world of the creeds, as they run through a narrative of what God has done and will do from creation through surprising restoration all the way to final consummation in the world to come.[2] Hence, adoption of these themes is embarrassingly and critically dependent on the creeds; it is the creeds that lie in the background and without them the choice of loci ceases to make sense.

On the other hand, the contemporary systematic theologian cannot really start from anything even indirectly related to the creeds with a good conscience. If we do, we are immediately thought of as being archaic, of being hopelessly repetitive, and, surely, worst of all, doomed to begging the whole question of truth from the outset. A minority, perhaps more than a minority, would go so far as to be hostile to the creeds. At best, any kind of creedal materials, even their schema, can start the conversation. At worst, they get in the way of truth, and maybe they are morally poisonous. It is small wonder that many private universities that have Christian foundations refuse to allow theology as a genuine academic discipline with its own place in the curriculum for undergraduates. The interest in truth is thought to be entirely secondary.

The standard way to resolve the dilemma just articulated is to work up a prolegomenon where, among other things, you provide a method for getting at the truth or, better still, a criterion for settling issues of truth and falsehood in theology. You seek to work out an epistemology of theology. In this you critically explore how theological assertions are to be grounded, what warrants should be deployed, how you arrive at truth, and the like. With a brief or not-so-brief epistemology in place, you work through the loci ultimately arising from reception of the creed in baptism and defend them by appeal to Scripture if you are a conservative. You rework them if you are a revisionist, doing your best to keep the themes intact, even if you have to do some fancy footwork, or even if you lose a doctrine here or there, like Friedrich Schleiermacher (1768–1834) did with the Trinity in the nineteenth century. Some toggle back and forth between conservation, rejection, and revision, never really thinking about what they are doing with the loci.[3] They flit back and forth

---

[2] It is common to trace the narrative to speculative Greek notions of exit and return from the One to the Many and to secure the loci by reference to Peter Lombard's *Sentences* (*Libri Quattuor Sententiarum*) in the twelfth century. The former is too remote in conception and the latter too late in development. As we shall see, the explanation lies much closer to hand in the catechetical schools of the patristic period.

[3] One of the more remarkable examples is to be found in the fine two-volume work where the authors move straight from the treatment of the person and work of Christ to the church and

with nowhere to lay their heads. Many lean in to a great figure from the past or turn to an identity group in the present and shelter under their wings.

What has to be faced here is this: there is no guarantee that the epistemology of theology adopted will secure any of these themes in any robust sense. Either the epistemology will be finessed to give you the results you want, so the epistemology is artificial and constrained; or, if you keep the epistemology independent of the results it yields, you will have to shoe-horn the tradition and its themes into the epistemology adopted. There are subtle difficulties in play here, for the sensitive epistemologist must pay attention to the subject matter in hand in order to deploy apt means of epistemic evaluation.

We have a very serious dilemma staring us in the face right at the start of our work. Surely something has gone badly wrong. Let me sketch out what has gone wrong, where and how it has gone wrong, and then begin to indicate my own way out of this dilemma. To be more precise, I shall indicate that we need a new sub-discipline within theology as a whole called the epistemology of theology. Beyond that, I shall argue for a vision of systematic theology as post-baptismal, university-level catechesis.

Let me begin with some historical remarks.[4]

The church gathered around the apostles erupted in an outburst of evangelistic activity after Pentecost.[5] Empowered by the Spirit, she took on the might of the Roman Empire and eventually broke its persecuting power and zeal, winning hosts of its citizens to become disciples of Jesus Christ. Evangelism had two components or hands. With one hand, the church reached out to gossip and herald the good news of the kingdom of God. This heralding was accompanied by healing, by miracles, and by exorcism. From the beginning the church was a dynamic, charismatic community proclaiming the Gospel by word and deed. With the other hand, the church reached out and brought new converts into the church. This was the task of catechesis. Once Gentile converts multiplied, there had to be substantial, lengthy, serious formation. Folk had all sorts of intellectual, moral, and spiritual baggage that had to be

---

leave out entirely the topic of the Holy Spirit. See Francis Schüssler Fiorenza and John P. Galvin, eds., *Systematic Theology: Roman Catholic Perspectives*, 2 vols. (Minneapolis: Fortress Press, 1991).

[4] In what follows I rely on work already covered elsewhere: *The Logic of Evangelism* (Grand Rapids, MI: Eerdmans, 1989), *Canon and Criterion in Christian Theology: From the Fathers to Feminism* (Oxford: Clarendon Press, 1997), *Crossing the Threshold of Divine Revelation* (Grand Rapids, MI: Eerdmans, 2006), *Divine Agency and Divine Action, Volume I: Exploring and Evaluating the Debate* (Oxford: Oxford University Press, 2017), and *Divine Agency and Divine Action, Volume II: Soundings in the Christian Tradition* (Oxford: Oxford University Press, 2017). I also draw on William J. Abraham, Jason E. Vickers, and Natalie B. Van Kirk, eds., *Canonical Theism: A Proposal for Theology and Church* (Grand Rapids, MI: Eerdmans, 2008).

[5] Here and elsewhere the use of the term "church" rather than "Church" is deliberate. The latter usage sends theological signals about identity and exclusion that I reject; the rationale for this usage will become clear when I take up the topic of ecclesiology.

sorted out. The kind of wishy-washy initiation we find, say, in much of the contemporary church would have struck our ancestors in the faith as ludicrous. The faith represented, for example, in the Apostles' Creed handed over to the convert had to be learned, tried on like a new dress, and worked into the fabric of one's existence. Catechesis and formation were crucial. This was the second component of evangelism. Taken as a constructive practice, evangelism was constituted by both proclamation and catechesis.

Systematic theology began as a further exploration, unpacking, and defense of the faith of the church as laid out in the creed. This was the case, for example, in the great school of Alexandria led by Clement (150–215) and Origen (185–254). Origen states the issue succinctly as follows.

> The holy apostles, when preaching faith in Christ, took certain doctrines, those namely which they believed to be necessary ones, and delivered them in the plainest terms to all believers, even to such as appeared to be somewhat dull in the investigation of divine knowledge. The grounds of their statements they left to be investigated by such as should merit the higher gifts of the Spirit and in particular such as should afterwards receive through the Holy Spirit himself the graces of language, wisdom, and knowledge. There were other doctrines, however, about which the apostles simply said that things were so, keeping silence as to the how or the why; their intention undoubtedly being to supply the more diligent of those who came after them, such as should prove to be lovers of wisdom, with an exercise in which to display the fruit of their ability. The persons I refer to are those who train themselves to become worthy and capable of receiving wisdom.[6]

This sort of creedal development was entirely natural. A robust creed does not close off inquiry. Take it seriously and it will engender an acute pain in the brain. Receiving the creed of the church, and then thinking seriously about it, is like taking a subject to a deeper and higher level. The lower levels both prepare for this work, and they provoke this work. To use a different analogy, it is like getting married; the hard, intellectual work already begun becomes even more intense after the ceremonies are over, not least for those called upon to teach the faith of the church.

I propose up front that we do not need an explicit epistemology to do this work in systematic theology, that is, the work of exploring, unpacking, explaining, and defending the faith of the church. We can even leave open how we should specify the desiderata of a good epistemology. Whatever decisions we make about epistemology, we can become a Christian in good standing without buying into any epistemology.[7] We receive the faith and then, willy-nilly,

---

[6] G. W. Butterworth, *Origen On First Principles* (Gloucester, MA: Peter Smith, 1973), 2.
[7] This has long been the claim of "methodists" in epistemology; you cannot know if any proposition is true unless you have the correct method or criterion for determining what is true. Of course, you then have to find the right second-order method to determine this first-order

we get to work with the materials to hand. We go deeper into what we have already been doing, that is, we start paying attention to the church's faith owned in Christian initiation and celebrated liturgically every Sunday. We naturally go to work intellectually on this faith: making distinctions, following through on certain insights, looking for internal connections, dealing with objections, discovering arguments which support our initial conversion and attraction to Christ, wondering what counts as a good argument, pondering whether we need any arguments, identifying problems that we and others have noted, making a speculative move here and there, tracing connections and contradictions between our Christian faith and other beliefs we have when we wake up in the morning or when we read our chosen non-Christian authors.

Push this line further. Christians got their faith in baptism within Christian initiation from the tradition of the church that emanated in one way or another from the apostles.[8] The church gave us that faith without giving us an epistemology. The church gave us food for thought straight from the kitchen; she did not give us a recipe on how she got that faith. The church in her faith gave us a bridge to the living God; she did not give us a course on engineering on how to build bridges. The church gave substance rather than process, content rather than form, meat rather than meat-producers. The church laid out what it was convinced it knew and for which its members and leaders were often prepared to die in martyrdom; it did not in the same way lay out how it knew what it knew. In fact, the church never initially worked out an agreed criterion of truth, or a reflective theory of rationality, or a theory of justification or knowledge. This observation is deeply instructive and unbelievably illuminating for the predicament sketched at the beginning of this chapter.

Let me approach this suggestion from a different and more traditional angle. Many theologians think that the church had from the beginning a criterion for its theology, and that criterion was its canon of Scripture. Most proponents of traditional Protestantism and Roman Catholicism agree on this.[9] Scripture, the biblical canon, it will be said, is the foundation, the

---

method, and on and on ad infinitum. Particularists, by contrast, begin with particular assertions they find to be true and work dialectically to figure out relevant and appropriate methods of inquiry.

[8] There is, of course, a stark contrast between the seriousness of Christian initiation in the life of the church prior to and immediately after Constantine and what prevails in much of the church today. Happily, serious efforts are afoot to fix this problem given the advance of secularization and the arrival of rival religious claims in the public square.

[9] Popular apologetics in the West systematically ignores this historical observation. Somehow Scripture alone and Rome alone are pitted against each other. What is left out is that Rome carefully guards the claim that her complex network of offices operates hermeneutically rather than epistemically, so the crucial warrants for theology proper must go back to Scripture. The details are worked out at Vatican II in *Dei Verbum*, a jewel of a work in the doctrine of revelation in the last century. The fruit of this vision is available in the flourishing of splendid biblical

criterion for Christian theology. This is the proper norm (the norm that is not normed) of all good theology. If I am right in what I have just said, then this claim is clearly false. I am claiming the church officially adopted its doctrines without first coming up with a Bible and then developing the former from the latter.

The argument in favor of this account of the Bible in theology is cumulative. The leaders and members of the church were doing theology long before there was any fixed canon. This practice would be impossible if the theory under review were true.[10] Further, the church was far more concerned to secure the content of its creed, its list of teachings or doctrines, than it was in fixing the limits of its canon of Scripture. Also, the church's rule of faith was critical in deciding the content of the canon of Scripture, so the relation is the reverse of what we usually claim. One of the reasons why the church rejected various Gnostic gospels was precisely because they contradicted its developing doctrines. In addition, when it came to the epistemology of theology, the great theologians of the church were simply not on the same page; the church tolerated significant diversity. Finally, even the very text of Scripture may have been reworked to fit its developing doctrines.[11]

We can pursue our quarry in traditional terms by looking at a word that we generally associate with Scripture, namely, the word "canon." What does the word "canon" mean? Is it a criterion? Is it a standard or measure? Well, it can, and it sometimes did, mean this. However, I do not think that this was the primary meaning. The primary meaning of "canon" is a list. The canon of saints is a list of saints. The canon of Scripture is a list of books to be read in worship.

In developing its faith, as the church went along merrily evangelizing the Roman Empire and moving over into the bogs of Ireland, the church put together what I want to call its canonical heritage. The bigger picture is that the canonical heritage consists of generally agreed lists of materials, persons, practices, and events.

Think of the canon of Scripture. Recall how this arose. The story is complicated, so I shall have to cut corners to make my central point. Marcion (85–160) brought out his own canon; he dropped the Old Testament and went with Luke and selections of Paul. As a serious thinker and generous donor to

---

commentaries, which, taken in the round, provide a fine integration of theological and historical materials.

[10] The debate about the final texts included in the canon of Scripture in the West was not resolved until the Reformation and Trent; the East operated with the Septuagint and, in many respects, was not really bothered about the borders of the canon of Scripture.

[11] See the textual debate about 1 John 5:7–8. Former fundamentalists find this sufficient evidence to detect intellectual corruption; the more plausible explanation is that folk felt secure enough in the faith of the church to fix what they considered to be a wayward text here and there that they had received.

his local church in Rome, he was a force to be reckoned with. The church competed with him at his own game by gradually identifying its own canon of Scripture, determined by its resolution to keep the Jewish Scriptures and by its widespread usage of the books that are now in the New Testament. The book of Revelation barely made it in by the skin of its teeth. Maybe we should have left that one out; we would not have had to deal with the folk who have killed its brilliant literary power by reading it like they read the *Wall Street Journal*. On the other hand, if we had left it out, we would have not been able to cope so well with the horrors of World War II when European Christians realized that the drama of the book of Revelation really was onto something crucial in the way it depicted the drama of good and evil in the world.

Now it is tempting, given our formation in Western Christianity as whole, to believe that the Bible is all we need spiritually and intellectually. Actually, this is an illusion. At a minimum the church developed all sorts of aids to help us make sense of it. The Bible is a big book; it is not all bedtime reading; parts of it are hair-raising in form and content; it is a small library of books collected over centuries from different places. Hence we need something alongside Scripture if we are to grasp the intellectual core of the Christian faith. More accurately the church already developed its creed, and it used this as an aid both for determining the content of the canon of Scripture and for reading Scripture as a whole.

The church learned this hermeneutical lesson from hard experience. Its chief rivals in the ancient world were various religious sects known collectively as Gnostics. Their equivalent in our day is the various New Age movements. There were and are both low-brow and high-brow versions readily available. It was central to the Gnostic claim that they really had access to the truth about the world; so they knew what Scripture truly said. Give them any book or text, and they could show how their creed or vision was to be found in it. This was a tremendous challenge to the church. The leaders of the church solved it, in part, in a brilliant and economical manner. They developed over time what they called a canon of truth or a rule of truth. They formally drew up their own creed. Note how the word canon crops up here. They drew up a list of convictions or beliefs. Such a list cuts off the Gnostic move at the pass.

Actually, this partial development of a creed was already present in the church independently of the challenge from the ancient New Agers. The church found that it had to draw up a short meaty summary for converts. Most folk want important information in summary form; books and explanations tend to come later. When we hear some item of news about a crime, we want to know two things: "Who did it? And did he get caught?" A library of books will not deal with this necessity. So out of pastoral commitment the church developed its creed, its canon of truth, its rule of faith.

It did not leave this sort of thing to a committee of experts or academics working on tenure. The creed was hammered out by experienced evangelists and teachers. Over time it formally adopted a single creed, a creed we know by its shorthand name as the Nicene Creed, simply because some of the crucial decisions were made in the fourth century at a place called Nicaea in Asia Minor. This is the only creed that has received formal approval by the church universal. Sometimes churches use the Apostles' Creed in church, and this is fine. However, the only creed agreed by the whole church was and remains the Nicene Creed. It is a brilliant summary of the faith.[12]

We now have two sorts of materials: a list of books and a list of teachings.[13]

There were other materials developed in a canonical way. Thus, the church developed iconography, where those trained in art and prayer paint the truth in pictures for all to see and take in by the eye. Interestingly the technical term for producing an icon is that you write an icon. There is other critical doctrinal material, like the Chalcedonian definition, where the church lays out what it believes about the person of Christ. There are also various lists of persons. There is a canon of saints who represent what is true as opposed to fake holiness. Over time a canon of Fathers emerges. This is not a sexist notion; it identifies great spiritual leaders who were adept at handing over the faith. There is even a canon of theologians. Initially there are three in number: John the Divine (the writer of the fourth gospel), Gregory of Nazianzus (329–90), and Symeon the New Theologian (949–1022). These clearly take the church's teaching to a whole new level and deftly preserve the truth of the Gospel. There is a canon of bishops, that is, a list of those who are called to exercise oversight over the church. Their job in part was to guard the store and to stop somebody moving in their alien proposals and planting them firmly in the church's living room.

---

[12] The Nicene Creed runs as follows. "We believe in one God, the Father Almighty, creator of heaven and earth, of all things visible and invisible. And in one Lord Jesus Christ, the only begotten Son of God, generated from the Father before all ages, light from light, true God from true God, begotten not made, one in being from the Father, through whom all things were made. For us men and for our salvation he came down from heaven and became flesh from the Holy Spirit and the Virgin Mary and was made man. For our sake, too, he was crucified under Pontius Pilate, suffered and was buried. On the third day he rose again, according to the Scriptures, ascended into heaven, and is seated at the right hand of the Father; and he will come again in glory to judge the living and the dead; to his kingdom there will be no end. And (we believe) in the Holy Spirit, the Lord and Giver of Life, who proceeds from the Father, who together with the Son is worshipped and glorified, who has spoken through the prophets. And (we believe) in one, holy, catholic, and apostolic Church. We acknowledge one baptism for the remission of sins. We await the resurrection of the dead and the life of the world to come." See Heinrich Denzinger, *Compendium of Creeds, Definitions, and Declaration of Matters of Faith and Morals* (San Francisco: Ignatius Press, 2010), 65–6, 43rd edition, revised, enlarged, and in collaboration with Helmut Hoping, edited by Peter Hünermann in the bilingual edition.

[13] The church sometimes called these teachings dogmas; this designation has absolutely nothing to do with being dogmatic. Dogmas are simply official, public teachings of a community, as opposed to private opinions. Heresies are private opinions masquerading as official, public doctrines of a community.

Already we are moving into canonical practices, for episcopacy is a practice; it is a job of oversight that has to be carried out by a living, breathing person. A book or a creed, on its own, cannot take care of moral or intellectual problems that are in and around the faith of the church. Only persons can really do this, and, even then, it is extremely difficult to do so. More generally the job of the bishop was to ordain, to teach and hand over the creed, to encourage, to lead, to protect the church from moral and intellectual poison, and the like. This was no sure-fire practice; bishops themselves can readily become a menace in the life of the church. Even popes can become heretics as happened in the case of Honorius I (585–638) in the seventh century.

More regular practices that all agreed to were the celebration of the canonical sacraments and other rites, chiefly, of course, baptism and Eucharist. There developed canonical liturgies that provided patterns for a right way to choreograph our worship of God. Here the Jewish tradition was a pivotal starting point and model.[14] We could also say that preaching was a canonical practice with its own unique place in the life of the community. We might even go so far as to say that the sermons of Augustine are canonical in the West, and the sermons of John Chrysostom are canonical in the East.[15] Finally, there were canonical events: the great ecumenical or canonical councils where these sorts of issues were hammered out or endorsed. The councils were charismatic events where the church prayed for and expected the Holy Spirit to lead her into the truth and into right practice as Christ had promised. There were minimally seven of these in all in the first millennium with the Apostolic Council of Acts 15 providing the model for this.

Of course, there are many who tend to see the Nicene Creed and all the other elements of the canonical heritage of the church as a terrible imposition, perhaps, imposed on the church by the powers that be, or imposed by nasty church leaders trying to inflict their ideology on the rest of the church forever. This is not an accurate rendering of what actually happened. This whole way of seeing the developments in the early church gets things back to front. Donald MacKinnon expresses the issues at stake succinctly.

> The whole exterior framework of the Christian Church is the poor man's protection against the tyranny of the wise who would rob him of the heritage of the Gospel. In a sense one might say, too, that her visible structure, her articulate doctrinal standards, her ordered sacramental life, represents the very lashing of the Church herself to her historical moorings. The whole Church is an

---

[14] Indeed, the first instantiation of the life of the church after the coming of Jesus was what we now call Messianic Judaism. The reappearance of Messianic Judaism is one of the seminal theological events of the contemporary scene; it undercuts standard exclusivist claims to represent today the faith of the apostolic church whether they be Protestant, Eastern Orthodox, or Roman Catholic.

[15] *The Standard Sermons*, forty-four in all, of John Wesley are canonical for many Methodist churches to this day.

organ of the Gospel... Those aspects of her life that most perplex hankerers after 'spiritual religion' are due to the fact that she proclaims, not a possibility of spiritual achievement, but a work of redemption wrought by the Son of God in human flesh and blood.

Again and again we have seen the pressure of external circumstances upon individual members of the Church, who have held high office within her and have usually been endowed with great personal gifts, a pressure which issues in individual demands that the Gospel of God be transformed in a human philosophy. And it has been the external organization of the Church, in itself attesting the character of the Gospel, that has preserved its saving truths for Christ's little ones. It is through the institutions of the Church that the Gospel is preserved from the idiosyncrasies of its members.[16]

At one level, all of these developments are contingent developments; other means could have been used to perform the same functions. Across history, various Christian communities have in fact found various ways for securing the ends sought by the relevant choices made with respect to each of these elements in the canonical heritage. Not surprisingly, some Christian communities have sought to preserve exactly the original network of canonical materials, practices, persons, and events. They have gone far beyond this in excommunicating communities that do not share their exact vision of the history. In the West, we have long had exclusive claims advanced on behalf of the Bishop of Rome where whole networks of Christian communities continue to be downgraded because they do not accept the precise way in which Roman Catholicism has interpreted its own unique configuration of canonical materials and practices. This represents one of the great tragedies in the history of the church; things are not going to change on this front. However, we can readily agree that the developments sketched above are not merely contingent developments; they are indeed the work of the Holy Spirit in the life of the church. It is another matter entirely to claim that the action of the Holy Spirit is exclusively tied to these precisionist accounts of the early history. We need a hermeneutic of charity in evaluating the official teachings and practices of the vast array of Christian communities that exist across space and time.

Moreover, in one respect, namely, in the overreach to canonize a particular epistemology of theology, we can say this. The church never canonized any epistemology, any theory of reflective rationality, any agreed upon method for getting at the truth. She never canonized any theory of revelation or inspiration, no more than she canonized any theory of the atonement. She left this issue open; some went this way; some went that way. The church allowed all sorts of epistemic insights and suggestions to fructify in her womb. Even though there was deep general agreement that revelation was

---

[16] D. M. MacKinnon, *The Church* (London: Dacre Press, 1940), 54–5.

essential, even this was left in the bosom of the church without being formally defined or adopted.

Perhaps we can find this observation more attractive if I clear up one loose end at this point. What was the overall purpose of the canonical materials, persons, practices, and events? Or, to put the same question in a different form, what was the purpose of the church in using these materials, in deploying these practices, in designating and appointing these persons, in sustaining these treasures in its life and ministry? Their purpose is simple: rightly working together, they bring us to God, heal us of our troubles and corruption, and make us divine. They make us like Jesus Christ; they turn us the right way up; they restore us to the image of God. They create in us the mind of Jesus Christ, who for our sakes became poor that we through his poverty might become rich. They enable human beings to find their true destiny as designed and appointed by God.

We can state the same point conventionally by claiming that we have here means of grace. Working together these varied materials, practices, and persons makes us wise unto salvation. They mediate prevenient, justifying, and sanctifying grace. They make available the truth that sets us free; they attract us to the amazing generosity of God; and they make available the power of the Holy Spirit in bringing victory over evil. Hence, they need to be handled with care and spiritual sensitivity.[17]

Consider, for example, the way the content of the creed was handed over. The church knew that the seeker had to be pretty far along to even begin to grasp its content. Hence inquirers were not allowed to write it down and take it home. They were warned not to share it with outsiders. If one did, folk would laugh and jeer, for how could anyone even begin to understand the creed if they had not come to terms with the Gospel? One received the creed after one was introduced to the Gospel and while one was on the way to conversion. The reception of the creed was an art. Let me explain this more fully.

In coming to encounter the God of the Gospel in the creed, we also come to understand ourselves. As we explore who God is, we also explore who we are as children of God, made in his image and liberated from sin by Christ. Hence prospective converts had to go away and mull over the faith. Startled by the Gospel, they worked up to God from their condition and then down to a revised understanding of their condition after hearing the good news of the Gospel of God. Otherwise the creed was just abstract God-talk, mere religious mumbo-jumbo, or silly theological nonsense.

---

[17] The over-determination, their multiplicity, means that one can come to a true and living faith even though one only has access to parts of the canonical heritage of the church. Russia effectively came to faith through access to the four canonical gospels, iconography, baptism, and extraordinary sanctity as represented later by Seraphim of Sarov. Many are coming to faith today in Nepal in similar circumstances, in this instance mediated by various forms of Protestantism.

At the heart of the creed is Jesus Christ. In meeting the testimony about him in the church we come to meet God. We do not go above, or around, or below him to meet God. The church really believed that anyone who encounters Jesus Christ encounters God. We do not have to be trained in epistemology or in philosophy to meet God and be healed. In fact, the church was bold enough and confident enough to tell this to philosophers to their face. This is a staggering claim; it has and always will be a matter of intellectual offense.

Now, consider this: in coming to Jesus Christ we all need the help of the Holy Spirit. The Spirit repairs our sight and enables us to see who Jesus truly is. There is more here than some rickety intellectual argument. There is the illumination of the Holy Spirit. Just as the sun helps us to see the world as it is, the Spirit helps us to see Jesus Christ as he is, the eternal Son of God. In turn we cannot be drawn into the life of the Son through the Spirit without obedience, humility, and repentance. It is those who are poor in spirit who see God.

There is more to ponder. The church insists that as we come to meet and know God, we will never fathom the final mystery and beauty of God. In God's essence, God forever lies beyond the reach of our concepts and ideas. Our knowledge of God melts in wonder, in love, in silence, and in praise.

I want now to cut to the chase and simply declare that this internal ordering of the life of the church got turned inside out over time. The drive to get the epistemology right and to show that we are in the right and the other fellow in the wrong is intimately related to the divisions that break out in the church over time. I think it applies to the first really big split in the church, the split between East and West, but I will not get crucified on that cross in these preliminary remarks. I will instead settle for a rendering of the effects of the divisions in and around the Reformation. Let me put the issue simply and sharply without any qualifications.[18]

The Reformers, whatever else we say about them, tried to recover the Gospel and the proper usage of the Scriptures. They rediscovered the sheer beauty and wonder of the Gospel for themselves. As they pursued this recovery further, they were faced by opponents who required them to supply an epistemology. They were pressed to supply a criterion and to answer the question of authority. Their favorite slogan at that point was some version of *sola scriptura*.[19] Their hopes in this respect failed. They failed to reach consensus on the Trinity, the sacraments, the nature of church order, the relation between church and state, and so on. In time, they took to killing one

---

[18] For an earlier assessment of the state of recent theology see my "Oh God! Poor God! The State of Contemporary Theology," *The American Scholar* LVII (1989): 557–63.

[19] There are, of course, narrower and more expansive versions of this slogan. I am deploying a narrower one for the sake of emphasis.

another. In disgust their children looked for a better foundation in reason or experience. They created the Enlightenment in its various manifestations. The second and third generation schooled in the Enlightenment turned their epistemological weapons back on the church. From then on theology has been on one wild goose chase after another to fix the foundations and get the epistemology straight. All along the church is now hostage to experts in the philosophy department. When this fails, and philosophy refuses to oblige, her teachers turn to ancillary disciplines and pseudo-disciplines like cultural studies, literary theory, gender studies, and the like.[20] In the meantime the children look up and are offered stones when they ask for bread. The church is in danger of becoming spiritually and intellectually bankrupt. By the time we arrive at the nineteenth century, there are so many intellectual options all claiming to rest on the right foundations that the Mormons invent their own revelation. They want a sure-fire way out of the terrible pain and confusion, a way determined by a new revelation for today. Not surprisingly contemporary nominal Christians are drawn to Islam because of its simplicity and certainties.

The net result of this obsession with epistemology is modern Protestantism in the West. It is a kind of credit-card Christianity without any money left in the bank. Hence we are constantly looking for a reliable source of really good money. Epistemology has turned out to be much more difficult that we thought it would be. There is no agreement in the field as a whole that the theologian can rely on. This is not to say that we have not made progress in epistemology, for we have. However, one person's progress is another person's regress. Some, under the name of post-modernism, have tried to write obituary notices of the subject. There is no self or subject who can do any knowing, for all selves are really creations rather than stable creatures. There is no truth outside what your friends will let you get away with, that is, there is no justification outside the conventions of community. There is no objective reality to which language corresponds or refers; there is simply the incessant play of metaphor harnessed perhaps to interest, materiality, and power. These are what we might call anti-epistemological epistemologies.[21]

Here is the irony. We are still working overtime to get the right epistemology or anti-epistemology at a time when the culture has become post-Christian, as in Europe, or hopelessly confused and divided, as in the United States of America. Hence we have denominations fighting it out over the right criterion or correct epistemology, when we need to be able to preach and teach

---

[20] This is not a blanket condemnation of these kinds of inquiry; even pseudo-disciplines depend on important insights that can be mined by the theologian.

[21] The crucial strategy is to undercut the very conditions of rational assessment and then quietly introduce the favored alternative ontology and politics, generally Marxist in orientation, while the critic is still pondering the counterintuitive proposals on the table.

the faith with confidence and humility. Modernity has not lived up to its promises;[22] postmodernity is often simply the playground of the intellectual elite.[23] Evil is as real as ever it was at home and abroad. I have no brief for sensationalism, but the reality and power of evil in the world is as great as ever it was after two centuries of Enlightenment. We have not arrived at the various utopias of blessing promised by modernity. The need for redemption, for the salvation of our souls, for the healing of the nations, is as great if not greater than ever. Hence the church must recover its intellectual and evangelistic nerve. If the church fails in this task, it will cease to fulfill its missionary obligations. Continuing to be stuck in epistemology is only of limited help at this point in our journey.

I offer two proposals to move us forward at this point.

We need to put epistemology in its place. The obvious way to do this is to create a new sub-discipline within theology but outside systematic theology called the epistemology of theology.[24]

We need to reinvent systematic theology. We need to reconceive systematic theology as post-baptismal, university-level catechesis in the church.

Note carefully what I am doing here. I propose we relax about epistemology in systematic theology; we can take up that work as time and aptitude allow. More importantly, I am inviting Christians to step afresh into the waters of baptism and explore what lies on the other side of that immersion. This invitation is not given in smugness or in intellectual laziness but in fear and trembling. This is not some new form of ecclesiastical fundamentalism; it is not giving vent to a new round of gloomy conservative instincts. It is a hard-won conviction derived from wrestling with the faith as honestly and rigor-ously as I can. It is an act of faith in the God of Israel and of the church who in Jesus Christ has come to redeem the world and who has sent the Holy Spirit to lead it into the truth it needs to do its work. I am inviting the reader on a journey into the loci of systematic theology. With the church in its diverse manifestations I am promising that if we make this journey then we will come to know, love, and serve God better. I am proposing that we view systematic theology as an extension of the catechetical life of the church. It is serious,

---

[22] For one overview see the tetralogy by Michael Burleigh, *Earthly Powers: The Clash of Religion and Politics from the French Revolution to the Great War* (New York: HarperCollins, 2005), *Sacred Causes: The Clash of Religion and Politics from the Great War to the War on Terrorism* (New York: HarperCollins, 2007), *Blood and Rage: A Cultural History of Terrorism* (London: HarperCollins, 2008), and *Moral Combat: Good and Evil in World War II* (New York: HarperCollins, 2011).

[23] For a penetrating if somewhat polemical exposition of postmodernism see Stephen R. C. Hicks, *Explaining Postmodernism: Skepticism and Secularism from Rousseau to Foucault* (Roscoe, IL: Ockham's Razor Publishing Company, 2017). Compare Roger Scruton, *Fools, Frauds, and Firebrands: Thinkers of the New Left* (London: Bloomsbury, 2015).

[24] This is pursued in William J. Abraham and Frederick D. Aquino, eds., *The Oxford Handbook of the Epistemology of Theology* (Oxford: Oxford University Press, 2017).

rigorous, university-level catechesis. This is the formal claim I mentioned at the outset.

My initial comment on the second material claim lies close at hand. The loci allow us to identify and articulate a network of divine actions neatly summarized in terms of creation, freedom, fall, redemption, and consummation.[25] They speak of a God who created the universe; who chose a particular people, the Jews, as the bearers of divine revelation and divine life; who came to earth in the person of his Son, Jesus Christ; who sent the promised Holy Spirit to secure a whole new era of God's kingdom through the church; who transforms sinners into saints; and who will bring his purposes both on a personal and cosmic level to final fulfillment in the world to come. We are dealing with divine action from creation through redemption to final fulfillment of God's good purposes for the created order. Keeping divine agency and divine action in mind as we proceed will help us to secure our bearings and to keep our intellectual nerve intact. In the end this material proposal is best defended by execution in what follows rather than by formal defense.

---

[25] Note that far more is at stake than a sophisticated commentary on either the Apostles' or Nicene creeds. We go so far beyond them that we need a fourth volume to pursue the metaphysical and other ancillary investigation our work begins to pursue.

2

Prolegomena

Presuppositions and Tasks

I hope to come to you soon, but I am writing these instructions to you so that, if I am delayed, you may know how you ought to behave in the household of God, which is the church of the living God, the pillar and bulwark of the truth. Without any doubt, the mystery of our religion is great: 'He was revealed in flesh, vindicated in spirit, seen by angels, proclaimed among the Gentiles, believed in throughout the world, taken up in glory.'

1 Timothy 3:14–16.

Systematic theology is essentially an intellectual discipline for insiders. Outsiders are welcome to participate but they are seriously handicapped if they do not understand the Gospel or if they do not understand the demands of basic Christian formation. This should not surprise us in the least. Historians assume that there is a past and get on with understanding what happened. Natural scientists assume that there is a natural order and set about explaining how it works. Ordinary people have to be initiated into the relevant modes of thought and understanding. In that sense, they are outsiders. Moreover, they have to learn that you do not figure out how to cure cancer in the same way you figure out why World War I happened. The subject matter of a discipline determines how you resolve fundamental disputes that crop up across the generations. Theology assumes the reality of divine agency and divine action; it has its own modes of understanding and explanation. Let the work begin.

Immediately, of course, we reach for distinctions. History is about the past and natural science is about the natural order. Ordinary folk do not need introductory remarks about whether they exist or not. This is not the case in theology; theologians have an extra intellectual burden to carry. They cannot assume the reality of God. Empirically, this is in fact only partially true. The default position for most people is that they believe in God; generally, they have to be dispossessed of their religious beliefs, however vague and implicit they may be. However, given the cognitive effects of sin and given a prevailing skeptical culture, these counter-assertions do not count for much. Theologians have, in fact, readily assumed this additional responsibility across the ages. The fecundity of the history is astonishing. Yet there is a snake in the grass. The immediate danger is that we turn aside and deal with skeptical worries and never leave the scene of their distraction. Hence, there is a lot of throat clearing on norms and sources before we get down to work. My solution to that has already been made clear. The issues here run so deep and the history is so fascinating that we need a division of labor. We take up these matters with enthusiasm in the sub-discipline of the epistemology of theology.

Yet we are not in the clear just yet. Theology, broadly conceived, is not just about divine agency and divine action. It is constituted by an array of sub-disciplines that take up a multiplicity of data and warrants: biblical studies, church history and the history of doctrine, moral theology, philosophical theology, systematic theology, and practical theology. If one wants a simple life, then it would be wiser to sell insurance or become a particle physicist. Better leave theology aside, for the intellectual demands are staggering in the extreme. The solution to this cognitive overload in the modern period has been to begin with biblical studies, move up through the church history and the history of doctrine, perhaps add a course in the philosophy of religion, and then tackle the problems of moral theology and systematic theology. Practical theology is often left aside like an orphan starved of sustenance.[1]

At least two assumptions govern this conventional picture. First, there is an implicit epistemology in place, namely, an epistemology that sees the Bible as foundational and which insists that all theological claims must minimally be tested by rigorous exegetical work in the original languages. What is really at stake here is a vision of Scripture as a form of or witness to divine revelation, supplemented as taste will have it, say, with tradition, reason, and experience. Second, there is an implicit Whig interpretation of the history of doctrine which looks to every new generation either finally to attain the truth about God or to state the church's teaching about God in terms intelligible to each new generation of seekers and believers. Today the second is clearly the favored option. Hence, there is a deep skepticism about the truth and stability of Christian claims.

What we see here is that conventional theological studies are embedded in highly contested epistemological claims which are rarely identified, much less pursued with care. Suffice it here to say that the results of this arrangement are bound to be not just chaotic but intellectually insecure. Biblical studies now has many lives of its own that cannot carry the burden assigned by theology;

---

[1] Once we think of practical theology as the critical examination of the ministerial practices of the church then clearly we have a very serious intellectual sub-discipline on our hands. For a fine exposition of this vision of practical theology see Schubert M. Ogden, "Prolegomena to Practical Theology," in *On Theology* (Dallas: Southern Methodist University Press, 1992), 94–101.

these lives display rival ontological and epistemological commitments. The history of doctrine in play is equally insecure. Like biblical studies, historical study of doctrine will depend on a host of prior philosophical commitments. Moreover, it takes nerve to believe that we have to wait until today to find out the truth about God. Hence, before we get to normative work in moral and systematic theology, we remain subject to intense cognitive dissonance. Add in the inevitable role for philosophy at that point and the cognitive overload is unbearable.[2] We can do what we can to make a virtue of this situation, but the time has arrived to reject it and find a better way forward. Given the weight of convention in theological studies and given the contested character of our claims, I make no pretense of establishing a better alternative; yet those who share my deep distrust of the standard picture may be open to what follows.[3]

Systematic theology rests on prior commitment not just to some vague moral theism or to some superficial vision of the meaning of life. It rests first and foremost on the Gospel; secondarily, it presupposes initiation into the church by basic catechesis and baptism. Once we sort through these desiderata, we can identify the central tasks that are characteristic of its integrity. In turn, this can pave the way for an alternative vision of theological studies and a final note on the epistemology of theology.

It is not difficult to identify in summary form the heart of the Gospel.[4] The heart of the Gospel is the astonishing news that God has inaugurated his kingdom in the life, death, and resurrection of Jesus of Nazareth. We begin not with the creeds or with some moral code but with an announcement: "The time is fulfilled, and the kingdom of God has come near; repent, and believe in the good news."[5] The fundamental image in play is political; God's sovereign rule in creation and history has come in a fresh and powerful manner. Yet the fuller content of that message transcends politics and cannot be reduced to politics. The content reaches back into eternity before creation in the councils of God and it stretches forward beyond history into eternity with a radically transformed creation. The kingdom is partially already present in creation and providence; it took specific shape and promise in an everlasting covenant with Israel; it has become radically present in Jesus of Nazareth; it is brought close since Pentecost through the work of the Holy Spirit in the life and practices of

---

[2] The temptation at this point is to outsource our work to some great theologian of the past or to whatever church with a strong pedigree in hand will promise us rest for our weary souls. But what theologian shall we choose? And what do we do when the church we choose turns out to have to do theology just like everyone else?

[3] This does not mean that the current arrangement is devoid of use or lacking in fruitfulness. On the contrary, we are faced with a wealth of material that can surely hold its own in any intellectual arena. My ultimate concerns relate to the order in which we pursue the many questions that are engendered by theology.

[4] For a fuller account see my *The Logic of Evangelism* (Grand Rapids, MI: Eerdmans, 1989), chapter 2.

[5] Mark 1:15.

the church; it spills over into every nook and cranny of the world; and it will be fully realized for humanity and the cosmos in the future.

Consider the following important passage from Matthew.

> Then Jesus went about all the cities and villages, teaching in their synagogues, and proclaiming the good news of the kingdom, and curing every disease and every sickness. When he saw the crowds, he had compassion for them, because they were harassed and helpless; like sheep without a shepherd. Then he called to his disciples, 'The harvest is plentiful, but the laborers are few; therefore ask the Lord of the harvest to send laborers into his harvest.'[6]

This is the second time that Matthew pauses to summarize the activity of Jesus.[7] The initial good news is that God is dramatically at work in Jesus in word and deed to establish his kingdom. The deeper story that unfolds is that of God's work of redemption in the passion and resurrection of Jesus. The gospels of John and Luke make it clear that even this work continues in the coming of the Holy Spirit in power at first upon and within the first followers and disciples and then upon and within those who repent and enter the kingdom of God through the ministry of the church.

Paul does not repudiate this vision of the Gospel. Like John who uses the language of eternal life to speak of the kingdom of God, he deploys his own semantic resources.

> For I am not ashamed of the gospel; it is the power of God for salvation to everyone who has faith, to the Jew first and also to the Greek. For in it the righteousness of God is revealed through faith; as it is written, 'The one who is righteous will live by faith.'[8]

Paul strikes here the same note of victory that we find in the canonical gospels. God's righteousness is not just a moral attribute like goodness; it is also God's victory over evil now made available to all through faith. Luke is careful to identify Paul's evangelistic work as focused precisely on the arrival of the kingdom. Paul was in no rush to move on until that element of his work was secure.[9] Once the foundation of the Gospel was in place, his vocation as a recipient of divine revelation was to begin to explain more fully what God has done and to explore the ramifications of this momentous good news to those who had come to believe it and base their lives upon it.

The canonical ordering of the New Testament makes it clear that the Gospel begins with Jesus, with his life, death, and resurrection. Luke follows up in Acts with the continuation of what God began to do in Jesus in the early assemblies that came into existence after Pentecost. The epistles and Revelation provide brilliant snapshots and expositions of the consequences and challenges that

---

[6] Matthew 9:35–8.   [7] Compare Matthew 4:23–5.   [8] Romans 1:16–17.
[9] In Corinth, he stayed a year and six months. See Acts 18:11.

ensue. Clearly these texts and their predecessors in the Old Testament are absolutely pivotal for all future understandings of what God has done in history for the renewal of the world. The Jewish Scriptures cannot be jetti-soned; taken with the Gospel mediated by faithful followers and by Paul himself, they are utterly indispensable. "All scripture is inspired by God and is useful for teaching, for reproof, for correction, and for training in right-eousness, so that everyone who belongs to God may be proficient, equipped for every good work."[10]

If the Gospel centers on the arrival of the kingdom of God, then a helpful way to think of our relationship to that kingdom is that of entry. We speak not just of believing certain propositions but of embracing the good news of the kingdom in such a way that we actually enter into the kingdom. Of course, we believe certain propositions; without hearing the good news and getting hold of the relevant information, we cannot even begin the process of entering into the kingdom. However, mere belief is not enough; we receive an invitation to repent and be born again; we are called to exercise faith and trust. The announcement of the Gospel requires a definite human response. Divine action is met with human action; human action in turn is met with further divine action.

> Therefore, my beloved, just as you have always obeyed me, not only in my presence, but much more now in my absence, work out your own salvation with fear and trembling; for it is God who is at work in you, enabling you both to will and to work for his good pleasure.[11]

Already we can feel the pressure to take off into one of the great themes of Christian theology. How should we think of the interaction of divine and human action in salvation? How do we handle the dilemma of divine grace and human freedom? If salvation is entirely a matter of grace, of divine generosity and divine energy, what room is there for genuine human action? Yet we must not move so fast. Questions like these belong downstream from entry into the kingdom. They became acute in the history of theology in the work of Augustine at a time when the crucial doctrine of the Trinity was already in place. If we move too fast, we are likely to lose our bearings and reach for all sorts of philosophical tools that can readily engineer other crucial

---

[10] 2 Timothy 3:16. The Scriptures mentioned here are the Septuagint, the standard Bible of the early church until the New Testament was added. Notice that the relevant action-predicate is "inspired" not "authored," "spoken," "dictated," or other speech-actions beloved of later theology. Notice also that the purpose is to give corrective information with a view to making believers both proficient and equipped for every good work. Speaking technically, the purpose is soteriological. Moreover, a text can give information and be used for correction without reaching for the kind of inflated account of normativity that has bedeviled the discussion. It is one thing to give information; it is quite another to claim that this constitutes a norm in the epistemology of theology.

[11] Philippians 2:12–13.

elements in our thinking before we are properly equipped. In this case, the temptation is not so much to turn to epistemology, but to metaphysics, and reach for some favored notion of action or double-agency to carry the day. Before we know what has happened we are hostage again to the philosophy department.

What is needed at this point is to pause and think briefly about entry into the kingdom of God for the first time. The obvious concept to deploy at this point is the concept of initiation. Think of being initiated into a special society, or being initiated into a specific academic discipline, or being initiated into a complex skill, like taking up the trumpet, learning to play it, and then joining an orchestra. Each of these will require its own combination of information, understanding, practices, values, skills, dispositions, and the like. Entry into these specific worlds requires time; it depends on proper curiosity; it demands the development of crucial attitudes; it mandates the internal appreciation of what is appropriated. The early church tacitly understood that something similar was essential to Christian discipleship. It began with extensive initiation with Jesus by the apostles, who in turn carried through a similar program with new disciples.[12] This ministry became especially critical in the evangelization of the Greco-Roman world. This is precisely what is needed in our increasingly post-Christian world of today. Older methods of initiation which assume significant immersion in a Christian society are simply obsolete.

Two sorts of questions arise immediately, one conceptual and the other practical. On the conceptual side, we need a rough outline of the diverse features of initiation into the kingdom of God; on the practical side, we need to work through effective practices that really establish folk in the faith. I leave aside the practical and pick up the conceptual challenge.

Consider the following critical elements in any serious account of initiation into the kingdom of God.[13] Let's assume at this point that folk already have some understanding of the kingdom of God. I also assume that there has been a genuine turning in repentance to welcome this good news; folk have genuinely changed their mind in order to align themselves with the news they can scarcely believe.

Entry into the kingdom will surely require some sense of the moral requirements that they will take on board. We can begin with the straightforward command to love God and love our neighbor as ourselves. Perhaps we add for good measure that Christians will develop a particular concern for the poor. They will also begin to see that sexual morality is not some kind of indoor sport where nobody gets hurt and where all have to agree in advance to the boundaries permitted; it involves a vision of celibacy or marriage rooted in the

---

[12] A classic text in evangelism that explores this theme is Robert E. Coleman, *The Masterplan of Evangelism* (Grand Rapids, MI: Revell, 1993).

[13] I have argued for this account in *The Logic of Evangelism*, chapters 5–7.

covenant love of Christ for the church. Once these are in place then the journey into justice and love can be picked up and pursued in the future. Equally important, Christian initiation will involve characteristic but diverse experiences represented by repentance, conversion, reception of the Holy Spirit, and the like. Folk get to start all over again, to be born again from above; they need some initial guidance on what that may mean for them. This can run all the way from dramatic conversions to the quiet reception of the faith from childhood in a Christian family.

Entry into the kingdom will also involve baptism and reception into the church. The kingdom has a specific community, the church, instantiated in local assemblies with various forms of ministry. This is not an option that can be left to the individual. The kingdom has a people; Christ has a body. To reject the church is to try and have Jesus but reject his body. As a corollary, folk cannot have the body and settle for nominal membership and reject Christ. Hence, there is an inescapable social or corporate dimension to initiation. Closely connected to this dimension, there is clearly a need to find one's place in the varied ministries of the church. There are gifts of the Spirit to be appropriated according to the sovereign decisions of the Spirit. These are for all, so that sorting out how these varied ministries of the church dovetail with the offices of the church will require serious attention at some point. The crucial initial point to be learned is that the division of clergy and laity is only part of the story; each must find their unique place in the body and begin to learn how to exercise the person-relative ministry given to them.

Furthermore, entry into the kingdom will involve owning the spiritual disciplines that are indispensable for maturity and development. Consider the place of fasting and charitable giving; or think of the importance of prayer and the study of Scripture; or ponder the place of self-denial, spiritual fellowship, and study. Above all think of the critical importance of regular worship and the regular reception of the Lord's body and blood in the Eucharist. The latter is especially important for it is at once an exercise in repentance, in thanksgiving, in communion, and in regular reception of the very life of God. Taken in the round, the spiritual disciplines are essential to survival whatever the cultural or contextual challenges in play.

There is one last dimension which I have deliberately left to the end. Consider the critical importance of intellectual initiation, that is, the initiation into the core elements of Christian teaching that are spelled out succinctly in the creeds. A creed is not the Gospel; it arises precisely because the Gospel engenders a definitive vision of faith that makes available the identity of the God of the kingdom, together with other immediate matters essential for getting our intellectual bearings. It provides an initial map that acts as a critical starting point for further reflection. It anchors our understanding of God, provides an anti-virus that enables us to identify alien claims about the divine, and makes clear the object of our love and commitment. It is akin to the Lord's prayer in our devotional life; it is the functional equivalent of the great commandment to love God and neighbor in our moral life; it mirrors the summons to faith, hope, and love in the spiritual life.

The foregoing is not offered as a definitive vision of Christian initiation. However, the big picture is clear. Moreover, I am convinced that failure in any one respect will lead to obvious malfunction across the board in the church. To take but two examples, if we focus on characteristic spiritual experiences without, say, intellectual formation, we will create disciples who crave sporadic sensations and eventually wither on the vine. If we focus exclusively on intellectual formation, we will end up with dead orthodoxy and bigotry. The aim is to insist on proper formation, a challenge the early church took with radical seriousness and without which it would never have evangelized the Greco-Roman world. Our fundamental problem at this point is that we want the ends without the means; we do not believe in causation; we practice pseudo-spiritual magic. We can no longer depend on the culture to do this work for us. If we take it seriously then we can be relatively hopeful about the prospects of long-haul renewal.[14]

My aim thus far is to underscore the two prerequisites for doing systematic theology. I have argued that we need to have in place a relatively robust account of the Gospel and a serious commitment to initiation into the kingdom of God. Once the latter is in place, we already have initial immersion into the intellectual core of the faith as represented by the creeds. It is these, I argued earlier, that are the background music for doing systematic theology. The Nicene Creed, for example, gives us our bearings; now we find ourselves drawn into a whole new world that deserves our attention over a lifetime.[15]

It was this new world that Origen and the other founders of systematic theology sought to explore with all the tools at their disposal. Their favored site of investigation was Scripture. This was where they settled in to find answers and confound their critics. Yet they did not limit themselves to this source. They used any and every data and warrant they deemed relevant. In doing so they never agreed on some grand theory of rationality or epistemology; these became obsessions most especially after the Reformation when rival theological proposals shook society from top to bottom. Even then, theological claims cry out for articulation and defense; so epistemological queries naturally arise and can no more be shut down than we can stop hurricanes coming in from the sea. I am drawn back again against my will to the place of epistemology in theology. Before I take leave of that topic let me stay the course and do the

---

[14] I take up a critical examination of this topic in *The Logic of Renewal* (Grand Rapids, MI: Eerdmans, 2003).

[15] The church assumes at this point serious usage of the canon of Scripture; yet this cannot take the place of the creed. Scripture has its own unique role in formation; it is like a spiritual handbook always on hand to be read again and again. The issue is not one of clarity or perspicuity; it is a matter of appropriate fit for the work in hand in serious catechesis.

following: offer a summary definition of systematic theology, make some general comments, and identify the central tasks of systematic theology.

Systematic theology is the articulation and self-critical appropriation of the canonical doctrines of the church as related to the ongoing spiritual formation of Christians in the church.

If readers need a handy designation, then I am a retrievalist and a renewalist. I like the aphorism of Erasmus: "To restore great things is sometimes harder and nobler than to have introduced them."[16]

Let me explore this proposal with a series of comments. There are four in all.

First, systematic theology is a form of faith seeking understanding. We begin by taking testimony seriously. Initially we depend on the testimony of families and friends who bring us the Gospel. This then shifts to the testimony of the "undivided" church, for it is this church that has preserved the Gospel and worked out the canonical heritage in which we are formed as Christians. The church testifies to the work of God in history and under God develops its canonical commitments. We begin with the faith of the church and we enter into that faith to understand it more fully and deeply. This is often contrasted to understanding seeking faith, but we must handle this contrast carefully. In coming to faith, we already have some understanding and in seeking understanding we move to a fuller and richer faith. Perhaps we should say that all the way along there is both faith and understanding, each illuminating and increasing the other. I put faith first because at the beginning stages of systematic theology I think that it is with faith more than with understanding that we do in fact start.

Second, implicit in this vision of systematic theology is the conviction that the new world opened up to us in the church is utterly real, and that in confessing its faith the church speaks the truth about this divine world. The church in faith declares as best it can the truth about creation and redemption. Indeed, commitment to the truth was in part the driving force of the work of evangelism. The church confesses that the truth about God had been given to her in all its mystery and fragility. Here there was a kind of bedrock conviction at work. The task of the theologians was to unpack this truth with all the skill and flair they could muster. That this truth was rejected by the world, or that it was difficult to secure by public argument, did not inhibit them. It drove many of them to develop complex accounts of the relation between faith and reason, even though there was no agreement on this matter. As I keep insisting, such epistemological work is secondary. Primarily, we stand in awe and worship in the presence of God. Then, in fear and trembling, and in company of the whole church in heaven and on earth, we seek to delineate what we see.

---

[16] Found in a letter to Pope Leo X, February 1, 1516.

Third, systematic theology is pursued within the church to the highest intellectual levels possible. It belongs naturally, therefore, in the university.[17] In fact, universities in the West invariably grew out of the work of theology, for exploration of the faith inevitably involves all sorts of information and intellectual skill which needs extended attention and institutional support. Systematic theology is a field of inquiry. It is more like geography than like physics. It is glad to draw on other relevant disciplines for its work. It is, however, a field of inquiry in its own right.

Fourth, within systematic theology we stand currently at a time of tension and renewal in the church. We live for the most part in a pluralist world. We also live in a world that has to be evangelized; and a world where the church is in need of comprehensive renewal. In some circles the opposition has become paranoiac. There is tension because Christians still want to hold on to their older privileged position as chaplain to the culture and hence are tempted to go wherever the culture goes. There is renewal because without renewal we will not be able either to survive in a healthy manner or do the difficult work of evangelism. The systematic theologian needs to keep a wary eye on these developments without becoming distracted or obsessed by them. In other words, we need to pay attention to the particular missionary situation in which we now find ourselves. We not only need robust initial formation; we also need sensitivity and flair in relating the canonical doctrine to the new missionary situation.

In the modern period this was viewed predominantly in terms of some kind of translation into the idiom of the unbeliever. This was a fatal mistake, for the discourse and claims of Christianity have their own integrity and logic. Translation means surrender to the forms of intelligibility and credibility which cannot in the nature of the case contain the intellectual treasures of the church. What is needed is fresh statement and creative engagement with the challenges of the culture in which we live.

Already we are embarked on an account of the tasks of the theologian and the norms of theology. Let me tackle these topics more directly. The work of the theologian is manifold; there is not one task but many. The different tasks will call for different sorts of methods. The challenge is to stay resourceful and versatile on all fronts. Consider four central tasks. Which one we take up with regard to the various loci is a matter of judgment.

---

[17] John Henry Newman in his magisterial *The Idea of the University* (San Diego: Ubi Caritas Press, 2017) makes the case for this with characteristic flair. He notes, for example, that the rejection of theology requires a prior and thoroughly contested commitment to skepticism. He also deftly argues that when theology is omitted, adherents of other disciplines will readily overreach beyond their competence to fill the ensuing vacuum. It should also be added that theology suffers precisely because it does not have to wrestle with colleagues and issues in other disciplines.

One task is expository. A theologian will expound and clarify and articulate the canonical doctrines of the undivided church. Here the work is primarily exegetical. The focus is historical. We seek to get hold of the central concepts and claims of the tradition. In this work exploring the origins of this or that doctrine is essential.

A second task is hermeneutical. In this case, we go beyond exegesis and try and ferret out the deeper issues that lie beneath and around the canonical material. We explore the issues and questions addressed by the doctrine. We go beneath the surface of the tradition. We look at the alternatives which were canvassed and why they were received or rejected. We explore what insights may lie buried in material that was ultimately rejected. We look at ideas in the neighborhood of the canonical doctrines. We seek to explore how the doctrines hang together and relate to each other.

A third task is constructive. Here we make proposals and suggestions for the church as whole on how to best interpret and receive the canonical doctrine. The aim here is revision of understanding, reception, and application. We propose how the church might better understand the Trinity, or better understand mission and evangelization, or better understand life after death. In some cases, we pick up topics that remain unspecified and expand on them, like atonement. Or we resolve long-standing controversies, like the Augustinian–Pelagian controversy on grace and freedom. Or we suggest better ways to think of God's relation to the world; perhaps we think that some particular philosophical trajectory helps us here. Or, we say that there is a better way to work out how to relate the Gospel to the oppressed peoples of the world; or that here is a creative way to handle gender predicates as applied to God. The theologian works sometimes as a kind of physician or surgeon, seeking to bind up the wounds of the tradition. At other times, he or she may work as a prophet, calling the church to radical obedience. At other times, he or she may work as an expert consultant, drawing on specialized skill or information to help the church sort through how best to think of the topic in hand.

A fourth task is apologetic in nature. One part of this is to defend the church against objections and maybe even slander. In this instance, we assume the role of a defense lawyer, seeking to clear the church of false intellectual charges made against her. Another part of this is to explain and explore how the church grounds its convictions about God. This can all too quickly go all the way from sorting out what is involved in the appeal to faith, revelation, reason, and experience, to working on full-scale theories of rationality, justification, and knowledge. This is where the spill-over into epistemology is inevitable, and perceptive readers will already be aware of how I propose to deal with this challenge. In order to forestall worries about evasion let me take up that issue again for one last time.

A clear-headed theologian will assume a whole host of epistemological proposals that can be left to the work of philosophy. In this instance, we are in the same boat as the historian, or the natural scientist, or the lawyer, or the ordinary citizens of the world. Theologians should not get uptight about this sort of dependence; other perfectly respectable intellectual disciplines take this course without fuss or a bad conscience. We assume that we can trust a host of cognitive capacities, dispositions, practices, and virtues. For example: we trust memory, perception, conscience, intuition, the laws of logic, induction, deduction, and the like. We rely on cumulative case arguments, arguments to the best explanation, and the like. We assume the cultivation of intellectual virtues in the acquisition and maintenance of our beliefs. We assume the cultivation of attentiveness, of courage in following the truth, of persistence in holding on to the truth, of discernment, of wisdom, of fruitful curiosity, of discretion, of intellectual humility, of creative imagination, of teachableness, of foresight, of honesty, of consistency, of comprehensiveness in covering the relevant data, and so on. Equally, we assume in theology that we will seek to eliminate intellectual vice. We will resist closed-mindedness, obtuseness, gullibility, superficiality, wishful thinking, self-deception, dogmatism, idle curiosity. These matters belong in epistemology proper. There is no need to sort out all these issues before we proceed. This is a standard that is not met in a host of disciplines; we deploy an intellectual double standard if we require this in theology. We can help ourselves at the outset to all sorts of platitudes with a good conscience.

It is especially important for the theologian to pay particular heed to those epistemological issues that are unique to theology. This is surely one reason why the issue of norm or norms in theology crops up in the arena of prolegomena. Many of the norms taken up in this arena are general in nature. For example, consistency, comprehensiveness, coherence, fittingness to situation, and the like are really general intellectual norms that are not unique to theology. Again, we fall back into the arms of the epistemologist and should gladly welcome any help we can receive. Other norms are not general. In particular, it is obvious that the topic of divine revelation is an issue of exceptional importance to the systematic theologian, a fact that is readily manifest in most volumes of systematic theology. I mean here revelation of either the nature and character of God or of the purposes and will of God. In the neighborhood of divine revelation, we need also pay attention to the potential place of experience of God; both are normally contrasted with reason or inference. So clearly the theologian should be aware of the nature and relations between natural theology, religious experience, and revelation. In turn this discussion will spill over into the relation between these phenomena and Scripture and tradition.

It is fanciful and unrealistic to think that we can avoid these topics altogether, or even that we should avoid them. Inevitably, we shall find that we deploy epistemological proposals either tacitly or in an ad hoc manner in our work in systematic theology. We shall be drawn into epistemological matters by way of appropriate digression or by way of necessary explanation for other things we want to say. This is exactly as it should be, so we should relax and not be afraid to speak of divine revelation, religious experience, proper inference from features of experience and the world, and the like. Similar kinds of moves will occur when we deploy other philosophical considerations, say, crucial conceptual and material considerations about identity, action, meaning, contingency, necessity, and the like. We should operate the same way here: be aware as best we can of such claims and their import for theology.

All I insist on is that we not make these moves on the cheap. We recognize their place in our work; we gladly remember the constraints imposed on us by the aims of systematic theology; we come clean on the experts and authorities that we rely on; and we insist on appropriate and rigorous evaluation of all the philosophical assumptions we deploy. Failure to face the music here is one of the more embarrassing features of much contemporary systematic theology. There is far too much sloppiness, moralistic hand-waving, declamation, super-cilious sarcasm, question-begging slogans, whistling in the dark, and outright self-deception. I have fallen into a jeremiad. I repent and move on. We should readily avail ourselves of all the philosophical help we need in systematic theology, but we must do so with the clear acknowledgment that somebody somewhere has to foot the bill. Sooner or later, if we fail to do this, we will be confronted by the bill-collectors or mugged by their collection agencies.

As to sources, effectively there is no boundary that can or should be set as to which ones we can draw on. Sources simply refer to any material we choose to use to achieve the end in view. Norms are different: they refer to the grounds or warrants for theological claims. Frankly, it is in the use of sources where the cultivation of creativity is crucial. Anything within our overall purposes which staves off boredom, which fosters cheerfulness, and which keeps us focused and engaged is to be welcomed.

I mentioned, nay, lamented, the fragmentation that confronts us in the sub-disciplines that make up theological studies today. We have biblical studies, church history and history of doctrine, philosophical theology, moral the-ology, systematic theology, and practical theology. Within this the crown jewels belong to biblical studies. Yet this field no longer is in the mood to deliver the resources theologians at one time ordered for timely delivery at the outset of their journey. Furthermore, biblical studies has become so diverse and contested, not least because of prior ontological and epistemological commitments that are in play. The same applies to the history of doctrine and, most certainly, to philosophical theology. Of late we have seen in the latter case the emergence of a whole new effort to deploy the resources of analytic philosophy within the heartlands of systematic theology.[18]

---

[18]   See Oliver D. Crisp and Michael C. Rea, eds., *Analytic Theology: New Essays in the Philosophy of Theology* (Oxford: Oxford University Press, 2009).

Given what I have argued in this chapter it is tempting to call for a reordering of the sub-disciplines in theological studies. It would be nice if biblical scholars read Scripture with appropriate theological sensitivity; after all, these texts are robustly theological. If we read the Scriptures as functional atheists, we can predict that the results are likely to be meager in the extreme. The same applies to our understanding of the history of the church and her teaching. If we study church history and doctrine with a hermeneutic of suspicion rather than a hermeneutic of openness to divine action, then it will be no surprise that our resources in that arena will be in short supply. Hence, it is tempting to turn the current arrangements on their head. Begin with proper grounding in systematic theology and then follow up with extensive work in the sub-disciplines.

The crucial field is, of course, biblical studies. Søren Kierkegaard once judged that the situation was so bad that drastic action should be taken. He gave an explicit order: "Kill the commentators."[19]

> Today's mass of Bible interpreters have damaged, more than they have helped, our understanding of the Bible. In reading the scholars it has become necessary to do as one does at a play where a profusion of spectators and spotlights prevent, as it were, our enjoyment of the play itself and instead we are treated to little incidents. To see the play one has to overlook them, if possible, or enter by a way that has not yet been blocked. The commentator has indeed become a most hazardous meddler.[20]

We live in fact in much more propitious times; there are whole series of biblical commentaries that are providing rich theological interpretations of Scripture. In the future, we are even likely to have to hand rich philosophical readings of Scripture that open up new vistas for the theologian.[21] More broadly, it was essential that biblical studies cut its apron strings from theology in order to make room for much more accurate readings of the biblical material in their historical context. Moreover, the theologian is now free to take up Scripture without requiring that Scripture be manipulated into saying what later developments on theology rightly require. Scripture has its own

---

[19] Søren Kierkegaard, "'Alone with God's Word' and 'Kill the Commentators'," in Charles E. Moore, ed., *Provocations: Spiritual Writings of Kierkegaard* (Walden, NY: Plough Publishing House), 196. I discuss the significance of this observation in "Scripture," in Joel D. S. Rasmussen, Judith Wolfe, and Johannes Zachhuber, eds., *The Oxford Handbook of Nineteenth-Century Christian Thought* (Oxford: Oxford University Press, 2017), 628–42.

[20] Kierkegaard, "'Alone with God's Word' and 'Kill the Commentators'," 195.

[21] A pioneering work is that of Yoram Hazony, *The Philosophy of Hebrew Scripture* (Cambridge: Cambridge University Press, 2012). See also Kenneth Seeskin, *Thinking about Torah: A Philosopher Reads the Bible* (Lincoln: University of Nebraska Press, 2016). Consult also the splendid commentaries of Rabbi Jonathan Sacks on the weekly readings of the Jewish Bible. Sacks trained initially as a philosopher at Cambridge before become a distinguished Torah scholar. Four volumes are currently available: Genesis, Exodus, Leviticus, and Numbers.

unique place to play within the rich canonical heritage of the church. So too do the creeds. As a medium of divine revelation, biblical teaching will always play a pivotal role in systematic theology. However, this vision of Scripture is only a half truth, for its primary purpose is soteriological. Moreover, the creed is not a portable scripture; it has its own integrity and its own unique place in the formation of disciples of Jesus Christ. As we have seen, it paves the way for the work of the systematic theologian, an operation which is quite different from that taken up, say, in what is called biblical theology.[22]

We can leave this kind of rumination to posterity. In the meantime, we make a virtue of necessity and get on with our work. There are in fact signs that the long night of functional atheism or agnosticism in theological studies is coming to an end. Even so, theologians have learned long ago to plunder the Egyptians and take captive foreign materials. "Therefore every scribe who has been trained for the kingdom is like the master of a household who brings out of his treasure what is new and what is old."[23]

---

[22] For a seminal treatment of this enterprise as it applies to the Old Testament in the modern period see James Barr, *The Concept of Biblical Theology: An Old Testament Perspective* (Minneapolis, MN: Fortress Press, 1999). While there is much to learn from biblical theologies, they cannot replace the work of systematic theology; nor are they some kind of required prelude.

[23] Matthew 13:52.

3

The Divine Trinity

Now the eleven disciples went to Galilee, to the mountain to which Jesus had directed them. When they saw him, they worshipped him. And Jesus came and said to them, 'All authority on heaven and on earth has been given to me. Go therefore and make disciples of all nations, baptizing them in the name of the Father and of the Son and of the Holy Spirit, and teaching them to obey everything that I have commanded you. And remember, I am with you always to the end of the age.'

Matthew 28:16–20.

In a remarkable thunderbolt Jesus gives his disciples a dire warning: "If anyone of you put a stumbling block before one of these little ones who believe in me, it were better for you if a great millstone were fastened around your neck and you were drowned in the depth of the sea."[1] There are, no doubt, many ways in which we can cause one of these little ones to fall or stumble. We can cause them to stumble by ridiculing them in public, by shaming them into thinking they are stupid and naïve. Or we can cause them to stumble by our sin, leading them to doubt if holiness is really possible or to give up on the church as crucial to the work of God. Or we can cause them to stumble by confusing them, by rambling all over the place in our teaching. In this instance, we cause them to fall by our own intellectual laziness and indifference. We fail to think things through, throw out a few theological platitudes, and then find other things to do. Or we can cause them to stumble by introducing all sorts of false ideas about God and about ourselves. In other words, we become incompetent theologians, teachers who are entirely sincere and well-intentioned but who ultimately shoot wide of the truth and thus mislead the rational sheep of Christ in faith and practice. The words of our Lord strike me as applying to all of these cases and more.

As the church went from Jerusalem to Judaea and then on out to the ends of the earth, she took this warning seriously. She developed what I have identified as a rich canonical heritage in order to enable people to come to faith and then

---

[1] Matthew 18:5–7.

to survive in a world that readily ridiculed those who were baptized and often persecuted and killed them. Within this canonical heritage of materials, persons, and practices, the creed had a pivotal role. The creed is more than a map; it is also a kind of *curriculum vitae* for God. The heart of the creed is a vision of God. It is a threefold confession: We believe in God the Father; we believe in God the Son; we believe in God the Holy Spirit. The church signals here in an unmistakable fashion that its core vision of God is Trinitarian. God is Triune. The proper name for God is the Trinity: Father, Son, and Holy Spirit. God has one nature in three mutually interrelating persons. The Father is God; the Son is God; the Holy Spirit is God; yet there are not three gods, but one living God.

This vision of God as Triune is clearly a challenge to our intellects. To many it is an absurdity; others worry that idolatry lurks in the neighborhood. However, let's not move too fast just yet. We need to feel what is at stake. One way to do this is by way of contrasts. Consider the alternative visions of God we meet in popular culture and even in the academy.

God can readily be construed as a designer God carefully constructed to fit our churches and our sub-cultures. God is a Gummy Bear deity. God is a cosmic granddaddy waving in the background to pat us on the back and talk nicely to us; God is a grandma deity ever ready with a consoling word of kindness and comfort to keep us from being unhappy and depressed. God is the God of the instant platitude, of just the right list of little principles that will fix our lives for the coming week. Alternatively, God is a Robin Hood deity on hand to redistribute wealth, power, and status; God is a kick-ass deity ready to destroy the bastions of neo-liberal states and to unhinge the battalions of corrupt capitalist systems.

This tragedy is sometimes borne out by our worship. Given the Santa Claus deity of crucial sectors of popular religion, given this Gummy Bear deity, people literally saunter into church and lounge around. There is no sense of awe or fear; there is no sense of deep reverence; there isn't even any love. God is like grandma: she is to be tolerated in a kindly sort of way; after all, there might be something in the will; and there is always the insurance money to fall back on. In this instance worship smells of pious sentimentality. Hence, people come looking for bread and are given candy; they come looking for wine and are given stale, fizzy lemonade.

Alternatively, given the Rambo deity or the Amazonian deity incarnate in the poor and oppressed, given the warrior deity already at work in the revolution, worship becomes an occasion for multi-cultural self-congratulation. Worship in this instance is marked by moralistic sermons that repeat the pious political slogans of self-designated, self-appointed pseudo-experts on economics and politics. This god, we soon discover, has called and appointed a new group of prophets and priests to chastise the unrepentant and to provide the inside track on what Scripture really means. In this instance worship rapidly becomes tedious and suffocating. We come looking for bread and are given stones to throw at our enemies; we come looking for wine and are given burning oil to scald the rich.

There is one other popular picture of God that is worth mentioning. Call this deity the Good Samaritan God. We might call this God the nice God of popular piety. In this case, we think of God simply as good. God is here to help people. And we should help people, too. So let's develop strategies to build houses for Habitat, to help children in inner cities, to build orphanages in the Third World, to be generally kind to our neighbors, and thereby to transform the world. In this instance, we are constantly bombarded by psychological and moral exhortation, something that over time becomes dull and asphyxiating. We come looking for eternal life and are given merely temporal prophylactics; we come looking for a Word from God and are given well-meaning human advice and moral exhortation; we come looking for deliverance from evil and the salvation of our souls and are given pious schemes to transform the world and helpful hints from the latest manual on how to succeed in life. We come looking for God and are given a toy religion.

Compare all these with the God of the Exodus. Whatever we may say about the God of this little slice of the canonical heritage, we cannot say that this God is boring or operates at our behest. This God is an extraordinary agent who makes covenants with a people not just for their sake but for the sake of the whole world, who shows up in a burning bush, who argues with Moses until he is speechless, who ingeniously hardens Pharaoh's heart, who keeps promises to a group of despairing workers who have forgotten their ancestral birthright, who sends plagues in the dead of night, who thunders in lightning from Sinai, and who then turns around and gives in to Moses when he argues that Israel should be spared an act of divine genocide, and on and on. This is an awesome deity, a deity surrounded at once in light and darkness, a deity who is at once known and unknown, a deity who is both hidden and revealed, a deity under no human control and yet subject to human persuasion.[2]

I juxtapose these various descriptions, nay caricatures, of God for a purpose. There is constant danger that the concept of God suffers massive disintegration. In contrast to this, the church has to hand in her canonical heritage a

---

[2] "How should the Hebrews be other than terrified at that which they knew to be other than themselves, being humans judging it good to honor a golden calf? Such as they were, they did well to be afraid . . . Fear is nobler than sensuality. Fear is better than no God, better than a god made with hands . . . The worship of fear is true, although very low: and though not acceptable to God in itself, for only the worship of spirit and of truth is acceptable to Him, yet even in his sight it is precious. For He regards men not as they are merely, but as they are now growing, or capable of growing, toward that image, after which He made them that they might grow into it. Therefore a thousand stages, each in itself all but valueless, are of inestimable worth as the necessary and connected gradations of an infinite progress. A condition of declension would indicate a devil, may of growth indicate a saint." George MacDonald, in C. S. Lewis, *George MacDonald: An Anthology* (London: Collins, 1946), 2–3.

vision of God that can heal our souls and drive out the weather-beaten deities of the academy and the culture. So let's get down to business and do the best we can to retrieve and articulate the nature of the God of the canonical heritage.

The first and basic assertion to make about God can be put on a postcard: God is a unique, mysterious, tripersonal Agent.

As already noted, the canonical way to identify this vision of God is in terms of the doctrine of the Trinity. To speak of God as unique is to insist that he is not one more item in the universe; God does not belong to any genus that fits with a catalogue of entities in the created order; in fact, the universe totally depends on him. To speak of God as mysterious is to alert us to the fact that we will never fathom the reality who has inaugurated the kingdom of God in Christ through the Holy Spirit; we can comprehend God but never fully understand him. To speak of God as an Agent is to identify the ultimate ontological category in play; God is not Being, or Process, or Event, or Serendipitous Creativity, and the like.[3] The fundamental, ultimate category for understanding God is that of an Agent. Now that the initial assertion is in place, we can take up the exegetical, hermeneutical, and apologetic tasks of explicating this amazing vision of the divine. I shall take up two questions initially. First, how and why did Christians develop this side of their doctrine of God? Second, was the church right to make the decisions that it did canonically?

The crucial clue to start with is the claim that the Christian community developed a Trinitarian doctrine of God because of an accumulation of data and warrants; it was a creative effort to relieve an acute pain in its corporate brain.

The acute pain had three dimensions or poles. On the one side, the followers of Jesus inherited a Jewish monotheistic heritage. The earliest Christians were rooted in a Jewish matrix of experience and reflection. Even the Gentiles who joined were Gentiles who had come to God through a thoroughly Jewish carpenter from Palestine. Monotheism was therefore non-negotiable. The second side or pole of the issue is Christological. The early Christians were convinced that in meeting Jesus Christ they had encountered God. In fact, nowhere else had they come face-to-face so fully with the reality of God. In this Jewish day laborer, crucified and risen, they had met the awesome, mysterious divine reality. Consequently, they began in their worship, prayers, liturgy, and the like, to respond to Jesus in the same way that they responded to God, that is, in terms of total, unconditional surrender and obedience. This extended all the way to martyrdom.

---

[3] The move to this fundamental metaphysical category is deliberate. Its articulation and defense can be found in volume IV of this tetralogy. As with epistemology, we need to keep the metaphysical moves in their proper place so that we can engage in theology proper.

The third pole of their dissonance was their experience of the Holy Spirit in salvation and empowerment for obedience and ministry. Let me dwell on this for a moment. According to the primary narratives and literature that was circulating among them, their experience of the Holy Spirit began in their encounter with Jesus. Jesus was himself immersed in the Holy Spirit. He had been conceived of the Spirit, he was immersed in the Spirit at his baptism, he was transfigured in the light of the Holy Spirit at the transfiguration, he did his mighty works through the agency of the Holy Spirit, he offered himself up to God on the cross through an act of the Holy Spirit, and he promised that the disciples would enter into new dimensions of the reality and work of the Holy Spirit after the resurrection.

Moreover, from the beginnings the early church was a charismatic community. It was a community of the Holy Spirit. Her members were brought to birth into the kingdom through the Holy Spirit; her very understanding of Christ was a gift of the Holy Spirit; and her life of love and ministry and service were made possible through the active presence of the Holy Spirit.

With these three streams—Jewish monotheism, encounter with Jesus, and experience of the Spirit—coming together under one roof, we have an intellectual revolution waiting to happen. Sooner or later, one has to face the question of how these poles are going to be integrated or balanced. There are four ways to deal with the challenge.

The first option is to abandon monotheism and become tritheistic or polytheistic. The problems in this are obvious. It goes against the monotheistic developments inherited in the Old Testament. It goes against the anti-polytheistic thrust of the doctrine of creation. It also goes against the inherently economical character of monotheism.

The second option is to deny the divine character of Jesus and the Holy Spirit. One treats talk of the Son of God in more prosaic fashion as when, for example, the Old Testament speaks of Israel as a Son of God. This is not an ontological, but a functional title. Treat the Holy Spirit along the lines suggested in the Psalms as an aspect or attribute of God. In both cases, insist that while both kinds of discourse are crucial, they do not involve any unique ontological consequences for our thinking about God. The problem in this is clear. One has to play down the evidence for unique divine action in Jesus and in our lives through the Spirit displayed in the new materials emerging in the aftermath of the coming of Jesus in the gospels, epistles, and the like, and also captured in the uniquely Christian experience of God.

The third option was and is to deny any real distinctions between the Father, Son, and Holy Spirit. One could say, for example, that God is made known in three modes, as Father, Son, and Holy Spirit. These are really three names for God; they are three ways in which God appears to us; but there is no distinction in God per se. The problems here are much the same as in the second option. It is incompatible with the new canonical material emerging (the gospels, and the normative letters of Paul). One has to engage in forced exegesis of the dialogue between Jesus and God. It has obvious existential conundrums: if Jesus is a mode of God, *simpliciter*, without qualification, what happened to the universe when he was crucified? This sort of move would clearly have a major impact on the doctrine of creation.

The final and better option is as follows. Find a way to modify, to enrich, to transform monotheism so as to incorporate the reality of the Son and the Holy Spirit. There is ample precedent for that in wisdom traditions of the Old Testament. For Wisdom was seen as distinct yet united with God. This is precisely what we find in the tradition, for example, in the writings of the second and third centuries. There was a tendency initially to move in a hierarchical direction in order to incorporate the Son and the Holy Spirit. God the Father is the fountainhead of Unity; the Son and Holy Spirit are treated as subordinate. Already there is a profound, informal stretching of the concept of God. This worked until it was deeply tested by Arius in the fourth century. Arius pushed the hierarchical motif to its limits and applied the consequences to his account of the Son. He proposed that God is supreme; the Son is pre-temporal creation of God; divinity as applied to Jesus is a courtesy title. Everything else is created through the Son. Athanasius made the sharpest and most pertinent response to this. There were at least two central issues: the nature of soteriology and the indispensability of divine power in salvation and incarnation. The logic of this: Christ must be truly human if humans are to be truly saved, Christ must be truly divine if it is God who is truly our savior. The Son must be truly human and truly divine if we are to be saved. So, the nature and extent and origin of the divine healing of the human condition are at stake. Moreover, God is the kind of Agent who has it within his power to become incarnate within his own creation.

All this was hammered out in and around the Council of Nicaea in 325. The deposit of this debate shines through brilliantly in the Nicene Creed. Here there is a pulling back on hierarchy within God and an insistence that whatever God is, the Son is. As a further subplot, a similar move is implicit in the church's thinking on the Holy Spirit.

The end product is a very careful network of concepts. Three crucial technical moves were made in terminology. The first is Christological: Christ is of the same substance as the Father. Thus, a sharp contrast is drawn between *homoousios* (one in essence, consubstantial, of the same nature) and *homoiousios* (of similar nature). The second move is Trinitarian: there is one substance (*ousia, substantia*) (nature, substance, essence, being) and three Persons (*hypostasis* (pl. = *hypostases* or *persona* (pl. = *personae*)) in the Godhead. So, in the West, we have the formula of *una substantia et tres personae* (one substance and three Persons). In the East, we have the formula of *treis hypostaseis, mia ousia*, three hypostases (what stands under a given set of properties, a particular embodiment of certain qualities, or individual being) and one being. The third move speaks of the intra-Trinitarian relations: the Son is eternally begotten of the Father; the Spirit proceeds eternally from the Father.

I shall explore aspects of this very dense depiction of God in due course. Prior to that let's tackle briefly the question: Was the church right to say all this? The answer should be given in the affirmative. The church was not only right to accept the challenge it faced when it began to reflect on what to think and say about God, the church was fundamentally correct in what it said about God, given its prior commitments to Jesus and the Holy Spirit. Expressed negatively, the church could not accept a simple unitarianism or binitarianism in the doctrine of God, if it was to do justice to its encounter with Jesus and its experience of the Holy Spirit. Expressed positively, we might say that the doctrine of the Trinity is a brilliant, creative, and economical solution to the intellectual challenge embodied in the appearance of Jesus Christ in history and in the distinctively Christian experience of the Spirit of God. There is never any proof for such a subtle and ingenious piece of theological reasoning. The grounds for the correctness of this judgment are threefold: revelation, reason, and experience.

The doctrine of the Trinity is by far the most economical way to do justice to five sets of phenomena: the revelation of God in God's word and deed in Israel; the revelation of God in God's mighty acts in Jesus of Nazareth; the revelation of God to chosen apostles like Paul, called and appointed by God to interpret God's acts in Christ; the experience of the apostles in their encounter with Jesus of Nazareth/the experience of generations of Christian converts in their encounter with the apostolic and post-apostolic memory and witness to Jesus; the experience of Christians at Pentecost and thereafter, that is, the multiple and manifold experiences with God here and now which are naturally identified as experiences of and encounters with the Holy Spirit of God. In this analysis the place of reason is regulative rather than informative. The data are derived from revelation and experience; reason enriches the creative categories and the form in which the data are organized and held together.

We can express the crux of the matter in this way. Grant the revelatory and especially Christological premises, and grant the experiential premises, and the doctrine of the Trinity is a fitting and apt way to recognize the penultimate truth about God.

Notice two other considerations that are critical here. We are not here operating or thinking synchronically but diachronically. It is not as if we are surveying a body of data at one moment in time and making a judgment; we are not engaging in some sort of argument worked out by a single theological genius. We are following a line of development that takes place in a community over generations. Notice also this: the interpretation of this complex body of data is not gathered up by mere human ingenuity; we are also dealing with the divine assistance of the Holy Spirit in the church. It is the Holy Spirit in the church over time that, drawing on this kind of data and supplying badly needed cognitive cleansing, guides the church to this extraordinary vision of God.

The promise in play is given in the gospel of John:

> I have many things to say to you, but you cannot bear them now. When the Spirit of truth comes, he will guide you into all the truth, for he will not speak of his own, but will speak whatever he hears and he will declare to you the things that are to come. He will glorify me, because he will take what is mine and declare it to you. All that the Father has is mine. For this reason I said that he will take what is mine and declare it to you.[4]

John's gospel plays a pivotal role in the development of both the doctrines of the Trinity and the doctrine of the incarnation. This is not to say that the other gospels do not provide relevant material for these teachings. On the contrary, all of the gospels supply accounts of the life of Jesus and the action of the Holy Spirit which press us to move forward and think deeply about the nature of God. However, from the beginning it was recognized that the gospel of John stood apart from the other three in its daring theological assertions. Even then, John insists that there is more intellectual work to be done in the future. However, this can only happen after the earlier material has been digested. There is an essential process of incubation and explicit reflection. In this instance, we meet a familiar reality: some things can only be said after other things have been said. Moreover, given that what is at issue is the very nature of God, divine help is needed to fathom the truth of the matter. We cannot simply look up the relevant texts, apply standard logical rules, and immediately reach the truth about God. We are faced with another familiar reality: some truths are a matter of discernment rather than formal reasoning.

Paul takes a similar line when challenged about the place of the crucifixion of Jesus in his preaching to the Corinthians. On the one hand, he too draws attention to a distinction between initial teaching and later teaching in the formation of believers.

> And so, brothers and sisters, I could not speak to you as spiritual people, but rather as people of the flesh, as infants in Christ. I fed you with milk, not solid food, for you are not ready for solid food. Even now you are still not ready, for you are still in the flesh. For as long as there is jealousy and quarrelling among you, are you not in the flesh, and believing according to the human inclinations?[5]

However, the issue is not simply one of our cognitive malfunction due to vice; if that were the case all that would be needed is relevant repentance and good will. We also need divine assistance to fathom the deep truth about God. Paul

---

[4] John 16:12–15.   [5] 1 Corinthians 3:1–3.

works off an analogy related to the difficulty of understanding features of our own, all-too-human lives.

> For what human knows what is truly human except the human spirit that is within? So also no one comprehends what is truly God's except the Spirit of God. Now we have received not the spirit of the world, but the Spirit that is from God, so that we may understand the gifts bestowed upon us by God. And we speak of these things in words not taught by human wisdom but taught by the Spirit, interpreting spiritual things to those who are spiritual.[6]

The claim that the work of the Holy Spirit is crucial to our understanding of God was taken to a whole new level by Symeon the New Theologian. Drawing on Paul's image of the body in Romans 12:4–5, Symeon identifies various roles that the members of the body play in the proper functioning of the church. One important role is played by those especially gifted with creating the crucial concepts needed to understand God. Some fulfill the role of hands; others the shoulders; others the breast; others the legs and feet; others still the belly.

> Others, again, take the function of the thighs since they carry in themselves the fecundity of the concepts adequate to God of the mystical theology. They engender the Spirit of Wisdom upon the earth, i.e., the fruit of the Spirit and His Seed in the hearts of men, through the Word of their teaching.[7]

This is an astonishing and daring vision of the work of the theologian which calls for a deflationary vision of our standard conception of theology. For the most part, the theologian is a competent teacher of the tradition, although we should take the full measure of what that means as I indicated in the previous chapter on the tasks of theology.

The language used in the doctrine of the Trinity has been a challenge to those who want to work out everything strictly from Scripture. Thus, many have lamented the use of language derived from Greek metaphysics to delineate the nature of God. They have protested that we have left behind the language of Scripture and drifted perilously close if not completely into the language of pagan thought. There is no doubt but that the church has indeed adopted the categories of Greek metaphysics. Nor should we deny that we have gone above and beyond the language of Scripture. I grant both these obvious assumptions. However, this is by no means the end of the matter.

To begin, this worry will only hold initially if we have a strict, rationalistic vision of the appeal to Scripture. There would have been no interest in developing the doctrine of the Trinity if a clear-headed reading of a wide

---

[6] 1 Corinthians 2:11–13.
[7] Symeon the New Theologian, *On the Mystical Life, The Ethical Discourses, Vol. 1: The Church and the Last Things*, trans. Alexander Golitzen (Crestwood, NY: St. Vladimir's Seminary Press, 1995), 43.

range of biblical passages had not created precisely the dissonance that called for intellectual resolution. The doctrine is broadly scriptural but not precisely scriptural. However, this does not mean that the doctrine was a matter of simple deduction, or a matter of an argument to the best explanation intended to make best sense of the relevant scriptural texts.

Augustine states this point plainly.

> If we say that there are three persons in God, as a way of expressing what is common to the Father, the Son and the Holy Spirit, why do we not also say that there are three gods? The Father is a person, the Son is a person, and the Holy Spirit is a person. The Father is also God, the Son is God, and the Holy Spirit is God. Why then are there not three gods, or conversely, if all these are one God, why is there not just one person? . . . We use the term 'person' of the three not because Scripture does so but because otherwise we would have no way of describing them. Scripture does not authorize us to do this, but neither does it forbid us, and herein lies the difference, because Scripture does forbid us to say that there are three gods.[8]

Furthermore, we need to draw a distinction between the verbal reproduction of this or that passage of Scripture and the conceptualization of what is at stake in the articulation of the teaching of Scripture. I do not want to exaggerate the importance of this distinction; the doctrine of the Trinity goes beyond the teaching of Scripture. However, it is a mistake to insist that we adhere slavishly to the precise language of Scripture when the issue of how best to understand the nature of God was not the one under discussion. Once the question of the nature of God was pointedly raised by Arius, then the church discovered that it needed to borrow the language of philosophy to capture what was really at stake. Omit this language and we end up with language which is even less adequate. There is, therefore, no need to see the language of philosophy in crude and simple terms as pagan and thus alien to the church's vision of God. This observation rests on much too negative a view of the work of Greek philosophers. There is a mixture of sense and nonsense in their deliberations. Moreover, to claim that divine insight is totally absent from the better wisdom of philosophy works off much too narrow a vision of the relation between divine action and culture. We might say that God gave the pagan philosophers of old good dreams; that divine providence stretches all the way to the life of the mind across the world. Even so, it is clear that the church in borrowing this language baptized and transfigured it. It digested the relevant concepts and refashioned them to fit its own intellectual agenda. This is especially visible in the use of the term "Person." What was originally used to describe the mask of an actor in the theatre and was thus pretty thin in content, was enriched by divine revelation and experience of God and stretched to describe the inner

---

[8] Augustine, *On the Trinity*, 7.4.8.

relations within the divine life. Once we add that human agents are made in the image of God, the next step is to allow language that was originally invented to speak of God to enrich our conceptions of human agents. It is perhaps no accident that the loss of a deep vision of God as Trinity leads in time to a loss of a deep vision of human agents as genuine persons.

At least two other considerations need to be in place to appreciate what is going on in the development of the doctrine of the Trinity. First, consider the use of the terms "begetting" and "proceeding" to describe the relations between the Persons of the divine Trinity. John of Damascus astutely noted the significance of this distinction for securing the identity of the second and third Persons of the Trinity.

> In the case of the Godhead, we confess that there is only one nature and maintain that there are three subsistences actually existing in him. Everything related to the nature and existence of God is simple, the difference of the subsistences being recognized only in three properties that distinguish them—unbegottenness in the case of the Father, begottenness in the case of the Son and procession [in the case of the Holy Spirit]. We also know that these three are indivisible and inseparable from each other, united in one and interpenetrating each other without confusion. Nevertheless, they remain three distinct subsistences, even though they are united without confusion or separation. Each has an independent existence and individuality of its own—its own mode of existence—but they are one in their essence and in the properties that belong to that.[9]

Thus, we can distinguish the Persons by certain essential properties: the Father is unbegotten, the Son is begotten of the Father, and the Spirit proceeds from the Father.[10] However, even so, notice that this is language carefully drawn from Scripture; and it is left strictly undefined even in the most metaphysically inclined theologians who insisted on its canonical adoption by the church. It is as though we have simply reached a limit in our thinking and the church is content to rest with the language of John. For this reason, I eschew efforts to work out a vision of social Trinitarianism where speculation tends to move all too quickly in the direction of tritheism.

This semantic reserve is no mere casual affair. Theologians queue up to insist on the limits of our understanding, as they do with the doctrine of the incarnation when they insist that there are two natures—the divine and the human—fully present in the Son. These are the two great mysteries of Christian theology that must be faced head-on.[11] In part the issue is that our

---

[9] John of Damascus, *The Orthodox Faith*, 3.5.

[10] Later efforts to add the *filioque* clause and to insist that the Holy Spirit proceeds from the Father and the Son are mistaken in thinking that this new formula is essential in order to distinguish the Spirit from the Son. John of Damascus is exactly right in the way he formulates the distinction. I shall take up the issue of the *filioque* clause when I deal with the ontology of the Holy Spirit.

[11] I shall take up the general issue of mystery in Christian teaching in volume IV.

linguistic resources are tied to our earthly existence. Hence we rightly draw a distinction between cataphatic discourse and apophatic discourse when it comes to God. In the use of cataphatic discourse, we insist on substantial, positive comments about God; in the use of apophatic discourse, we insist on silence before the ineffable reality of God.

Gregory of Nyssa provides a telling description of the apophatic nature of our discourse.

> Imagine a sheer, steep crag, with a projecting edge at the top. Now imagine what a person would probably feel if he put his foot on the edge of this precipice and, looking down into the chasm below, saw no solid footing nor anything to hold on to. This is what I think the soul experiences when it goes beyond its footing in material things, in its quest for that which has no dimension and which exists from all eternity. For here there is nothing it can take hold of, neither place nor time, neither measure nor anything else; our minds cannot approach it. And thus the soul, slipping at every point, from what cannot be grasped, becomes dizzy and perplexed and returns once again to what is connatural to it, content now to know merely this about the Transcendent, that it is completely different from the nature of the things that the soul knows.[12]

Symeon the New Theologian is equally illuminating.

> Think of a man standing at night inside his house, with all the doors closed; and then suppose that he opens a window just at the moment when there is a sudden flash of lightning. Unable to bear its brightness, at once he protects himself by closing his eyes and drawing back from the window. So it is with the soul that is enclosed in the realm of the senses: if ever she peeps out through the window of the intellect, she is overwhelmed by the brightness, like light-ning, of the pledge of the Holy Spirit that is within her. Unable to bear the splendor of unveiled light, at once she is bewildered in her intellect and she draws back entirely upon herself, taking refuge, as in a house, among sensory and human things.[13]

Note carefully that it is an elementary semantic mistake to think that in the use of masculine imagery we are importing alien categories of sexuality into the church's teaching about God. The language of "fatherhood" is analogical; it suggests an analogy between God and the best human father we can imagine; if we miss this we are handicapped by the kind of literal mentality that is clearly ruled out by the apophatic character of our discourse. The language of begetting is also analogical; it references the ontological continuity between the Father and the Son. Animals and humans do not create their offspring; they beget them and are identified ontologically by precisely this language.

---

[12] Quoted in Kallistos Ware, *The Orthodox Way* (Crestwood, NY: St. Vladimir's Seminary Press, 2002), 29–30.
[13] Quoted in ibid., 30.

So the concept is now stretched to bring home the ontological identity of the Son as divine, surely a deft move to make.

Even more important in the contemporary scene, we poison our doctrinal claims by systematically reading sexual or gender categories into the canonical doctrine of the Trinity. Such interpretation was rejected with derision by the best teachers of the church.[14] Consider this pithy remark by Arnobius of Sicca:

> When we speak of God, we use a masculine word, but let no thoughtless person accuse us of saying that God is a man. It is not gender that is expressed but rather his name, its customary meaning and the way in which we habitually use words. The deity is not male, even though his name is of the masculine gender. In contrast, [pagans] attribute gender to the gods, by calling them either 'god' or 'goddess.' We cannot believe that God has a body because if we did, he would have to be male or female.[15]

Gregory of Nazianzus is even more forthright.

> Now for your say! Let the slings and the subtle inferences be drawn! 'The Holy Spirit must either be ingenerate or begotten. If he is ingenerate, there are two unoriginate beings. If he is begotten, we again have an alternative: either begotten of the Father or from the Son. If from the Father, there will be two sons who are brothers.' Make them twins if you like, or one older than the other, since you have a penchant for corporeal ideas. If he is begotten from the Son, our God apparently has a grandson, and what could be odder than that? We certainly have the arguments of people 'wise to do evil,' but unwilling to write what is good. For my part, if I saw the necessity of the alternatives, I should accept the realities without being put off by the names. But because the Son is 'Son' in a more elevated sense of the word, and since we have no other term to express his consubstantial derivation from God, it does not follow that we ought to think it essential to transfer wholesale to the divine sphere the earthly names of human family ties. Do you take it, by the same token, that our God is a male, because of the masculine nouns 'God' and 'Father'? Is the Godhead a female, because in Greek the word is feminine? Is the word 'Spirit' neuter in Greek, because the Spirit is sterile? If you want to take the joke further you could say, as the trashy myths of old did, that God coupled with his own will and fathered the Son. We should be faced with the bisexual God of Marcion, who pictured those out-landish aeons.[16]

Does all this matter? Indeed it matters. To begin we can express the significance of the doctrine of the Trinity negatively. Once the church loses this intellectual jewel, it will lose its moorings. It will lose its Christological heritage and suffer grievous loss overall, or it can keep its Christological heritage and be guilty

---

[14] I shall take up this concern in some detail in volume IV.
[15] Quoted in Gerald L. Bray, ed., *Ancient Christian Doctrine, I: We Believe in One God* (Downers Grove, IL: IVP Academic, 2009), 38.
[16] Gregory of Nazianzus, *Theological Orations*, 31.7.

of idolatry. Equally, the church will cease to foster deep and intimate experience of God in salvation; or keeping these, it will be bereft of adequate conceptual resources to speak about its deepest experiences of God. The doctrine of the Trinity holds all these together, insisting that all three Persons of the Trinity find their rightful place in the life of the church. It is no accident that the doctrine has been upheld across the great divisions of the church across the centuries. Churches instinctively know that they cannot dispose of it without shedding theological tears.

Speaking more positively, it must be said initially that the doctrine of the Trinity arises out of the narrative of divine action in creation and redemption. The Triune God who created the universe has healed it in the activity of the Son and the Holy Spirit. The essence of God has been cautiously but forth-rightly conceptualized in such a way as to depict accurately the divine action named in the Scripture and in the experience of the church. There is no other God above or behind the mighty acts of God; God is Triune all the way to the bottom. Even then, beyond insisting that all the actions of the divine persons are one in operation, that issue is left as a piece of unfinished business in the life of the church.

This depiction of God as Triune shows up again and again in Christian devotion and in the church's worship. Consider just two examples from two great hymn writers, Isaac Watts and Charles Wesley.

> Almighty God, to thee
> Be endless honours done
> The Undivided Three,
> And the mysterious One:
> Where reason fails with all her powers,
> There faith prevails, and love adores.[17]

> Eternal, triune Lord!
> Let all the hosts above,
> Let all the sons of men, record
> And dwell upon thy love.
> When heaven and earth are fled
> Before thy glorious face,
> Sing all the saints thy love has made
> Thine everlasting praise.[18]

A third consideration is brought to mind in the naming of two attributes of God by Watts and Wesley. They speak God as "almighty" and as "love." This is not accidental. The doctrine of the Trinity in referring us back to divine action picks out these two attributes almost as a matter of course. God is

---

[17] Isaac Watts, in *Hymns and Psalms: A Methodist and Ecumenical Hymn Book* (London: Methodist Publishing House, 1983), number 18.
[18] Charles Wesley, in ibid., number 4.

almighty in what he has done for us in creation and redemption; only a God with almighty power can perform such actions. Equally, God displays his love in what he has done for us in creation and redemption; only a God of extraordinary love can perform such actions. Scripture goes further on this front by awkwardly noting that God is love, a sentence which makes no grammatical sense. "Beloved, let us love one another, because love is from God; everyone who loves is born of God and is known of God. Whoever does not love does not know God, for God is love."[19] The temptation to read this as requiring that God must of necessity create the universe has been a perennial one. After all, if God is love, and God is necessarily and everlastingly love, there must, so it is argued, be a creation to love. The more astute observation is this: in the three Persons of the Trinity we already have to hand an obvious way to capture this awkward grammatical expression in its full intensity. The love that is poured out in creation and redemption already has a home in the very essence and heart of God. We are already drifting nicely into a new phase of our work, a treatment of the attributes of God.

[19] 1 John 4:7–8.

4

The Attributes of God

I pray that the God of our Lord Jesus Christ, the Father of glory, may give you a spirit of wisdom and revelation as you come to know him, so that, with the eyes of your heart enlightened, you may know what is the hope to which he has called you, what are the riches of his glorious inheritance among the saints, and what is the immeasurable greatness of his power for us who believe, according to the working of his great power.

Ephesians 1:17–20.

I was born in the bogs of Ireland underneath a small mountain called Topped Mountain. I continue to climb it from time to time when I go back. The journey during my adolescent years was simple. I would take my bicycle with my friends along the narrow back roads, and then we would leave them on a curve on the road where the footpath to the mountain began. On the journey up the mountain, we were sheltered in a deep dip or bowl hollowed out on the south side of the mountain; all we could see was the path behind us, the little lake at the bottom of the bowl, and a farmhouse over on the other side. We steadily climbed the south side, looking out for the rabbits, the sheep, the wild flowers, and the cattle quietly grazing in the gorse. Then we came to the last short stretch to the top and suddenly we were right at the top, right on the peak, and, in an instant, we were confronted with a dazzling sight. We could see the full horizons on every side and catch a glimpse of a world that until then was completely hidden from view. The sight on a good day was extraordinary in its range and richness. We could see as far as the eye could see in every direction; the sight before was breathtaking; yet we knew there was always more to see and no map would even begin to capture it.

Discovering the canonical heritage of the church has been like this for me. I was first introduced to faith by ordinary farmers and preachers, who lovingly began to open up the treasures of the faith. Many would dismiss these people as narrow and ignorant; they had limited theological training; and, truth to tell, some of them were not very worldly-wise. One of my uncles used to make fun of them. He especially disliked the amount of hair-oil sported by one of them, a humble farmer called Willie Darragh. My uncle used to say in his lilting accent: "The oil was shining on his head like raindrops on the tar." Then he would burst out into his uproarious laughter. However, the humble farmer with the hair-oil in his little rural church had built a road to God as best he knew how. Even though I lost my way for a time and became an atheist, I never want to forget him and the others who taught me. Following the road that they set me on has taken me far away from the bogs of Ireland. That same road has taken me over time to the vast treasures of teaching and instruction embedded in the canonical heritage of the church. Crucial to systematic theology is finding a way around that world, pausing to identify its riches with care and affection.

The crucial first step is to become familiar with the doctrine of the Trinity. This is not just a matter of logical priority; it is also a matter of spiritual priority. We are baptized in the name of the Holy Trinity. In the initial phase of the Christian life in and around baptism we come to terms with entry into the kingdom of God by responding to the arrival of the kingdom in the death and resurrection of the Son of God in history through the working of the Holy Spirit within us now. Here we discover that God is absolutely and resolutely turned towards sinners and utterly determined to reorder our lives for the good. Hence, we come to experience the love and power of God in its most intense form. Hence, the Gospel itself and our response to it naturally lead to a ready embrace of the doctrine of the Trinity. There is a pleasing correlation between our intellectual and spiritual priorities: the Trinity operates both as the name of God we receive initially in the church and as the intellectual horizon of life in the kingdom of God.

I am assuming afresh here that the ultimate category for understanding God is that of a unique, mysterious, tripersonal Agent. Agents are made known through what they do. Thus, in coming to know God as Father, Son, and Holy Spirit, we also come to know the intrinsically attractive love and the almighty power of God. These two pivotal attributes are manifest in the divine actions that were critical in the construction of the doctrine of the Trinity. So, indirectly, the doctrine of the Trinity launches us into a treatment of the attributes of God. However, we need to hesitate before we move on, for it is common knowledge that once we take up an exposition of the attributes of God it is easy to get lost in a laundry list of abstractions. Moreover, the deep connection between the doctrine of God and intimate devotion to God can readily be severed. One strategy to overcome this is to make clear the obvious connection between the attributes of God and radical trust in God. I shall take up this challenge in due course.

The problem, however, runs much deeper than one of abstraction, boredom, and spiritual malfunction. The problem is that standard accounts of the attributes of God run into two sorts of difficulties. First, they do not connect naturally with the doctrine of the Trinity and therefore introduce an unfortunate disjunction and contrast in our vision of God. Second, certain attributes begin to show up, most notably impassibility, immutability, and simplicity, that do not seem to square with the vision of God required by the doctrine of the Trinity. The result is that treatment of the attributes comes across as a hodgepodge of concepts only loosely if at all connected to the deep faith of the church. I have sought to alleviate this problem initially by noting that the doctrine of the Trinity naturally requires us to take up the attributes of power and love because they arise felicitously from exactly the same sources as the doctrine of the Trinity. Yet this is little more than a gesture in the teeth of the difficulties just enumerated.

Happily, there is an easy diagnosis and correlative solution to our predicament with respect to the attributes of God. The acute problems just noted arise because we have imported alien conceptions of the divine into our vision of God. Rather than think of God as an Agent we have turned to various unbaptized philosophical notions, like Being or Being beyond Being, and then looked to these as the source and warrant for our account of the attributes.[1] This fatal strategy not only means that the account of the attributes loses its proper grounding in the agency and action of God; it also means that alien notions readily get introduced and become the cause of endless confusion. The solution is to return to the rough ground of divine agency and divine action and explore from that ground what we should say with respect to the attributes of God. Furthermore, this strategy will give us clues as to how to order our account of the attributes of God. We begin with those at the heart of divine agency and divine action given to us in divine revelation and work out from there to the wider horizon of divine action that a full account of the attributes will give us.

It is important we understand the diagnosis and solution I am adopting. I am not rejecting the use of philosophical categories in the articulation of the attributes of God. I am rejecting alien philosophical categories that are derived from a merely philosophical conception of God borrowed from philosophy without due caution. First, I am insisting on deriving our vision of the attributes from a vision of God clearly identified at the outset as a unique, mysterious, tripersonal Agent. This is, of course, controversial and, as already promised, will be defended elsewhere. Second, I am prospectively insisting that it is good and proper to make use of philosophical reflection in our account of the attributes. The warrant for this is already to hand in the worship of the Holy Trinity. Here, the relevant clue is found in the brilliant insight of Anselm when he noted in worship that the God he worshipped—and this God was none other than the Trinity—was rightly conceived as that than which none greater could be thought. Anselm is here providing a splendid way to

---

[1] This is the constant danger also of a natural theology that seeks to build a conception of God that will provide an explanation for the universe and varied features we find within it like consciousness, order, beauty, religious experience, and the rest. For a brilliant articulation of this vision see Richard Swinburne, *The Existence of God* (Oxford: Clarendon Press, 1979).

make explicit the long-standing practice of theologians who articulated various accounts of the divine perfections. These perfections in turn were often derived from the practice of worship. Consider Psalm 145.

> One generation shall laud your works to another, and shall declare your mighty acts. On the glorious splendor of your majesty, and on your wondrous works, I will meditate. The might of your awesome deeds shall be proclaimed and I will declare your greatness. They shall celebrate the fame of your abundant good news, and shall sing aloud of your righteousness. The Lord is gracious and merciful, slow to anger and abounding in steadfast love. The Lord is good to all, and his compassion is over all that he has made.[2]

Note the close connection of the attributes applied to God here to divine action, to God's mighty acts. Note also here and throughout the Psalm the span of divine attributes. God is awesome, great, righteous, gracious, merciful, slow to anger, abounding in steadfast love, good to all, compassionate, powerful, faithful, gracious, just, and near to all. Anselm's mode of thinking is precisely the kind of philosophical reflection that is not only welcome but mandated. At one stroke, it allows us to take on board many of the traditional attributes of God without losing our moorings in the faith of the church already expressed in worship.

I have already noted that the order of presentation is important. We begin at the heart of the faith; we move outward into a wider horizon. It may help if we gather together our catalogue of attributes in two clusters. As a point of entry into the first cluster consider the amazing account of the theophany given to Moses on Sinai.

> Moses said, 'Show me your glory, I pray.' And he [the Lord] said, 'I will make all my goodness pass before you, and will proclaim before you my name, "The Lord"; and I will be gracious to whom I will be gracious, and will show mercy to whom I will show mercy.'[3]

The revelation is repeated almost verbatim a short time afterwards.

> The Lord passed before him, and proclaimed, 'The Lord, the Lord, a God merciful and gracious, slow to anger, abounding in steadfast love and faithfulness, keeping steadfast love for the thousandth generation, forgiving iniquity and transgression of sin, yet by no means clearing the guilty, but visiting the iniquity of parents upon the children and the children's children, to the third and fourth generation.'[4]

The initial predicates applied to God here are these: good, gracious, merciful, faithful, forgiving, and slow to anger. This suggests a cluster of attributes that we might more formally identify in and around the goodness of God.

---

[2] Psalm 145:4–9.   [3] Exodus 33:19.   [4] Exodus 34:6–7.

1. God is all loving. God is unsurpassing in his love. There are no limits to God's love. God's love knows no bounds; its length, depth, breadth, and height are inexhaustible and limitless.

2. God is the source of all true human happiness and human welfare. As creatures, we find our true destiny and wellbeing in our relation to God.

3. God is worthy of worship. God is the kind of Agent whose nature and attributes naturally and rightly evoke in humans such dispositions as: respect, reverence, awe, fear, attraction, love, and deep delight. God is intrinsically beautiful.

4. God is just. God is no respecter of persons. Jew and Gentile stand equal before God. God is committed to the rescue of all, regardless of history or background or pedigree. There are no special arrangements due to status, gender, race, age, ethnicity, biology, or social location.

5. God is holy. God is radically opposed to human evil and cares about the suffering of the oppressed and beleaguered. God displays his disapproval and wrath against human sin by handing us over to our own desires and passions individually, corporately, and across the generations.

6. God is righteous, intervening in history to fulfill his covenant promises, to put things right when they go wrong, and to vindicate those who put their trust in him.

7. God is free. When God acts or engages in any activity, God freely and fully forms God's own intentions in such action or activity. God reacts just as God deems appropriate to events in the world. God finally determines how God reacts; this is not the case with creation or with creatures God has made.[5]

As a point of entry into a second cluster of attributes, consider the following manifestation of God to Moses.

> Say therefore to the Israelites, 'I am the Lord, and I will free you from the burdens of the Egyptians and deliver you from slavery to them. I will redeem you with an outstretched arm and with mighty acts of judgment. I will take you as my people, and I will be your God. You shall know that I am the Lord your God, who has freed you from the burden of the Egyptians. I will bring you into the land that I swore to give to you for a possession. I am the Lord.'[6]

---

[5] Consider the way C. S. Lewis captures what is at issue here: "Perfect goodness can never debate the end to be attained, and perfect wisdom cannot debate about the means suited to achieve it. The freedom of God consists in the fact that no cause other than Himself produces His acts and no external obstacle impedes them—that his own goodness is the root from which they all grow and His own omnipotence the air in which they all flower." Clyde Kilby, ed., *A Mind Awake: An Anthology of C. S. Lewis* (San Diego: Harcourt, Inc., 1968), 80.

[6] Exodus 6:6–8.

This passage suggests a cluster of attributes that can be grouped in and around the power of God.

1. God is omnipotent. There are no non-logical constraints or limits on God's power other than those accepted by God. God is able to bring about those states of affairs that are logically possible and that fit within God's purpose. This is not to be confused with divine causal determinism, the view that all events are caused by God. The property of "being omnipotent" has no such entailment; it is simply logically confusing to say that it does.[7]

2. God is both eternal and everlasting. God transcends all time and yet, whatever time there is in our earthly existence, God exists throughout it. God both transcends and indwells time and space.

3. God is omniscient. God knows everything it is logically possible to know. If the future can be known (a claim I take to be true), then God knows the future.[8] We can go one step further. Consider this proposition: God knew twenty-four hours ago that I would freely work on this chapter today. This is an entirely coherent proposition. Whatever happens to me, or whatever I do after completing this chapter, God surely knows what is the case with respect to the future. And God's knowing in the future does not mean or entail that God determines the future.

4. God is omnipresent. The agency of God is extended throughout the entire universe simultaneously. God both creates space and indwells it. If God stopped breathing, the whole world would fall apart.

5. God is impassible. God is not like fickle human agents or many of the Greek and Roman deities who are subject to the ebb and flow of their emotions and passions. God is steadfast and firm in total, irreversible faithfulness to the covenant of love and grace in Israel and in Jesus Christ. God will have mercy on whom he will have mercy; there is absolutely nothing we can do to stop that. God is impassible to our attempts to limit grace to this or that select group.

---

[7] There is significant confusion between divine omnipotence and divine sovereignty in some quarters. Thus it is sometimes claimed that omnipotence means that God is sovereign, and to claim that God is sovereign is to claim that God causally determines all that happens. The mistake here is this: there is a failure to note that these properties are logically independent properties. Properties A and B are logically independent properties if the statement that X has property A neither entails nor is entailed by the statement that X has B. The properties of "being omnipotent," "being sovereign," and "causally determining all that happens" when applied to any entity X neither entail nor are entailed by each other. It is even false to assert that if X conjunctively has the property "being omnipotent" and the property "being sovereign" then X must also have the property of "causally determining all that happens." These are logically independent properties.

[8] It is sometimes thought that if God knows the future then the future is determined. This proposition is clearly false. I know that the sun will come up tomorrow but this in no way entails that I determine that the sun will come up tomorrow.

6. God is immutable. In his essential attributes, he does not change. God does not grow or wear out. God does not change in his character. God's fundamental character remains fixed and dependable.

7. God's existence is a necessary existence. No other agent, or natural law, or principle of necessity, or the like, is responsible for the existence of God. God is radically independent. Everything non-divine could disappear and God would still exist in all the fullness of the divine being. God cannot go out of existence; this is causally impossible; there are no causally sufficient conditions for bringing about the end of God's existence.[9]

No classification of the divine attributes can begin to do justice to the richness of the comprehensive account of divine attributes that is needed to describe adequately the God made known in the canonical heritage of the church. Taken together, lists like these begin to summarize the crucial ingredients that constitute a Christian doctrine of the attributes of God. The doctrine of the attributes is rich, complex, subtle, and dense. Furthermore, whatever predicates we use need to be constantly heard in, with, and through the rich materials made available in the Scriptures, the lives of the saints, the great hymns and liturgies of the church, and above all in our constant immersion in the Gospel itself. I introduced my account by a quotation from Scripture (Ephesians 1:17–20) in part to make precisely this point. Yet it is important to step above and beyond Scripture in order to pause and get a firm grasp of the nature of the God we worship and serve. This practice will ensure that our theology remains vigorously theocentric. It will also enrich our reading of Scripture because it will alert us to features of the text we might otherwise overlook.

In order to ensure that our theology is indeed theocentric it may be helpful to work through a number of hermeneutical comments at this stage in the presentation. We need to cleanse the theological stables of alien material that can readily get in the way of spiritual nourishment.

For a start, we need to avoid the equivocation and double-speak that all too often shows up in expositions of the attributes. The attributes of God really do give us a faithful and accurate account of who God is. They are not mere accounts of the divine worked up from below from pious feelings. To be sure, meditating and encountering this God—the God depicted in the foregoing descriptions—readily brings about a host of feelings by way of response. We naturally develop a sense of awe, love, fear, and penitence. However, these

---

[9] This observation has fascinating implications for the place of theology in bringing explanations to closure. The proposition "God exists" is neither analytic nor logically necessary. However, in providing explanations for states of affairs, if the chain ends with the proposition "God exists," we have reached the final resting place of explanation. The assertion that God is a necessary being means that some proposition referring to God is the final answer to our search for explanation. This is one of the deep insights buried in the ontological argument for the existence of God.

feelings and dispositions are evoked by the object of our affections and passions; the object is not somehow created out of those feelings by way of projection. The referent for "God" is God in all his glory, not our feelings about God.

Equally, the attributes of God are not mere conventional assertions reflecting our all-too-human perspectives about some kind of Infinite or Absolute or other philosophical entity dragged into theology as a substitute for the Living God.[10] There are, of course, various philosophical speculations that would seek to veto any serious effort to speak of God as he really is. Theologians have been quick to follow suit and launch into lush discourse that tells us of the utter incomprehensibility of God. Consider a passage from Ephrem the Syrian.

> It is an aberration if we try and examine what God is and what he is like. For how can we describe the image of his being in us, which is similar to the mind? We cannot examine his appearance in such a way as to describe it in our intellect. He hears but without ears, he speaks without a mouth, he works without hands, and he sees without eyes. Our mind cannot understand this, and for that reason it stops trying to do so.[11]

The incoherence of this observation is obvious. We are initially forbidden to inquire about what God is like and in the next breath we are told that there is a similarity between God and mind. There is also a crude semantic claim to the effect that action-predicates like "hearing" and "seeing" cannot apply to God because God does not have a body. This is an interesting premodern version of more recent positivist arguments. Similar incoherence shows up in one of the best recent treatments of the attributes. Consider the following introduction to a splendid summary of the attributes of God. "What God is is indeed unspeakable in human language and unknowable by human minds. The task, however, is to find words adequate to God."[12] Either our account of the attributes captures the truth about God or it does not. Equivocation and double-speak are fatal at this point. Philosophical objections can and should be dealt with in a proper forum. The theologian should stay the course in this discussion and insist that in speaking of the

---

[10] This was a major feature of nineteenth-century European theology where notions like the "Infinite" and the "Absolute," which had no causal powers and therefore could not have any causal interaction with the world, were taken as the primary categories for understanding God. This drove the ingenious Dean Mansel to treat Christian doctrine about the agency of God as merely regulative and not truly descriptive of God. For a fine discussion see Henry Sheldon, *System of Christian Doctrine* (Cincinnati, OH: Jennings and Graham, 1912), 160–3.

[11] Quoted in Gerald L. Bray, ed., *Ancient Christian Doctrine, I: We Believe in One God* (Downers Grove, IL: IVP Academic), 48.

[12] Stephen R. Holmes, "The Attributes of God," in John Webster, Kathryn Tanner, and Ian Torrance, eds., *The Oxford Handbook of Systematic Theology* (Oxford: Oxford University Press, 2007), 69.

divine attributes we refer to God in all his abundance rather than our concepts about God.[13]

Theologians, however, need to keep their nerve at this point; and that for two reasons. First, the Gospel requires that we deliver good news. News necessarily implies that we have accurate information. The truth about the world, for example, is not confined to the brutality of Herod in slaughtering the innocents; it also includes the news that God has entered into human history in Jesus of Nazareth; indeed, this is by far the more important news. Equivocation and double-speak undercut the proclamation of the Gospel at the outset and should be rejected. Second, revelation delivers knowledge. God in mercy is utterly committed to saving the wayward creatures he has created; this cannot happen if there is no revelation of who this God is and what he has done. The equivocation in this instance is to grant the revelation and then tell us that we cannot really understand it because of our finitude or because of divine transcendence. What we really then have is a God who is either incompetent or is indifferent. He is incompetent because he makes creatures who cannot understand what he reveals to them; or he is indifferent because he does not undertake what is essential to redeeming his wayward creation. The Gospel, in contrast, assures us that God can indeed get through to us and provides the radical assistance of the Holy Spirit to enable us to appropriate his great act of grace and love in the coming of the Son. If a philosopher or theologian argues that this is impossible, we reply: the impossible on your terms has happened; so, let's now think through what has gone wrong and find a better way to deal with the relevant phenomena.

Perceptive readers will have noted that while I included "immutability" and "impassibility" in my list of divine attributes I did not include "simplicity." I could readily have included this attribute by noting that God is one. God is not a compound of various parts. I could even have quoted John of Damascus to good effect when he noted:

> The divine attributes must be understood as common to the deity as a whole and as containing the notions of sameness, simplicity, indivisibility, and union, while the names of Father, Son and Holy Spirit, causeless and caused, unbegotten and begotten, and procession all contain the idea of separation, for these terms do not explain God's essence but the mutual relationship and manner of existence [of the three persons].[14]

The notion of "simplicity" is entirely innocent if we deploy it to describe the unity of the Godhead. God is not composed of different elements in some kind

[13] For a spirited defense of this position see Alvin Plantinga, *Warranted Christian Belief* (New York: Oxford University Press, 2000), chapter 2.

[14] Bray, ed., *Ancient Christian Doctrine, I*, 58, quoting John of Damascus, *The Orthodox Faith*, 1.10.

of compound substance or entity. However, theologians have wished to go much further than this. Here is a classical statement from Augustine.

> There are many ways in which God is rightly called great, good, wise, blessed, true and so on, but his greatness is the same as his wisdom, for he is not great by size but by power. Likewise, his goodness is the same as his wisdom and greatness, and his truth is the same as all those things, so that in him it is not one thing to be blessed and quite another thing to be great, wise, true or good.[15]

This is a dense passage, but it is generally taken to signal a view of the semantics of the divine attributes which insists that there is no difference in meaning between the various predicates we apply to God. God's wisdom is the same as his love, is the same as his power, is the same as his righteous anger, and so on. Even more dramatically God's existence is identical with being itself; there is no ontological gap between God's existence and his essence. To say the least, these are puzzling assertions. The puzzlement is not relieved by appeal to the famous revelation of the tetragrammaton in Exodus when God names himself as "I am who I am."[16] The text can also be rendered as "I am what I am or I will be what I will be." In the context, the claim is much more plausibly read as an expression of the divine commitment to be and remain to be whatever God needs to be in order to keep his covenant promise and deliver Israel from bondage. It is a stretch to read it as an enigmatic expression that captures a later metaphysical vision of God that underwrites a doctrine of divine simplicity.

Be that as it may, the obvious problem initially is that this version of divine simplicity is incoherent. It makes no sense to say that each of the attributes when ontologically applied to God is identical in meaning with each other and that all of them are identical with the very being of God. We should resist at this point—as I have done above in the case of anti-realist doctrines of the attributes—the move to draw a distinction between God and the categories we apply to God. If these do not map unto God and thus render the truth about God, the game is up. We have once again lost our intellectual nerve and gone the way of skepticism. The other problem with this position is that it is incompatible with the crucial distinctions required to sustain the doctrine of the Trinity. We cannot, on the one hand, say that all our predications as they relate to God are identical and then insist, on the other hand, on the relevant distinctions within the Godhead required by our doctrine of the Trinity. These distinctions go all the way to the bottom; there is no god above, below, behind, or beyond them.

What is needed here is the standard distinction between the cataphatic and the apophatic in our discourse about God. We boldly speak of who God is, what he has done, and how we should best describe him. However, experience

---

[15] Augustine, *On the Trinity*, 6.7.8.   [16] Exodus 3:14.

shows that in encountering God we are eventually reduced to silence in our wonder, love, and praise. This is true in the case of many of our ordinary human deliberations. We cannot fully capture the beauty of a great piece of music or the wonder of friendship. Even less can we know what it is to be a bat or an energetic English cocker spaniel dog. The principle applies even more radically in our understanding and speech about God. We do indeed understand but we do not fully comprehend. We must beware of paying God empty metaphysical compliments in our semantic and ontological deliberations. Hence we should avoid the confusions introduced by pious but inflationary accounts of divine simplicity.[17]

I have just taken something of a detour into the outskirts of the philosophy of language as it pertains to theological discourse. All that I want to say here is that any substantial doctrine of God will make use of a variety of linguistic strategies. The intellectual moves made in the tradition need to be read sensitively taking each element on its merits. Sometimes our language will be figurative, sometimes literal. No theory which posits a single way of construing discourse about God is adequate; say, a theory of analogy, such as we find in Aquinas. We need a repertoire of linguistic devices to achieve our ends.[18] Within this we need to make sure that the conceptions of the attributes we develop are constantly renewed and corrected by our account of what God has done for us in Christ and our experience of the Holy Spirit. Thus, our vision of divine love, for example, may well begin with everyday conceptions of love as we find them in our daily experience; they must then be refigured in the light of the costly love of God made manifest in the life and death of Christ.

It is time to turn to more rewarding observations that take us back into theology proper. What is at issue is a fertile account of the God we encounter in the gospels and in the rich and complex heritage developed in the church to bring us back to God and to create within us the very mind of Christ. To that end let me ruminate on four additional comments on the vision of God that shows up in the doctrine of the Trinity and in the varied accounts of the attributes of God that can be developed. Recall again that I am working with a conception of God as a radically unique, mysterious, tripersonal Agent.

---

[17] The obvious historical explanation for this development is the uncritical adoption of the concept of simplicity derived from Plotinus in his account of the One. See the *Enneads*. Note again that I am not rejecting the deployment of philosophically engineered concepts; I am simply insisting they be integrated faithfully into the mind of the church. Properly baptized, simplicity can be used to describe the unity of God noted above.

[18] For splendid treatments of the issues at stake see Janet Martin Soskice, *Metaphor and Religious Language* (Oxford: Clarendon Press, 1985), and William P. Alston, "Functionalism and Theological Language," in *The Concept of God*, ed. Thomas Morris (Oxford: Oxford University Press, 1987), 21–40.

First, a clear grasp of the attribute of divine power can help in providing relevant background beliefs for the treatment of miracles. Given the descriptions of God enumerated in the attributes, it should not surprise us that miracles are a significant element in the redemption of the world. By miracles I mean, for the sake of exposition here, violations of laws of nature brought about by God for certain intentions and purposes. Given that God is omnipotent it is unreasonable to think that these are not possible. God has the requisite power to perform such acts. Of course, this does not mean either that God of necessity must perform such acts; or that God has actually performed such acts. All God's acts are genuinely free; they depend on the divine will. I am pressing here formal claims about God in terms of divine omnipotence and divine freedom. Materially, the issue is different. Whether we have to deal with miracles in reality depends on the array of divine actions actually carried out by God in the establishing of his kingdom and the work of redemption. I think that God has indeed performed miracles in the course of the inauguration of his kingdom. At that point we have to come to terms with what God has actually done. However, the formal point in play is crucial: God has the relevant powers to perform miracles should God decide to do so.[19]

Second, we should not be surprised that Scripture often depicts God in anthropomorphic terms that can readily appear embarrassing to those who are used to more abstract, philosophical descriptions of God or to those reared on a diet of scientific accounts of the universe. Thus God is depicted as walking in the cool of the Garden of Eden, as coming down to Mount Sinai to speak face to face with Moses, as having bowels of compassion, as having breasts like a mother, and so on. There is clearly at times an element of deliberate semantic exaggeration and overkill in speaking of divine action; there is a scriptural hagiography that imaginatively casts what God is doing in ways that are intended to awaken us from our spiritual boredom and set our minds on fire.

Consider the dramatic way in which Leviticus speaks of the anger and wrath of God. If Israel disobeys God, then God will be hostile in his fury towards them. "I will in turn punish you myself sevenfold for your sins."[20] As part of this, God will "unsheathe the sword against you; your land shall be desolate, and your cities a waste."[21] So far so good. Before and after these warnings we are given dire predictions of what God will do.

> I will bring terror on you; consumption and fever that waste the eyes and cause life to pine away. You shall sow your seed in vain, for your enemies shall eat it. I will set my face against you, and you shall be struck down by your enemies; your foes shall rule over you, and you shall flee though no one pursues you. . . . I will break your proud glory, and I will make your sky like iron and your earth like

---

[19] I shall take up the wider topic of divine action and miracles in volume IV.
[20] Leviticus 26:28.   [21] Leviticus 26:33.

copper. Your strength shall be spent to no purpose; your land shall not yield its produce, and the trees of the land shall not yield their fruit. . . . I will let loose wild animals against you, and they shall bereave you of your children and destroy your livestock; they shall make you few in number, and your roads shall be deserted.[22]

And as for those of you who survive, I will send faintness into your hearts in the lands of your enemies; the sound of a driven leaf shall put them to flight, and they shall flee as one flees from the sword, and they shall fall though no one pursues. They shall stumble over one another, as if to escape a sword, though no one pursues; and you shall have no power to stand against your enemies. You shall perish among the nations, and the land of your enemies shall devour you.[23]

These are hair-raising accounts of divine wrath and punishment. God is depicted as intervening to punish directly his wayward People. Compare them with the more prosaic account of divine wrath developed by Paul.

For the wrath of God is revealed from heaven against all ungodliness and wickedness of those who by their wickedness suppress the truth. For what can be known about God is plain to them, because God has shown it to them. Ever since the creation of the world his eternal power and divine nature, invisible though they are, have been understood and seen through the things he has made. So they are without excuse; for though they knew God, they did not honor God or give thanks to him, but they became futile in their thinking, and their senseless minds were darkened. Claiming to be wise, they became fools; and they exchanged the glory of the immortal God for images resembling a mortal human being or birds or four-footed animals or reptiles. Therefore, God gave them up in the lusts of their hearts to impurity, to the degrading of their bodies among themselves, because they exchanged the truth about God for a lie and worshipped and served the creature rather than the Creator, who is blessed for ever! Amen.[24]

Paul follows with a catalogue of the effects of God giving them over to their degrading passions as expressed in sexual immorality and all kinds of wickedness. In this famous passage the wrath of God is depicted not as the direct intervention of God but as the withdrawal of God from human agents and thus human agents, after they suppress the truth about God, becoming enslaved to their passions and where they lead them.

The solution to this contrast is surely to read the first as a dramatic way of bringing home the drastic consequences of disobedience. As is the case more generally with anthropomorphic depictions of God, the point is to send a siren call to the hearer and reader as to what is at stake. The rhetoric matches the intention to give a dire warning that should be heeded.[25] The text works to provoke the relevant emotions that will motivate a change of direction and a return to spiritual sanity. Working through the notion of divine wrath becomes

---

[22] Leviticus 26:16–22.   [23] Leviticus 26:36–8.   [24] Romans 1:18–25.
[25] The latter part of Leviticus 26 brings out the positive divine intention to bring Israel to her senses, confess her iniquity, and return to the covenant relationship with God.

a salutary exercise that prevents a misreading of the scriptural text, a warning we surely need in the contemporary scene with the appearance of theologically motivated terrorism.

Third, a comprehensive vision of God will, if taken seriously, deepen our trust in God. In a way that awaits further explanation, our faith is created by the object of our faith, that is, by hearing who God truly is. The deeper and more comprehensive the vision of God, the deeper our faith will be over time. We hear the Gospel and then call upon the name of the Lord. " . . . If you confess with your lips that Jesus is Lord and believe in your heart that God raised him from the dead, you will be saved."[26] "Everyone who calls on the name of the Lord will be saved."[27] Once we put that in place, we have a whole new way of thinking of the divine attributes. These are then no longer conceptual abstractions, a neat laundry list of attributes to be divided up according to further abstract schemes of classification. Once they are integrated into the life of faith on the other side of our turning to God in Christ, they become living realities rather than dead concepts and abstract schemes.

Luther brilliantly captured this with characteristic boldness.

> Since He (God) is omnipotent, what can I lack which He cannot give me or do for me? Since He is Creator of heaven and earth and Lord of all things, who will take anything from me or harm anything mine? Indeed, how will all things not be for my benefit and serve me if the one to whom they are all obedient and subjected grants goodness to me?[28]

Luther is here reaching into the doctrine of creation and providence. However, he is making a more radical conceptual shift, one fraught with danger, but one we surely must take despite the risk. What we need to do at some point in our theological journey is look at all the other attributes of God in terms of this startling insight. In this way, we bring together the God of the philosophers and the God of the Bible, the God of reason and the God of revelation. Our God is omnipresent: he can meet our needs wherever we are. Our God is omnipotent: he has the power to meet our needs. Our God is eternal and everlasting: he is always available to help in time of need. Our God is omniscient: he knows all about us and knows how to meet our needs. Our God is immutable: he remains unmoved in his commitment to meet our needs. Our God is impassible: he stands firm in his commitment to our welfare. We can apply this, insight *mutatis mutandis*, all the way to cover all the attributes of God.

We thereby establish an intimate connection between the attributes of God and our trust in God. We have solved the problem of the yawning gap that has bedeviled treatment of the attributes of God for so long. We retain a theocentric focus of our faith, even as our trust of God in our hearts and minds is

---

[26] Romans 10:9.   [27] Ibid.
[28] Martin Luther. Unfortunately, I have misplaced the origin of this quotation.

enlivened. In fearing and loving this God—the God with the litany of attributes enumerated above—we are given courage to endure in the midst of opposition and hostility.

> Who will separate us from the love of Christ? Will hardship, or distress, or persecution, or famine, or nakedness, or peril, or sword? As it is written, 'For your sake we are being killed all the day long; we are accounted as sheep to be slaughtered.' No, in all things we are more than conquerors through him who loved us. I am convinced that neither death, nor life, nor angels, nor rulers, nor things present, nor things to come, nor powers, nor height, nor depth, nor anything else in all creation, will be able to separate us from the love of God in Christ Jesus our Lord.[29]

We see here the love of God integrated into the immeasurable greatness of God's power. Add in the other attributes explored and we have additional resources to feed our souls and minds.

This kind of deep faith and trust does not come easily. It will never come from mere philosophical speculation about the attributes of God. Philosophy may clear roadblocks in the way of faith but it cannot create deep trust in God; on this front, it is impotent. Deep trust is mediated through the life, death, and resurrection of the Son. The life of Jesus is our pattern for coming to trust God. It is by the cross of repentance, of suffering, of inward agony, of terrible spiritual pain, and of piercing wounds that we come by deep trust in God. Through this pilgrim way we are resurrected not just to the love of God but also to the power of God who gives us the life that was the heartbeat of Jesus. This kind of spiritual life is only made possible by God through the inner working of the Holy Spirit who brought Jesus to birth in the womb of Mary and who raised him from the dead. Blessed are those that find it. In the end, we can only come to true faith in God through a massive immersion in the life God made manifest in the cross of Jesus Christ and made available in the Holy Spirit. We begin with the love of God in the Trinity and end with the immensity of God depicted accurately in his attributes.

---

[29] Romans 8:35–9.

5

The Person of Christ

Jesus went out with his disciples to the region of Caesarea Philippi; and on the way he asked his disciples, 'Who do people say that I am?' And they answered him, 'John the Baptist, others, Elijah; and still others one of the prophets.' He asked them, 'But who do you say that I am?' Peter answered him, 'You are the Messiah.' And he sternly ordered them not to tell anyone about him.

Mark 8:27–32.

Consider at the outset a parable. A couple of years ago I found a stray dog, a beautiful golden retriever. He had no owner, so we decided to adopt him. I got him neutered, paid for his shots, christened him "Plato," and took him into our home. Everything went pretty well until I tried taking him for his walks. I had great trouble getting him past lampposts. Despite all my efforts, his lead got entangled around the lampposts; I wanted to go one way; he wanted to go another. There was only one solution. I had to find a way to get him to retrace his steps, to go back around and start again. It is like that in Christology. Folk too readily go around and a round in circles with the material from Scripture and the theologians of the early centuries until their heads are in a spin. The only solution is to go back around once more and keep doing so until we can see what was going on. Like dogs at lampposts, we resist this; but there is no alternative. In the case of Christology there are not four lampposts but seven. When we line them up straight, it is amazing the light that shines forth from these lampposts. By lampposts I refer here to the first seven ecumenical councils of the church.

In opening up with this bold statement about the significance of the ecumenical councils of the church, I run an immediate risk. We seem to be rushing beyond the Gospel and our initial formation in the church to a history of hair-splitting debate that will ruin our spiritual appetite. However, perceptive readers by now will readily perceive that this way forward represents exactly what I mean by systematic theology as post-baptismal, university-level instruction in Christian teaching. We have seen in the case of the doctrine of the Trinity that this requires wrestling with the deliberations of the councils of the fourth century. Furthermore, I have already indicated that systematic theology calls for a variety of tasks: the exegetical, the hermeneutical, the constructive, and the apologetic. It is the first two of these tasks that will detain us in this chapter, and that requires some detailed historical excavation.

The first critical question we face in Christology is this: Who do you say that I am? The follow-up question then asks, given a proper answer to this question: What is the role or work of Christ in the salvation of the world? The first question, which Christ directed to his disciples[1] and to the leaders of the church in all generations, is at the very heart of the Christian doctrine of God. Take this question out of the center of Christian proclamation, of Christian teaching and preaching, and Christianity becomes a salt that has lost its taste. One cannot be a faithful servant of Jesus Christ and at the same time remain profoundly agnostic about who he was. One cannot witness about a person whom one does not know. The second question tackles more directly the questions of relevance. What has Christ done that we should be in the least interested in him beyond finding out what the church has said about him? I will take that issue up in the next chapter where the task will be fundamentally constructive. To use traditional language, I aim to give a fresh account of how to think about the great work of atonement.

One way to prepare us for the material to follow is to consider this objection to the very place of Jesus at the heart of the Gospel. Ponder the following bold comment.

A particularly difficult problem for Christian feminists is the centrality of Jesus as a male savior. Although attempts have been made to redefine Jesus Christ in ways that de-emphasize his maleness—as a 'feminist,' as a model of the 'new humanity,' as liberator or Suffering Servant—such efforts leave two major difficulties unanswered.

The first of these is the use to which the maleness of Jesus has been put by the Church. The historical fact that Jesus was male continues to be used to deny women access to positions of religious and spiritual authority. Implicit, if not explicit, in this position is the message that maleness is more like God than femaleness, since God chose to be incarnate as male rather than female. This view appears to grant spiritual superiority to male embodiment and to devalue female embodiment. Theological claims that Jesus is God or reveals God reinforce this negative view of female bodies. Feminist spirituality, by contrast, affirms and values female embodiment, refuses to define it as a disability, and in some visions of goddess religion, claims that the ability of women's bodies to give birth and nurture young makes female embodiment superior to male embodiment.

The second problem for Christian feminists is the role of Jesus as male savior. The feminist emphasis on women's autonomy and freedom rejects dependence on

---

[1] Mark 8:29.

men as saviors. A male savior appears to deny women's religious authority, autonomy, and moral agency. The further emphasis of some forms of Christian piety on 'submitting to Jesus,' 'yielding to his will,' and so on, deepens the dilemma for women who are struggling to name our own experience and claim our own authority. Models of submission to male authority are not emancipatory for women. Traditional language naming Jesus as 'Lord,' 'Master,' and 'King' are not regarded as useful.[2]

Rather than address this worry head on, I propose to take a wide-angle lens and approach it indirectly. I propose we take seriously that to speak at all of Jesus Christ always has been, is, and always will be, an offense. One minor test of this is how awkward people feel when anyone mentions Jesus in polite company. Compare the mention of the following: Plato, Cleopatra, Queen Elizabeth, Tom Wolfe, Hillary Clinton, Winston Churchill, Martin Luther King, or Barack Obama. People think you are informed or maybe even interesting if you bring up these sorts of names. They do not quite know what to do if you bring up Jesus. Frankly, they find it embarrassing if not offensive.

Paul warns of this possibility in his letter to Corinth.[3] Søren Kierkegaard provides a brilliant clue as to how to express this pointedly.[4] Kierkegaard provoked us to imagine Jesus not as a figure in the past, but as a contemporary figure. Imagine the Jesus of the gospels living among us now as our contemporary. Kierkegaard is thinking here not of some historically reconstructed person, beloved of nineteenth-century European scholarship, but as the Jesus portrayed in the gospels. Imagine that Jesus is among us now. It shocks us into facing up to the strangeness and offense of Jesus.

Imagine Jesus applying for a job in the local school of theology. Think of the consternation on the search committee. There is no way he could come up for tenure. There is not a single book review with his name on it. Suppose Jesus meets some leaders in the business community. What will they do with him? He has no theory of capital and he hasn't got a video on management skills. Why bother any further? Suppose he meets some modern philosophers. Why, he does not have his natural theology in order! And he has not got a solution to the mind–body problem. Good grief! He has not even mentioned the words "epistemology" or "metaphysics"! Suppose we take Jesus to the singles class in one of the larger local churches. He is going to be an acute embarrassment. Here's an eligible bachelor who doesn't believe in free love. He does not

---

[2] Marjorie Procter-Smith, "Feminism and Spirituality," in *Spiritual Traditions for the Contemporary Church*, eds. Robin Mass and Gabriel O'Donnell (Nashville, TN: Abingdon, 1990), 438–9.

[3] 1 Corinthians 1.

[4] See Søren Kierkegaard, *Training in Christianity* (New York: Vintage Books, 2004).

subscribe to the standard view that sex is nothing more than a good indoor sport where anything goes so long as everybody consents and no one gets hurt. Suppose we introduce him to our politicians. They have a heart attack. The man is ambivalent about democracy and revolution! The best policy in this case is silence. Keep your mouth tightly shut; he might expose you. You might say something that would get in the papers. So keep your distance. Stay clear of him. Suppose he meets a local bishop. Heavens above! He does not know about the relevant book of canon law! He has not had the right psychological tests. If he comes into the area, he will have to start at the bottom. We cannot rock the ladder of promotion. Sorry, Jesus!

Jesus really is a problem. He is not acceptable to the rich because he is poor. He is not acceptable to the poor because he has no scheme to milk the rich. He is not acceptable to Gentiles because he is a Jew. He is not acceptable to Jews because he is favorably disposed to Samaritans and Gentiles. He is not acceptable to women because he is a male. He is not acceptable to males because he insists on the dignity of females. He is not acceptable to religious people because he is not conventionally pious. He is not acceptable to the unconventional and the radicals because he insists on total obedience to God. He is not acceptable to the comfortable because he wanders around as a vagabond teacher. He is not acceptable to vagabond teachers because he goes to synagogue every Saturday and insists that the classical institutions of Judaism really were given to the people by God.

In the light of this very general observation about the offense of Jesus, the one rock-like piece of information we have about him is surely correct: Jesus was offensive enough to a lot of people to be crucified ignominiously. In the Synoptic gospels, the final spark that lights the fire is the cleansing of the Temple. But the fuel was already there to catch alight. He was perceived as an offense and a threat from the very beginning of his ministry when Herod slaughtered the innocents. Jesus as our contemporary really is a problem and an offense.

When you look closer, the offense goes even deeper. This Jesus, according to the Christian Gospel and the faith of the church, really is our contemporary. He is not dead, he is risen, and he is coming again as our judge. Treating these as mythology is our modern way of taming the offense of Jesus. "Mythology" is a safe, intellectual, cognitive category to relieve the offense and to tame Jesus. It is our way of keeping guard on the tomb so that he is not let loose from death. It is a wonderful way to keep Jesus at a very safe distance: buried in the past.

The other side of the offense is every bit as difficult to assimilate. It is this offensive and utterly human Jesus who is divine through and through. It is not a macho, muscular Jesus who is divine, but a humble, elusive, uncontrollable, crucified Jesus who is divine. This is a scandal to end all scandals. It is in this offensive person that we ontologically encounter God. It is not just that we meet a prophet, or a priest, or a king, or a healer, or an exorcist, or a religious genius, or an adopted saint. Here we come face to face fully with God. This is the core of the canonical claims about Jesus.

My claim is that the first thing that we need to do is to listen to the teaching of the church, expressed in her councils. Here there is an important distinction. The church works through the first question about the person of Christ resolutely and precisely; she leaves the second question about the work of Christ wide open in its details. There is no specific canonical doctrine of the atonement. There is a definitive, carefully worked out doctrine of the person and nature of Christ. In this chapter I concentrate on the issue of the person and nature of Christ.

The seven ecumenical councils may be viewed as the decisive turning points in the life of the church at which the teaching of the apostles received more and more definitive expression. At the councils, the key question "Who do you say that I am?" was restated in two major ways: What is Christ's relationship to God the Father? What is Christ's relationship to us, humans?

Some historians have attempted in the past to reduce the issues at stake in the councils to a mere power play, to a sad spectacle of the worst human passions, to empty quibbles about outdated Greek metaphysics, and to the old prejudices of local theological schools. I start with the presupposition that any reductionist account, whatever its accidental merits, must be rejected as a piece of bad history. That is too big a topic to unpack here so I set it aside. However, I do want to make one critical historical comment as we proceed. All seven councils were gathered because the church's implicit, workaday answer to the question "Who do you say that I am?" was at risk. The preservation and further elucidation of the apostolic tradition was a matter of life and death. It was a matter for which the blood of the martyrs was shed in the first three centuries of the church. It was an issue intimately related to human salvation and to our basic orientation in the world. It was a topic that was directly related to the church's worship, to the ways in which Christians were baptized, and to the ways in which they praised and prayed to their God.

The opponents of the church's position rightly saw that critical issues were at stake and tried very hard to win the polemical and public-relations debate. They still do today. The Jesus seminar, for example, is a very carefully funded and orchestrated campaign with very clear ecclesial and theological intentions. The basic assumption is that the church got it wrong in what it said about Jesus and therefore needs to be corrected by proper historical investigation. To return to the past, Athanasius of Alexandria (296–373) complained that Arius (256–336) composed Christological hymns and set them to popular tunes. Arius hired an army of sailors and virgins to sing them on the streets and at the sea ports of Alexandria. Half a century later Gregory of Nyssa (335–94) complained that Arianism continued to be a hot topic of public debate:

> The whole city is full of it [controversy], the squares, the market places, the cross-roads, the alleyways; men in old-clothes, money changers, food sellers: they are

all busy arguing. If you ask someone to give you change, he philosophizes about the Begotten and the Unbegotten; if you inquire about the price of a loaf, you are told by way of reply that the Father is greater and the Son inferior; if you ask 'Is my bath ready?' the attendant answers that the Son was made out of nothing.[5]

The decisions of the councils made it into the wide public arena. These were not just technical debates among the experts; they were picked up and discussed by ordinary folk on the streets and in the public baths.

I will now tell a historical story that will have many familiar elements; yet it is a story worth repeating. I shall focus on the critical Christological issues throughout. My treatment will be very uneven because I want to draw attention to the thread that runs through them all. I will give special attention to Nicaea I (325) for reasons that will be clear as we proceed.

Usually we come at Nicaea I with Trinitarian interests in hand. We can just as easily come to Nicaea I with Christological issues in hand. The crisis that precipitated the gathering of the first ecumenical council is well known. Arius, a presbyter of Alexandria, started to preach that since Christ in the gospels is depicted in typically human terms, he cannot be equal to God the Father. Christ was God's special creature, instrumental in fashioning and ordering the world. At best, he was semi-divine.

Arius' proposal had several components. He noted that the ancient creeds were characteristically imprecise about the divine status of Christ. The ancient creeds called him Lord and spoke of his exaltation, but they did not explicitly equate him with God the Father. Furthermore, Arius turned to the passages of Scripture where Christ says: "The Father is greater than I," where Christ professes his ignorance of future events, and those that speak of typically human weaknesses: hunger, thirst, shedding tears, grieving, and the like. The High God, Arius argued, could not experience all that. In addition, Arius pointed out that the Son derives his being from the Father. God, on the contrary, is unbegotten; he cannot be generated by anything else. Besides, the effect, Arius argued, could not be greater than its cause. Arius appealed to a commonsensical observation: before one is born, one does not exist.

Then Arius worried about the central terms deployed: *ousia, homoousios, homoiousios.* How far should the analogy from human generation be applied to the case of the divine generation? So he tried to make nonsense of his critics' position on the eternal generation of the Son out of the Father's essence. This position was too crudely materialist; it was as if the Father was tearing apart some stuff out of himself in order to produce the Son.

Finally, Arians argued that the custom of triple immersion had an exclusive meaning of being a symbolic reenactment of the three days that Christ spent in

---

[5] Nyssa, *On the Deity of the Son* (PG 46:557B).

the tomb, not with the three Persons of the Trinity. He argued that since a believer is buried with Christ, he has to be dipped three times in commemoration of Christ's resurrection on the third day. This analogy, as the opponents were careful to point out, was founded on a miscalculation: strictly speaking, Christ rose on the third day, which meant that he spent in the tomb no more than two full days, perhaps even less. Later Arians (the so-called Eunomians) decided to abrogate the practice of triple immersion altogether.

The upshot of all this was that Christ was neither fully human, nor fully divine. He was a passible created Logos who assumed human body, without human soul. Clearly, Arius' proposals had to be met and fought on all of these grounds. The great advocate for the alternative vision was Athanasius.[6]

Athanasius pointed out that it was the intention of the most ancient creeds to celebrate God as Triune, as Father, Son, and Holy Spirit. From the most ancient times the Christians sang hymns to Christ "as if to a God" and worshipped him above all prophets, heroes, and martyrs.[7] He also pointed out that the Scripture has to be interpreted in such a way that the passages that speak of Christ's human weaknesses apply to the limitations of the incarnation to which God freely submitted himself, having assumed human flesh. These limitations do not apply to the Son's eternal being with the Father.

In response to the metaphysical considerations, Athanasius argued that it is totally arbitrary to think that the effect is somehow less significant than the cause. Furthermore, it is inappropriate to introduce temporary relations into the inner life of the Trinity. The meaning of the relevant terms needed more nuanced interpretation; and he offered a defense of the fact that the word *homoousios* was not biblical.

It is interesting that Athanasius did not quite want to play by the rules set up by Arius and added a new and pivotal soteriological dimension to the components listed by Arius: Humanity cannot be saved by a mere man, or by a superhuman individual. The breach between humanity and God can be bridged by God alone. "God became man in order that we may be deified." God became what we are in order that we could partake of what he is. Later Anselm of Canterbury attempted to tighten this statement appropriately. We needed salvation, but cannot redeem ourselves; God could redeem us but did not need to do it. Therefore, the God-man was chosen, who did not need to be saved and could save.[8] The theologians could not settle the matter by

---

[6] I will not repeat here the reading I gave in volume II where I bring out the persuasive way in which Athanasius deploys arguments about divine agency and divine action to secure his claims on the person of Christ.

[7] See a report from Pliny's *Letters to Trajan,* Book X, letter 96, written in 112.

[8] Notice that this is not a mathematically tight formula. God could so ordain that we were saved by a mere mortal. To deny that this was possible would be tantamount to denying the power of God. Duns Scotus (1266–1308) argued that God could have ordained to become incarnate in a donkey or a stone, and, in this way, he could save us. This was an extreme form

appealing to the scriptural exegesis alone. The appeal to select scriptural passages was not sufficient, although indispensable, to settle this controversy. Athanasius continually spoke of the mind and the main intent (*skopos*) of the Scripture that Arius, in Athanasius' judgment, has missed entirely.

The outcome of the Council of Nicaea I was the affirmation that the incarnate Son was of the same essence with God the Father. The ontological consequences of this are revolutionary. The divine realm was purged of demigods and pseudo-deities. Christ was not a centaur, half-divine and half-human; he was fully divine and, as the next council will insist, fully human. He was not a divinity inferior to the Father. The full humanity of Christ was affirmed, while the question in what sense Christ may be considered human was not the focus of theological attention.

The consequence of the council was that the Arian controversy raged mightily until the Council of Constantinople I in 381 put an end to it theologically. In this case the crisis led to the second ecumenical council which gathered in order to respond to the view of Apollinaris (310–90). Apollinaris taught, following Arius, that Christ was not fully human; the Logos in Christ replaced human rational soul, or reason. He could not imagine how two minds, human and divine, could reside in one body. He also insisted that his proposal allowed for the Logos' fuller and more direct participation in the human experiences of Christ.

The opposition, more particularly Gregory Nazianzus (329–90), argued that "that which was not assumed was not healed," only that which is appropriated by the Godhead is saved. Notice, again, that the decisive argument was soteriological. If Christ assumed imperfect humanity, then he restored to incorruption only imperfect humanity. So the Council of Constantinople restated the creed of Nicaea and expanded the article on the Holy Spirit. The Council declared that Christ is of one nature with us in everything, excluding sin. Apollinarianism, unlike Arianism, proved to be rather easy to defeat: it died out soon.

Once the full divinity and the full humanity of Christ were in place, the issue became how the two are to be held together. This was effectively taken up at Ephesus in 431. In this case the crucial figure initially was Nestorius (386–451), who, following his teacher Theodore of Mopsuestia (350–428), proposed that there were two subjects in Christ: divine and human. The divine subject was responsible for miracles, exorcism, foreknowledge, authority over nature, and the like. The human subject was responsible for birth, suffering, ignorance, human emotions, and the like. The story of the gospels, according to Nestorius, had two quite distinct narratives, human and divine.

---

of voluntarism. The argument in Athanasius was not a necessary deduction, but one articulated in terms of fittingness of a particular way of salvation.

One narrative concerned the divine subject; the other narrative concerned the human subject. Nestorius appealed to the patristic distinction between the Creator and the creature and argued that there is a sharp line of separation between the two and that this gulf is not bridged in the incarnation. Nestorius, therefore, attempted to resolve the difficulties involved in relating the human and divine natures of Christ by making a sharp separation between them. As a corollary, he suggested that Mary could not be called God-bearer, but only man-bearer, or at best, Christ-bearer. She did not give birth to God, for God is without beginning and immortal; she gave birth only to a human being called Jesus.

Cyril of Alexandria (378–444) responded to this proposal that it goes against the intention of the Nicene Creed and against the great Christological hymn in Philippians 2. According to both the creed and the hymn, it was God who voluntarily chose to be subjected to the experiences of the incarnation. God did all of this through and in his human nature. Yet, because of the incarnation, it was possible to predicate all human experiences directly to the divine Logos, with the understanding that these characteristics apply to the Logos in his incarnate state. One could not split the hero of the gospels into the two subjects, for then there would be no divine emptying (*kenosis*) and no real participation in the human condition.

The question of how precisely the two natures are related was never spelled out. Cyril insisted that this question needed to be treated on a par with the question of how the soul is related to the body. Since the latter was a mystery, it was to be expected that the nature of the union of human and divine in Christ would also remain a mystery.

We may conclude that at the third ecumenical council the unity of the human and divine natures was proclaimed against the Nestorian attempts to split Christ into two subjects or agents. Cyril of Alexandria taught against the Nestorians in his *Twelve Anathemas* and *Two Letters* that the Son of God has made human nature entirely his own. That human nature in Christ did not have any independent existence prior to the union. Furthermore, this union should not be conceived in terms of some kind of "inspired man" Christology. This teaching also has a significant soteriological dimension. God united himself to that which was truly human and bridged the gap between the Creator and the creatures. The ecclesiastical outcome was that eventually those who favored the clarity of the Nestorian position, primarily the Persians, split from the church, engaged in missionary work in China, and built an independent institution that survives till the present day.

The crisis that precipitated Chalcedon in 451 had to do with the so-called Robber's Council, which was summoned in 449 by Dioscorus, patriarch of Alexandria (444–51). We owe the nickname of the Council to Pope Leo the Great (390–461) because it violated all acceptable legal procedures and was rather violent. Bishops present were forced to sign the conciliar decree.

In a nutshell, Dioscorus, who died in 454, represented a party that took the view of Cyril of Alexandria to its extreme and affirmed that human nature was mingled with the divine in such a way that after the incarnation one could speak only of one nature, the human nature being absorbed by the deity.

In response to this view, the Council of Chalcedon, which gathered two years later in 451, decreed that the two natures were united in Christ: "without confusion, without change, without division, [and] without separation"; the peculiar property of each nature being preserved and being united in one *prosopon* and in one *hypostasis*. Notice the apophatic (all four qualifying adjectives are negative) and the balanced character of the Council's language. The first two statements, "without confusion" and "without change", are directed against Dioscorus. The last two, "without division" and "without separation", are directed against Nestorius, who attempted to separate the two natures. The long-term ecclesiastical outcome was that fifty years later those who agreed with Dioscorus' interpretation of Cyril split from the church. The Monophysites are present till this day in Armenia, India, Ethiopia, Egypt, and other countries.

The fifth ecumenical council, Constantinople II, was summoned in 553 under the Emperor Justinian (482–565) in response to the crisis generated by the circulation of the so-called *Three Chapters*: the writings of Theodore of Mopsuestia (350–428), Theodoret of Cyrus (393–457), and Ibas of Edessa (died 457). These authors were widely read in Syria. In a nutshell, these writings offered a Nestorian interpretation of Chalcedon in which they tended to separate the two subjects in Christ and overemphasized the distinction between two natures. The council was an attempt to win back the Monophysite wing that did not accept the Chalcedonian definition of the church which by that time separated into a parallel institution and called itself Jacobite. However, this attempt failed.

The sixth ecumenical council (680–1) was summoned in response to those who taught that the unity of one person in Christ requires that he had one divine–human will.

The fathers of the council insisted that in order to speak of full humanity, one has to include together with the body and rational soul also a fully human will. Likewise, in order to speak of divine nature one inevitably had to presuppose a distinct divine will. The issue was the preservation of the full divinity and the full humanity of Christ. Those who defended two wills regarded the teaching of Monothelites (those who defended one will) as Monophysitism ("one nature") revisited. The question was this: Does will belong to nature, or to person?[9]

---

[9] For a defense of the crucial figure in this debate, Maximus the Confessor, who died in 662, see the relevant chapter in volume II.

An excerpt from the definition of the sixth ecumenical council supplies the answer.

> We likewise declare that in him are two natural wills and two natural operations indivisibly, inconvertibly, inseparably, inconfusedly, according to the teaching of the holy Fathers. And these two natural wills are not contrary the one to the other (God forbid!) as the impious heretics assert, but his human will follows, and that not as resisting and reluctant, but rather as subject to his divine and omnipotent will. For it was right that the flesh should be moved but subject to the divine will, according to the most wise Athanasius. For as his flesh is called and is the flesh of God the Word, so also the natural will of his flesh is called and is the proper will of God the Word, as he himself says: 'I came down from heaven, not that I might do mine own will but the will of the Father which sent me!' where he calls his own will the will of his flesh, inasmuch as his flesh was also his own. For as his most holy and immaculate animated flesh was not destroyed because it was deified but continued in its own state and nature, so also his human will, although deified, was not suppressed, but was rather preserved according to the saying of Gregory Theologus: 'His will [i.e., the Savior's] is not contrary to God but altogether deified.'

The important corollary of this definition was what is known in the East as the doctrine of synergy, or divine–human cooperation. According to this doctrine, the human will cooperates with divine will on the path to salvation. If we eliminate the participation of human will, we eliminate the participation of fully human nature in salvation. This doctrine is usually and rightly contrasted with the "Augustinian" view, according to which salvation is entirely the work of divine grace and in no way depends upon human cooperation.

At the seventh ecumenical council (787) the unity of God with the material creation in incarnation was firmly reasserted. If God has truly become man, and dwelled among us, then the incarnate God can be depicted and represented in colors on wood. By becoming incarnate God has sanctified the whole material creation. Yet we do not worship the material images of God, but venerate them with awareness that worship belongs alone to their prototype. At the same time, the acceptance of images was the denial of the Monophysite error according to which humanity was fully absorbed by divinity. Those icons are one means of grace which the church grants us on the path to sanctification and salvation.

As one may see from this hang-glider overview, in articulating its views the mind of the church moved following a remarkable dialectical pattern: from the acknowledgment of Christ's full divinity (first council) to the acceptance of his full humanity (second council); then to the affirmation of the closest union of the two natures in one person (third council); then to a clearer distinction between the two natures (fourth council); then again, reaffirming the unity of person on the basis of Chalcedon (fifth council); returning to the emphasis upon the distinction of two natures, only now expressed in the form of two wills (sixth council); then, at last, reemphasizing the unity of Christ's person in stating that it is the person of the incarnate God which can be depicted on the icons, not human nature in separation from divine nature (seventh council). No contemporary proposal, in my judgment, surpasses in cogency, symmetry, and beauty the words of the Chalcedonian definition:

> Following, therefore, the holy fathers, we all teach with one accord one and the same Son, our Lord Jesus Christ, perfect in His Godhead and perfect in His manhood, true God and true man, consisting of a reasonable soul and of a body, of one substance with the Father as touching the Godhead, and of one substance with us as touching the manhood, like unto us in everything, yet without sin.

During the cause of this development certain extreme positions were stated, for it is common to humans, imperfect as we are, to be tempted to the extremes. Yet, thanks to the assistance of the Holy Spirit, those extremes were rejected, and more balanced options appeared as the answers to the church's prayer, as the fruits of patient work, of polemical correspondence, and, indeed, of bitter controversies. These were nothing new in the church. We see controversy in the life of Jesus, and we see it in the letters of the New Testament. It is no different now from what it was then.

In conclusion let me make some final comments on the significance of the church's vision of the person of Christ.

First, we can readily see why some communions concentrate on the first four councils. The core issues are really all resolved by then. The others are a kind of mopping up and reassertion. Yet it is a great disservice to ignore the full seven councils, so we should not let our intellectual trials and tribulations stop at Chalcedon.

Second, we can readily see why the doctrine of the virgin birth, or better, the virginal conception, of Jesus fitted so aptly with these developments. To baulk at the virgin birth after one has accepted the incarnation makes no sense intellectually. If one buys into the incarnation, the virgin birth is "small fry" divine intervention. It is baulking at a gnat while swallowing a camel. Moreover, there is surely an aptness about the doctrine of the virgin birth; there is a beautiful coherence between incarnation and virgin birth. The same applies to the doctrine of the Theotokos. Baulking at this doctrine shows that we have not grasped the deep import of the incarnation; that we are only half-heartedly coming to terms with its nature and significance.

Third, consider an existential comment. Each of us has our own intellectual crosses to bear in our journey of faith. There are parts of the canonical faith we readily embrace and others that cause us acute intellectual pain. Some have no difficulty with belief in God, the one and only Creator of the universe. They are naturally happy theists. Others may have come to faith through a vivid experience of the Holy Spirit, say through a weekend retreat or their own experience of God. In both cases, they find a pain in their stomach trying to figure out what to do with Jesus. This has not been my experience. My problem from the beginning was God. I could not believe in God simply because I was a straightforward empiricist. Only what was available to the senses could be real; I was a materialist; in the end, all we had was physics and chemistry. What broke the hold of materialism on me was the reality of evil. Evil would not fit into my materialist universe. Indeed, I suddenly discovered that I had no conceptual problems with the demonic.[10] Once that was in place then belief in God became an option for me. This struck me like lightning; I could take readers to the very spot where I worked this out. But all that this gave me was the possibility of an invisible, personal God; it did nothing to tell me anything substantial about this invisible God; much less had I a clue how to relate to this invisible God. And then the lightning struck twice: in the incarnation, I saw into the heart of the Christian faith. In Christ, the invisible had become visible. In this figure in human history, bone of our bone and flesh of our flesh, we meet the invisible God. Once I had crossed that threshold, the game of sitting on the fence was over; my life was wrecked; all my plans had to be rethought; and I began an intellectual journey that is still very, very far from over.

Fourth, wrestling with this long stretch of history matters. Here is one reason why. To attain sensitive historical knowledge means to enter sympathetically into the thoughts and intentions of those people who were involved in certain historical actions and events. To study the canonical doctrine of the church is to enter the mind of the church that participates in the mind of Christ. Entering the mind of the church requires from us humility, patience, and compassion with the thoughts and doings of those holy teachers who are very distant and whose thought forms are sometimes very foreign to us. A mature theologian knows how fragile our fathers and mothers are; these theologians are not perfect either in their lives or in their thinking; we have to follow the inner developments carefully; we have to see the whole lineage of thought and conviction in the church; hence in love we bind up the wounds of the tradition.

Fifth, and finally, let me comment on the relevance of historical investigation for our understanding of Jesus. As I noted at the outset, in speaking of Jesus as the Son of God, fully human and fully divine, we are clearly speaking of a real historical figure who is liable to cause offense in every generation and in every culture. Moreover, I also noted that our readiness to write off substantial claims about divine action in Jesus as "mythological" represents a modern way of keeping him at arm's length. The crux of the issue is that we cannot make decisions about Jesus without exercising deep theological discernment and judgment. The New Testament writers are witnesses to the

---

[10] I will take up the issue of divine action and the demonic in volume IV.

activity of God in Jesus. The documents are kerygmatic, homiletical, pastoral, and spiritually educative. These writers are not "secular" historians. This is not in the least a fault or a problem theologically. It has become a deep problem for Western Christianity. Hence we have had a succession of quests for the historical Jesus. In fact, we have had three of these.

There is the famous nineteenth-century quest predicated on secular and metaphysical assumptions that reject the classical self-understanding of the church. If Jesus is not the Son of God, who is he? That was the issue. This quest collapsed due to a radical failure to find any kind of critical consensus. Indeed, it engendered a deep skepticism about Jesus. There is the second, or so-called "new quest" for Jesus, which appeared in the searches predicated on an attempt to unpack the self-understanding of Jesus brought to expression in the *kerygma* critically reconstructed. This has had a very limited acceptance.[11] Finally, there is the third quest initiated in the 1960s at Oxford by George Caird (1917–84) and currently pursued by his former students and others.[12] Here the crucial issue is to recover the Jewishness of Jesus. In some cases, scholars in this tradition have gone back to the first sort of quest with similar sorts of results to those proposed by Albert Schweitzer (1875–1965), namely, Jesus turns out to be surprisingly like the kind of figure a scholar in North America in late modernity wants to find. Sometimes he turns out to be a kind of iconoclastic, "hippy" Jesus who works from the margins.

None of these proposals are able adequately to cope with Jesus theologically. To cope with Jesus, we need a twofold narrative. We need a human-historical narrative that is the standard territory of the historian. Here we speak of human actions: of Palestine and Pontius Pilate. We also need a theological-historical narrative. Here we have to speak of what God is doing in creation, in history, in Israel, in the church, and in our own lives, and in Jesus of Nazareth. For example, when we speak of the resurrection, we are inescapably dealing with what God has done. We have to spell out the deep intentions of God in acting in Jesus for the salvation of the world. This radically alters how we deal with the human-historical materials related to the resurrection narratives, that is, the empty tomb, the appearances, and the radical change in the early disciples. The claim is theological: "God raised Jesus from the dead." This is a theological claim first and foremost. What on a secular and humanistic understanding of the world appears weird and impossible becomes in this altered perspective fitting and appropriate. Thus Peter insists that "God raised Jesus, having freed him from death, because it was impossible for him to be held in its power."[13]

Hence, the mature Christian theologian will avoid two extremes. She will not simply hand this over to the historians and build her theology on what is

---

[11] It is associated with James M. Robinson and Ernst Käsemann.
[12] Tom Wright, Marcus Borg, Ed Sanders, Ben Meyers.   [13] Acts 2:24.

handed back. Nor will she in the fashion of the modern fundamentalist refuse to exercise a deeply informed and reflective judgment about the events mentioned in the tradition bequeathed to her. Taking her life in her hands, she will venture forth to articulate and express what God has done in and through Jesus of Nazareth. In my judgment, such work will ultimately vindicate the conviction of the church that saw in Jesus a single person who was at once fully human and fully divine. If this means that we have to conceive of yet another quest, a fourth quest for the historic, biblical Christ of both faith and history, so be it. Clearly such a quest calls us to think through afresh the action of God in Jesus.

"Who do you say that I am?" To use a hackneyed phrase, the church had to fish or cut bait on this. Right from the beginning the church confessed the full humanity and divinity of Jesus Christ. She reiterated this crucial judgment in varied and different concepts and forms. With controversy at every step, she kept her nerve on this issue. The invisible had become visible. God had become man. A cradle was the birthplace of God. The cross was the deathbed of God. The Creator had become a creature. Through this extraordinary journey God himself had rescued us from misery and evil. Through the unjust murder of a just man, the world was redeemed once and for all. With that we enter the threshold of the work of Christ, but that, of course is a topic for another chapter.

6

Atonement and the Work of Christ

For while we were still weak, at the right time Christ died for the ungodly. Indeed, rarely will anyone die for a righteous person—though perhaps for a good person someone might actually dare to die. But God proves his love for us in that while we still were sinners Christ died for us. Much more surely, then, now will we be saved through him from the wrath to come. For if while we were enemies, we were reconciled to God through the death of his Son, much more surely, having been reconciled will we be saved by his life.

Romans 5:6–10.

Consider this historical observation. In the construction and canonization of Christian doctrine in the patristic era definitive commitments were made on the person of Christ; in contrast, there were no definitive commitments on the work of Christ. Various proposals abounded yet no single theory was agreed; there is no equivalent of Chalcedon; and no consensus has ever been reached. Put sharply, there is no canonical doctrine in this arena. In keeping with this historical observation, it is common, and correct, to develop some kind of historic typology. Hence it is usual to insist on three types: the classic (Christus Victor), the Latin (Penal Substitutionary), the subjective (Moral Influence Theory). Theologians are deeply divided about what to do in response to this body of material. Should we pick one and reaffirm it? Should we invent a new theory? Should we seek a unified theory which sets the three types in a larger horizon? The latter option is stressed in a pleasing manner by the great English theologian, P. T. Forsyth (1848–1921). Forsyth speaks of the early church stressing the triumphant aspect of the work of Christ, the medieval and Reformation church its satisfactory aspect, and the modern church its regenerative aspect. He then says this:

And it is a good test of the native aptitude of the theologian, and of his evangelical grasp, that he should find them all necessary to express the fullness of this vast work, and [to express] its adequacy to anything so great and manifold as the soul.[1]

---

[1] Forsyth continues: "But what we do not find in the classical theologians of the past is the co-ordination of the three aspects under one comprehensive idea, one organic principle,

I do not intend here to meet the detailed conditions for success that Forsyth proposes but I want to register agreement with his claim that we cannot just leave our account of the work of Christ as a loose bundle of metaphors and themes. We need some kind of central narrative around which we can arrange our thinking. Beyond that we need to see how we might make vigorous sense of the host of ways in which Christian theologians have tried to develop their favored vision of atonement. For example, how do we handle the language of debt or the language of animal sacrifice?

My aims in this chapter are these: to suggest the crucial axis around which I think atonement should revolve; to flesh out some crucial dimensions or issues which inform and shape the axis; to sketch out why the way of Jesus Christ's death is of special significance in atonement; and, finally, to indicate what we should do with the varied materials bequeathed to us in the tradition.

As we proceed one of the first things to do to achieve our first goal is to depietize our discourse. We have made the term "atonement" into a pious, technical term far removed from our everyday experience and discourse. We need a bonfire of the pieties. Here we need some strong etymological disinfectant. Atonement is an Anglo-Saxon word. It is a simple compound: at-one-ment. It suggests something crucial in our social relations, namely, "The personal reconciliation of responsible people who had been violently and even morally opposed to one another."[2] There are two dominant emphases in the background: personal relationships and reconciliation of estrangement. In the history of the concept, however, this broad conception has been narrowed. The focus has shifted from the mending or reconciliation of relationships, and what this generally might mean, to the means used to bring about the reconciliation of relationship. Hence atonement has been narrowed to mean such things as propitiation, satisfaction, expiation, and reparation. So, we have had a drastic decline of emphasis on the repair or reconciliation of a relationship and a steep rise of emphasis on the means of at-one-ment.

---

corresponding to the complete unity of Christ's person, who did the work. We do not find such a unitary view of the work as we should expect when we reflect that it was the work of a personality so complete as Christ, and so absolute as God who acted in Christ. Yet we must strive after such a view by the very nature of our faith. A mere composite or eclectic theology means a distracted faith. A creed just nailed together means churches that cannot draw together. We cannot, at least the Church cannot, rest healthily upon medley and mortised aspects of the one thing which connects our soul with the one God in one moral world. We cannot rest in unresolved views of reconciliation. As the reconciliation comes to pervade our whole being, and as we answer it with heart and strength and mind, we become more and more impatient of fragmentary ways of understanding it. We crave, and we move, to see that the first aspect is the condition of the second, and the second of the third, and they all condition each other in a living interaction." P. T. Forsyth, *The Work of Christ* (London: Independent Press Ltd, 1938), 200.

² Robert S. Paul, *The Atonement and the Sacraments* (Eugene, OR: Wipf and Stock, 2002), 23.

I propose that we return to the core, root meaning: to the righting of relationship between estranged persons. This provides the framework for our reflection. Atonement is fundamentally concerned with the repair of broken relationships.

How might we unpack what is at stake in atonement once we stake out the basic assumptions governing this notion? We need to begin with ordinary examples of estrangement and then move to the estrangement between our-selves and God. Let me give a mundane example of the former from my own family. When my father, a bog-Irish farmer and day-laborer, was killed in a bad truck accident, various uncles on my father's side arrived during the wake and laid claim to various pieces of property, or so my mother told me. They insisted that various pieces of farm machinery really belonged to them, that the horses belonged to them, that even the winter fuel, the turf from the bog, was theirs. It took firm intervention from others outside the family circle to push back and make sure that my uncles did not strip my mother of what little was left after her devastating loss. The aftereffects of this lived on in my mother's life, even to the point where she vigorously forbade me from acting as best man at a cousin's wedding. I am not at all sure that my mother ever got over this experience; my generation still feels the effects of it even to this day. At best, I would say that there has been partial reconciliation.

Doctrines of sin in the Christian tradition spell out the estrangement that has emerged between human agents and God. All I need register at this stage is that we take radically seriously the estrangement involved. We can express it in terms of radical distrust, human hubris, ingratitude, disobedience, rebellion, treachery, idolatry, deliberate distortion of divine intentions, and the like. There are many ways to spell this out, not least by our readings of Genesis 1–11.[3]

When we look below the surface at dramatic accounts of estrangement and reconciliation we can quickly see the dimensions that need to be identified.

Consider first the bad news. First, there is a profound break in the relation-ship between us and God. The breach has subterranean consequences for the relationship: for the divine–human relationship initially, the human–human relationships, and then the human–creation relationship. We are not dealing in trivialities but the stuff of human sin and evil. Second, there is a clear sense that both an objective and subjective wrong has been committed. The object-ive wrong is this: God has been wronged in that he has been rejected as our creator, sustainer, friend, provider, and the like. The subjective wrong is this: the evil we have done has been done intentionally, deliberately. We did not drift casually into sin; we plunged headlong into it. Third, the actions and the ensuing estrangement cannot be ignored. It is not enough to brush all this off

---

[3] I shall take up this material when we turn to the doctrine of sin.

as trivial. It is a moral outrage and an affront to do so, however unpleasant it may be to acknowledge that this is the case.

Consider now the good news. First, the relationship is ultimately put right, so the Christian theologian insists. It is really put right. The estrangement is removed; literally, there is a return to communion. There is now at-one-ment. Second, speaking generally, the relationship is put right in a very particular way. The two sides to it are these: first, confession and a turning to the one who was wronged, that is, to God in Christ; and second, the response of absolution and reconciliation from God through Christ. Third, atonement is bilateral. If there is to be atonement, both sides must move towards each other; if only one side moves, then there is no at-one-ment. Both sides have to make decisions; indifference on either side is fatal to the relationship. Where there is apathy and indifference there is then no personal relationship at all; there is no sharing of purposes and intentions.

A doctrine of the action of God in Christ is an attempt to sketch out the divine side of the bilateral action that is constitutive of atonement. That is why, as we shall see, historically speaking, incarnation is constitutive of atonement for Christian theology. Our vision of the person of Christ gets caught up in our account of the work of Christ, even though theories of the latter are left in the bosom of the church for endless reflection and review. Once we reorient our discourse properly, the crucial theological issues we have to bring to the surface are these: What generally is Christ's role in atonement? And what is the role of Christ's death in atonement?

A parenthesis is essential before we proceed. These questions in turn force us to deal with the more general questions of how we can restore our broken relationships, including our relationship with God, in a morally acceptable way. Atonement deals with violent moral disagreement and estrangement. It is obvious that three commonly accepted paths in the folk religion of our day are not satisfactory solutions to the problems that have to be faced. The first I shall call the answer of the moral sentimentalist. In this case, one dismisses the reality of sin and the ensuing estrangement. This will not work because it does not take evil seriously. The second is similar to this. Let's call it the solution of the theological sentimentalist. In this case, one trivializes it from the side of God. God winks and passes over our sin. God, we claim, is silent about our violent disagreements with him; he has other more important issues on his mind than snooping around to see what we are doing. Against this, we must surely insist that there must be passion on the divine side if the reality of evil in us is to be acknowledged. The God of Scripture is a passionate deity, passionate in righteous judgment and in love. Given the actual estrangement that exists between us and God, can God just forgive and pass on and there be genuine renewal of the relationship? To say "yes" is to trivialize God's judgments on evil; it is to have a frivolous doctrine of God. We need to deal with the depth of human sin and evil.

The third unacceptable answer is to resolve the issue by making moral reparations on the human side. This is rampant in countries with a long history of Christianity, like Ireland in the early twentieth century before she lost the civilization she saved. Dedicating the next set of royalties to the Center for Philosophy of Religion at Notre Dame does not repair the relationship. It may help the Center; it does not resolve the tear with the relationship. Nor is it enough to claim that God will give me "A" for effort. One problem here is that in this solution we do not address the matter of psychological bondage; there is no at-one-ment in the relationship. Negatively, there is a fear and distance that has to be overcome; positively, these need to be replaced by appropriate assurance and intimacy.

So what do we need if we are to have a vision that will work? What conditions need to be satisfied if any vision of atonement is to work? I think there are three conditions that must be met beyond these fuzzy elements in the underworld of Christian piety. First, our vision of atonement must be rooted in the mercy, compassion, loving-kindness, and utter goodness of God. If our vision of the atonement makes God out to be a monster, then something has gone wrong. If it casts even a shadow on the unceasing generosity of God, then we need to back up and see what has gone wrong. Second, our vision of God must not trivialize evil. It must take the full force of sin in all its destruction seriously. And it must take seriously God's estimate of the depths of human sin and evil. If it leads us to underestimate the depths of sin or to turn God into a sentimental grandma, then we need to back up and think again. And third, our vision of God must spiritually and psychologically foster the deep healing of the human soul. If our vision of the atonement leads to abuse or violence or the maltreatment of women and children we need to back up and see where we have gone off the rails.

Once we grant the reality of evil and the moral discernment of God, there has to be bilateral action. On the human side there has to be acknowledgment of evil, a real return to face the estranged party, a real confession of evil and request for forgiveness, and a real move to renew the relationship, to have fresh communion. On the human side these have to be objectively and subjectively in place. These involve both behavior (outward action) and subjective intention (real decision). They also involve extensive divine action within and without human agents, a requirement that will take us deep into doctrines of grace, salvation, and ecclesiology. Equally, there has to be objective and subjective action on God's part. Human action or change is not enough. Subjective views of atonement are weak here. Atonement has necessarily got both objective and subjective dimensions on the divine side too. Putting the matter plainly, there must formally be a decision, a turning, and a moving towards us on God's side. Without this objective movement from God, there is no atonement; there is no communion. This is logically required if we are to speak of at-one-ment.

What we cannot say is exactly how God is required to act on God's part. To insist on some particular requirement is to try and control God and how God must act. We cannot make God's decisions for God. We cannot undercut the freedom of God on God's side of the relationship.[4] Yet we can surely expect that what God does will be apt to the human predicament, to the depth of human sin and evil. If sin were merely trivial, then atonement would be a relatively minor affair; it could be brushed off like we brush off this or that minor spat we have with a friend. If we have a realistic vision, or better still an ultra-realist vision, of our situation then fixing the relationship really is costly; it cannot be had casually or on the cheap.

We can begin to make headway, as the tradition has done, by noting that reconciliation cost Christ his life. Every vision of the atonement that is serious about Christ and about sin will insist on this. But how are we to speak aptly about this? Surely we must take seriously at this point the way Christ died. If Christ had died of the measles or a bad cold, we are not likely to say that this reconciled us to God. We have to look at how he died. It is not just any death that saved us; it was the actual death on Golgotha. That death was a voluntary death; it involved agonizing decision on the part of Christ, so much so that he sweated great drops of blood. We need to ponder this very carefully before we reach for any theory of the atonement.

It is easy to say Jesus had to die; but what kind of necessity is in view here? There is more than one kind of necessity, so we must think through what kind of necessity is involved. We need to begin with a straightforward analysis of why Christ died historically. Any account of atonement should begin with the history involved and must be compatible with it. If we read it even half right, we cannot say that God was killing Jesus or punishing Jesus. Jesus was an innocent agent who was brutally executed for a host of actions that caused him trouble even as they attracted others to become his disciples. There is no need here to get psychologically caught up in an inflated account of what happened so beloved of a certain kind of pious preaching. What is difficult to sustain is this: in and through the human actions of those who killed Jesus God was the crucial Agent engaged, say, in an act of punishment. To claim that the real action here is that of divine punishment, an action that supervenes on the human actions involved, is morally intolerable. Moreover, it requires spelling out an instance of double-agency that has not even been acknowledged much less justified. However, my main point here is this: any account of why Christ died must be compatible with the human actions performed in the events of the crucifixion.

---

[4] Here I have less confidence than Anselm in untutored human reason immersed in faith. As a theologian I stand across the threshold of divine revelation inside the canonical faith of the church.

Rendering the historical story is difficult and it is even dangerous given the way the death of Christ became a pretext of anti-Semitism. But we must not lose our nerve here. We need to step out in fear and trembling. And there is initially no great problem in answering the question why Christ died. Fundamentally, Jesus died because he was an offense. Human agents just like us in the Roman and Jewish world could not abide what he did, what he said, what he stood for, and what he was. It was an accumulation of things that brought his death. Little things like healing on the Sabbath (he did not keep appropriate office hours), like identifying with the outcast and those outside the system, like daring to forgive people their sins directly. Confronting corruption head on, alone, without an army, and without an organized committee, actions like this brought about his death. Consider the simple act of cleansing the Temple. Jesus was calling into question the misuse of the Temple, the abiding place of God, for commercial purposes. It was this that was simply the last straw. The final act was left for the Roman administration of the day which required crucifixion as the appropriate punishment for the crime supposedly committed.

It is tempting to leave the death of Jesus at this level and simply see him as one more martyr, or persecuted prophet, or as one more victim of political and religious corruption. If we do, we will simply have an exemplary vision of what his death means. Of course, at a technical and even spiritual level this is correct; Christ's death is exemplary. However, this is radically incomplete once we ponder who Christ is. Jesus is not just one more human martyr; this is the Son of God who has come to restore our fellowship with God. It is God who is dying on the Cross.

> We see a strange and fearful mystery accomplished today.
> He whom none may touch is seized.
> He who looses Adam from the curse is bound.
> He who tries the hearts of men is unjustly brought to trial.
> He who closed the abyss is shut in prison.
> He before whom the hosts of heaven stand with trembling stands before Pilate.
> The Creator is struck by the hand of His creature.
> He who comes to judge the living and the dead is condemned to the cross.
> The Conqueror of hell is enclosed in a tomb.
> O Thou, who has endured all things in Thy tender love,
> Thou hast saved all men from the curse,
> O long-suffering Lord, glory to Thee![5]

The point of his dying is enfolded in the wider point of his coming in the first place in the incarnation. The gospels are very, very clear about why Christ

---

[5] *Vespers of Holy Friday* (Syosset, NY: Orthodox Church in America, 1982), prepared by David Anderson and John Erickson, 24–5.

came. Consider the normative witness of John the Baptist: Christ came to baptize us in the Holy Spirit. However, if we are ever going to get within earshot of this, then God will have to confront us and deal with our rebellion and our sin. The problem of sin and guilt will have to be tackled. So it was not that Jesus came to die. Fundamentally, God came in Jesus to enter into communion with us. Jesus came to turn us back and ultimately to baptize us in the same Spirit which animated Christ's whole life from conception to resurrection. Consider the powerful message of Mark 12 in the parable of the vineyard where the move to bring us back is brought out with incredible force. The vineyard owner sends his son in the hope that they will turn the tenants around and get them to see sense; instead they see this as their chance to steal the vineyard once and for all; so they seek to kill the son who is sent. God takes their opposition and uses it as the chief cornerstone in his temple of the Holy Spirit, a temple constituted by both Jews and Gentiles.

We can now begin to see why his death was necessary. Staying the course to the point of death was an apt way of bringing death to an end, of getting us to face up to the depths of human evil, and of bringing us to see how utterly forgiving God is towards us. Without coming to terms with sin and forgiveness there is no possibility of being baptized in the Holy Spirit and having communion with God. In the end God's coming among us in the incarnation led to the death of the Son of God. Full incarnation in the world, as it actually is contingently, meant standing up to death itself and bearing the full cost of atonement from God's side. It involves real decision on the part of God; it requires generosity, patience, ingenuity, and compassion. This involves radical sacrifice on God's side. And surely God knew where it would end; it would end on Good Friday and Golgotha.

Here we must distinguish resolutely between God planning the death of Christ and God anticipating the death of his Son and turning that into an act of redemption from evil. What we need to say is not that God had to come in Christ and die if we are to be saved. Rather, the measure of God's action in moving towards us in communion is that God has freely and fully come to us as a matter of contingent, historical commitment and action. The price he paid for that action was the death of his Son. Both the coming and the dying are genuinely free acts of God. God does not have to come towards us morally or theologically. The Calvinist sense that it is utterly amazing that God should show grace to anyone at all, least of all his elect, and even less to the whole created order is on to something really deep and mysterious. My point here is that anyone with a serious sense of sin knows that they do not have a leg to stand on. So actually, the coming of Christ highlights the extraordinary generosity of God. This is an act of stupendous supererogation. It is an act that is morally amazing in its generosity, but it is in no way morally required of God; it is an act of grace from top to bottom. The necessities are real; if God is to save sinners like us, this is a maximally apt way to act; but they are radically contingent; and it is because the necessities are contingent that they are utterly amazing.

The language used to express this mystery of divine compassion and humiliation is daring in the extreme. Classical theories of the atonement are wrestling with the rich imagery used to map out the amazing way God stands up to evil in human history and what it is for us, his wayward creatures, to be the beneficiaries of this sacrificial act. The classical theories operate on a simple principle: pick out an image that fits the work of Christ and then upgrade it into a grand theory. So they develop theories around the concept of ransom, or of sacrifice, or of satisfaction, or of debt, and then look to these to be the scaffold for further reflection. Popular piety, most especially in hymnody, press these further by developing additional imagery that speaks in very powerful ways to the human condition.

We can catalogue the great varieties of imagery in the following manner. They began with a sense of what has gone wrong in the world, a depiction of sin, and then relates this to the death of Christ in very powerful ways. So we have commercial imagery. Sinning is like accruing debts innumerable; Christ's death is akin to having our debts paid once and for all. The pounds and pennies we owe have been paid in full; the credit card debit has been paid off at great cost by a wonderful benefactor. We find the imagery of cleansing. To reflect seriously on sin is to develop a sense of being soiled, foul, unclean, and stained; to see and take in the full force of the love of God expressed in the incarnation and death of Christ is to be cleansed and washed in the blood of Christ. There is psychological imagery. Sin has become a burden to us and, like the casting of our sins on the scapegoat in the Jewish sacrifices, the burden has been loaded up on Christ and carried away never to return.

There is military or criminal imagery. Sin is like being captive to enemies who have taken us hostage and enslaved us. Christ's death is like freeing us from enemy territory and captivity by the paying of a ransom. We run across satisfaction imagery. In human relations, we make up for the wrong done by doing something that will bring satisfaction to the person wronged. By joining ourselves to what Christ has voluntarily offered in his death to the Father, we render satisfaction to God and thus mirror what we do in human cases of satisfaction. There is the language of propitiation. In doing wrong we feel that God is entitled to be angry with us and we desperately desire to propitiate and turn God's anger aside; Christ has done that on our behalf and speaking in this way expresses our sense of relief that God is no longer angry with us.

There is the imagery of warfare with the demonic. In Christ's death, we are, as it were, delivered from the powers of evil let loose in the world. This is the ultimate sting operation and the Devil has been shown to be the fool that he is. We find eschatological imagery. Christ bore for us the wrath of God. The Son of God bore in his body the full consequences of estrangement from God for we live in a godless world that is violent and murderous. God's anger is expressed in terms of the withdrawal of his grace and we become slaves of our passions, worldly ambitions, and hatred of the divine. Christ bore the full brunt of this in his death at the hands of sinners, of whom we are chief. There is apocalyptic imagery. Nature itself groans as it watches the torment of God in his efforts to reach us in Christ. What is happening in the death of Christ works itself out ultimately in cosmic redemption of the whole created order and we are stunned by its extension.

We run into juridical and legal imagery. Given what we have done, we find ourselves in the divine court and deserve to be punished. But Christ has borne our punishment for us in dying for us. And last but not least there is the language of sacrifice. "Behold the Lamb of God who takes away the sin of the World."[6] In an agricultural society, the best lambs were the backbone of the economy and financial welfare. In the sacrifices made to God, one expressed how much God meant to one by sacrificing the best lamb. God has his lamb, his Son, given to restore communion. Here is the sacrifice to end all human and animal sacrifices. The sacrifice of Christ rises as a pleasing odor and scent to God on our behalf.

Theories of atonement, as already noted, simply pick up one or two of these themes, argue for their primacy, and then go to work to spell out the relevant divine action brought about in the death of Christ. There is merit to this exercise. It is simply impossible to keep all of this network of images in mind when thinking through what God has done in Christ. We naturally gravitate to a few of them for the sake of simplicity. Moreover, different images will appeal to different elements in our experience of evil and the way in which these experiences become embedded in our minds. We are gripped, say, by sin as a burden, or sin as a debt, or sin as a deep violation of the law of God, deserving punishment. Not surprisingly, whole cultures can become saturated with quite specific conceptions of estrangement that govern how we read the traditional materials that we pick up in our moral and spiritual formation. Some cultures are riddled with a sense of shame and develop honor codes; others become flooded with a sense of social injustice that cries out for satisfaction; others are waterlogged with a terrible consciousness of victimhood. We cannot avoid these personal and cultural developments; they speak too accurately and too persistently to the human condition. Yet there is the constant danger of narrowness of focus where we become obsessed with one or two elements of the picture as a whole; in some cases, we fall headlong into bigotry, so that everything, including our theological sensibility, becomes focused on merely one element in the total horizon. We become fixated on one concept so that everyone we meet, every conversation, every topic in theology, every reading

---

[6] John 1:29.

of Scripture, every interpretation of the history of doctrine, has to be brought around and connected to it. This is not a pleasing sight to behold.

One antidote to this intellectual vice is to note the tendency to reduction, take a season to enter into the nooks and crannies of each image, and then to move on over time to the full range of images and their scaffolding that are available. Two other considerations are important. We need to resist the temptation to reduce the work of Christ in atonement to the particular means that captures our attention. The overall focus remains that of reconciliation between ourselves and God. Equally, we should bear in mind that the incarnation of the Father in the Son through the Spirit means that God has already enacted a dramatic union or atonement before we tackle the crucial place of the death of Christ in securing reconciliation between alienated human agents and God. God's commitment to union has already been secured in the Son, fully human and fully divine; the death of Christ makes manifest just how costly that commitment is from the divine side. Expressed differently, no human opposition can stand in the way of God's love for the world. On the contrary, God allows the human opposition and in an extraordinary act of ingenuity and providence works a wonder of wonders in the death of his Son.

Let me formally identify what I am doing here. On the one hand, I am refusing to abandon the rich body of discourse that shows up in debates and treatments of the atonement. Even the reduction to three grand theories is an historical and theological mistake. On the other, I am transposing the language into a new key. Let me risk a name for this: let me call it an expressivist-cognitivist account of the language of atonement. To develop an account of the rich discourse that shows up in descriptions of the life and death of Christ and that are identified in the various doctrines of atonement is to do the following: it is to give expression to the reception of the good news of the Gospel that begins to capture the sense of liberation, release, joy, and gratitude that naturally arises when one sees what God has objectively done in coming to us in Christ. Thus, there is an expressivist core to each of the images deployed. However, there is also a cognitive core, for the expressions used depend upon an apt network of description of our alienation and estrangement from God. They relate to and depend upon fitting ways to spell out the host of ways in which sin can be depicted phenomenologically and truthfully. Even more important, they supply us with a dense network of divine actions to describe what God is doing in the incarnation and in the death of his Son.

Let me supply but one example from a hymn by Charles Wesley.

> O love divine, what hast thou done!
> The immortal God has died for me!
> The Father's co-eternal Son
> Bore all my sins upon the tree;
> The immortal God for me has died!
> My Lord, my Love is crucified—

Is crucified for me and you,
To bring us rebels back to God;
Believe, believe, the record true,
We all are bought with Jesus' blood,
Pardon for all flows from his side:
My Lord, my Love is crucified.[7]

In this instance, Wesley weaves together the identity of Jesus as the second Person of the Trinity with the action of the Son in death in taking our sins upon himself, in dying for us, in bringing us back to God, in buying our redemption, and in pardoning our sins. It matters both who died—it was the co-eternal Son of God—and it matters what God did in his dying. And in the latter case we have a whole network of divine actions to ponder. Note also how the hymn displays the integration of the vision of Christ's death into the depths of the human heart.

To bring home the methodological point at stake in this chapter let me make it explicit with respect to a standard way of deploying the penal substitution theory of atonement. The elements in that theory are elegant and straightforward. Here is Thomas Schreiner:

> The Father because of his love for human beings sent his Son (who offered himself willingly and gladly) to satisfy God's justice, so that Christ took the place of sinners. The punishment and penalty we deserved was laid on Christ instead of us, so that in the cross God's holiness and mercy are manifest.[8]

Central to Schreiner's account is the further claim that the kind of justice involved is retributive in character. "Since all human beings have sinned and God as the Holy One judges retributively and does not merely overlook sin, sin must be atoned by sacrifice. There must be a penal substitute."[9]

Let's grant the contested critical place of retribution in any morally robust vision of punishment. I take it that retribution minimally involves the following: that the person punished deserves to be punished (neither the innocent nor those disposed to commit a crime can be justly punished); that the punishment must fit the crime (neither deterrence nor therapy can secure this condition); and that after punishment the person punished is free from further intervention by the state. The problems that arise when this is applied directly to the penal substitutionary theory of atonement are these. First, it is not legitimate to transfer the punishment from the guilty to the innocent. Retribution requires that the guilty be punished not the innocent. Even if the

---

[7] Charles Wesley, in *Hymns and Psalms: A Methodist and Ecumenical Hymnbook* (London: Methodist Publishing House, 1983), number 175.

[8] Thomas R. Schreiner, "Penal Substitution View," in James Beilby and Paul P. Eddy, eds., *The Nature of Atonement: Four Views* (Downers Grove, IL: IVP Academic, 2006), 67.

[9] Ibid., 82.

innocent offers freely to take the place of the guilty, this will be immediately rejected as undoing the first condition of any serious doctrine of retribution. Second, there is then a radical shift of categories, for we move from the language of punishment to the language of sacrifice. The implicit assumption would appear to be that Christ's death is a form of punishment inflicted on him by God in order to keep intact the theory of punishment involved.

The problems in this are obvious. The switch in categories is illegitimate; we need an explanation for this change in orientation, once we remember that these are drawn from radically different social and semantic contexts. As already noted, retribution requires that the guilty rather than the innocent party be punished; but this is totally rejected in the theory before us. Moreover, in the human situation we recognize the place of amnesty where punishment is set aside in order to achieve other goals in the repair of nations and societies. So we have to consider the possibility of amnesty in addition to the require-ment for retribution if we are to run with the language of punishment. We also face the difficulty of who is the agent of punishment. In the gospels, it is human agents who crucify Jesus; it is not the Father. Luke records that in dying Jesus voluntarily gave himself up into the hands of his Father. Mark makes clear that in death Jesus recites a psalm of radical trust in God. To speak of the Father punishing Jesus does not fit the historical record available. If we insist on this claim, then the Father is intimately involved in horrendous crime of judicial murder of an innocent man. The Father, then, does not just use evil providentially to do good; he actually engages in evil to do good. These are, surely, unacceptable consequences.

In addition, the implications of this for our doctrine of salvation are obvious. If we allow, for the sake of argument, that Christ takes our punish-ment, then we have one of two options. Either Christ does so for everybody or he does not. If the former, we must commit to a universalist vision of salvation and also reject the option of human agents saying a radical no to God and thus reject the robust freedom this entails; if the latter, then the punishment is efficacious only for the elect and the mercy of God is severely restricted. We enter, of course, well-known contested territory, but one has to follow the lights one has. For my part, God is radically committed to the salvation of all his creatures; human agents really are genuinely free and can indeed reject the will of God for themselves; and the significance of the death of Christ is not local but universal, up to and including the redemption of the cosmos. So these commitments require that one follow the argument back to its initial premises and start again.

Rather than reject the language of penal substitution, I propose that we retain it. The reasons for retaining it are these. First, the language shows up again and again in theology; it is an essential element in the rich variety of concepts that are available. Second, the language speaks in a very powerful way when we see ourselves as those who have systematically violated the law of

God. This language too is ineradicable; it will always speak to the human condition formed in the deep faith of the Scriptures and the church. The language also helps to put names to the diverse set of divine actions visible in the death of Christ. The solution is to set aside the quest for a formal theory of atonement. Theories in this case obscure as much as they reveal; they create intellectual dissonance that cuts sharply into our moral vision of God. Thus, there is always the suspicion in this instance that God is on the lookout for us so that he can drag us into his court and mete out the punishment we all deserve. To be sure, we can always double down on the theory and find a way to ward off such a suspicion. We can say that when it comes to our relationship to God, the normal rules do not apply. The innocent in this case can indeed take the place of the guilty. And we can double down on either universal salvation or on limited atonement only for the elect. We need a different strategy: retain the imagery and find a better way to interpret it.

We read the penal imagery as a magnificent way to capture the sense of joy and gratitude that emerges when people look upon themselves as guilty lawbreakers before God, are exposed to the objective action of God in Christ, and find the language of penal substitution a fitting analogical way to express their sense of relief and release. It is likewise for all the other rich ways of speaking of what the life and death of Christ means to us when we seek to provide a dense account of estrangement and alienation from God. Hence I readily endorse the wisdom of the church in not canonizing any specific doctrine of the atonement and in thus opening up her treasures in ways that can be applied to the varied conditions of human agents in sin across space and time.

7

The Person of the Holy Spirit

I have said these things to you while I am still with you. But the Advocate, the Holy Spirit, whom the Father will send in my name, will teach you everything, and remind you of all that I have said to you.

John 14:25–6.

Many Christians are not too sure what to say about the Person of the Holy Spirit. They know that somehow the Holy Spirit is important; but, if asked to indicate who or what the Holy Spirit is, they hesitate. I once heard a distinguished New Testament scholar refer to the Holy Spirit as "the spook factor" in Christianity. He had in mind the bizarre claims often heard on religious television. Yet teaching on the person and work of the Holy Spirit constitutes a palpable element in the full contours of the Christian faith. In this chapter I shall explore the ontology of the Holy Spirit. I want to know what we should say about the being of the Holy Spirit before I take up the topic of the action and activity of the Holy Spirit. More specifically, I shall investigate the central concepts we need to put in place to secure the identity and character of the Holy Spirit.

Consider the splendid advice of Austin Farrer at this early point.

Moralists and philosophers bid us to reflect, they would have us do the supremely reasonable thing. Our religion also bids us reflect, but not at all in the same way. We are to think once, and think twice, and think twenty times, not about our actions, but about our God: we cannot too much consider his honour, and his kindness; we may very easily consider too long how we should respond.[1]

Farrer's cryptic comment is salutary in so far as it refers to material on the Holy Spirit. It means initially that we insist that any doctrine of the Holy Spirit be located firmly in our thinking about the Trinity. It also means that we should not make haste to speak about the action and activity of the Holy Spirit without a firm grasp of what is at stake when we speak of the Person of the

---

[1] Austin Farrer, *Words for Life* (Eugene, OR: Wipf and Stock, 2012), 59.

Holy Spirit. Above all, it means that we should not hurry off to focus on our response to the work of the Holy Spirit.

To be sure, our response to the Holy Spirit matters; and that response deserves extended reflection. There is a wealth of informal and formal material devoted to our response to the Holy Spirit in the literature of monasticism and of revivalism. To take the latter, Jonathan Edwards has given us an outstanding account of the religious affections which stem from the extraordinary outpouring of the Holy Spirit in and around his ministry in the first half of the eighteenth century.[2] John Wesley's sermons show a similar interest. The same occurs today in the many works available from within Pentecostalism and the Charismatic Movement. The besetting temptation in this complex tradition has been that we begin wonderfully, focusing on the reality of God, and within that giving special attention to the work of the Holy Spirit, and then we change gears to focus on ourselves responding to God. Thus, there is a disastrous shift away from a theocentric theology to one that drifts naturally into an anthropocentric obsession with ourselves. In turn, this anthropocentric focus splits into a damaging division between those who attend to personal experience in our response to God and those who spotlight the moral and political consequences of our response to God. The wild human intellect takes hold of our egocentric passions and readily undermines our best intellectual and spiritual intentions.

It is crucial, therefore, to recover our nerve and refuse to move too quickly from sustained ontological reflection on the Person of the Holy Spirit before we even take up the challenges related to the action and activity of the Holy Spirit. Recall immediately that the central teaching of the church is that the Holy Spirit is the third Person of the Trinity who proceeds eternally from the Father. This claim is not uncontroversial, but it is where we must begin, stand our ground, and even end our deliberations. This claim—that the Holy Spirit is a Person who proceeds eternally from the Father—is the irreducible and irreplaceable foundation of our reflections. Maybe this is all we need; we shall see if this is so before the end of the chapter.

We can fix our attention resolutely at this point by revisiting and updating the historical story behind this development. It is easy to rush this story because the church did not have to spend as much time thinking through the Personhood of the Holy Spirit in the life of the Trinity as happened in the case of the Personhood of the Son. Once the crucial conceptual breakthrough had been made by Athanasius, it was relatively easy to make the relevant application to the ontology of the Holy Spirit. Athanasius saw that the church could not say what it did about the actions of the Son without making significant adjustments in the monotheism inherited from Israel. To take the simplest of cases, if Jesus in his ministry forgave the paralytic his sins, this

---

[2] Jonathan Edwards, *The Religious Affections* (New Haven, CT: Yale University Press, 2009).

required either an admission of blasphemy or a radical rethinking of the nature of the divine. This is precisely what happened over time. Actions constitutive of the identity of the God of Israel were being predicated of Jesus; the solution was to speak of two divine Persons in the One God, the Father and the Son, related by way of eternal generation. The Father and the Son were of one divine substance but differentiated by way of two Persons. The crucial conceptual and intellectual move was now in hand to develop a similar solution to the challenge posed by the activity of the Holy Spirit. The Holy Spirit imparted divine life to those who put their faith in the Son; this was an act constitutive of the divine; so the solution was to expand the ontology to include a third Person, the Holy Spirit who proceeds eternally from the Father.

My aim here is to capture the critical conceptual revolution in play in the debate. This should not be read as an effort to neglect the other factors that were crucial in the origination of the doctrine of the Holy Spirit. Thus, already in the Old Testament and in the New Testament there were significant references to the Holy Spirit that had developed over time. The most obvious claims already in play that indicate the deeply personal character of the Holy Spirit speak of blaspheming the Holy Spirit,[3] quenching the Spirit,[4] grieving the Holy Spirit,[5] putting the Holy Spirit to test,[6] and outraging the Holy Spirit.[7] Moreover, there were at times vivid and dramatic experiences of the Holy Spirit that required adequate description and explanation in terms of personal agency. There was also a desire to preserve intellectual coherence at the heart of the church's confession of faith. So, there was a wealth of diverse, confusing, and even incoherent data scattered hither and yon that came into play in providing warrants for the faith that emerged over time in the church. Yet the data remained a mere constellation of materials, a ragbag of themes and experiences, that would have remained precisely that but for the conceptual breakthrough picked up and brilliantly developed by Athanasius.

Even so Athanasius and the theologians working in his slipstream were extremely careful to state their position with modesty and reserve. What they could not allow was that the Holy Spirit be identified as a creature; it was especially exasperating that some had even toyed with the language of grandson as a possibility.[8] The challenge was how to introduce conceptual innovation adopted at Nicaea I into the formal teaching of the church at Constantinople I. The actual language adopted is instructive. The church confessed: "The Holy Spirit is the Lord, the Giver of Life, who together with the Father and Son is worshipped and glorified, who spoke by the prophets."

---

[3] Mark 3:29.   [4] Ephesians 4:3.   [5] Acts 5:9.   [6] Ibid.
[7] Hebrews 10:29.
[8] My favorite bizarre example from the ancient world is supplied by an eccentric group called the Elchesaites who identified the Spirit as the female companion of the angel (twenty miles tall) who delivered a book of revelation to the founder of their sect. See G. W. H. Lampe, *God as Spirit* (Oxford: Oxford University Press, 1977), 217.

The earlier language that expressed the deity of the Son (the language of *homoousion*) is not used. However, there is no doubt about the content of the material. The Holy Spirit is clearly identified as divine for the Holy Spirit is Lord and Giver of Life and is worshipped and glorified with the Father and the Son. If this was intended to satisfy the large group of Macedonian bishops who either rejected the divinity of the Holy Spirit or felt it was unwise to say so publicly, it failed, for they refused the olive branch and quietly vanished in time from history. In the official teaching we see here important pastoral concerns in operation. We also see that the divinity of the Holy Spirit could be couched in varied forms and that underneath the doctrine were all sorts of implicit warrants that were vital in the initial debate. It is no accident that the doctrine has continued to carry the day across the churches down through history. The epistemological backing is by no means insecure; it has been revisited and upheld again and again, even though everyone agrees that we are dealing here with a mystery that shatters our categories.

My concern here is ontological. Perceptive observers will already have noted that I have thus far stood by the original reading of Constantinople I. Thus, I have not spoken of the Holy Spirit proceeding from the Father and the Son, the famous *filioque* formula. The history behind this addition in the West and its rejection is both complicated and contentious; it remains a very significant factor in ecumenical discussion. Various reformulations have been canvassed but none has secured consensus. The intention behind the change was clearly a good one; theologians were seeking to uphold the full divinity of the Son in the teeth of fresh forms of Arianism in Spain. They reasoned that if they spoke of the Holy Spirit eternally proceeding from the Father and the Son, they could then ensure that the Son received the same honors and status of the Father. The obvious danger was that now the divinity of the Holy Spirit was at risk. If his full divinity required that the Son be an originating source of the Spirit, then the full divinity of the Holy Spirit required that he be an originating source of the Father and the Son, a move that clearly contradicts the core elements in the doctrine of the Trinity.

This ongoing debate about the ontology of the Holy Spirit has thrown invaluable hermeneutical light on a distinction that is crucial to observe. Many have argued that because the Holy Spirit is sent at the request of the Son, and because the Holy Spirit is a gift of the Son bestowed upon believers by the Son, then the inference is thought to be obvious: the Holy Spirit proceeds from the Father and the Son. Thus, if we follow this reasoning, the church in the West was correct to make the relevant change. The problems in this line of reasoning are equally obvious. First, the Holy Spirit is intimately involved in the sending of the Son to earth in the virginal conception, thus, if we follow this logic, we will have to say that the Son is eternally begotten of the Father and the Spirit. Few are prepared to make this radical alteration. Second, and more importantly, the argument confuses the eternal procession of the Spirit from the Father in eternity with the temporal sending of the Holy Spirit by or through the Son in time. In this instance, there is no simple line of reasoning that can take us from the actions of the Son in time to the eternal relations within the very being of the Trinity in eternity. Indeed, once we pursue this line of argument, we open a Pandora's box of speculation in which everything that occurs by way of the temporal actions of the Persons of the Trinity quickly has to be replicated within the eternal life of God. Thus, if there is an incarnation of the Son in time, there will have to be a pre-temporal "incarnation" of the Son in eternity. If the Son endures a cross of suffering on Golgotha then there will have to be a suffering on a cross in the immanent Trinity. To put the issue sharply, we have lost the apophatic dimension of our discourse about the Trinity and abandoned the crucial element of reserve that was built into the exposition of church teaching on the Trinity from the beginning. Put differently, we have ignored the crucial distinction between the eternal relations within the Trinity and the temporal missions of the Son and of the Spirit in time.

The categorical reserve in play here shows up in one other historical episode that deserves brief mention. In rendering the doctrine of the Trinity, some theologians in Syria readily deployed the grammatical pronoun "she" when they referred to the Holy Spirit. Not surprisingly, this has been used as a warrant for thinking of the Holy Spirit as feminine. The hope was that this would go some way to deal with the heavy male imagery embedded in the doctrine of the Trinity. The underlying argument was that the Hebrew for Spirit was grammatically feminine. However, grammatical usage provides no such warrant in that grammar and gender are distinct categories. Theologians are clutching at straws to make bricks at this point, as many contemporary languages other than English attest. In the original context treatments of the Holy Spirit as ontologically feminine died out over time because of their associations with heresy. More importantly, this argument introduces sexual categories into the core of the doctrine of God that were expressly forbidden and even ridiculed by those who recognized the real possibility of paganism lurking in the speculative weeds. We see again how firm and circumspect the church was in its deliberations. The church confesses the divinity of the Holy Spirit, and insists on the Holy Spirit as a Person who proceeds eternally from the Father. If we say less than this, we are not doing justice to the reality of God, and we also run the risk of folk making up nonsense; if we go beyond this, we are beyond the bounds of our conceptual resources, and we also run the risk of teaching nonsense.

Both the content and reserve in our discourse rule out immediately any decision to reach for the generic language of energy, personality, force, or impersonal power, in our thinking about the Holy Spirit. It also challenges the reduction of the Person of the Holy Spirit to such religious phenomena as divine presence, God in action, divine energies, or divine grace. Still less should we think of the Holy Spirit as a personification of a network of personal or cultural attitudes, say, like the spirit of Dunkirk or the current spirit of the Notre Dame football team. We are dealing with the Person of the Holy Spirit, a Person integrally related by the most intimate bonds of unity with the Father and the Son. None of these concepts do justice to the strength of this claim. Nor will it do to reduce the Person of the Holy Spirit to a relation within the Godhead, say, the relation or bond between the Father and the Son. Again, it must be reiterated, we are dealing with a fully divine Person who proceeds from the Father.

However, rejecting false trails like these is by no means the end of the matter. Two considerations come into play at this point. First, there are a network of descriptions and symbols of the Holy Spirit that deserve our attention. Surely, these can help us make progress on reflecting on the Person of the Holy Spirit. Even though they readily spill over into descriptions of the action or activity of the Holy Spirit, it is useful to tarry for a time. Second, given that the church was prepared to go beyond scriptural language to express its faith about the Trinity, can we not do the same today and thus deepen our understanding of the Person of the Holy Spirit? Let's take these suggestions in order.

The obvious place to begin is to pick up the language of the Holy Spirit as the "Giver of Life." We have a neat group of symbols of the Holy Spirit that give us a thick description of this designation for the Holy Spirit. We can begin with the idea of the Holy Spirit as *rûach*, that is, the breath or wind of God moving over the face of the waters at the beginning of creation to bring energy and life.[9] We can add the startling observation that God breathed into Adam the breath of life and he became a living soul.[10] Likewise, the wind of the Spirit that appeared at Pentecost signifies the Holy Spirit breathing life into the waiting disciples to give energy to their lives and witness.[11] Furthermore, the wind of the Spirit, Nicodemus is told, blows where it wills to bring new birth, to enable those who hear the Word of God to start all over again.[12]

In the neighborhood of the metaphor of breath we encounter the image of the Holy Spirit as rain and water.[13] These images speak of the Holy Spirit initially bringing life and energy to replace the lethargy, boredom, and listlessness we associate with dry ground and with dry spells in our moral and spiritual lives. We are in a wilderness where we struggle through merely to survive. Water is needed to fertilize new growth. These images also highlight the promise of Jesus that the Spirit will come like rivers of living water within us, and thus becomes manifest as a Person who indwells us so that life gushes forth naturally from within as a source of fresh hope and motivation for

---

[9] Genesis 1:2. [10] Genesis 2:7. Compare Ezekiel 37:9. [11] Acts 2.
[12] John 3. [13] Isaiah 44:3–4; Joel 2:23, 28–9.

ourselves and others.[14] So the Holy Spirit as wind and water draws us also into an understanding of the Person of the Holy Spirit as Giver of Life.

A very different image gives us a very different picture, namely, the Person of the Holy Spirit as fire.[15] In this case the fundamental idea is that of purging, where elements of our lives are burned off so that the life of God may have space to grow and flourish. The Holy Spirit is not just a judge who identifies what is wrong but a cleansing agency that begins the deep and painful process of repentance and reorientation. There is also a sense of the Holy Spirit as a powerful Person who cuts through our excuses and nonsense in order for new growth to sprout and develop. Think of a brush fire that clears a public space for a new beginning in nature. Such an image rightly evokes a sense of holy fear mixed with fruitful anticipation.

In addition, there is the symbol of the Holy Spirit as a dove, a symbol that has rightly gained its popularity because of the theophany at the baptism of Christ.[16] In this case the fundamental idea conveyed is that of a supremely gentle Person who operates peacefully and gracefully. Doves indicate a Person with a caring, soft disposition. Where the Son is depicted as a lamb in the world of animals to indicate his sacrificial character in dealing with our sins, the depiction of the Spirit as a dove indicates supreme gentility in order to handle the delicate, fragile, and fearful elements in our lives.

Finally, there are the less popular images of the Holy Spirit as wine[17] and oil.[18] Properly received wine gladdens the heart, destroys our shyness, and brings a sense of freedom. The image of the Spirit as oil brings to mind associations with fuel that provides energy; with medical practices that bring healing; and with the practice of consecration where the Spirit supplies wisdom and inspiration over the long haul.

With the exception of the symbol of the dove, all these images are impersonal in nature. Their purpose is to speak to the nature and character of a Person within the Holy Trinity. This semantic strategy is nothing unusual, for the same strategy shows up in our thick descriptions of the Father and the Son. It also shows in our everyday usage in applying impersonal metaphors to describe human agents, say, as rocks or mountains. We often describe a friend as a force of nature, for example. We are not tempted to take these literally; we know instinctively how to deploy them to understand our friends. Likewise, this rich network of concepts helps us to understand the kind of Person we encounter when we speak of the Holy Spirit. They also form a bridge to our analysis of the characteristic actions and activity of the Holy Spirit for they can be cashed out semantically in terms of the role of the Holy Spirit in the inauguration of God's kingdom and the experience of salvation.

---

[14] John 4:14.   [15] Matthew 3:11; Acts 2:3–4.   [16] Matthew 3:11.
[17] Acts 2:12–13.   [18] 1 John 2:20; 2 Corinthians 1:21–2.

In exploring the symbols classically associated with the Holy Spirit, the theologian is not engaging in a hit-and-run exercise in biblical exegesis. The goal is to gather together salient analogies from Scripture that fill out our account of the Person of the Holy Spirit. This clearly requires exercising theological judgment; we need apt selection and reflection above and beyond a mere inductive study of Scripture. Gregory of Nazianzus captures what was at stake.

> The Old Testament proclaimed the Father openly, and the Son more obscurely. The New Testament manifested the Son and suggested the Deity of the Spirit. Now the Spirit Himself dwells among us and supplies us with a clearer demonstration of Himself. For it is not safe, when the Godhead of the Father was not acknowledged, plainly to proclaim the Son; nor when that of the Son was not yet received to burden us further (if I may use so bold an expression) with the Holy Ghost.[19]

Gregory insists here on the need for apt patience. The same observation applies to the second strategy we can use to fill out our understanding of the Person of the Holy Spirit, namely, the turn to wider philosophical considerations. Given that this step has already been taken in the development of the doctrine of the Trinity, then there can be no objection in principle to this procedure. What is needed is critical assessment to ensure that our deliberations cohere with our foundational commitments to the doctrine of the Trinity, and thus to the Holy Spirit as a Person; and that they actually take us deeper in our understanding rather than lead us astray. In the following I shall explore three efforts to make progress, two more ancient and one of more recent vintage. In turn they pick up the language of force-field, love, and light. I shall deal with the first two rather briefly; the last one at greater length.

I begin with the language of force-field, a concept that is widely discussed in the current literature.[20] The central concept in play here is drawn from physics but the initial rationale is drawn from the use of the term *pneuma* as used within Stoicism. The original aim behind the idea of *pneuma* was that of a very fine stuff that permeated all things in the cosmos and that gave rise to the different qualities, changes, and movements of things. This notion was picked up by Philo and then by some early Christian theologians to refer to the working of the Holy Spirit in creation. The obvious problem with this borrowing is that the Stoic position was entangled with a version of materialism, a claim that was incompatible with any serious account of the Holy Spirit. However, the impulse to turn to the Stoic tradition was on target once it was

---

[19] Gregory of Nazianzus, "On the Holy Spirit," *The Nicene and Post-Nicene Fathers* (Grand Rapids, MI: Eerdmans, 1983), vol. 7, 326.

[20] In what follows I pick up this proposal as developed by Wolfhart Pannenberg. See his *Systematic Theology Volume 2* (Grand Rapids, MI: Eerdmans, 1994), translated by Geoffrey W. Bromiley, 79–102.

cleansed of its material associations and spelled out in terms of a better account of material reality supplied by modern physics. Medieval theology turned to the notion of motion as a way to capture the causes of material change, that is, to the idea of a non-bodily cause of material movement. In time the notion of motion was replaced by Leibniz and others by the idea of force; this in turn was a precursor of the concept of field theories of scientists like Newton and Faraday. The central idea here is that bodily phenomena are the manifestation of force-fields which comes to a climax in the idea of one cosmic force-field. So, beyond the singular force-fields represented, say, by gravity or by magnetic energy, there is one force-field underlying the whole of the cosmos, a proposal introduced by Faraday.

The application of this concept to theology is neither naïve nor reduction-istic. Nor should we suspect pantheism lurking below the surface. The one reality is described accurately in entirely naturalistic terms. However, the theologian's description in terms of creation supervenes on this initial de-scription and sees the same phenomena in terms of the working of the Holy Spirit. In doing so theologians deploy their own warrants for their account of the world; they are not simply picking up crumbs from the physicist's table. Moreover, the connections historically run deep.

> We see that the reality is the same [nature understood in terms of field theory and creation] because theological statements about the working of the Holy Spirit go back to the same philosophical root that by mathematical formalizing is also the source of field theories of physics, and the different theories give evidence of the same emphases that we see in the same metaphysical intuitions. We see also that the reality is the same because the theological (as distinct from the scientific) development of the concept is in a position to find a place in its reflection for the different form of description in physics, for which there can be empirical dem-onstration, and in this way confirm the coherence of its own statements about the reality of the world.[21]

The rationale for the relevant theological description is supplied by the concept of God as Spirit. However, what operates at this point is not a generic conception of God but a Trinitarian conception which sees the Holy Spirit as one of the concretions of the essence of God as Spirit in distinction from the Father and the Son.

> The person of the Holy Spirit is not himself to be understood as the field but as a unique manifestation (singularity) of the field of divine essentiality. But because the personal being of the Holy Spirit is manifest only in distinction from the Son (and therefore from the Father), his working in creation has more of the character of dynamic field-operations.[22]

---

[21] Ibid., 83.   [22] Ibid., 83–4.

The fundamental issue to be noted is both simple and attractive. We can lay aside both the semantic origins of the proposal and its potential apologetic value in sorting through the relation between science and theology. The crucial question is whether the image of a force-field, impersonal as it is, helps us expand our initial descriptions of the Holy Spirit drawn from Scripture. As it stands, this way of thinking about the Holy Spirit provides food for the imagination in giving content to features of the Holy Spirit we might otherwise miss. It brings home in a vivid way the presence of the Holy Spirit throughout the created order. And it does so as an enrichment of the church's vision of the Holy Spirit rather than as a replacement of that vision.

The language of love in contrast to that of force-field has an ancient and honorable pedigree that was developed by Augustine. Augustine builds his account of the Holy Spirit as love not from Scripture[23] but from his account of the double-procession of the Holy Spirit from the Father and the Son. This latter doctrine he does take to be a scriptural doctrine.

> Nor can we say that the Holy Spirit does not proceed also from the Son, for it is not without reason that the same Spirit is said to be of both the Father and the Son. Nor do I see what else he intended to signify when he breathed in the face of the disciples and said, 'Receive the Holy Spirit.' For that bodily breathing, proceeding from the body of the sensation of bodily touching, was not the substance of the Holy Spirit but a manifestation through a fitting sign that the Holy Spirit proceeds not only from the Father but also from the Son.[24]

We have here the familiar argument that we can arrive at the truth of the inner life of the Trinity from the actions of the Persons of the Godhead in history. Here is one way Augustine seeks to press the issue towards a vision of the Holy Spirit as love.

> The Holy Spirit ... is properly called the Holy Spirit relatively, since He is referred to both the Father and the Son, because He is the Spirit of both the Father and the Son. But the relation is not itself apparent in that name, but it is apparent when He is called the gift of God, for He is the gift of the Father and of the Son, because 'He proceeds from the Father,' as the Lord says, and because the Apostle says, 'He who does not have the Spirit of Christ does not belong to him,' he certainly says of the Holy Spirit. When, therefore, we say the gift of the giver, and the giver of the giver, we speak in both cases relatively in reciprocal reference. Therefore, the Holy Spirit is certain unutterable communion of the Father and the Son.[25]

The next move is twofold. First, the joint giving of the Spirit (the ground for the identity of the Holy Spirit with communion of the Father and the Son) in time mirrors an eternal relation of communion between the Father and the Son. Second, we can readily substitute love for communion and thus think of

---

[23] Augustine is quite explicit about the non-scriptural basis of his position.
[24] Augustine, *On the Trinity*, 4.20.29. [25] Ibid., 5.11.12.

the Holy Spirit as the reciprocal love that eternally exists between the Father and the Son. Both these moves are nicely captured in the following.

> Therefore the Holy Spirit, whatever it is, is something in common between the Father and the Son. But this communion itself is consubstantial and coeternal; and if it may fitly be called friendship, let it be so called; but it is more aptly called love.[26]

As it stands, both the effort to secure the doctrine of the double-procession of the Spirit from the Father and the Son and the conceptual decision to construe communion as synonymous with love are deeply flawed. This is not to say that alternative arguments for the *filioque* clause are not available; nor is it to say that we could drop the language of communion and simply retain the language of love. Let's grant that all this could be done.[27] The fundamental problem with the identification of the Holy Spirit with the love that exists eternally between the Father and the Son is that it is an obvious category mistake. It would be bizarre to deny that there is love at the heart of the Trinity. However, love is essentially a relational disposition between two or more subjects. It is simply incoherent to identify love as the subject rightly identified as the Person of the Holy Spirit. The most we can gain from this exercise is a reminder of the eternal love that exists at the very heart of the Godhead. Reminders like this are always welcome in theology; the danger is that they will redirect our attention away from the Person of the Holy Spirit and the correlative role in salvation that is all too readily marginalized or forgotten. However, this was not either the intention of Augustine or the result of his ruminations on the nature of the Holy Spirit as a Person in the Trinity, for he developed extraordinarily important insights on the doctrine of salvation that will detain us later in our work.[28]

Let's now turn to the language of light and see where that might take us. I refer to an image of light that was central to Symeon the New Theologian in his deliberations on the Holy Spirit. Compared to Augustine, Symeon, outside certain esoteric circles, is barely known as a significant figure within contemporary theology, much less in the churches at large. This is unfortunate because he is recognized as not just a great Father of the church but as a canonical theologian. Thus in the East he stands with John, the writer of the fourth gospel, and with Gregory of Nazianzus, who was pivotal in securing the doctrine of the Trinity in the fourth century, as one of the three great

---

[26] Ibid., 6.5.7. Later Augustine says this: "And if the love by which the Father loves the Son and the Son loves the Father ineffably demonstrates the communion of both, what is more suitable than that He should properly be called love who is the Spirit common to both?" Ibid., 15, 19 (37).

[27] For a concerted effort to find a better way to secure and spell out the doctrine of the Holy Spirit as love see David Coffey, "The Holy Spirit as the Mutual Love of the Father and the Son," *Theological Studies* 51 (1990), 193–229.

[28] I eschew at this point the standard polemics between East and West that attempts to trace supposed neglect of the Holy Spirit to the work of Augustine.

theologians of the first millennium. Indeed, Symeon himself identified a true theologian as a gift of the Spirit in the church whose central task is to provide apt concepts for describing the experience of God in the church as a whole. This vision of a theologian differs sharply from our common understanding of a theologian. We might say that the regular theologians of the church are essentially creative teachers of the Christian tradition. This is not an unworthy designation; but it is clearly a very different one from that advocated by Symeon. If Symeon is on the right track as to what a true theologian is, then he has raised the stakes as to what we should expect. Applied in the current context, we should expect him to supply fresh light on the nature of the Holy Spirit that might well lead us to a fresh and more accurate reading and reception of Scripture. The result, in fact, is dramatic and calls for a fresh look at a central episode in the life of Jesus and the disciples.

We can go straight to the heart of his contribution by looking at the remarkable testimony to Symeon's personal experience of the Holy Spirit. He addresses the reader in the third person; this is clearly a strategy to deflect attention away from himself and towards the Holy Spirit.

> One day, as he stood and recited, 'God, have mercy upon me, a sinner' (Luke 18:13), uttering it with his mind rather than his mouth, suddenly a flood or radiance appeared from above and filled the room. As this happened the young man lost all awareness [of his surroundings] and forgot that he was in a house or that he was under a roof. He saw nothing but light all around him and he did not know if he was standing on the ground. He was not afraid of falling; he was not concerned with the word, nor did anything pertaining to men and corporeal beings enter his mind. Instead, he was wholly in the presence of immaterial light and seemed to himself to have turned into light. Oblivious to all the world he was filled with tears and with ineffable joy and gladness. His mind then ascended to heaven and beheld another light, which was clearer than that which was close at hand. In a wonderful manner there appeared to him, standing close to that light the saint of whom we have spoken, the old man equal to angels, who had given him the commandment and the book.[29]

What are we to make of this astonishing episode of a relatively young Christian? The crucial observation to make about this experience is that Symeon is here describing his own experience of the Holy Spirit and that the relevant description is in terms of light. He intends us to take this description utterly realistically; indeed, he supplies a sophisticated epistemological account and defense of the veridicality of this description.[30] In the wake of this it is not surprising that the depiction of the Holy Spirit as light is central to his

---

[29] Symeon the New Theologian, *The Discourses* (Mahwah, NJ: Paulist Press, 1990), 245–6. The saint referred to here is the Elder Symeon who had been instrumental in providing spiritual direction to him prior to this experience.

[30] I provide a critical overview of the relevant epistemology in "Symeon the New Theologian," in William J. Abraham and Frederick D. Aquino, eds., *The Oxford Handbook of the Epistemology of Theology* (Oxford: Oxford University Press, 2017), 382–94.

theology of the Holy Spirit. It is much too weak to think of this language as a metaphor or image. The language cuts much deeper into the reality of the Holy Spirit. We might say that the Holy Spirit is not merely described as light in the way we might think, say, of the Son as the light of the world, but rather the Holy Spirit is manifest as light, or, more precisely, as immaterial light. Just as the Son is manifest in history in the flesh as genuinely human, the Holy Spirit is here manifest in history as light.

This may come as a startling suggestion. However, consider this account of the transfiguration.

> Six days later, Jesus took with him Peter and James and John and led them up a high mountain apart, by themselves. And he was transfigured before them, and his clothes became dazzling white, such as no one on earth could bleach them. And there appeared to them Elijah with Moses, who were talking with Jesus. Then Peter said to Jesus, 'Rabbi, it is good for us to be here; let us make three dwellings, one for you, one for Moses, and one for Elijah.' He did not know what to say, for they were terrified. Then a cloud overshadowed them, and from the cloud there came a voice, 'This is my Son, The Beloved; listen to him!' Suddenly when they looked around, they saw no one with them anymore, but only Jesus.[31]

The contemporary reader is as puzzled as Peter in this episode. Symeon goes a long way to resolving the puzzle. This is surely a theophany of the Trinity where the Holy Spirit is graphically described in terms of light. For those who want scriptural warrant for this claim, here it is in full sight. However, this is not the best way to treat the issue of warrant. This account of the Holy Spirit is not true simply because it is in Scripture; it is in Scripture because it is true. The deep warrant here is that of perception of the divine. Moreover, that perception has been sporadically confirmed by the testimony of others across the centuries.[32] We might say that they have followed the encouragement that Symeon himself supplies.

> Do not say: 'It is impossible to receive the Holy Spirit.'
> Do not say: 'Without Him it is possible to be saved.'
> And so do not say that that one can possess Him without knowing!
> Do not say that God is not seen by humans.
> Do not say: 'Human beings do not see the divine light,'
> or that it is impossible in the present times.
> This is never impossible, friends,

---

[31] Mark 9:2–8.

[32] I will pick up the remarkable testimony of Seraphim of Sarov in a later chapter. I have heard two persuasive testimonies across the years that fit with this account of the experience of Symeon. One was from a friend from Georgia, in the old Soviet Union; the second from a fine Anglican priest from Malaysia. The first testimony involved an ordination conducted by a priest who had spent years suffering in the Gulag. The second testimony involved an experience of divine light at the Eucharist. I leave it to historians to reread the history of spirituality to find more examples of this kind.

but it is very possible for those who wish it,
but only for as many as life has provided with a purification to the passions,
and has made pure the eye of the intellect.[33]

It is time to bring our reflections on the ontology of the Holy Spirit to a conclusion. The church's confession is at once dense and limited. The Holy Spirit is a Person within the Trinity who proceeds from the Father. The density is expressed in the language of Person; the limitations in the language of procession. In my judgment, we can make no further progress in articulating or expanding the language of procession. We simply stipulate that this distinction is real and is to be contrasted with the eternal generation of the Son from the Father. We have reached the end of the line here; the apophatic triumphs over every cataphatic effort to unravel the depths of this mystery. With respect to the language of Person, we are on somewhat firmer ground. In this instance, we do have a network of significant scriptural images to fill out our reflections. Thus, we can deploy the language of wind, breath, fire, dove, and the like. Beyond that we have little to go on. The image of the Holy Spirit as a force-field will have some purchase; but an image like this is person-relative; it will help some and be useless for others. The best that the language of love can do for us is to act as a reminder that God is love, a scriptural assertion that grammatically makes no sense, but which brings home the depths of love at the heart of the life of the Trinity.[34] I ended on a more positive note. The concept of light in the hands of Symeon brings us up short as we pause for breath; when we relax, and take it seriously, we have a wonderful depiction of the Holy Spirit that strangely brings us back down into the history of revelation as it shows up dramatically in the life of the Son.

It is no surprise that Symeon is not well known outside certain esoteric circles. His account of the ontology of the Holy Spirit can readily set our teeth on edge. The issue here is not one of skepticism; that has always been a factor, and Symeon responds to it by his own astute vision of knowledge of God in terms of perception of the divine. The issue is one of spiritual challenge and disorientation. We shall meet this all over again as we turn to reflect on the characteristic actions and activity of the Holy Spirit.

---

[33] Symeon the New Theologian, *Divine Eros* (Crestwood, NY: St. Vladimir's Seminary Press, 2010), 208.

[34] In working on the ontology of the Holy Spirit I turned with eager anticipation to the work of Philip Clayton in order to see if the language of spirit would enrich our understanding of the ontology of the Holy Spirit. Regrettably, I was disappointed. See his "In Whom We Have Our Being: Philosophical Resources for the Doctrine of the Spirit," in Bradford E. Hinze and D. Lyle Dabney, eds., *Advents of the Spirit: An Introduction to the Current Study of Pneumatology* (Milwaukee, WI: Marquette University Press, 2001), 173–232.

8

The Work of the Holy Spirit

And when the day of Pentecost had come, they were all together in one place.... And all of them were filled with the Holy Spirit and began to speak in other languages, as the Spirit gave them ability.

Acts 2:1, 4.

My superstitious friend Seamus had a dream. A mean little demon appeared to him as a witty leprechaun and made him three promises: he will give Seamus the ability to turn toilet paper into dollar bills; he will give him the capacity to score three goals in the upcoming final of the Gaelic football season; and, last but not least, he will ensure that Seamus is elected as mayor of Dublin in the elections two years hence. The only condition of reception is that Seamus swear to serve him for the next ten years. Seamus was tempted to take all of these offers. However, he hesitated; and not because he was super-spiritual. He hesitated because he knew instinctively the identity and character of the agent who was sucking him into a poisonous and destructive life. If he agreed, he would have sold his soul to a life of unending misery. What stops us in our tracks here is not just the misery involved but the identity and character of the agent who has made the offer. We do not need to know very much at this point; all that we need to know is the ontology of the agent; we are dealing with a demonic agent who is out to destroy us in the end. The ontology has serious consequences.

Here is a paradox. We have seen that the Holy Spirit is nothing less than the third Person of the Holy Trinity who proceeds from the Father. We even speak of the "Holy" Spirit and thus draw attention to the moral qualities of the Holy Spirit. We are equally taught that the internal life of the Trinity is a life of perfect love. Yet we hesitate when it comes to embracing the work of the Holy Spirit in human history. Given some of the images that show up in depicting the being of the Holy Spirit, we can understand why. The images of wind, fire, and water can readily threaten us. However, these are readily offset by the complementary images of dove, wine, oil, and light. The bigger picture is clear; our ontology of the Holy Spirit signals works of holiness and love. So the paradox remains. Given what we know of the nature and identity of the

Person of the Holy Spirit, our immediate response should be one of faith and eager anticipation. Yet what we find is hesitation and fear. The ontology fails to register.

I exaggerate. Happily, recent theology has engaged in a significant quest for the reality and activity of the Holy Spirit. Contemporary Christians are keen to explore the work of the Holy Spirit in three radically different arenas. There is a quest to identify the presence and power of the Holy Spirit in ministry in the church. We see this in the search for a new Pentecost, in the striving for renewal in the church, and in the struggle to identify the gifts of the Holy Spirit in ministry. In contrast to this, we find a quest to identify the work of the Holy Spirit in the drama, misery, and trauma of human history. We seek to explore the work of the Holy Spirit in the struggles for justice, liberation, and the care of the environment. There is also a fine cottage industry devoted to exploring the work of the Spirit in world religions. Compare these sites of investigation with several other more familiar sites: the work of the Holy Spirit in the production of Scripture, the work of the Holy Spirit in the sacraments and ordained ministry of the church, the work of the Holy Spirit in conversion and sanctification, the work of the Holy Spirit in creation, and the work of the Holy Spirit in the life and ministry of Jesus. We are immediately in deep trouble, for attention to all of this will quickly barrel out of control in a catalogue of action and activity where we will be subject to cognitive overload. We need a strategy that will provide an ordered account of the work of the Holy Spirit. Most importantly, we need an account of the priorities of the Holy Spirit.

We faced a similar challenge in dealing with the work of the Son. Our strategy there was to find a center of gravity furnished by a broad vision of atonement and reconciliation. With this in place, we could organize the many theories of atonement that are available to us. We were also creating a platform for further exploration of the work of the Son, say, as a teacher, or as prophet, priest, and king. We can go on beyond the crucial initial staging to fill out the manifold actions and offices of Christ. In other words, we got hold of the mission of the Son as sent from the Father through the Holy Spirit. I propose a similar strategy for securing a center of gravity for understanding the work of the Holy Spirit. We seek to get hold of the mission of the Spirit sent from the Father by the Son. Hopefully this will give shape and order to our deliberations.[1]

As we proceed, we set aside generic talk about the action and activity of the Holy Spirit. Such language turns out to be a lot of talk and very little action, for

---

[1] This is how I aim to give content to claims about the mission of the Holy Spirit. Sometimes the term is used to designate the visible effects of the Spirit. See Kilian McDonnell, *The Other Hand of God: The Holy Spirit as the Universal Touch and Goal* (Collegeville, MN: Liturgical Press, 2003), 82. However, this alternative way of proceeding gives us a much better angle of vision, not least because it allows us to think of the priorities of action related to the sending of the Spirit.

these nouns (action and activity) are radically open and need to be filled in by way of identifiable actions. This does mean that we cannot sketch a wider horizon in which to locate the relevant actions. In fact, the crucial first step is to connect the action of the Holy Spirit to the inauguration of the kingdom of God announced and enacted in the life of Jesus and then brought forward in history at Pentecost and its aftermath. These are anchors that tether our deliberations. Two points deserve mention. First, the coming of the kingdom is initially enacted and therefore governed by the actions of the Holy Spirit in the life and ministry of Jesus. Second, the coming of the kingdom of God is further enacted through the bestowal of the Holy Spirit on the apostles at Pentecost. These considerations provide crucial normative constraints on discerning the priorities that govern the activity of the Holy Spirit. In what follows I shall reverse the historical order and take first the bestowal of the Spirit at Pentecost. However, before I do this, a further preliminary comment is in order.

This contextual approach will go a long way to undermining the suspicion that has recurred again in the history of the church with respect to claims about the Holy Spirit. The examples are well known, stretching from the Montanists in the early period,[2] through mystics in the medieval period, on up to and including Methodist enthusiasts in the modern period, and Pentecostals in the contemporary period. There has been a natural suspicion about claims about the Holy Spirit as found in all of these groups; in some cases, there has been outright hostility and ignorance. However, we are called to test the spirits, so we can leave all this to the historians to sort out. Theologically, we can move forward in confidence. The Holy Spirit does not show up in a vacuum; our vision of her work should be governed by our normative convictions about the kingdom of God; and the kingdom has a Messiah, one anointed by the Holy Spirit, who is therefore a paradigm for our assessment of claims about the working of the Spirit. Indeed, the Spirit is the Spirit of Christ and is thus intimately related to the work of Christ.

To speak of the mission of the Holy Spirit is to speak of the ultimate purpose of the Holy Spirit in her coming decisively in history at Pentecost.[3] This is not something we can identify by way of intuition or theological speculation. We need divine revelation. More specifically, we need to be both shown and told what that mission is. Interestingly, the specific action attributed to the Holy

---

[2] For a revisionist and more accurate account of the Montanists than is commonly known see William Tabbernee, "'Will the Real Paraclete Please Speak Forth!' The Catholic-Montanist Conflict over Pneumatology," in Bradford E. Hinze and D. Lyle Dabney, eds., *Advents of the Spirit: An Introduction to the Current Study of Pneumatology* (Milwaukee, WI: Marquette University Press, 2001), 97–118.

[3] We owe the prominence if not the origin of talk of the mission of the Spirit to Aquinas who used this expression to speak of the visible effects of the coming of the Spirit. See the *Summa Theologiae* I, question 43.

Spirit in the Nicene Creed is that of speaking by the prophets. Contrary to standard interpretations, we should not confuse this action with the action of inspiration. Speaking predicated of the Holy Spirit is no more like inspiration than is the case of human agents. While human agents indeed can inspire through what they say to us, the two are not the same. In the case of the prophets the critical action is that of speaking. They hear a word from God of interpretation, say, of other actions of God; or they hear a word of promise or judgment. In the case of securing the identity of the mission of the Holy Spirit, the obvious place to seek for this is in the teaching of those designated as prophets who proclaim the purpose of the coming of the Spirit. As we shall see this observation has significant implications for claims about the work of the Holy Spirit, say, in society and politics today.

The crucial prophetic figure initially is John the Baptist. In all of the gospels John the Baptist gives four clear signals as to how we should think of the work of the Spirit.[4] First, he couples the coming of the Spirit with his announcement of the kingdom of God and repentance. Second, he insists that the ultimate goal of Christ's coming is the bestowal of the Holy Spirit. Third, he uses the language of baptism to describe the effects of the coming of the Spirit. Fourth, we need to relate the work of the Spirit to the coming of the Holy Spirit at Pentecost. All four of these elements deserve attention. I take them in turn.

If we take the kingdom of God to mean the sovereign rule of God, then the work of the Spirit can readily be viewed as one if not the most important manifestations of the rule of God in history. Thus, before we think of the rule of God in, say, the church or in politics, we need to anchor the work of the Spirit in the bestowal of the Spirit at Pentecost. The kingdom is inaugurated in the coming of Christ whose ultimate purpose is to baptize us in the Holy Spirit. It is thus not at all surprising that we find rare but highly illuminating renderings of the relevant request for the coming of the Holy Spirit ("Your kingdom come, your will be done in earth as it is in heaven") in terms of the coming of the Holy Spirit.[5]

Furthermore, given that both John the Baptist and Jesus share the same theological horizon on the fundamental significance of the kingdom of God, it is not surprising that the purpose of the work of Christ is intimately related to the bestowal of the Spirit. While the work of Christ in reconciliation and atonement is pivotal in the purpose of Christ, this work has as its ultimate goal

---

[4] I follow here mainly the material in Matthew 3.

[5] The alternative reading for the petition "Your kingdom come" runs: "Your Holy Spirit come upon us and cleanse us." This shows up in Gregory of Nyssa and Maximus the Confessor as well as in two ancient manuscripts (ms 162 and ms 700). It is also found in Marcion's *Euangelion* as reported by Tertullian who did not question this usage. For support for this account of the original rendering of the Lord's prayer in Luke see Robert Luney, "The Lucan Text of the Lord's Prayer (Lk xi 2–4)," *Novum Testamentum* 1.2 (1956), 103–11, and Jason DeDuhn, *The First Testament: Marcion's Scriptural Canon* (Salem, OR: Polebridge Press, 2013).

the bestowal of the Spirit. It is not enough that we be forgiven and reconciled to God; it is pivotal that there be genuine at-one-ment between human agents and God. The rule of God signals the possibility of human agents actually enacting the rule of God in human history. This will clearly require the post-resurrection activity of the Son, activity designated as the bestowal of the Holy Spirit.

At this stage the language of baptism becomes important. The original language at this stage is rich. It can literally mean scuppering a ship, immersing or dipping a piece of cloth in a vessel of dye, sinking in mud, and, when used passively, being overwhelmed or perishing. The language of baptism in the main suggests that the bestowal of the Spirit involves a deep immersion in the Spirit, an immersion that means death to the rule of our wayward passions and desires, and an immersion that results in visible changes in the person immersed. The image of a cloth being dipped in a dye speaks dramatically to the latter reality. This naturally links up with the reference to fire in connection to the language of baptism. John the Baptist makes the point graphically. "He will baptize with fire. His winnowing fork is in his hand, and he will clear the threshing floor and will gather the wheat into the granary; but the chaff he will burn with unquenchable fire."[6]

The language of fire also shows up in the fulfillment of the promise of the bestowal of the Holy Spirit as we find it in Acts. Luke is quite specific that Pentecost represents the fulfillment of the promise originally announced by John and clearly endorsed by Jesus. The apostles chosen were

> not to leave Jerusalem, but to wait there for the promise of the Father. 'This', he said, 'is what you have heard from me; for John baptized with water, but you will be baptized with the Holy Spirit not many days from now.'[7]

Moreover, what was scheduled to happen was not necessarily some blueprint for Christian experience but a turning point in the work of God in history. Other times and periods were to be left in the hands of God; the apostles were to attend to the events related to Pentecost. The risen Lord was about to leave, for his definitive work on earth was now complete; the next step in God's management of the kingdom awaited the bestowal of the Holy Spirit.

Given this turning point in history it is important we pause and take note of Luke's account of what happened.

> When the day of Pentecost had come, they were all together in place. And suddenly from heaven there came a sound like the rush of a violent wind, and it filled the entire house where they were sitting. Divided tongues, as of fire, appeared among them, and a tongue rested on each of them. All of them were

---

[6] Matthew 3:11–12.   [7] Acts 1:4–5.

filled with the Holy Spirit and began to speak in other languages, as the Spirit gave them ability.[8]

The effect in the lives of the apostles was twofold: they discovered that they were proclaiming "God's deeds of power" in languages they had never learned; and they appeared to those present to be drunk with new wine. Peter corrected the latter impression with a prophesy from Joel that used apocalyptic language to bring home that a whole new era of divine action in history had been inaugurated.[9] A great and glorious day of the Lord had dawned in which everyone who called on the name of the Lord could be saved.

It is easy to gloss over the specificity of the events related to Pentecost because of historical skepticism. We are dealing here with a radical intervention of God in human history that is every bit as real, and as challenging, as the events related to the coming of Christ in his birth and resurrection. We run into the familiar problems of the treatment of divine action in history where we readily reach for generic talk about divine action to avoid the epistemological problems that have been so central over the last two centuries. It is also easy to gloss over what happened by drifting into a world of pious escapism that misses the mundane reality of exuberance reflected in the language of drunkenness. Austin Farrer, despite his desire to reach for a theory of double-agency to resolve the former difficulties, can help us avoid the latter temptation.

> What happened on the first Christian Pentecost? Something invisible happened, and something visible. The invisible event was a moving of the divine life; the Apostles who had been watching and waiting began to be moved and used by God. But that was what no eye could see, what even the men concerned would have been at a loss to describe. Yet there was also something perfectly visible which many eyes in Jerusalem saw, many critical and laughing eyes; a roomful of sober, earnest-minded citizens bundled out into the street and shouting as if they were drunk. This is the sort of thing that never fails to amuse, 'Well, really,' you say, 'just think of old Peter,' or whoever it is, some worthy candidate for Holy Orders, on an occasion like a college reunion, balanced on the top of a roof and yelling his head off.[10]

So much for the insistence that Pentecost represents a new phase in the coming of the kingdom in history. Note that recording this pivotal event does not mean that the Holy Spirit was absent from history before Pentecost;

---

[8] Acts 2:1–4.

[9] Such language should not be read in a flat-footed manner as if we were picking up a copy of a high-brow newspaper. Even in common English we use apocalyptic language to describe pivotal events in our personal and social lives. I take up this topic later in the material on eschatology.

[10] Austin Farrer, "Pentecostal Fire," in *A Faith of Our Own* (Cleveland, OH: World Publishing Company, 1960), 115.

the relevant distinction at this point is between the ongoing presence of the Holy Spirit and the specific actions performed by the Holy Spirit. To be sure, if we constantly translate all specific action-predicates into generic talk about the activity of the Holy Spirit, we will not be able to state precisely what is at stake in the events related to Pentecost. We will switch to talk about the human agents involved; or we will reach for a theory not of special action but of special discernment or perception of the generic action of the Holy Spirit. This, no doubt, will be done with the best of intellectual and spiritual intentions. However, these strategies are serious mistakes in this case. We cannot dismiss a pivotal moment in the history of God's relation to history by invoking such semantic strategies. The solution is simple: we register a distinction between presence and action. We have no difficulty doing this in the case of other agents. We can readily record, say, that Mary was present at an important meeting but decided to do nothing for very good reasons. Likewise, we can readily think of the Spirit being present and not performing this or that specific action. So, insisting that the Holy Spirit was turning the page of salvation history at Pentecost does not for a minute mean that she is absent elsewhere from God's manifold work in creation and in human history.

We can exemplify the distinction between presence and specific action afresh when we turn our attention to the action of the Holy Spirit in the life and ministry of Jesus. Here we can be brief and provide a short catalogue. We record the action of the Holy Spirit in his conception in the womb of Mary;[11] in his anointing for the service of the Father;[12] in his testing in the wilderness;[13] in his being led in his movements from one place to another;[14] in his speaking the words of God;[15] in the performance of his exorcisms and miracles;[16] in the provision of wisdom;[17] in his offering up of himself as a sacrifice for the sins of the world;[18] and in his resurrection from the dead.[19] We might say that the whole life and ministry of Jesus was saturated with the activity of the Holy Spirit. In him we see the Holy Spirit as *Paraclete*, as one who comes alongside as a helper, before we see the same kind of activity in the life of the early church in figures like Paul. Thus, we have a paradigm case of the work of the Holy Spirit already in place in Jesus which then is picked up, beginning at Pentecost, in the church's history across space and time. Thus, the church is not whistling in the dark when she speaks of the work of the Holy Spirit in her life and witness. She has to hand in the portrait of Jesus a rich account of characteristic actions of the Spirit. Cries of subjectivism, emotionalism, and "enthusiasm" will certainly be heeded; however, these are often means of denial and avoidance rather than a call for critical discernment. It is

---

[11] Luke 1:35.   [12] Acts 10:38.   [13] Matthew 4:1.   [14] Luke 4:1.
[15] John 3:34.   [16] Matthew 8:28.   [17] Isaiah 11:2–3; 52:1; Matthew 12:17–18.
[18] Hebrews 9:14.   [19] Romans 8:11.

no accident that we are given an account of the life and ministry of Jesus before we are told the story of Pentecost. After all, the Spirit is indeed the Spirit of Christ; his life provides an objective anchor for discernment and deliberations. Perhaps we should say that he displays a life that is fully immersed in the life of the Holy Spirit; in turn, he then baptizes us in the very same Spirit that is manifest in him. Nothing less than baptism in the Spirit was the ultimate goal of his own coming in history.

With this vision firmly in place, we can begin to plot the work of the Holy Spirit in the lives of the individual and in the life of the church. We are now, of course, wandering into territory that will be taken up afresh in later chapters. My aim here is to connect the varied activity of the Holy Spirit in these domains with this ultimate goal of baptism in the Spirit. Immediately this allows me to take up the fascinating text in John where the work of the Spirit is described in these terms.

> I tell you the truth: it is to your advantage that I go away, for if I do not go away, the advocate will not come to you; but if I go, I will send him to you. And when he comes, he will prove the world wrong about sin and righteousness and judgment: about sin, because they do not believe in me; about righteousness, because I go to the Father and you will see me no longer; about judgment, because the ruler of this world has been condemned.
>
> I still have many things to say to you, but you cannot bear them now. When the Spirit of truth comes, he will guide you into all the truth; for he will not speak on his own, but will speak whatever he hears, and he will declare to you the things that are to come. He will glorify me, because he will take what is mine and declare it to you. All that the Father has is mine. For this reason I said he will take what is mine and declare it to you.[20]

It is tempting to make this remarkable statement about the work of the Holy Spirit and give it priority in our thinking about the mission of the Spirit. We should resist this temptation for a very obvious reason. The theme of baptism in the Holy Spirit is given to us right at the opening of the gospels where the obvious intent is to get clear at the outset the big picture involved. What this means is that we should see this account of the action of the Holy Spirit as crucial in the journey to the ultimate goal of Christ's ministry already identified earlier in the tradition in terms of baptism and immersion. We noted this when we took up the issue of the place of atonement in the mission of the Son. The ultimate purpose of his coming is baptism in the Holy Spirit. However, this cannot be accomplished without first dealing with the acute problem of sin and alienation, precisely a central element in the work of Christ. Just as there can be no baptism in the Spirit without the work of atonement, so likewise there cannot be baptism in the Spirit without this crucial work of the

---

[20] John 16:7–16.

Holy Spirit identified in the gospel of John. This is a matter of both logic and empirical necessity.

If we take the last promise in the Johannine declaration first, we see that the work of the Holy Spirit will be vital in providing the truth about Christ for the disciples once they are able to grasp what is at stake. Given their current state of understanding not much could be said about the deep significance of the cross and resurrection. It will take prophets like Paul and inspired authors whose writings will later be canonized as Scripture to carry out the task of disclosing the glory and proper understanding of these profound mysteries. We can surely add to this the work of the Spirit in providing continued guidance of the church as she seeks to explore the profound ramifications of Christ's life for understanding the identity and nature of the God of Israel and its modification in the doctrine of the Trinity.

The much more puzzling elements take us back up into the work of the Holy Spirit in proving the world wrong with respect to sin, righteousness, and judgment. The term "prove the world wrong" clearly relates to the task of persuasion. Given that Christ is no longer there in person on the ground, and that the disciples are called upon to bear witness to the work God has done in and through him, there is a need for significant help in bringing home the truth about the reality of sin and the divine victory over sin now offered in the preaching of the Gospel. It is not enough merely to report what has happened or to mount various arguments about the truth of these claims; there is the need for the Holy Spirit to speak to the conscience and heart of the hearers. The declaration of victory over sin is in turn reinforced by the work of the Spirit in convincing the hearer that the ruler of the world has been judged and condemned by God.

There are significant underlying epistemological issues in play here. Human sin and desire can lead folk not only to dismiss the claims of God's work in Christ as false but to see it all as much too demanding to be taken seriously. Equally, it is easy on hearing the Gospel to give up in despair of any real change in our lives and our world; the information comes across as make-believe and wishful thinking. For those who take the demonic seriously, this possibility becomes even more incredible. If we are to be persuaded, we need more than the appeal to human reason, or to textual sound bites, or to learned discourses. The point is well made by the Irish Methodist writer William Arthur in his extended treatment of the narrative of Pentecost in Acts 2.

> We know that many who speak the truth as accomplishing all, do not mean the truth without the Spirit to apply it; but what is meant ought to be said. Hold fast the truth as an instrument divinely adapted and altogether necessary; but in magnifying the instruments, never forget or pass by the agent. The Spirit in the truth, the Spirit in the preacher, in the hearer; the Spirit first, the Spirit last, ought to be remembered, trusted in, exalted, not set aside for any captivating name. There should never be even the distant appearances of wishing to avoid avowing a

belief in the supernatural, or to reduce Christianity to a system capable at all points of metaphysical analysis. If no supernatural power is expected to attend the gospel, its promulgation is both insincere and futile.[21]

In the Johannine account of the activity of the Holy Spirit, we can detect already the role of the Holy Spirit in opening up the way for conviction of sin, for declaring the prospect of a whole new future involving victory over evil, and for the fostering of the hope that a whole new life is being offered to those who hear and believe. What we see here are the beginnings of a journey that must start at this critical turning point before it can move forward to the eventual reality of baptism in the Spirit. The same line of reasoning should be applied to the varied actions that show up as further elements in this journey. We can deal with this briefly, for the crucial point is to secure the angle of vision. We need to take note of the relevant actions of the Spirit and leave till later a further analysis of what is involved when we take up the topic of salvation.

Consider first the actions of the Holy Spirit related to all that the Spirit does in order to bring about Christian initiation. Aside from baptism in the Spirit, here is a cluster of significant actions: inner conviction, illumination, and enlightenment; regeneration and new birth; justification and acquittal; heart-felt assurance of forgiveness and inner witness to being a child of God; sanctification and recreation in the image of God.[22] As a consequence of the Spirit's manifold actions, there is a cluster of virtues identified as the fruit of the Spirit: love, joy, peace, patience, kindness, goodness, faithfulness, gentle-ness, and self-control.[23] More generally, as a result of these actions of the Holy Spirit, a profound ontological bond is created between the soul and God; the Spirit indwells and fills the believer. We are surely here in the neighborhood of the language of immersion in the Holy Spirit. Just as a cloth dipped in dye is marked with the color of the dye, so the person is now marked with the stamp and seal of the Holy Spirit. We have circled back to the ultimate goal of the work of the Holy Spirit: the goal is to create human agents who are fully immersed in the life of the Holy Spirit, a life marked by faith, hope, and love. This will always be a matter of degree, to be sure. We catch a dramatic glimpse of what is at issue not in speaking in tongues (a significant but incidental gift of the Spirit) but in those rare cases of transfiguration that show up in the tradition. Such cases pull back the curtain and show us that even our bodies, not just our souls, can and will ultimately be so immersed in the Spirit that we

---

[21] William Arthur, *The Tongue of Fire, or, the Power of Christianity* (New York: Carlton and Porter, 1859), 185.

[22] Given this cluster of actions it is no surprise that the work of the Holy Spirit can readily collapse into talk about grace understood as the generosity and power of God. Indeed, this is one way to avoid the embarrassment of speaking of the Holy Spirit.

[23] Galatians 5:22.

shine with divine glory. This is a complex journey of initiation into the very life of God; sorting out the psychological dimensions of this is the delicate task of ascetic theology. What matters here is to get hold, if only partially, of the ultimate mission of the workings of the Holy Spirit, namely, the creation of saints who are not just intoxicated with the love of God but are so immersed in the Spirit that they exhibit the very mind and life of Christ.

The immediate worry that will crop up at this stage is that this account of the work of the Holy Spirit is hopelessly individualistic, fueled perhaps by membership in a consumer society hooked on personal fulfillment and pleasure. Where in all of this is the work of the Holy Spirit in the church? There is no merit to this objection. For one thing, what is at issue is the painful reorientation of human passions and desires. The Spirit burns off all sorts of sinful elements in our lives, even as there is, on the human side, the kind of repentance that involves cross-bearing and death. Second, this objection conflates the personal and the individual in that it contrasts what is individual with what is social. As human persons, we are inescapably social. There is no need to set up an opposition between the work the Spirit does within us and the work the Spirit does in, with, and through the life and ministry of the church. In fact, in one Spirit we are all baptized into one body.[24] The church plays a vital role in the reception of the Holy Spirit, not as an exclusive reservoir and dispenser of the Spirit but as an instrument of the Holy Spirit in the service of the kingdom of God. In a clear sense, it is obvious that the church is intrinsically important. The church is the body of Christ, and as such we are morally and spiritually obliged to be members and loyal servants. Indeed, I hold that the church is the most important social institution bar none in the world. However, there is also a clear sense in which the church is penultimate; she subsists in the agency of the kingdom of God; she is subordinate in her life and ministry to the work of the Holy Spirit in the inauguration of God's kingdom on earth.

This is the time to take up, as promised, the working of the Holy Spirit in the church. Again, I am content to provide a summary of the relevant actions of the Holy Spirit. Consider the following: the work of the Holy Spirit in the creation of the church; in the call of the apostles; in the elaboration of apt institutional structures; in the development of ongoing oversight; in the provision of guidance in the councils of the church; in the provision of offices and ministers in the church; in the various diverse gifts of the Holy Spirit scattered throughout the membership; in the sacraments of the church, such as baptism and Eucharist; and in the laying on of hands for special service. To use contemporary jargon, the life of the church is charismatic all the way from the top to the bottom. We are taking seriously the charismatic activity of the

---

[24] 1 Corinthians 12:13. For a fine treatment of Pentecost that takes this theme seriously see Raniero Catalamessa, *The Mystery of Pentecost* (Collegeville, MN: Liturgical Press, 2001).

Holy Spirit manifest not just in the spiritual and moral lives of this or that believer, but in the corporate phenomena of councils and conferences, orders of ministry, canon law, the practices of preaching and teaching, sacramental exercises, and the like. All of these phenomena are directed to the mission of the Son, that is, the bestowal of the Spirit. Because they are given to us by the Spirit, they can never be seen as mere instruments. To do so is to insult the Giver and to ignore their intimate role in securing the life of Christ within us. Yet to treat them as intrinsically worthwhile apart from the life of the Spirit is to risk the judgment and fire of the Spirit among us.

We can put this issue simply as follows. The church exists as a servant and manifestation of the kingdom. As such she exists therefore to serve the Holy Spirit who has a pivotal role in the inauguration of the kingdom here on earth and its consummation in heaven. Failure on this front is all too real in her life; and that failure is not just in ordinary members but at the highest levels of leadership. However, there is always hope for the church, for the church with her manifold life and practices is the creation and instrument of the Spirit. The Spirit, therefore, can readily find ways to renew her life by fire and living water for ontologically the Holy Spirit is nothing less than the Giver of Life.[25]

Having moved from the work of the Spirit in the life of the church, I have opened up another line of objection to my analysis. The natural query that arises at this point is this: where is there any mention of the work of the Holy Spirit in the great social crises of our times, in the struggle, say, for justice and care of the environment? If focus on the work of the Holy Spirit in personal salvation suggests a lack of interest in the work of the Holy Spirit in the church, merely adding the latter is not going to do justice to the crying need for help in naming the activity of the Holy Spirit in the social and political arena. Given the alignment of churches with oppressive regimes, given the church's moral failure in the treatment of children, women, outsiders, and minorities, given the crass injustice permitted and perpetuated by the church, my position looks hopelessly pietistic and escapist. This is a serious objection and I am happy to deal with it, albeit briefly.

I stand by my account without reservation in three respects. First, any account of the work of the Holy Spirit must reckon with the work of the Spirit in our personal lives and in the corporate life of the church. Our bodies are a temple of the Holy Spirit; the church is the creation of the Holy Spirit. Second, my earlier distinction between the presence of the Holy Spirit and the specific action of the Holy Spirit holds in this arena as well. Thus, to make claims about the action of the Holy Spirit in our personal lives and in the life of the church, in no ways entails that the Holy Spirit is not present in the great struggles of human history. Thirdly, and most importantly, the initial theological decision to

---

[25] I explore the topic of church renewal in my *The Logic of Renewal* (Grand Rapids, MI: Eerdmans, 2003).

be made is this: are there clear priorities in the working of the Holy Spirit that must be named and articulated first, before we move on to delineate the working of the Holy Spirit in the struggles of human history? My claim is that there are such priorities and that these are constituted by the work of the Holy Spirit in the life and agency of the church as these relate to the salvation of every human agent across the globe. So, my potential critic has read my position accurately.

However, I need to do more than repeat what I have already proposed in some detail. Here is my rationale for this decision and the implications of the rationale for the objection before us. First, this ordering of our priorities is warranted by the Word of God given by the Holy Spirit to the church. If we want to know how to order the working of the Holy Spirit, then it is the Holy Spirit who is in a position to tell us what the ordering should be. This is not a matter of intuition or speculation. The Holy Spirit has clearly told us through John the Baptist and through the Son what her mission is; our task at this point is to listen, understand, and obey.

Second, it is not therefore surprising that the focus across the years in treatments of the working of the Holy Spirit has fallen broadly where I have placed it, that is, on the work of the Holy Spirit in the life of salvation and in the life of the church. What is new and perhaps alarming in my presentation is that I have insisted that the ultimate goal of the bestowal of the Spirit is nothing less than baptism in the Holy Spirit. Thus, the network of actions related to personal salvation and the life of the church are subordinate to this ultimate horizon. Again, my warrant for this is precisely the claim that this is what the Holy Spirit has revealed to us. Agents are entitled to tell us what they take to be most important in their work; the Holy Spirit is no exception to this principle. My aim at this point is faithfulness to what the Holy Spirit has revealed through the prophesy of John the Baptist, endorsed by the Son, rightly interpreted in the inspired reflection on that revelation in the Scriptures and canonical theologians of the church. Of course, it is an added bonus that it also shows up in the life and teaching of a host of great saints and the experience of ordinary believers.

The obvious rejoinder is that I have systematically ignored other materials that should be discussed. I have in mind most especially the declaration of Jesus in Luke:

> The Spirit of the Lord is upon me, because he has anointed me to bring good news to the poor. He has sent me to proclaim release to the captives and recovery of sight to the blind, to let the oppressed go free, to proclaim the year of the Lord's favor.[26]

---

[26] Luke 4:18.

We can also add in various texts that speak of the work of the Spirit in political leaders in the Old Testament;[27] or we may ruminate on "the economics" of Pentecost when the early church for a period decided to hold all things in common.[28] What is most prominently in place at this point is to insist that it is liberation understood in material and political terms that should be presented as the first and foremost work of the Spirit rather than baptism in the Holy Spirit.

I leave for the next volume a fuller treatment of the theme of divine action in liberation. It will suffice here to undermine this whole line of thinking in a preliminary fashion. I agree, of course, that the arrival of the kingdom has enormous political significance. Indeed, this is one reason why I have deliberately used this language. Thus, I have not opted for softer terms like "realm," "kindom" (sic), "dominion," "rule," and the like. I want to retain the awkward, troublesome political imagery that is in play. Furthermore, I agree that the intersection of theology and politics is a matter of enormous significance in our current context.[29]

However, I reject the primary alternative before us for compelling reasons. First, we cannot set aside the wider context in which the proclamation of Jesus as liberator is located. The issue is liberation from sin and death, not merely liberation from political oppression. Indeed, on this front, Jesus was an abject failure for his People were decimated by the Romans in the destruction of the Temple in AD 70. There was no freedom from oppression; there was, in fact, more oppression. It is not often that a clean theological claim about divine action is falsified, but here it is in plain sight.

Second, the general argument in favor of liberation as the primary work of the Holy Spirit is an interesting one. It runs something like this. The God of Jesus is also the God of the Exodus. The God of the Exodus is a liberating God. Therefore, every act of liberation is an action of the God and Father of our Lord Jesus Christ. Given that the Holy Spirit is the Spirit of Christ, then the work of the Spirit first and foremost is that of engaging in liberation from every and any form of oppression. The flaws in this line of reasoning are obvious. It quietly ignores those actions of God represented, say, by the exile of Israel, where what we find is not liberation but judgment. Thus, it ignores the full range of divine action in Israel and sets aside the very particular setting of the liberation of Israel from Egypt. Furthermore, it is also mistaken in the

---

[27] These texts are discussed in the splendid work of Michael Welker, *God the Spirit* (Minneapolis, MN: Fortress Press, 1994). See also the rich treatment of our theme in Anselm Kyongsuk Min, "Solidarity with Others in the Power of the Holy Spirit," in Hinze and Dabney, eds., *Advents of the Spirit*, 416–43.

[28] See Amos Yong, *Who is the Spirit? A Walk with the Apostles* (Brewster, MA: Paraclete Press, 2011), Part Three.

[29] I tackle some of the issues involved in my *Shaking Hands with the Devil: The Intersection of Terrorism and Theology* (Dallas, TX: Highland Loch Press, 2013).

warrants deployed. Israel was able to discern what God was doing in its midst because of the prophetic word given to identify and interpret the divine action in Egypt. There is no equivalent, credible prophetic Word given in the present on the part of those who advance liberation as the primary work of the Spirit. Indeed, it is not too difficult to trace the political and philosophical sources of these claims in nineteenth- and twentieth-century ideologies of class and empire.

As I have already noted, the objection before us deserves a fuller defense of my position than fits my purpose here. That purpose has been to lift up the work of the Holy Spirit in immersion and baptism in the Holy Spirit, characteristically but not exclusively brought about in the life and ministry of the church. Put succinctly, I have been arguing for a retrieval and renewal of Pentecost as a turning point in creation and history. Pentecost is a critical element in the coming of God's kingdom to be celebrated, welcomed, and sought with all our hearts by voluntary submission to God's ordinances and commandments.

> Thus, indeed, God does reign in those in whom He did not reign before, in those who are in the process of purification through tears and repentance, and who are made perfect by the wisdom and knowledge of the Spirit. So, too, do human beings become like cherubim in this world bearing aloft on the backs of their souls Him who is God above all. Who then would be such a fool, or so unfeeling, as to desire power, or glory, or riches to the sight and experience of this glory? Indeed, who would be so insane and foolish as to imagine that any other glory, or kingdom, or wealth, or honor, or rule, or luxury, or any other benefit said or thought to be on earth or in heaven, could be greater than the Kingdom and glory of God, so as to choose the first in preference to the second? Truly, there is nothing else preferable to this for those who have any sense.[30]

---

[30] Symeon the New Theologian, *On the Mystical Life, The Ethical Discourses, Vol. 1: The Church and the Last Things* (Crestwood, NY: St. Vladimir's Seminary Press, 1995), 138.

9

Divine Creation

By faith we understand that the worlds were prepared by the word of God, so that what is seen was made from things that are not visible.

Hebrews 11:3.

The doctrine of creation can be stated in one simple sentence: The Triune God created everything there is *ex nihilo*, out of nothing.

Perceptive readers will note immediately that this doctrine is not derived from the text of Genesis 1:1: "In the beginning God created the heavens and the earth." For one thing, it would be anachronistic to read the doctrine of the Trinity back into Genesis 1. As we have seen, the doctrine of the Trinity was arrived at through a long and tangled process of theological reflection and development. Equally, it is not the case that Genesis 1:1 gives us, at a glance, the doctrine of creation *ex nihilo*. It would be convenient if this were the case, but the text is ambiguous. The text certainly allows this option; but it does not mandate it. The Hebrew can be and has been rendered as: "When God began to create the heavens and the earth, the earth was without form and void." To be sure, once we have arrived at a doctrine of creation *ex nihilo*, given a positive view of divine inspiration and a correlative vision of interpretation, we can re-read the text to mean creation *ex nihilo*. Equally, once we have arrived at a doctrine of the Trinity, we will also naturally re-read the text in terms of the action of the Triune God. However, this involves a radical re-contextualizing of Genesis that moves us beyond its original meaning. The crucial initial point is that the Christian doctrine of creation *ex nihilo* is not merely an exegetical decision; it is a crucial theological decision. In this chapter I shall argue precisely that it is a true judgment.

In noting the importance of the theological decision in play, I intend also to marginalize the initial input from empirical considerations in the doctrine of creation. We need to keep our nerve at this point and not be intimidated by apologetic worries or by the noisy debates about cosmology and evolution. The rush to find incompatibility or compatibility at this point should be resisted. If we want to reach a considered account of the relation between theology and natural science, then the first item of business is to provide a clear account of what should be said on the theological side of the discussion. I will not be timid about the consequences of my position for the conversation with science; in fact, I think that the crucial issues of principle can be dispatched relatively quickly. However, everything depends at this point on how we understand the doctrine of creation; hence that will be my main focus in what follows.

When I was first introduced to the notion of creation *ex nihilo*, the introduction came with a warning. This is a mystery, and never forget it. I was puzzled then and have remained puzzled ever since with this warning notice. The considerations in play were enumerated in terms of two platitudes. In the case of "create" as predicated of human agents, we always assume that human agents begin with raw materials and can then go to work to create this or that object. This is not the case with God. Furthermore, in the case of God, we are dealing with a transcendent agent, so we have no way of understanding what it means for God to create. We are finite; God is infinite; so even though we speak of divine creation, we really have little or no clue what it means as applied to God. I agree to both these platitudes but I reject the standard conclusions that are generally drawn from them. The conclusion strikes me as a total failure of intellectual nerve. Of course, in the case of human agents we rely on prior materials for standard acts of creation. However, it does not follow that somehow creation *ex nihilo* is not intelligible to us. Moreover, it is surely correct to say that we have no idea of the divine "psychology" in creating *ex nihilo*. However, this applies across the board to all our action-predicates as applied to God. I know no more about what it is to be God than what it is to be a dolphin or dog. Yet we say a host of things about divine action despite this failure. So, this premise is irrelevant. Moreover, even if we have to work with faint analogies from our own acts of creation when we think of divine creation, we have a straightforward way of conceiving of creation *ex nihilo* in terms of this act being a basic act of God.

A basic act is one that we carry out without doing another act; we do it straight off. Many of our acts are done in, with, and through other acts we perform. I shut the door by pushing it with my hand. I write this chapter by gathering my thoughts and sitting down to write. However, I simply use my hand to push the door shut without any intermediary acts. Moving my arm in this way is a basic act. Forming new thoughts are basic acts in my mind. Leaving aside the fact that God creates human babies by creating human agents who procreate, the idea of creation *ex nihilo* as applied to the universe as a whole is entirely intelligible once we realize that it is a basic act, brought about straight off without any intermediate actions. Given the attributes of God (his power, intelligence, wisdom, love, and the like), we should take creation *ex nihilo* in our stride conceptually. The problem at this point is that we import all sorts of irrelevant considerations, like, whether we can imagine such an action. Once we abandon such semantic requirements and come to terms with the basic act involved, we have said all that needs to be said to capture what is at stake.

To reiterate, God, given his attributes, can create the whole universe straight off *ex nihilo*. To speak in graphic terms: logically speaking, the universe did not exist; then it existed; and the only bridge between these states of affairs is divine creation *ex nihilo*. Looking for more is a bogus enterprise; crying mystery, whatever we take it to mean here, cannot mean that we cannot grasp conceptually what is at stake. Either we grasp this or we do not; there is nothing more to be said to those who want more, or to those who think that it is especially deep and pious to prevaricate, or to throw semantic dust in our eyes. The Triune God created the universe out of nothing. This is where we begin and end our deliberations. The doctrine can be put on a postcard.

One further note of elaboration is needed. How should we explain this basic act of God? There are a variety of strategies we deploy in order to explain our actions. In rare cases, we simply perform the act involved and the only explanation is that we did it. There are no goals or reasons or motives beyond the performance of the act. If we are to speak of an explanation, then we might call it an expressive explanation. So, Murphy simply gives a dollar bill to the beggar on the corner on the way to work as an act of generosity. He has no intention of helping the beggar find a meal, no goal of transforming the world through charity, no grand design to bring glory to himself among his friends, and the like. He just did it as an expression of generosity. In other cases, we speak of explanation of actions in terms of practical reasoning. I move my finger at an auction as a basic act because I want to make a bid on the red mini car that has come up for sale. I have the goal of buying a car and making a bid by raising my finger is the means by which I achieve my goal. If we are in doubt about the explanation, we can always ask what is going on.

It is entirely natural to ask why God created a world at all. We can work with a number of options. We can say that God has the goal of making a world that will express his goodness and ingenuity; he achieves that end by creation *ex nihilo*. So, he just did it. We can say it is simply an act of stupendous generosity, an expression of the love and power of God, a love and power that God uniquely possesses as an Agent. There is a faint analogy in the action of great artists who just create as an expression of their genius and talent. They find it odd to think of their work in terms of ordinary means–end explanations. Or we might say that God took delight in the thought of a magnificent, complex world that would one day bring forth creatures made in his own image and created the universe to achieve that end. Or we could say that God thought that making a world would provide an arena in which one day he would be incarnate in his Son through the Spirit, so creating the universe out of nothing was a means of achieving that end. These are speculative options. We could adjudicate between them if God were to reveal to us why he created a universe. The record of divine revelation at this point is sparse to say the least. Theologians, especially in the medieval period, have been divided on this issue. We are in no better position today. However, doctrines of creation can legitimately ask this question and my own hunch would favor an expressive account of the explanation of creation. God created the world as an act of sheer grace and generosity.

My reasons for this are soft as I do not think we have clear revelation on this topic. This way of thinking about creation links nicely with the policy of grace that is abundantly manifest in his covenant relation with Israel, in his work of redemption in Christ, and in his actions in salvation through the Holy Spirit. Furthermore, this way of thinking safeguards the transcendence and aseity of God in that there is no need in God that is satisfied by the creation of the universe.[1] God already possesses the perfections of his attributes without a world; creating a world adds not a whit to those perfections. Perhaps in the life to come we will discover the explanation for divine creation; imagine a seminar with philosophers and theologians discussing what the good Lord tells us at that point. Happily, the course involved will not be required or those attending might worry that they had been transferred to a less preferable option. Most believers are happy to leave the action to stand alone without explanation and revel in what God has given us in creation. They are none the worse for that. They find the claim intuitively attractive and are satisfied to rest with the claim that God created the world *ex nihilo.*

Of course, the story behind this astonishing claim about creation is far from simple. Many believers are shocked to find that it is not simply read out of Genesis 1:1 or other biblical texts. So, the next task is to spell out in some detail how the church arrived at this doctrine. With that in place we can then swing back around and deal with the relation between this claim and the wonders of creation made available in the natural sciences. I can also pick up how the doctrine can be related to Scripture and to the problem of evil.

The historical context for the development of the doctrine of creation out of nothing was the battle with Gnosticism, perhaps the greatest theological and philosophical rival to Christianity in the first three centuries after Christ. Gnostics, like contemporary New Age gurus, laid claim to having secret knowledge that was not vouchsafed to other mortals. They developed a variety of complex doctrines and saw themselves as the true successors to the apostles. In part, their appeal was that they offered substantial explanations for the way things were, not least for the recurring problem of evil. Thus, they developed narratives in which conflict in the spiritual arena resulted in the creation of a material world, which in turn helped folk come to terms with the grim reality

---

[1] Imagine for a moment that our creation satisfied some need in God. This is not exactly a comforting thought. Is God now going to use us as a means to the end of satisfying some need in the divine nature? God does not delight in his creation for its own sake, he creates us to foster his own happiness or undo his boredom. This whole line of thought is preposterous.

of evil. The intellectual challenge for the church was formidable; it was by no means a foregone conclusion that the initial theological alternative worked out by such figures as Tertullian, Irenaeus, Athanasius, and Augustine would win the day.

One way to see what was at issue is to lay out the options as they appeared for example to Tertullian, a hard-headed lawyer, in his debate with Hermogenes, a second-century Gnostic. Tertullian set out three alternatives. We could think of creation by way of emanation. Creation was out of God's own being. Or we could think of creation as creation out of preexisting material or stuff. Or we could think of creation *ex nihilo*. This is a wonderfully clear and compact way of going to the heart of the issue. Both Tertullian and Hermogenes ruled out the first option, for they believed that God was ontologically indivisible. In a certain sense, they insisted that ontologically God was simple; God was not composed of parts.[2] Hermogenes, akin to some contemporary biblical scholars in their reading of Genesis 1:1, took the second option: creation out of preexistent stuff. Tertullian took the third option, creation out of nothing. What is especially interesting is why Hermogenes rejected the third option. There were two problems that were acute for him. First, there was the problem of the absolute beginning. Why does God suddenly decide to produce a creation? Was he bored or fed up with being idle? Second, he was convinced that creation out of nothing, compared to creation out of preexisting stuff, failed to provide a solution to the problem of evil. The second option worked better on this score for it explained how that evil arose because of the preexistent stuff that God had to use.

These objections could not be ignored by those who preferred to think of divine creation as creation *ex nihilo*. On the first issue Augustine tried to resolve it by insisting that the question made no sense because time came into existence with creation, so it is senseless to ask what God was doing prior to creation. Strictly speaking this is true. However, if we frame the issue in terms of the explanation for divine creation, the issue remains and cannot be dismissed by appealing to debates about divine action and time, a matter that deserves attention in its own right. I have already indicated my own response to the issue when framed in terms of the explanation for divine creation; God acts out of sheer creativity and generosity. Once the issue is reframed then the very same question can be posed for the second option, namely, why did God create the world we inhabit from preexisting stuff? Thus, the second option is in exactly the same boat as the third. It cannot be used to rule out the option of creation out of nothing. As to the other problem, the problem of evil, this is a problem every theistic position faces and there are a variety of

---

[2] This claim should not be confused with neighboring claims that insist that God's existence and God's essence are identical, or that God's attributes are such that his love is identical with his power, which in turn is identical with his knowledge, and so on.

ways to deal with it that range from an appeal to the freedom of human agents, through an appeal to our ignorance, all the way to our finite and limited perspective on the world. Hence, again, the problem was not seen as excluding creation *ex nihilo*.

The positive factors in favor of creation out of nothing are cumulative. On the one hand, the Gnostic options all looked to internal conflict within the divine world of the Pleroma, Sophia, and various divine aeons, to explain the existence of the universe. The universe turned out to be the result of a battle within the spiritual arena and Gnostics bet the store on supplying an intricate analysis that would convey what they thought was a profound as opposed to a naïve narrative of creation and redemption. Over against this, creation *ex nihilo*, despite the absence of explicit explanations for the divine action involved, came across as much more economical and even honest. Irenaeus captures this with telling simplicity.

> For no question can be solved by means of another which itself awaits solution; nor, in the opinion of those possessed of sense, can an ambiguity be explained by means of another ambiguity, or enigmas by means of another great enigma, but things of such character receive their solution from those which are manifest, and consistent, and clear.[3]

The doctrine of creation from nothing cut through the tangle of speculation and cleared the air for the reception of a much simpler, clearer account of creation and redemption that was emerging in the proto-creeds of the church.

Two other factors were important in securing the third option. First, creation out of nothing captures the sense of the radical transcendence and sovereignty of God already embedded in the faith of those initiated into the life of the church in catechesis. The divine action in Israel and in incarnation and redemption indicates a God who is not limited by anything in the created order; creation out of nothing coheres nicely with this conviction. Second, creation *ex nihilo* captures afresh the idea of the unsurpassing omnipotence of God. To think of God as somehow dependent on preexisting stuff fails on this score; God's power, already manifest in Christ's resurrection and in the experience of new life in the Spirit, is better represented by a vision of creation out of nothing.

What I am proposing here is that considerations drawn from other developing elements in the faith of the church are tacitly at work in the adoption of creation *ex nihilo*. There is a tendency to think that doctrines of creation come first in the order of knowing. However, as we shall see shortly in the case of our reading of Genesis, we are misled at this point by the natural order of presentation. What is really doing the heavy lifting in the doctrine of creation is the experience of God in redemption. We begin in the world of redemption

---

[3] Irenaeus, *Adv. Haer.* II.x.3.

and then work back to what is likely to be the case of creation given what we have discovered in redemption. We can see this, once again, in the ruminations of Irenaeus when he examines the way Gnostics were handling the Scriptures compared to the broad reading of the Scriptures adopted by those who had been introduced to the rule of faith.

> He who retains unchangeable in his heart the rule of the truth which he received by means of baptism, will doubtless recognize the names, expressions, and the parables taken from the Scriptures [by the Gnostics], but will by no means acknowledge the blasphemous use these men make of them. For, though he will acknowledge the gems, he will not receive the fox instead of the likeness of a king. But when he has restored every one of the expressions quoted to its proper position, and has fitted it to the body of truth, he will lay bare, and prove to be without any foundation, the figment of these heretics.[4]

Irenaeus is cleverly deploying here his charge that the Gnostics read Scripture and come up with the picture of a fox; the faithful read Scripture but see an image of a king. What is salient, however, is that it is the narrative of creation now linked to redemption that is crucial in these alternatives. I am merely making explicit the implicit point made so graphically by Irenaeus.

Once the doctrine of creation is in place, it is natural for some theologians to ransack the biblical texts as the proper and true warrant for its truth. The results are a mixed bag. On the one hand, there are indeed texts that can be harnessed to support creation *ex nihilo*.[5] However, other passages compare creation to forming pots out of clay,[6] taming monsters,[7] or to setting boundaries to the forces of chaos.[8] Clearly, considerations above and beyond Scripture are in play in the appeal to these texts if we are to adopt creation from nothing. The crucial text, however, is, of course, the appeal to Genesis 1:1, rendered as "In the beginning God created the heavens and the earth." I promised to circle back to this text and it is time to fulfill that promise.

The whole of Genesis 1 is, of course, a magnificent portrayal of the work of creation. We need to pause and get the bigger picture. In terms of the book of Genesis as a whole, it is clear that chapter one is a prologue to a brilliant text whose focus is not at all creation per se but the amazing portrayal of the creation of human agents, their fall into sin and alienation, and the beginnings of the resolution of sin and alienation represented by the covenant with Abraham and its aftermath. Creation is an important but minor motif in the book as a whole; the book is in reality hopelessly anthropocentric. Furthermore, there is merit in the suggestion that Israel first came to know the action of God in redemption in history before she came to develop her vision of God

---

[4] Ibid., I.ix.4.
[5] 2 Maccabees 7:28; John 1:3; Romans 4:17; Colossians 1:16; Hebrews 11:3.
[6] Isaiah 64:8.   [7] Psalm 74:14–17.   [8] Psalm 104:9; Job 26:10, 38:8–11.

in creation. We see here a similar logic to the one just enumerated in the case of Irenaeus. This dovetails with the further suggestion that Genesis 1 was represented in priestly circles who base the ordering and rhetoric of Genesis 1 on the building and structure of the Temple. The message is clear: creation represents a sacred space of worship that supplements the sacred place of the Temple. Perhaps there is an even deeper message, in that the whole of Genesis 1–11 represents a daring account of what has gone badly wrong in creation and how God's various covenants with Israel represent the critical first step in providing an apt solution to what has gone wrong. Thus, what God has done in Israel is not just directed to Israel's woes; it is offered as a solution to the universal problem of human sin. This is not to say that the prologue on creation is secondary; however, it relocates the material where it belongs, that is, in a wider narrative of creation, freedom, fall, and redemption.

Consider now the potential historical setting for the material in Genesis 1. It has long been surmised that Genesis 1 is a counter-narrative to the prevailing stories of creation available in the Mesopotamian, Egyptian, and Canaanite traditions.[9] Most of these saw creation as arising out of the various battles between the gods, gods who in turn underwrote the various political schemes they were meant to serve. Genesis 1 represents a radical alternative to these options. We might say in vulgar terms that it provides a brilliantly inspired alternative propaganda for Israelite teenagers tempted to adopt the alluring and attractive images and stories of their hosts in exile. More grandly, we might say that Genesis 1 represents a splendid vision of God for the people of Israel as they prepare to return to their native land after their suffering in foreign parts. Or perhaps this is the point: in exile they can still worship God for creation itself is the temple of God.

The broad message of Genesis 1 is not difficulty to summarize. It upholds the simplicity of a network of basic acts of God represented as divine speaking who spontaneously and effortlessly creates all that is. It portrays the ingenuity of God in providing a creation that is beautifully ordered. It provides a climactic account of the special place of human agents created in the image of God as the apex of God's creative activity. Above all, it declares the goodness of creation from top to bottom. Once the background music of the numbers and structures involved are seen to echo the Temple and the seventh day of rest, it becomes an astonishing expression of wonder and praise to the God of Israel, already known in his mighty acts of generosity and redemption. Read against these themes and in this context, it will be entirely natural to read Genesis 1:1 as a statement of the doctrine of creation *ex nihilo*, which is exactly where the weight of tradition has been until recently.

---

[9] For a splendid treatment of the relevant issues see William P. Brown, *The Seven Pillars of the Universe: The Bible, Science, and the Wonder of Ecology* (New York: Oxford University Press, 2005).

Read in the context of the development of the doctrine of creation as outlined above, this option will be even further confirmed. The warrant in this instance stems from the way a text can be recontextualized when new information is added about the primary agent involved. To take a simple example, once Barack Obama became President of the United States, earlier stories that saw him as just one more politician among others will be reworked to include a reference to his later achievements in becoming President. In the account of his birth and childhood, he will be identified as President of the United States. Likewise, when folk become convinced that the God of Israel created the world out of nothing then they will naturally reidentify the God of Genesis which speaks of creation precisely in such terms. A sound theory of the inspiration of the authors and redactors of Scripture will not hesitate to endorse this reading strategy. So long as this reading is a possibility, the drive to this reading will not be stopped merely because it is not mandated by the exact grammar of the text. The rabbis were well aware of the difficulty in the text and were deeply puzzled by it. They rightly played with both options to see where it would take them. Contemporary Christian biblical scholars do exactly the same; and they are free to do so. However, if they are wise and reasonable, they will recognize that the doctrine of creation out of nothing does not stand or fall with their exegetical labors. It is a genuinely theological development that goes above and beyond some kind of fundamentalist reading of the Bible.

Before I turn to the relation of the doctrine of creation *ex nihilo* with the findings of natural science, consider four comments on the importance of the doctrine of creation. First, the doctrine of creation *ex nihilo* means that God should never be thought of as one more item alongside other items in the universe. God does not belong to a genus with a range of species. This language is drawn from the effort to divide biological creatures into a hierarchy where genus stands above species in a hierarchy of being. Thus, there is one genus of dogs which is divided into various species. No such taxonomy can apply in the relation between the Creator and creatures. If we were to even use this language as an analogy, then God would belong in a genus of one without differentiating the various species that belong in the genus. This makes no sense. Given that God is the Creator of everything we catalogue in terms of genus and species, this sort of distinction cannot logically arise. In this respect God is utterly unique, logically standing outside such categories. Pressing this may seem an abstract and irrelevant distraction. This is not so: to ignore this implication of the doctrine is to fall into paganism and idolatry.

Second, this doctrine is vital for a balanced devotional life. Meditation on the goodness of God and ingenuity of God in creation is a source of spiritual health. In Ireland, the annual Harvest Festival services have been a splendid source of edification in this regard. The doctrine of creation is a bulwark against anthropocentrism, the besetting temptation of the focus on salvation from sin. It wards off the need to be constantly taking our spiritual temperature; it is a way of starving the fat, relentless ego that is ever on the lookout for attention. Third, the doctrine of creation has deep ethical consequences that deserve extended treatment in the field of moral theology. This is not our world; it is God's world; and we are responsible for its care not just to our neighbors and to future generations, but to God, our just judge. Fourth, the doctrine of creation is essential to a viable doctrine of general revelation. The issue here is not natural theology but general revelation. Agents are known through what they do. There should be no surprise in Paul's assertion: "For what can be known about God is plain to them, because God has shown it to them. Ever since the creation of the world God's invisible nature, namely, God's eternal deity and power has been clearly perceived in the things that have been made."[10] In general revelation, we perceive God's deity and power in creation. In natural theology, we begin with certain features of the universe, say, its existence and order, and construct arguments to the existence of God. The doctrine of creation does not rule out natural theology; however, it does entail a doctrine of general revelation built on the platitude that agents are made known through their actions, a platitude that holds for God as it does for human agents.

Despite many obituary notices, natural theology continues to flourish in contemporary philosophical circles. We can understand why. The world as it appears to us phenomenally and as it is described by the extraordinary findings in natural science cry out for explanation. Kant's starry sky above and the moral law within continue to make us pause and ask, "where did all this come from?" To say that the world is created by God is one way to answer the queries that crop up. Scientific explanations come to an end at some point. The relevant explanations are causal in nature. On one standard reading they invoke a set of preceding conditions which when coupled with a set of relevant laws allow us to predict future events. On another reading, we think of nature as made up of entities with various powers which are instantiated in various states of affairs that are best expressed in terms of natural laws. Either way, the explanations assume the existence of the relevant states of affairs, entities, and laws of nature. We can then stop looking for explanations or look to an alternative way of explaining events, namely, the explanation of events in terms of the action and intentions of God. By this time, we are deep in the weeds of philosophical analysis. Suffice it to say that explanations in terms of agents and their actions are like banks too big to fail. So, the debate about natural theology rumbles on, even though theists themselves confess they fall short of what theologians want to and need to say; and even though they often

---

[10] Romans 1:19–20.

leave the seminar with a sense of disappointment about the spiritual value of the whole enterprise.

A more pressing issue for the theologian is how to integrate the doctrine of creation with the actual findings of the natural sciences as they show up in debates about cosmology and evolution. We need to cut through a lot of confusion at this point and keep our eye firmly fixed on the doctrine of creation *ex nihilo*. This is both an exceptionally fertile notion and an exceptionally limited notion when it comes to the relation between theology and science. On the fertile side, creation out of nothing highlights the radical contingency of the natural world. Creation might have been otherwise; hence, to discover how it works, we have to engage in empirical investigation to make progress on this front. We need a persistent inductive spirit, precisely what is needed to do good science. Furthermore, given that the world is radically distinct from God, it is permissible to investigate the world by way of experiments. Nature is demystified and desacralized; we can fearlessly put our questions to it and examine it. Again, this fits with the logic and spirit of science. Moreover, seeing the world as the effect of divine intelligence encourages us to look for order, regularity, and even design in the universe. We should look for laws and even surprising subtleties in those laws. So, the doctrine of creation provides a welcome intellectual womb in which science can flourish.[11]

Despite the conceptual and historical fit between creation and the logic and practices of science, we are accustomed to hearing about an extended warfare between science and theology. We need to understand why this narrative was developed from the theological side. The doctrine of creation *ex nihilo* became embedded in a very specific account of divine action that was developed out of a literal reading of the narratives in Genesis. The story of the creation of the universe emerged where God created the world in 4004 BC and where human agents were created miraculously from the dust of the earth on the sixth day of creation. Consequently, cosmological, geological, and biological discoveries came into conflict with these claims. This mingling of theology and empirical considerations was entirely natural in a culture which had not learned to distinguish scientific, historical, and theological questions. It is also natural because we will always embed our theological claims about creation within our empirical convictions about the world. Put sharply, if our ancestors in the faith had been confronted with what we now know, say, about the age of the earth, they would not have believed a word of what we would say to them. The doctrine of creation was expressed in the common sense of their day, as well as in the polemical interchange with competing accounts of creation available in the sagas and myths of their neighbors. As already indicated, their vision of

---

[11] Consider in this regard the title of Einstein's biography by Abraham Pais: *Subtle is the Lord: The Science and Life of Albert Einstein* (Oxford: Oxford University Press, 1982).

creation in Genesis, aside from its rhetorical beauty, is a brilliant antidote to the paganism of their time.

The issue here is not that theology answers the why questions and science answers the how questions. Scientists seek to know why things happen and have their own well-tested repertoire of explanatory strategies. To answer their why questions they supply answers in terms of how nature works. Theologians too ask why questions and the fundamental answer in relation to the universe is that it was created out of nothing by God. Given that this is a basic act of God, the how question takes care of itself. God did it as a basic act; there is no means–end answer logically available. We can then ask a further why question as to why God created the universe. As already noted, we are severely limited in answering this question not because there is some hidden mystery but because we have limited information on the part of the relevant Agent, namely, God. There is no serious difficultly here; we are dependent on what God has chosen to reveal.

However, there is a deeper and more important limitation in asserting the doctrine of creation *ex nihilo*. This assertion leaves open a host of possible options as far as empirical predictions are concerned. On the one hand, what is asserted is indeed substantial; to know that God created our universe is a shattering discovery. It has enormous consequences when related to other claims we make about, say, divine redemption in this life and the life to come. On the other hand, it is compatible with a variety of options on the empirical level. To be sure, there is a natural fit with theories that were inadvertently captured by the skeptical Fred Hoyle when he coined the term Big Bang. In fact, Hoyle resisted the Big Bang theory in part precisely because he thought it provided partial confirmation for the doctrine of creation.[12] He stuck to his steady state theory that posited that the density of matter in the expanding universe remains the same because matter is being continuously created from new stars and galaxies. But even this theory has to posit the continuous creation of matter; and the question of origins cannot be avoided. Even the more recent multiverse theory, where it is said that our universe is simply one of a host of parallel universes not available to detection, does not tell us where these parallel universes came from and the question of origins comes back to haunt us. On this scenario, we gain an even more amazing picture of the extraordinary power and ingenuity of God. There is no need for the theologians to panic or get ahead of ourselves. We can relax and wait and see what science tells us.

The same strategy works in the case of the debate about the origins of human agents as posited in, say, the standard accounts of evolution. There is no serious proposal from the theological side of the table on the issue of how

---

[12] For a fine account of Hoyle's determined opposition to the Big Bang theory see Jane Gregory, *Fred Hoyle's Universe* (Oxford: Oxford University Press, 2005), chapter 18.

God brought it about the human agents arose on the face of the earth. God creates each of us now through the agency of our parents. We are not directly created by immediate basic acts of God. Equally, it is clearly possible that God can bring about the emergence of human agents by working in, with, and through entirely natural processes. It would be foolhardy to say that we have heard the last word about how evolution works and how best to describe the processes involved. Eliminating design from science is as acute a problem in science as the problem of evil is in theology. What is needed is patience and reserve. It is often comical to watch folk try to weave this or that gap in the biblical account of creation in Genesis with this or that element drawn from science. This applies to non-fundamentalist as well as fundamentalist strategies. Equally, it is comical to watch atheists try to settle the complex issues involved, even as they ignore the crucial philosophical and metaphysical issues at stake.[13] We have to get beyond these stale debates both as an account of the relation between the doctrine of creation and the findings of science and as an account of our efforts to deal seriously with the differences between theists and atheists.

Systematic theologians should keep their nerve in all of this and stand by the core element in the doctrine of creation, namely, the claim that the universe was created by God *ex nihilo*. This is not a matter of false modesty or an effort to avoid awkward questions. We simply need to be aware of the deflationary character of our work and make sure that believers get hold of what really matters in this stage of the journey of faith. There is plenty of room for further exploration once the first things on the other side of our initial intellectual formation are more or less complete. I suggest a similar strategy in dealing with the other crucial problem that arises in thinking through the doctrine of creation, namely, the existence of angels and existence of evil.

Angels are best described as unseen, beautiful, incorporeal agents who engage in worship of the Trinity, who act as divine messengers, and who at times operate as warriors and guardians of the faithful. Without them our vision of the universe would be seriously impoverished. Just as there is a network of agents below human beings, there is a network above human beings in a celestial hierarchy that adds beauty and diversity to the created order. Brief as this is, it is enough for present purposes.

As to the problem of evil, given that my overall project rests on a robust vision of genuine human action, it will be obvious that I hold that much moral evil comes directly and much natural evil comes indirectly from human actions permitted by God. The challenge comes when we observe the amount of suffering that exists. Clearly, as in the case of creation from nothing, our

---

[13] Alvin Plantinga with characteristic ingenuity and clarity has rendered great service in identifying where exactly the real issue is in the debate between theists and certain schools of naturalism. See his *Where the Conflict Really Lies: Science, Religion, and Naturalism* (Oxford: Oxford University Press, 2011).

access to the divine reasons for such permission is limited. Recent work on divine hiddenness has rightly highlighted this feature of our situation. However, this strategy only takes us so far. It is a profound puzzle to me why God does not arrange a quiet heart attack here and there and bring, say, to a timely end, the lives of the moral monsters who have stalked through history and killed millions of innocent victims. In this respect, the problem of evil takes on added dimensions inside the canonical faith of the church and across the threshold of divine revelation that it would not otherwise have.

Similar considerations apply in the case of natural evil. We can surely see why natural evils are built into the universe by God in order for greater goods to be gained. Richard Swinburne has made a truly original contribution to this line of argument in recent years.[14] The basic story runs like this. God has created not a perfect world but a good world, a world that fits his purposes. This world is an incomplete and half-finished world in which there are human agents endowed with various capacities, intelligence, and freedom. This freedom is a substantial freedom that extends beyond our mere interaction with one another and encompasses the ability to explore how the universe works. Once we know how it works, we then have to decide how to use that information, whether for good or ill. The more we find out about the world, the greater our power and responsibility. Given the incomplete nature of the world, we can now decide whether to join in the care of the world exercised by God. The existence of widespread natural evil provides both the motive for, and the opportunity for, the exercise of a freedom that is staggering in its proportions. We are free as to whether or not to explore the world, and we are free as to whether or not we shall use the knowledge we garner from that exploration to bring God's universe closer to what God intends for it. Will we blow up the world in a nuclear holocaust? Will we destroy it by pollution of the atmosphere? Will we eliminate the diseases that we now understand through the exercise of our freedom to explore and explain? Will we join with each other and use our knowledge to bring the world to the destiny of goodness and harmony that God has planned for it?

What is at issue here is the matter of a credible theodicy. It is fashionable to make fun of theodicy in the twenty-first century. This is not advisable. Suffering is an inescapable part of life and it is insensitive to sweep it all aside as absurd and meaningless. Any theology or worldview that trivializes it, or refuses to find some sense in it, or sugarcoats it with pious nonsense, does not take suffering and evil seriously.[15] There are two sorts of instances where mature believers have always found some sense in suffering. One is in the case of personal providence where God clearly uses suffering to chasten us, to

---

[14] Richard Swinburne, *Providence and Evil* (Oxford: Clarendon Press, 1988).

[15] I take up the topic as it applies to deep grief in my *Among the Ashes: On Death, Grief, and Hope* (Grand Rapids, MI: Eerdmans, 2017).

deepen our faith, to make us holy. God clearly works through suffering and evil in this instance. Much religious experience testifies to this. The other is the case of the incarnation where God enters into the womb of human suffering and hangs on the cross of Golgotha. Again, God clearly works through suffering and evil in this case. Here we find significance in God working through heinous moral evil. Grant this and then the possibility is open for finding God's providence at work in even the worst kinds of moral evil.

Much hinges at this point on whether we stand outside the Christian tradition, say, in the world of atheism or in the world of mere theism. Atheists and mere theists will look at the phenomena of evil in a radically different way from someone who has been gripped by the work of God in his Son and in the Spirit as delineated in the earlier chapters of this volume. The atheist may be sure that she has decisive evidence against any serious doctrine of creation when she surveys the range and depth of moral and natural evil. The mere theist, in response, can always fall back on the hiddenness of the divine purposes after the standard strategies related to free will and soul-making have run out of steam. The debate rumbles on from one generation to another.

The canonical theist works off a wider range of divine action as spelled out in the work of the Son and the Holy Spirit. It is easy to be drawn into an obsession with the kind of critical inquiry that has no room for Christ or for the experience of grace. The result is intellectual tunnel vision. However, the action of God is not confined to that of creation *ex nihilo*. It includes the actions of the Son in reconciliation and the actions of the Spirit in our hearts in salvation. It also includes the planting of the wisdom of God in the Scriptures and practices of the church. Indeed, God has given us signs that speak to those who have ears to hear. The greatest sign with respect to evil is the sign of the cross, where the victory of God over evil is placarded before our eyes. This sign is then reenacted again and again at the table of the Lord. We are confronted with an abundance of divine actions wherever we turn, and our heads spin as we seek to unravel their content and their bearing on our lives.

It will always appear foolish and presumptuous to think we have fully understood what God has done. This applies to the phenomena of evil as we think about divine action in creation. It also applies to the other actions of God we are seeking to ponder. However, in Christ God has submitted himself in grace and mercy to be cross-examined and executed by his human creatures. In loving God with our minds and in coming to terms with all that God has done, we find more than enough to keep us in the way of faith and to celebrate his wondrous work in creating the world out of nothing.

10

Divine Providence

For we know that all things work together for good for those who love
God, who are called according to his purpose. If God is for us, who is
against us? He who did not withhold his own Son, but gave him up for all
of us, will he not with him give us all things? Who shall separate us from
the love of Christ? Will hardship, or distress, or persecution, or famine, or
nakedness, or peril, or sword? No in all these things we are more than
conquerors through him who loved us.

Romans 8:28, 31, 37.

John Wesley (1703–91) was a fastidious Oxford don who became one of the
greatest evangelists of the Western church. He was a Fellow of Lincoln College,
and went for a time as a missionary as a young man to the New World where
he failed abysmally. He also was a priest in the Church of England, as was his
brother Charles Wesley (1707–88), who served the cause of Methodism which
they founded with a repertoire of extraordinary hymns. At the height of his
powers John Wesley took ill in Newcastle, where he was nursed by a woman
called Grace Murray. She became his assistant, traveled with him as far away
as Ireland, and they became devoted to each other. They decided on marriage.
However, he and his brother had made an agreement that they would not
marry without consulting each other. When Charles got wind of what was
going on, there was no consultation. In a series of emotional meetings, he
convinced Grace Murray to marry another suitor, John Bennett, got Miss
Murray up on the back of his horse, and had her married off before John had
been informed. His motives were murky. Grace Murray was beneath the social
class of the Wesleys; marriage would ruin the work of John as the leader of
Methodism. Maybe Charles could not stand the woman. John arrived on his
horse half an hour after the deed was done.

What interests us here is John's response to the actions of his friends and
colleagues. He wrote a poem.

O Lord, I bow my sinful head!
Righteous are all Thy Ways with Man.
Yet suffer me with Thee to plead,

With lowly Reverence to complain:
With deep, unutter'd Grief to groan,
O what is this that Thou has done?

Teach me from every pleasing Snare
To keep the Issues of my Heart:
Be Thou my Love, my Joy, my Fear!
Thou my eternal Portion art!
Be Thou my never-failing Friend,
And love, O love me, to the End!

The striking feature of this expression of grief is that Wesley attributed what had just happened to God. His brother Charles had just betrayed him; his wife to be had deserted him to marry someone else; they had ruined his life. Yet he accused God of these actions. It is God who has betrayed him, deserted him, and ruined his life. This makes neither grammatical nor theological sense. However, John Wesley was no fool; he could have become one of the best theologians of his day if he had spent his days in a library rather than on horseback. So, we need to get beyond the surface grammar and see what is being asserted. Wesley was reinterpreting the human event of betrayal in terms of the action of God. He was deploying a repertoire of concepts to his experience even though initially they did not fit. He expected his life to be governed by a Divine Friend who looks out for his welfare. His Divine Friend had hurt him deeply by acting in a way that was emotionally devastating. In theological terms, he was tacitly deploying the language of providence. Indeed, the poem ends with a heartfelt resignation to the providence of God.

Wesley is coming at the concept of providence through the back door. Let's open the front door. The etymology (*providere*) means "to see beforehand"; thus, we could translate it as "foresight." The English picks up this history by speaking of "acting with foresight to provide for circumstances yet to come in the future." Applied to God, providence means that God acts for our good in ways that take into account his long-term goals for us. Thus, it takes on a whole new depth when linked to the notion of God's kingdom, that is, to God's rule that has been inaugurated in the coming of the Son and the bestowal of the Spirit. We might speak of God's governance wisely exercised with an eye to the future and not just to the events of the present.

Hence, the concept of providence also assumes the foreknowledge of God. God knows up ahead what is going to happen; he can act now in anticipation of the future. Initially, this means that God foreknows what human agents will freely do in the future. More dramatically, if we take into account the transcendence of God, God knows not just what Seamus will do if he goes to the pub on Saturday night, he knows what Seamus would do if Seamus were to go to O'Reilly's pub rather than Murphy's pub. In the first pub, the music would soothe his nerves when he got drunk: he would behave himself. In the second, the noise of the football crowd would get on his nerves and would lead him to punch his best friend Liam on the nose. We find a fascinating instance of this kind of knowledge in a comment of Jesus. "Woe to you, Chorazin! Woe to you, Bethsaida! For if the deeds of power done in you had been done in Tyre and Sidon, they would have repented long ago in sackcloth and ashes."[1]

We are also backing up into the doctrine of creation. For providence is going to require that God hang around, so to speak, after creating the universe and keep an eye on it. However, this little relic of deism where God creates *ex nihilo* and then takes a long holiday is much too thin a notion. God will have to have a hand in the created order, for looking after his human creatures and his People will require a much more intimate relation to nature. If creation is analogous to building a temple for worship, then creation will also need tending. The created order will need to be sustained and provided for as well. Thus, providence very naturally gets cashed out in terms of ongoing creation and preservation. The laws of nature will be seen as an instance of God keeping the whole show on the road. Providence understood under this description will be seen as a revelation of the wisdom and reliability of God.

We are headed for the theological quicksands. On the one hand, we enter a long-winded discussion of the relation of God to nature. The intellectual temperature rises as we hear the heavy breathing of science down our necks. Happily, there are famous foundations with lots of money to help us at this point. So, we set to work to develop a very general account of divine agency and divine action that we can use to unpack the concept of providence. Or maybe, the concept of providence is the key to unlock the notion of divine action; we look to divine action in providence as a window unto all divine action. I have already written the obituary notice on this strategy and will not repeat it here.

On the other hand, once we mention divine plans, we are drifting into the world of predestination, double or otherwise. In this case, the intellectual temperature rises because of at least three factors. First, we have hoary memories of Calvin and his scholastic followers, and we instinctively sense that we are going to be sent to hell for our sins, but sins which, if God had a tad more of concurrent grace and given it out more generously, we could have made it into God's good heaven, if only by the skin of our teeth. When the intellectual ingenuity of Thomas Aquinas and his Dominican friars are brought in to supplement the armies of Calvin, we know we are likely to lose the metaphysical battles about divine grace and human freedom that have been revived with gusto over the last generation.

Second, we will soon find that our old-time allies, the Jesuits, led originally by Louis de Molina, have joined real armies in the quest for liberation from oppression. They will warn us that the effects of the doctrine of providence

---

[1] Matthew 11:21.

have been devastating for the poor, for it has been a wonderful theological tool in the hands of capitalists and tyrants. The poor and oppressed are where they are because of the providence of God, the polluters and capitalists tell us; so, pass the Irish whiskey and plan that extra holiday in Las Vegas.

Third, when we get to Las Vegas, we run into a conference of Evangelical theologians who have become addicted to gambling because they are convinced that divine foreknowledge and human freedom are incompatible. God, of course, is better at card-playing because of his better memory of past hands. And God can think more quickly than his human creatures, but the future is open; so, he cannot but take risks once he creates genuinely free creatures. Thus, the concept of providence is beginning to disintegrate in the house of its friends.

Given, the formidable forces ranged against us, it is small wonder that recent academic theology has little to say about providence. To be sure, Stoic philosophers of old, who were good pagans, had a place for providence; and popular piety still clings to it like folk in rural Texas cling to their guns and their religion. However, this is mere hand waving before we bring out the white flag and surrender. Poor old John Wesley is turning in his grave; I am in no position to resurrect him but I will articulate and defend his wonderfully robust vision of providence. I shall do so by taking the worst-case scenario, that is, that rendering of the doctrine of providence where God is said to bring good out of evil. As to the armies ranged against me, let me send telegrams to keep them at bay for the moment.

In the case of the hoary concept of predestination, I shall take this up later in this volume when I deal with divine action in the Christian life; properly laid out, it is a doctrine of incredible joy and assurance, once we shore it of its Calvinist and Thomistic content. As to the fascinating metaphysical issues about divine foreknowledge and human freedom, and about divine action as it relates broadly to human action, I shall handle these in a subsequent volume. My goal here is to sort out first things first, even though well-informed critics will spot the metaphysical moves I am making. We need to get our bearings before we get too deep into philosophy.

Two more comments are needed at this point. First, like all doctrines, the doctrine of providence has been abused by wild human intellects fueled by the normal round of wayward human passions. The doctrine has been used to discourage political reform, to stop medical advances, and to excuse the abuse of children, women, and minorities. I got the memo on all these examples. However, all this is nothing new. Paul discovered that the doctrine of divine grace had been used to defend moral license. John Wesley knew only too well that his own account of the same doctrine of grace was used as an excuse for antinomianism; he immediately took steps to undercut the false inferences involved. In his own life, he was a champion of the poor; and he was fearless in the quest for social reform whatever the shortcomings of his political philosophy and theology. What is at stake here is a subtle set of concepts that have to be learned, marked, and inwardly digested. Wesley himself was taken up short in his account of providence in dealing with the shenanigans of his brother and his wife to be. However, he quickly made the necessary adjustments and went off to find solace in preaching and in taking care of his fragile converts.

Second, we do not arrive at the concept of providence from below by means of forming theological hypotheses about anomalous events; nor do we learn it by piling up scattered Scripture verses and coming to some kind of theory of divine agency and action. The former was the mistake of Liberal Protestants; the latter the mistake of various schools of Biblicism. We do find shining examples of providence in experience; and we do deploy the texts and stories of Scripture. However, the concept is not a bogus empirical hypothesis; nor is it in fact given in Scripture, as alert Biblicists are quick to realize. It is developed in the faith of the church; we receive it initially from above in our deep immersion in the faith of the church; we then figure out how to use it by living that faith in the hard knocks of human experience.

Consider the following episode and question.

> An intoxicated man at the railroad station in Scotland by mistake some years ago took the wrong train of two leaving the station in opposite directions. The train he should have taken was swept by the storm off the bridge into the Firth of Forth when all aboard were drowned. He escaped death because his intoxication led to his making the mistake. Many others, sober and sane, made no mistake, and were drowned. Shall the man whose escape from death was due to his intoxication call it a special providence in his behalf, and shall he further argue that divine providence had thereby approved of intoxication? Plainly we would say that this would be unwarranted and absurd inference, that no such interpretation is permissible.[2]

Now consider a summary of the subsequent development. Suppose, Wee Jimmy, our drunken Scot, should read this as a wake-up call to repent. He is converted to Catholicism, gets his life together, gives away all his money, enters the Franciscan Order, and spends the rest of his life in the service of Scottish drunkards. We hesitate to see this as an absurd reading of what happened. "As for me," he says, "I was working evil against myself; but God turned it into good, to bring to pass as it is this day, to save myself and through me to keep other people alive."[3] We might even be tempted to say that he was rational in reading his situation this way. This was not evidence of providence in any deep sense; but he had undergone an experience which, given later developments, called for an interpretation in terms of divine providence. Expressed

---

[2] Wilbur Fisk Tillett, *Providence, Prayer, and Power* (Nashville, TN: Cokesbury, 1926), 128.
[3] Ibid., 129. I have changed the details but made essentially the same point as Tillett does.

formally, this episode exhibited a purposiveness that made sense within a rich elaboration of the wider claims about God's purposes for the world and for Wee Jimmy.

We are now on the cusp of a more precise analysis of the concept of providence. Generally, providence is taken as involving three components. First, there is the active power of God at work in the world. Here the doctrine of creation is presupposed. Providence goes beyond mere creation to embrace God's active involvement in nature and history. Second, there is the foresight or foreknowledge of God. God acts in the world, taking into account what lies up ahead; hence God foresees the future and acts knowing what will happen. Third, there is the element of provision and purpose. In acting in the world in providence, God acts to achieve his good purposes for creation. This does not mean that all providential acts are directed to salvation; indeed, in speaking of an "awful" providence, believers sometimes want to draw attention to the judgment of God in providence. However, judgment is not at all necessarily to be set against God's goodness; all of God's acts of providence, even his acts of judgment, are an expression of God's goodness. This is absolutely crucial, and I will return to it briefly at the end.

We now have the bare-bones ideas that find their way into the concept or doctrine of providence. This kind of general information about the idea of providence is crucial, but it does not specify precisely how we are to understand God's working in the world in any detail. These conceptual components give us the bricks and mortar, but they do not provide any buildings. Another way to make this point is to say that the doctrine of providence is a very general claim that is meant to apply to *any* account of states of affairs or events that crop up. It is logically compatible with virtually any account you can imagine. This is exactly the strength of a doctrine of providence. It says that God is at work in the unlikeliest of processes, events, and people. God is not absent; God is intimately present whatever it may appear on the surface. For this reason, it can appear vacuous on the surface. Its strength is precisely its comprehensive reach so that believers can rely on God whatever happens.

Part of our difficulty with results of scientific inquiry may well be due to our loss of a doctrine of providence. The medieval and Reformation world was much more ready to speak of providence than we are. Johann Quenstedt (1617–88), a great Lutheran theologian, saw God's providence at work in a threefold way which dovetails with the central points made above about providence. We have: divine conservation and preservation of creation; God working concursively in and through natural causes; and God's active rule or governance of creation with respect to evil represented by: God's permitting evil; God's preventing evil; God's directing evil; and God's setting limits to evil. Beyond that, Quenstedt distinguished between ordinary providence, when God acts within the context and laws of nature, and extraordinary providence, when God in acting sets aside the laws of nature. The issue at stake in a doctrine of providence is simple: God provides for creation at every level, that is, at the level of sub-atomic, atomic, biological, up through the whole chain of existence, through humans, up to departed pilgrims, and right up to angels and archangels. The claim is general but it is not at all vacuous. God is actively involved to ensure the welfare of everything and everybody. "The very hairs of your head are numbered."[4] There is silence, however, on the exact sub-acts that make up the master act of providence.

Another way to put this is to say God works through what we call natural and human events and actions. This claim is kept at a respectable level of generality. Taken up in the arena of divine action in nature, it is enough to say that God preserves and sustains creation either in terms of sustaining the laws that govern its regular behavior or in terms of sustaining a host of enduring entities and the properties that constitute their identity. It is tempting to go beyond this specification and look for something more basic in terms of divine action. So, we look for some broader notion of divine action. There is nothing broader or deeper than God sustaining the world as a continuous basic action. Think of a singer sustaining the melody of a song and repeating it without interruption. So, God sustains the changes in the seasons year in and year out. It is also tempting to look for a gap between the divine action of sustaining and the operation, say, of the law of gravity. So, we posit some kind of causal joint; but there can be no causal joint in the case of basic activity of God like this.

The causal relation can be stated in terms of a simple conditional proposition: if God stopped breathing, the whole universe would fall apart. However, this formal account does not get us very far. We are constantly baffled when we try to work out what God is doing in providence; we readily reach for analogies that capture the unfathomable gap between what God knows and does and what we know and do.

> To the minnow every cranny and pebble and quality and accident of its little native creek may have become familiar; but does the minnow understand the ocean tides and periodic currents, the trade winds, and monsoons, and moon's eclipses; by all which the condition of its little creek is regulated, and may, from time to time (unmiraculously enough), be quite overset and reversed? Such a minnow is man: his creek the planet earth; his ocean the immeasurable All; his monsoons and periodic currents the mysterious course of Providence through aeons of aeons.[5]

If we took this too much to heart, then we would be tempted to stop our discussion right now. Yet this is too easy a way out. So, let's take a closer look at a hard case, that is, a case where God works through human evil. The matter can be nicely identified by referring to one of the favorite examples that shows

---

[4] Luke 12:7.   [5] Thomas Carlyle, quoted in Tillett, *Providence, Prayer, and Power*, 50.

up in discussions of providence: the Joseph narratives. I shall supplement this material with other familiar material.

On the one side: Joseph's brothers engage in acts of premeditated, deliberate, cunningly devised evil. They sin; and they sin deliberately. On the other side: God works through their evil to do good. "But Joseph said to them, 'Fear not, for am I in the place of God? As for you, you meant evil against me; but God meant it for good, to bring it about that many people should be kept alive, as they are today.'"[6] We have here a divine–human synergism which cries out for analysis and attention. In this synergism, you have two distinct elements working together. On the one hand, there is a commitment to the claims of full-blooded human action. You have the deliberate choosing and carrying out of human actions, actions that in this case are evil. On the other hand, there is a commitment to the claim that God is at work in, with, and through those same evil acts for the furtherance of human welfare.

Is there a way to unpack how God works so as to make sense of the kind of paradox I have just identified? Of course, in doing so we move in fear and trembling, for there is an air of comedy in trying to fine-tune the details of God's acting in the world to achieve his purposes. Let's begin by distinguishing between three different ways in which we might think of God's role in controlling events in the world.[7] We can think of three ways in which God might exercise power in the world. An agent controls an event *in the weak sense* if and only if (i) the agent does not bring about the event at all, but (ii) the agent could still have prevented the occurrence of the event. An agent controls an event *in the strong sense* if and only if (i) the agent brings about the event (ii) without the independent contribution of any other agents, and (iii) the agent could have prevented the occurrence of the event. An agent controls an event *in the middle sense* if and only if (i) the agent cooperates with another agent in bringing about the event, and (ii) the agent could have prevented the occurrence of the event.

These options suggest three different theories of providence: a Weak Theory of providence, a Strong Theory of providence, and a Middle Theory of providence. The really interesting options are the second and the third. The first (the Weak Theory) is coherent and possible, but it bears its main objection on its face: there is no real action of God in bringing about the event that is seen as subject to providence. Hence, it does not come close to tackling the kind of providential events that are common in the tradition. All we have is the bare possibility of God being in a position to prevent the

---

[6] Genesis 50:19.

[7] I follow here initially a suggestion by Scott A. Davison in "Divine Providence and Human Freedom," in Michael J. Murray, ed., *Reason for Hope Within* (Grand Rapids, MI: Eerdmans, 1999), 223.

occurrence of the event. This applies to all events in the world, so it does not help us to identify those events we demarcate as providential.

It is not clear if anyone has ever really held to the Strong Theory. However, we can catch glimpses of it at times in John Calvin (1509–64). Consider the following quotation.

> From furthest eternity, [God] ruled on what he should do, according to his own wisdom, and now by his power, he carries out what he decided then. So we maintain that, by his providence, not only heaven and earth and all inanimate things, but also the minds and wills of men are controlled in such a way that they move precisely in the course he has destined.[8]

This is clearly a very robust account of God's control over all events. Immediately folk object that this leaves no room for human freedom. Does this not make human agents into puppets? Calvin would disagree. He held the view that free human actions are not uncaused acts or undetermined events; indeed, if they were free in that sense, they would be chance events, they would be mere bolts from the blue; and no one could be held responsible for them. Free acts are voluntary acts. The mark of free acts is not that they are uncaused; rather they are caused by internal factors working within the agent, namely the agent's motives, desires, beliefs, dispositions, and the like. There are unfree acts, that is, acts that are brought about by coercion. In this case the cause lies outside the agent, and we do not hold folk responsible for such acts. However, what really matters is voluntary acts, acts where the causes lie within us, and these acts are determined. Hence determinism is compatible with genuine freedom. Applied to the issue in hand, agents act voluntarily; they act according to their desires and wishes; hence they are genuinely free. God also controls the minds and will of agents, but all that is needed for freedom is that agents act voluntarily according to their desires and wishes.[9] Their own passions, wishes, desires, and the like, motivate human agents; hence they are free, even though God controls in the strong sense.[10]

This view is making a comeback in both popular and academic circles. Perhaps it is the majority report in Western Christianity. The deep problem with the Strong Theory of providence is that it is not clear how genuinely free acts can be both determined by God and really free at the same time. If God really controls our minds and wills, then we have a form of hidden, "external"

---

[8] Quoted in ibid., 224. Book I, chap. xvi of Calvin's *Institutes* is devoted to a discussion of providence.

[9] Philosophically this is sometimes referred to as the compatibilist account of freedom and determinism; it is also sometimes referred to as soft determinism.

[10] This position also generally involves a robust conception of God's foreknowledge. God knows the future because he has determined the future from the outset of all creation in the way a teacher would know the questions on the final exam because she has already set the questions and she alone sets the questions.

coercion. The issue here is not whether we are puppets. We grant all the inner workings of desires, passions, acts of will, and the like, as essential to this position. The problem is that God minutely controls all of these. Hence the human agent is really a sideshow; the idea of the human agent is evacuated of real content.[11] If God is this deeply involved in the internal causes, then God is responsible for sin. God is the deep cause behind all human action, including sinful human action. Moreover, it is hard to see how there could be any evil at all in the world, if this account of the divine–human relation were to hold. All God has to do to change things from evil to good is to rework the inner causes so that evil is prevented and good is done. If God can really do this, then he can totally change the world and always bring about good without destroying freedom.[12]

Can the Middle Theory provide us with a better alternative? The crucial claim here is that God cooperates with other agents in bringing about events in the world. Obviously, the critical issue here is how we are going to spell out what is involved in God cooperating with other agents.[13] We can clearly think of a greater or lesser degree of cooperation. Cooperation could be either general or specific. Suppose you are fixing your car next door. I could cooperate with you in supplying you with electricity for your tools; or I could cooperate by helping you put in a new engine. So we can imagine God being involved in your performing various acts or projects in both ways. God might provide some background circumstances in which you can flourish in becoming a nurse or an architect by guiding your favored uncle or aunt to give needed funding. Or God might arrange for you to meet an expert nurse or

---

[11] No doubt some will want to add that evil and sin are nothing, deploying the notion of evil as the privation of the good.

[12] We begin to touch at this point some very deep issues in the metaphysics of human action that are best taken up in another venue, that is, a chapter in volume IV. I want to record, however, how much I admire the ingenuity that Calvinists and some Thomists have displayed in their defense of a strong theory of providence. Any deep analysis will have to tackle the following: (i) the clear and vehement rejection of any claim that God is the author of evil; (ii) the important distinction between the capacity to perform an action and the actual performance of an action; (iii) the adoption of a notion of "premotion" or "concurrent" divine action to bridge the gap between capacity and performance; (iv) the effort to sustain a strong doctrine of human responsibility for sin and evil; and (v) the extent to which the whole operation is governed by the desire to sustain a strong doctrine of grace. Francis Turretin's carefully worked out position is an intellectual marvel, deserving of our highest respect. See his *Institutes of Elenctic Theology*, vol. 1, ed. James T. Dennison, Jr. (Phillipsburg, NJ: Presbyterian and Reformed Publishing Company, 1992), 489–538. At times, I think that some of the differences are merely verbal; or that they are embedded in wider theories, say, of divine simplicity and immutability, that are the real bone of contention. At other times, I find this whole way of thinking so morally otiose and unworthy of God that I simply lose patience with its nooks and crannies.

[13] I shall assume here that God has genuine foreknowledge of what humans can freely do in acting, what humans would freely do under various conditions (the counterfactuals of freedom), and what they will in fact do in acting. Knowledge of the counterfactuals of freedom is often referred to as middle knowledge, following the suggestions of Louis de Molina (1535–1600). I am rejecting Calvin's view that God knows the future only because God has foreordained the future.

architect just at the moment when you are having a blockage in understanding a crucial idea or working out a crucial practice. These suggestions will work fine in unpacking the possibility of God working through the good actions of others. Surely God can do all sorts of nudging towards the execution of good actions voluntarily undertaken.

Can we apply this in the case where God might be involved in the evil acts or projects of others? Here it is helpful at this point to add a further factor in thinking about intentions. I can have an intention, say, to do evil, but I can execute that intention in a great variety of ways. So if, in a fit of jealousy, I decide to hit out at you, I can do that in many ways. I might spread rumors about your good name; or I might snub you at a party; or I might let down your car tires when you are visiting some friends. There is generally a host of ways I can carry out my intentions and projects. This provides for a whole range of possibilities, some of which, if carried out, might fit better with God's intentions and projects than others. So maybe God intervenes, nudging us when it fits his good purposes when we choose evil to express our evil intentions in one way rather than in another way.

Consider the following scenario. When I was a student, there was a group called the People's Democracy in my university in Belfast whose aim was to bring down the government, unite the working classes, and start a socialist revolution. One of their strategies was to hold marches in Belfast in order to provoke the authorities and destabilize what civil order there was. The hope was that this would pave the way for the uniting of the Protestant and Roman Catholic working classes and help create conditions for revolution. Endless debates were held in the student union to get various marches off the ground. All students were invited whatever their allegiance, and, since this was a People's Democracy, everybody could vote. I made a point of going to these meetings, even though I thought the whole thing was a dangerous farce and a sham. I was very careful to use my vote. We would first vote for or against a march. I voted against it on the grounds that these marches were generally occasions for riots where people were badly injured. Having lost that vote, I would then vote for the proposal that the march be held at 2.00 p.m. rather than 5.00 p.m. The earlier march would be much less likely be violent than a later march. In the later case shipyard workers, keen on confrontation with what they saw as elitist, lazy students, would be leaving work and would be very tempted to become violent. While I disagreed all down the line with the intentions behind these acts and the values on which they were based, I did not withdraw from the situation but did all I could to steer them in a direction that would do the least harm. I would use my vote for the earlier time, and as many others did the same, we sometimes prevailed.[14]

---

[14] A fascinating biblical example is given in the case of the choice of Saul to be the first king of Israel. God tries to persuade the people that having a king will cause all sorts of problems for

How might we think of this as applied to providence? Consider again the story of Joseph. At the end of it we find this fascinating remark: "You meant it for evil; but God meant it for good." Here is how we might construe it. In response to Joseph's arrogance, his brothers develop jealous attitudes and decide to take action against him. They can express their jealousy against him in any number of ways. Initially they decide to kill him. One of them, however, makes a different suggestion. Why not sell him into slavery instead? The others agree, happy that their jealousy has found an appropriate expression. What if this option better suited God's long-term plans? Suppose it does. Then God nudges them to take this option rather than the first option, paving the way for greater good in the years beyond in Egypt.

Or consider the story of Pharaoh. Pharaoh deliberately rejects and withstands the proposal to release the Israelites. He hardens himself against the Israelites. He insists, like most tyrants, that he runs the universe, and that he can do what he likes with his slaves. This prompts God to enter into a show of strength against Pharaoh and the Egyptian pantheon of deities in order both to free the Israelites and to show who truly is lord of the universe. Moreover, to do this in a dramatic and memorable way, God acts to give Pharaoh what he wants, namely, a hard heart, a heart of steel that is not going to give in to some upstart deity who has supposedly appointed Moses and plans to deprive him of his labor supply. Hence Pharaoh holds out longer than he might otherwise have done so that there can be a full display of divine power and grace acting on behalf of the undeserving Israelites. Indeed, God keeps Pharaoh alive precisely because in and through his stubbornness, God's mighty acts can be all the more visible.

> By now I could have stretched out my hand and struck you and your people with plague, and you would have been obliterated from the earth. However, I have let you live for this purpose: to show my power and to make my name known in all the earth. You are still acting arrogantly against my people by not letting them go.[15]

So, providence involves God cooperating with Pharaoh in his hardness, giving Pharaoh what he wants, keeping him alive, and then using his continued existence and his persistent and divinely assisted hardness to display his complete lordship over the whole Egyptian pantheon of deities.

Or consider the action of Judas in betraying Jesus. Judas decides he has been a fool in following Jesus, that Jesus must be opposed, so he makes a free decision to betray Jesus. This still leaves open how and where and when he will betray Jesus. Hence God could cause Judas to act at a time that would best

---

them. When this fails, God insists on staying the course and choosing Saul as their king. See 1 Samuel, chapters 8–9.

[15] Exodus 9:13–17.

bring out the deep meaning of the death of Jesus. Hence the timing of the death of Jesus would be associated with the temple sacrifices, which in turn would bring home the sacrificial character of the death of Jesus for the sins of the world. So Peter boldly says:

> This Jesus of Nazareth was a man pointed out to you by God with miracles, wonders, and signs that God did among you through him, just as you yourselves know. Though he was delivered up according to God's determined plan and foreknowledge, you used lawless people to nail him to a cross and kill him.[16]

In all of these cases we have the following combination of actions. Human agents freely decide to act in an evil manner and are allowed by God to carry out their evil intentions. The evil intentions can be expressed in a variety of ways, all of which are generally satisfactory to the human agents involved. God intervenes at crucial points to steer the expression of the evil acts in ways that can be woven into a wider network of events and actions that fit God's good purposes for the world. Throughout God acts only to bring about good.

This approach to providence in our lives strikes me as offering an entirely coherent set of propositions. We see God as deeply involved in the warp and woof of human history. This is not a God who stands aloof from human evil or a God who is intimidated by human evil; rather it is the picture of a persistent, compassionate, ingenious God who steps into the details of human history to constantly bring good out of evil.

Folk naturally worry that this provides a picture of a God who is too involved in human affairs. We prefer to stay silent; I understand this; in most cases of special providence, it is best to quietly ponder these matters in our hearts. Certainly, there is no need for God to act in this manner; we can be left to proceed in our merry sinful ways; divine permission to do evil may be perfectly adequate to suit God's overall purposes. Even with this qualification, some think that this whole operation makes God just one more agent operating alongside other agents in the universe and reach for their metaphysical rifles. Unfortunately for them, there are no bullets available; once we recall the crucial distinction between Creator and creature, this standard objection evaporates. Our option shows that God is extraordinarily ingenious. The wicked do not have the last word, as if they can thumb their noses at God on their way to their funerals and insist that they alone are in ultimate control. Even their last act of rebellion does not fall outside the divine capacity to bring good out of evil. So, this feature of the theory is surely an advantage rather than a disadvantage.

This vision of providence also insists that God is totally committed to bring good out of everything, and this, surely, manifests a God of unsurpassing

---

[16] Acts 2:22–3.

goodness. Yet it is hard to find a conception of power that does not contaminate our vision of providence. Recall that the first element in the concept of providence is that of the active power of God at work in the world. God's own action in history has to clean up our misuse of power, if we are to understand the love of God displayed in providence.

Here is why this is the case. We are used to the abuse of power even when it comes to acts of great generosity. We worry that below the surface we may be subject to manipulation; or we suspect that there are hidden motives that undercut the generosity on display; we may even resent that we are dependent on the generosity of others. This attitude can crop up in our attitude to God, even though we would not openly confess it. Austin Farrer captures this in his inimitable way.

> We have so mishandled the scepter of God which we have usurped, we have played providence so tyrannically to one another, that we are made incapable of an almighty kindness. Are not his making hands always upon us, do we draw a single breath but by his mercy, has not he given us one another and the world to delight us, and kindled our eyes with a divine intelligence? Yet all his dear and infinite kindness is lost behind the mask of power. Overwhelmed by omnipotence, we miss the heart of love. How can I matter to him? we say. It makes no sense; he has the world and even that he does not need. It is folly even to imagine him like myself, to credit him with eyes into which I could ever look, a heart that could ever beat for my sorrows or joys, a hand that he could hold out to me. For even if the childish picture be allowed, that hand must be cupped to hold the universe and I am a speck of star-dust of the world.

I noted earlier that in coming to understand providence we come to appreciate a concept that draws on the wider resources of Christian teaching. Farrer implicitly registers this when he follows up his skeptical questions with a telling comment about the incarnation.

> Yet Mary holds her finger out, and a divine hand closes on it. The maker of the world is born a begging child; he begs for milk, and does not know that it is milk for which he begs. We will not lift our hand to pull the love of God down to us, but he lifts his hands to pull human compassion down upon his cradle. So the weakness of God proves stronger than men, and the folly of God proves wiser than men. Love is the strongest instrument of omnipotence for accomplishing those tasks he cares most dearly to perform, and this is how he brings his love to bear on human pride—by weakness not by strength, by need and not by bounty.[17]

If we are to think aright about providence, then our conceptions of power have to be transfigured. Happily, they are transfigured when we reach for the full wealth of divine action showered upon us in the Son and in the Holy Spirit.

---

[17] Austin Farrer, *A Faith of Our Own* (Cleveland, OH: World Publishing Company, 1960), 41–2.

11

Human Agents Made in
the Image of God

So God created humankind in his image, in the image of God he created
them; male and female he created them.

Genesis 1:27.

Doing systematic theology is like rearing teenagers; they quickly grow out of
control; and they bring home friends who want to settle into the spare
bedroom. Changing the metaphor, doing systematic theology is like building
a house. You can begin with a basic and simple structure but, as time passes
and it changes hands, people are constantly building new rooms. They knock
out old walls and extend the living space. They bring in all sorts of exotic
furniture. Originally theology concentrated simply on God, especially on the
doctrine of the Trinity. However, over the years, theologians expanded the list
of topics, and very naturally so. Once you speak of God, you will speak not just
of the Trinity, but of creation, and once you mention creation, you will find
yourself dealing with providence. Then you realize there is something special
about human agents, their glory and their alienation from God, so you have to
take a step back and deal with the place of human agents in creation.

The doctrine of human nature has over the last century or so been
upgraded to include a wide variety of topics. Thus, theologians have looked
for fresh sources in the natural and social sciences; most recently there has
been a flurry of material on gender studies and disability studies. All the
while, philosophers have come bearing all sorts of gifts for sale; they are not
at knock-down prices for the consequences can mean lots of overtime pay.
As a result, theologians now find themselves between a rock and a hard place.
On the one hand, our theology looks terribly thin and emaciated if we stick
to, say, creation and sin. On the other hand, we look as if we are operating
without a license if we try and cover the whole range of topics that crop up.
The solution is simple: give up on the hard place and return to the rock. By
that I mean that the systematic theologian should stick to the two critical
themes of creation and sin. The rest can be shunted off into work in

philosophical psychology and theological anthropology.[1] The full range of topics now under review can come later, as time and talent allow. The first order of business both logically and temporally is to sort through the issues of creation and sin.

Why should we do this? Is it simply a matter of economy and convenience? Let me give two reasons for this decision.

First, we need to speak of creation and sin because this is precisely what Christian disciples need on the other side of conversion and baptism. These are the primary matters that need attention and that take precedence over everything else we should say. Indeed, anything else we say should be compatible with these two bedrock themes. Many modern Christians are disoriented because they muddle around without ever really coming to terms with these matters. As a result, the evangelistic work of the church can be very ephemeral.

Second, we focus on the image of God and the fall because this is precisely what we need to do to fulfill the soteriological intention of that heritage. The canonical heritage does not pretend to offer a rigorous philosophical or scientific account of the human person, although it invites us to explore a full ontology of the human person and therefore calls us to explore scientific and philosophical accounts of the human person.[2] What the canonical heritage does is to mediate salvation. In order to make best sense of salvation we need to know something about creation and sin as that pertains to the human situation.

Put another way, we might say that the canonical traditions require us to make certain references about the ultimate ontology or metaphysics of the human person but they do not dwell on this as an interest of the first degree. They do not offer, for example, any kind of detailed solution to the mind–body problem, yet they entail a position on this issue that is *prima facie* incompatible with certain solutions to the mind–body problem, for example, a thoroughly deterministic or materialistic account of the human person. Of course, there will also be opposition to purely idealist conception of the person, but outside of some declining Process traditions, that is not really a live worry for our times. We might even go so far as to say that the material bequeathed to us encourages Christian thinkers to work out an ontology of the human person, but any such account lies at the periphery of systematic theology rather than at its core and center.[3]

---

[1] David Kelsey, *Eccentric Existence: A Theological Anthropology*, 2 vol. (Philadelphia, PA: Westminster John Knox Press, 2009).

[2] See for example: John W. Cooper, *Body, Soul and Life Everlasting* (Grand Rapids, MI: Eerdmans, 1989).

[3] Richard Swinburne's *The Evolution of the Soul* (Oxford: Clarendon Press, 1986) is a very extensive treatment of some of the philosophical issues.

What these preliminary arguments suggest is that we should begin once again by exploring the internal logic of the Christian tradition rather than by borrowing some kind of scientific or philosophical explanation or theory of human nature. Our primary task is to pull together in a composite judgment that account of human nature which best captures the complexities of the canonical tradition. This is not just procedurally correct; it is also a good way to begin addressing the issue of the truth of our doctrine of human nature. What the canonical traditions seek to offer is an illuminating account of the human situation and of our predicament as sinners before God. As we explore the tradition, we are exposed to a searching light that in its own way makes sense of our lives and of our journey away from and back to God. This means, however, that our exploration of human nature will inevitably take up our own person-relative observations and appropriation of material at the margins of systematic theology.

Two further comments are in order before we go any further. First, the tradition has been extremely reticent to canonize any one detailed account of human nature. There is nothing equivalent to, say, the doctrine of the Trinity with respect to the nature of God. We can see a parallel with the doctrine of the atonement. Christian theologians were not diffident about atonement but they did not overcommit themselves in this arena.[4] Of course, major efforts were made, not least at the provincial Council of Orange in 529, to give a privileged position to Augustine on free will and grace. These notions carried with them complex and highly influential doctrines of human nature. Happily, these efforts failed to be taken to an ecumenical level, even though Western theologians have acted as if Augustine's views were canonical. Thus, they have ignored or neglected the very important insights of Irenaeus, the Cappadocians, and Symeon the New Theologian. This was a very serious mistake that has cost us dearly in terms of the credibility of our doctrine of human nature and of sin.[5]

Second, in dealing with human nature we are not dealing with a set of issues that can be addressed in a neutral fashion. We are speaking about ourselves and about the people with whom we live and move and have our being. Austin Farrer captured the point inimitably in the following comment.

> Our valuations of personal being are doubtless a different thing from what that being actually is, but unless they are founded on what it is, and in some way correspond to what it is, then we err in the whole focus of our lives, and might as well never have been born. If after my death I pass into a world of clear

---

[4] However, this should not be pressed too far: the issue is covered to a lesser or greater degree throughout the history of Christian doctrine and exactly the same could be said of a whole range of Christian doctrine, such as salvation, ecclesiology, and eschatology.

[5] The issue here is the artificiality and oddity of the vision of human nature, agency, and action that eventually emerges.

knowledge, and the angels come to me and say: 'Look, this is what the persons were in themselves whom you handled thus and so in life,' and I look, and perceive that my handling of these persons was an ignoring of what they really were, I shall be heartbroken.[6]

Suppose the following. Harvey Magpie O'Reilly has spent his life in Hollywood as a movie mogul, making films that have garnered millions in his bank account. He has made and unmade careers in the film industry. Unfortunately, he has been a moral sleazebag. He has used his power to abuse scores of young women desperate to make a career as movie stars. From the beginning of his own career he has looked on people as mere configurations of sexual energy who existed to satisfy his sexual appetite. Suddenly he dies. He is met by an angel who in an instant shows him the glory of what it is to be made in the image of God. He is stunned to discover this about himself and about the women he has abused; his punishment was to have a year-long, three-hour seminar on the doctrine of human nature before proceeding to other more fateful experiences. I will return to the cultural background music behind a story like this at the very end. The point of this little morality tale is that our attitudes to others are determined to a great extent by our vision of what they are. To put the matter technically, attitudes have intentional objects; they are directed to features of the human agents we are and meet. This directness of our attitudes to others means that in this chapter I shall take time to indicate some of the consequences of the theological account I shall now offer in some detail. We shall discover that O'Reilly badly needed that year-long seminar.

In our account of human nature, I shall first comment on how to think in very general terms about what it is to be made in the image of God. I shall then develop a rich account of what it is to be a human agent; then, with that in place, I shall identify those features that may be singled out as capturing what it is to be made in the image of God. So, there are four items up ahead in this order: an initial account of the language of imaging the divine, a broad description of human nature, a focused analysis of what it means to be made in the image of God, and a final section on the significance of my account for our treatment of others.

How are we to understand ourselves? What are we? "So God created humankind in his image; in the image of God he created them; male and female he created them."[7] The key to unpacking what is at stake here is to notice that there will be a material similarity between what we say about God and what we say about human beings and vice versa. This is an important methodological point. Drawing the lines of continuity is a delicate matter, but we need in the end to state as best we can in what way human beings

---

[6] Austin Farrer, *Reflective Faith: Essays in Philosophical Theology* (Eugene, OR: Wipf and Stock, 2012), 167.

[7] Genesis 1:27.

ontologically mirror God. In everyday language, for example, both God and human beings are conceived as personal agents.[8] This means that a fundamental analogue for God is that of the human person or the human agent. If we lose this connection, then the very meaning of our discourse about God collapses. The opposite also holds. A fundamental way of thinking of human persons is to see ourselves as mirrors of the agency of God. There is a dialectical and reciprocal relation between our vision of God and our vision of ourselves and vice versa. Thus, our vision of God as the Father of our Lord Jesus Christ cleanses and trumps our vision of human fathers, even though we rely on a certain vision of fatherhood to get an initial grip on our vision of God. We in no way mean here that God is just a bigger and better version of the human agent; nor that the human agent is simply a smaller and humbler version of the divine. Such moves deny the radical distinction that exists between the Creator and the creature. However, the claim I want to pursue is that there is a mirroring relation ontologically between God and ourselves. This is at the heart of being made in the image of God.

Let us now clear a space for getting to that goal by pausing and identifying the crucial factors that mark off persons from other elements in creation. I suggest that we should see the following network of ideas as pivotal in our understanding of what it is to be a person.

Persons are, first of all, agents. We are not simply an enduring succession of events or relations. Events and relations are episodic and derivative. Human agents are substances and continuants that transcend patterns of information, relations, and events; we possess a complex array of powers and capacities. We endure through space and time as centers of personal life and energy that are utterly unique and non-reducible. We are constituted by a mysterious unity and continuity that gives us identity over time. A person characteristically persists through time as a single person. We will change our physical bodies;[9] we become over time very different in our behavior, perspective, and moral outlook; we quite literally change our minds. Yet we remain recognizably the same person through all these changes. We are unique substances in the created order. We are not mere patients, or victims, or trousered apes, or complex configurations of physics and chemistry. We are mysterious personal agents. We are fearfully and wonderfully made.

---

[8] This insight is deeply ingrained in the tradition; it is so ingrained, in fact, that when a theologian says that God is not an agent, then that theologian has to provide a cogent and lengthy explanation for making such a move. So, if we think of God as Process, or the Absolute, or Being, or Ground of Being, or Pure Act, and so on, these notions come across as very odd indeed precisely because they either fudge on the concept of God as Agent, or they undercut the idea of God as Agent.

[9] We literally change all the cells in our bodies, including liver and brain, every six years.

Persons are, second, conscious, self-reflective agents. We possess some degree of intellectual awareness, including that kind of awareness we call self-consciousness. We are conscious self-reflective agents that operate in the realm of conscious thought rather than simply inbuilt instinct. We can think about thought itself, a capacity that leads not just to the existence of systematic theology but also opens up the whole world of philosophy, literature, history (and later psychology) that has been with us from the beginning of time. This feature about ourselves is something staggering and amazing. We are wonders of creation given to wondering about ourselves and about everything else round about us. Think of the beauty and marvel of historical investigation as integral to our understanding of ourselves. To be a human agent is something awesome and magnificent.

Persons are, third, embodied agents. We are from the earth. We are constituted in part by being of dust and ashes. We are from the earth and one day we give back our bodies to the earth. Even God does not escape this. God freely and fully comes to us embodied, not in the body of the world, but in the body of a person, Jesus Christ, who too gives over his body to be buried in the bowels of the earth. So, it is a gloriously good thing to be embodied, to inhabit a finite unit of physics and chemistry, exercising intimate control over a designated, personal unit of the universe.

Persons are, fourth, cognitive agents. As we are born and grow into maturity we find that we possess an astonishing array of cognitive capacities. We have sense organs that capture information from the world around us. Think of the extraordinary cognitive significance of sight, touch, smell, hearing, and taste. These sensory organs that we so readily take for granted are like thermometers. When functioning properly they record a vast range of data and information about the world round about us. We are amazing truth-detecting and truth-recording organisms that tap into the world around us and pick up intricate signals about what is happening. In addition, we have memory that mysteriously gives us access to the truth about the past. We have introspection so that we directly know what is going on inside our bodies, and hearts, and minds, and souls. Beyond that we have extraordinary powers of reason that go beyond the data received and enable us merely by thought to posit other potential truths about everything round about us. We invent over time the most intricate traditions of inquiry and investigation that extend our bedrock cognitive capacities into something utterly astonishing. Those same powers of reasons enable us to spot mistakes and false trails. So, we invent logic to codify and teach our best insights. Beyond that we have extraordinary powers of imagination that enable us to think up stories, myths, and fantasies, that are a delight, an endless source of satisfaction. Beyond that we have aesthetic capacities that enable us to recognize and appreciate beauty in all its fecundity and abundance. Beyond these capacities, we have a capacity to identify and grade things, events, actions, and behaviors according to certain values. We come into the world hardwired to perceive moral features of our lives and universe. We do not just desire, love, want, wish, dislike, abhor; we express in these emotions and dispositions deep valuations of the world; more formally we recognize good and evil. Properly functioning, we recognize good and evil, and we are drawn inwardly to the good and abhor the evil. So, we are amazing, superlative cognitive agents.

Persons are, fifth, moral agents. Persons are agents who actually perform actions and activities. We operate here both as individuals and as communities. We really are free to act or not to act. We can in a radical sense really do otherwise.[10] Personal actions are *sui generis*; they are not reducible to events and relations that are determined by prior causes. Actions are marked by unique forms of explanation. We explain actions not by citing the preceding events and laws governing them but by citing the relevant circumstances, beliefs, motives, goals, intentions, and purposes of the agent concerned. When we act, we characteristically act for certain purposes. Our actions express intentions that are intimately related to our desires and beliefs. Moreover, we explain or defend our actions by citing reasons and motives for our actions. It is a radical mistake to assimilate our explanations of actions to scientific explanations that would treat our motives and intentions as simply prior events and processes in a causal chain of events governed by law.[11] We really can do otherwise.

I have qualified the conception of freedom just enunciated because I think that there is a deeper freedom given to us as human agents, namely, the freedom to do things for the sheer hell of it, without there being any reasons involved. We might call this radical freedom. This freedom can be either positive or negative. In the positive case, we do good things just because we can do them. Thus, we can think of an act of sheer generosity that has no other reason than exercising the freedom to do so. The act is not rational in any normal sense of normal; the good undertaken is simply undertaken for its own sake. Equally, we can think of an act of radical evil in which there is no other intention than to do evil for its own sake; there are no considerations in play in terms of rational reasons or motives. This comes close, for example, to cases where individuals decide to invent their own lives as a sheer act of will without paying any attention to their place in the universe as created and redeemed by

---

[10] It is critical not to confuse this feature of our lives with bondage to sin. Even in our sin we make genuine decisions. So in an act of spite I can smear your good name or shun you in the hallway. In sinning we do not cease to be agents and become, say, stones. Luther would appear to have misled many at this point.

[11] We might capture this point by insisting that it is proper to speak, therefore, of persons as rational agents. This does not mean that human agents always act for reasons, or that when they do act rationally, they always act for good reasons. It simply means that one can always ask the question, "Why did you do that?" and always look for the citing of reasons as an answer to this question.

God. In fact, they see the whole theological enterprise as an effort to deprive them of their freedom to be whatever they decide or want to be. Their lives are like a novel that they construct rather than a broadly conceived plan given to them in creation. If they came to believe in God, this would be so intolerable that they would consider suicide. To be sure, all this is sheer illusion, for this choice in no way gives them the autonomy they crave; it simply postpones the discovery of their destiny as created by God. Yet we can surely make sense of this whole way of thinking and thus register a deeper notion of freedom than that governed by understanding and desire.

Thus, we rightly see ourselves as moral agents who can be held accountable for what we do. I do not hold my dog accountable for what it does. I do not hold my car accountable for what it does. We hold each other accountable for what we do. We reveal thereby that ontologically we belong to a wholly different order to the ordinary environment we inhabit. We are extraordinarily magnificent centers of energy and life. If we despise our free will, our capacity to act or refrain from various actions, we are self-deceived. If we see ourselves only and always as victims, we lose the precious agency given to us in creation.

Persons are, sixth, relational agents. We form friendships. We naturally come together in clans, in tribes, in nations, in ethnic groupings, in age groups, and in political communities that are deeply satisfying in themselves. We form clubs for any and every reason. Properly functioning, these are all great goods. We find deep satisfaction in belonging. We wither and suffer when we are isolated and neglected by others. The lack of bonding at birth between mother and child can be devastating. More particularly, for those called to holy matrimony, human agents come together to forms bonds that are the source of deep satisfaction and that are often the source of excruciating pain when they are ended or when they go horribly wrong. Those called to celibacy naturally seek out and become part of formal and informal communities that nurture their welfare as relational agents. We are loving agents. We are made by love and for love. If we despise our natural habitat as one of relationships and love, we deny a critical feature of our existence as made by God.

Persons are, seventh, spiritual agents or souls. We were made to know and love God. We are so designed that our best interests, our deepest welfare, and our fondest hopes are realized in and through a relation of love and trust towards the Triune God. We have the capacity to respond to God. While in the mercy of God we retain our agency as persons even when we rebel against God, outside of God we become in the end deformed and corrupt. We cease to function as we are meant to be. Rightly related to God we become fully and truly human. To be a soul is to be a unique and glorious reality in the order of creation.

Persons are, eighth, mortal agents. We are vulnerable. There are deep constraints built into the very order of our existence. Our minds and bodies are fragile, so they go wrong in all sorts of ways. We are delicate creatures subject to disease and malfunction. We suffer in a thousand and one ways. Our lives are often shot through with terrible tragedy and loss. We have no control over a host of matters. We have no control over our birth, or our parents, or our initial formation in families and societies. We have limited capacities that are irreducibly person-relative. Some cannot carry a tune; others cannot follow an argument; others have severe physical handicaps. We are critically dependent on others and on the environment round about us. We are subject to contingencies that can reduce us to vegetables over time or that can sweep us away in the twinkling of an eye. We are truly mortal; we all die. Some die young; others make it to a ripe old age; all of us die. We are mortal to the core. It is a good thing to live on this good earth for a finite limited time. While suffering is a problem for every theology and every worldview, this is no cause for lament about the ineradicable goodness related to being a mortal agent.

We now have a rich depiction and description of what it is to be human. We have critical information as we continue in our journey of faith. How do we pick out those features of human nature that reflect our being made in the image of God? In its original context, the claim that humans are made in the image of God is mentioned twice in Genesis 1:26–7. The intervening clause is instructive: "...let us them have dominion over the fish of the sea, and over the birds of the air, and over the cattle, and over all the wild animals of the earth, and over every creeping things that creeps upon the earth."[12] The natural reading of the text then is that the image of God is constituted by those capacities that enable human agents to exercise dominion. So, to be made in the image of God is to be precisely a personal agent that is conscious, cognitive, moral, relational, and spiritual. This is where we mirror the reality of God.

We differ from God in that we are embodied and mortal. There is no human agency without being embodied and mortal. Clearly, even when God becomes embodied and mortal in the person of His Son, God is not essentially embodied or mortal. God would still be essentially all that God is without becoming incarnate in Jesus of Nazareth. In contrast to this, we are essentially embodied and mortal; we would not be what we are if we were not embodied and mortal. Thus, there is a radical discontinuity ontologically between ourselves and God. However, there is also genuine continuity. God creates us with genuine personal agency to carry out the mandate given to us to exercise dominion within the created order.

What I have laid out as constituting what it is to be made in the image of God is what we might call the conceptual image of a person made in the image of God which is implicit in the Jewish and Christian traditions. This conceptual

---

[12] Genesis 1:26b.

image has informed our everyday understanding of ourselves over the centuries in the West and is embedded in many of our social situations, like our social relations, say between student and professor, between husband and wife, between judge and accused, and the like. It is a gift of divine revelation and of the church to civilization. However marred and impaired our enactment of this vision in the history of faith, it remains an intellectual and spiritual jewel that we neglect at our peril.

We feel very threatened when this vision is rejected or debased. We recoil when we are treated not as a personal agent, but as a consumer, or as cogs in the wheel, or as numbers in the system, or as a mere physical object, or as a mere higher primate, or as a mere patient, and the like. We do not always object if people view us along these lines for certain very limited purposes. We do not mind being seen as a door-stopper for a few minutes, but to be seen forever in these terms is dehumanizing. We prefer to see ourselves as active subjects, as persons who can really act in the world.

There is then available to us a very rich concept of ourselves as persons or personal agents. If we lose the Christian faith in our culture, then we are in danger of losing this deep notion of what it is to be a person. Of course, in the modern attack on the Gospel, many thought we could jettison this vision and substitute all sorts of secular conceptions of the person that would yield better goods in our personal and social lives. The track record over the last hundred years shows that these promises have turned out to be illusory. So, I repeat: this vision of human agents made in the image of God is an intellectual and spiritual jewel that we neglect at our peril. In so far as we lose or squander our theological heritage, we lose precisely this deep concept of the person.

We can put the matter simply. We are neither beasts nor angels; we are persons who as agents share in the very agency which God possesses and which God made manifest in the person of Jesus Christ in all its fullness in human history. We are not gods, but we are persons who are fundamentally god-like in nature. We are images and mirrors of the richness of divinity. This is the sober and wonderful reality we are. We are the climax of God's creation, planted as genuine agents in the midst of the world, endowed with conscience and reason, and appointed to make real decisions about our own lives, about our relationships with each other, about our relationship with the rest of creation, and above all, about our relationship with God, our merciful and all-good Creator and sustainer.

Much of this vision of the human person is beautifully captured in Genesis 1:26–7 and in the wonderful commentary on this in Psalm 8, when it is suggested that human beings are created and called upon to rule or have dominion. The context in Psalm 8 is a royal one. In remote parts of their domain, ancient Near Eastern kings would sometimes place a statue, an image of themselves, to represent their dominion. In Genesis, God appoints humans to be vice-regents. They are equipped to keep, control, and care for the earth.

To fulfill this vocation requires they be made in the image of God and that they be in action like God. The one sent to rule is to be like the one who sends. Their actions are to express the good purposes of God for all creation.

To be made in the image of God is to be like God in a rich variety of ways. Being made in the image and likeness of God is not just to share this or that attribute of God, say, the ability to think or to make moral judgments or to be self-conscious; it is to be like God in that human agents are persons. They are dynamic agents who are called to be God's vice-regents of creation. They are unique substances, persons, with unique forms of consciousness, cognitive capacity, moral sensibility, personal agency, relational integrity, and spiritual energy.

This vision of the human creature has significant implications; let me explore some of them if only briefly. First, the fact that humans are persons made in the image of God secures human rights. God saw humans as good. They have a right to life, to life-support, and security. Of course, such rights come with correlative duties. Moreover, we do not have a right to do wrong; wrongs are permitted; they are not mandated in the way that rights are. Ultimately, however we specify the relevant rights, they are undergirded by a robust vision of human agents made in the image of God. We can extend this line of thought into the political arena. Christians have been able to live in any and every form of political arrangement. Paul was so convinced of the dignity and importance of the political order in and of itself that he admonishes Christians in Rome to obey the Roman authorities even though he knew full well how brutal and inept they could be.[13] Yet it is no accident that Christians have been opposed to tyrannical regimes and have aided and abetted in the development of democracy. At the moment, it is fashionable in some circles to retreat into an adversarial relationship with our corporate, capitalist, democratic society. But even those who argue for an alternative in the name of socialism are quick to insist that they believe in democratic socialism. I understand the problems we have to face and the unique dangers that democracy brings with it. However, it is surely no accident that Christian nations have evolved towards democratic forms of government. Whatever their failings (and there are many), democratic forms of government give a dignity to human persons that fits nicely with our conception of human agents as made in the image of God. Certainly, our vision of the human person drives us out into the public square and encourages us to develop social, political, and financial institutions that have their own distinctive logic. There is such an entity as a Christian society as opposed to, say, a secular, or Islamic, or Buddhist society. It is the task of a robust political theology to spell out what that means.

---

[13] Romans 13.

Third, human beings are incurably religious. They are ineluctably drawn to God even when they reject God. Even in themselves, they sense the image of God. They have to be argued into atheism and secularism. They will become superstitious, polytheistic, idolatrous, and New-Agey, far more often than they will become skeptical and secular. This is why the continuation of religion and the revival of religion is such a puzzle to many secular intellectuals. Secularists and unbelievers often do not know what to do with the persistence of religion in North America and its extraordinary spread at present in the Third World.[14] But this should not in the least surprise us. We are made to know God. This is an ineradicable feature of human existence. We are incurably religious.

Fourth, human beings are inescapably creatures of hope. They are made for God so we cannot in this life kill their souls. Outside the terrible reality captured in the sin against the Holy Spirit, they are always capable of coming around, repenting, and returning to their proper vocation. That is why we can never give up on anyone. It is sin to give up hope, even though in reality we sometimes have to walk away from some people and shake the dust off our feet. When we are driven to despair, it is not our natural inclination. We are incurably creatures of hope, for we cannot eradicate our sense of agency without ceasing to be human.[15] That we again and again pin our hopes on illusory dreams and objects bears witness to our nature as creatures who are made to have a dignified place in the cosmic scheme of things.

Fifth, given that human beings are inescapably relational in orientation, loneliness, isolation, and distrust are deeply destructive. They kill the life of the spirit and destroy human community. Trust is an absolutely critical feature of human existence.[16] The loss of trust in contemporary society is a very unhappy development. Because of lack of trust we practice defensive medicine; we establish endless monitoring systems; we become swamped in oceans of paper that undercut the primacy of faith in other human agents. The consequences to these practices are real. We at once form and are formed by our relationships. We are persons, that is, unique agents who exist inescapably in a network of relationships with nature, with other human agents, with animals, and with God. Remove these and we die. Undermine them by destroying trust and we hurt. We cannot live outside these natural communities. They are the source of our deepest joy and our deepest pain.

---

[14] For a searing analysis of the ignorance and confusion involved see Lamin Sanneh, *Whose Religion is Christianity?* (Grand Rapids, MI: Eerdmans, 2003).

[15] For an extraordinary testimony to the resilience of human agents to withstand incredible degrees of domination see Maude Julien, *The Only Girl in the World: A Memoir* (London: Oneworld, 2018).

[16] See Onora O'Neill, *A Question of Trust: The BBC Reith Lectures, 2002* (Cambridge: Cambridge University Press, 2002).

Finally, human beings have dignity and honor. All of them have honor and dignity. They carry by design a weight of glory. They have weightiness and value. This is the deep ground for all opposition to abortion, racism, and sexism. These err by ignoring the primary and essential glory that everyone by nature possesses; they substitute biological realities as the essential reality. Racists treat a person in purely biological terms as designated, say, by skin color. Sexists reduce the person to genitalia. Abortionists treat the fetus as a mere physical appendage in the womb. In reality the fetus is not like a toenail or even like a delicate organ like the kidneys or the heart. The fetus is a new creation that already has a mother and father. To cast the issue as one of pro- or anti-choice is to set aside one of the critical issues at stake and reduce the fetus to a mere bundle of physics and chemistry. The language of choice is an ontological travesty at this point. The deep problem with racism, sexism, and abortion is the visions of the human agents at stake; they cut us down essentially to units of biology. Notice that in the cases of racism and sexism we do not allow ourselves the strategy of choice to evade what is at stake. No one will allow us to defend racism or sexism by retreating to the language of choice. "No, I am not for racism and sexism; I am simply pro-choice and want folk to have the right to decide for themselves on these deeply personal issues." We would not tolerate this kind of sophistry, once it is pointed out. Opposition to abortion, racism, and sexism is a seamless whole. They all deny that we are creatures made in the image of God.

It will not be easy to sustain a deep vision of human dignity, given the cultural climate as it relates to the place of the passions and sensuality in contemporary culture. Hume once noted that "reason is, and ought only to be, the slave of the passions, and can never pretend to any other office than to serve and obey them."[17] Modern philosophy has marginalized the potential consequences of this aphorism. Thus, it has quietly written out of its canon the work of the Marquis de Sade who took this theme and ran with it with gusto.[18]

More recent work has found a steadier voice in analysis and commentary. Consider in this context the telling phenomenological analysis of rape and pornography offered by Roger Scruton. It deserves to be quoted at length.

> Rape is a crime not because it involves force, but because it is a desecration, a spoiling and polluting of that which it is in a woman's nature to hold in reserve until it can be given freely. If sexual desire were merely the desire for sexual sensations, this ransacking of the body could not occur: to be raped would then be no worse than to be spat upon. It is precisely the existential seizure that

---

[17] David Hume, *A Treatise of Human Nature*, Book Two, Part 3, Section, 3.
[18] See Susan Neiman, *Evil in Modern Thought: An Alternative History of Modern Philosophy* (Princeton, NJ: Princeton University Press, 2004, 2015).

humiliates and destroys. For it is a kind of murder, a reducing of the embodied person to a corpse.[19]

Speaking of pornography, he writes:

The face is more or less ignored, and in any case is endowed with no personality and made party to no human dialogue. Only the sexual organs, construed not as agents but as patients, or rather impatients, carry the burden of contact. Sexual organs, unlike faces, can be treated as instruments; they are rival means to the common end of friction, and therefore essentially substitutable. Pornography refocuses desire, not on the other who is desired, but on the sexual act itself, viewed as a meeting of bodies. The intentionality of the sexual act, conceived in this disenchanted way, is radically changed. It ceases to be an expression of interpersonal longing, still less of the desire to hold, to possess, to be filled with love. It becomes a kind of sacrilege—a wiping away of freedom, personality and transcendence, to reveal the passionless contortions of what is merely flesh. Pornography is therefore functional in relation to a society of uncommitted partner-ships. It serves to desecrate and thereby neutralize our sense that the object of desire is made sacred and irreplaceable by our longing. By lifting the focus downwards, from the end to the means, from the object to the object, pornography diverts sexual feeling away from its normal course which is commitment, and empties it of its existential seriousness. Pornography is sex education for life, as it were.[20]

Scruton writes here as a philosopher not as a theologian. Yet he naturally reaches for language that is clearly religious in content. He speaks of desecration and sacrilege. Clearly, this cries out for a richer discourse that does not shy away from a vision of human dignity anchored in creation in the image of God.

Giving this amount space to sex in a chapter intended to bring out the marvel and glory of being made in the image of God may appear to be a wrong turn in the road at this point. I did promise earlier I would return to the behavior represented by Harvey Magpie O'Reilly; so, I can plead that at least I have fulfilled all righteousness on that front. The appearance of a wrong turn is, to be sure, an important half-truth; but who will deny that modernity and postmodernity have not taken us down this road with some enthusiasm. The church has across the years been acutely aware of the dangers that arise because of the varied passions and desires that are central to our existence. On the one hand, she has tended to overdo the warnings about sex. On the other hand, she has recognized the central place that sexual intimacy plays in procreation and as an image of the union between God and the human

---

[19] Roger Scruton, "Sacrilege and Sacrament," accessed September 8, 2007 at: <www.catholiceducation.org/articles/marriage/mf0081.htm>.
[20] Ibid.

creature. It is not easy to get the balance and good sense that is needed. Every student seems to know that the topic of sexuality has played a prominent role in theories of what has gone wrong in creation. Sin and sex have been like Siamese twins in the attention given to sin across the generations. I promise my readers that this will not be the case as I tackle the treatment of sin in the next leg of the journey.

12

Human Action in the Fall

The Lord saw that the wickedness of humankind was great on the earth, and that every inclination of the thoughts of their hearts was only evil continually.... Now the earth was corrupt in God's sight, and the earth was filled with violence. And God saw that the earth was corrupt; for all flesh had corrupted its ways upon the earth.

Genesis 6:5, 11–12.

It is often noted that the existence of evil can drive people to atheism; the reality of natural and moral evil is in fact generally taken to be the devastating argument against all forms of theism. It is the trump card in atheological apologetics. It is less often noted that taking evil seriously has been central in bringing a lot of people to faith. What struck me about Christianity when I took it seriously was that it looked on evil with radical honesty. The Scriptures from beginning to end are shot through with realism. As in the case of the history of Israel in the Old Testament, the pervasive presence of evil is recognized in all accounts of the history of the church. The core of salvation is located in an event of horrendous brutality, the crucifixion of Jesus; there is no effort to sugarcoat what happened. Human agents are depicted theologically as broken, wicked, diseased, contrary, nasty, and full of self-deception. Life as a whole is depicted as a drama between the forces of good and evil, of heaven and hell, of God and Satan, of creation and futility. Salvation is presented in terms of meeting this reality head on so that there is no cure without radical surgery made possible by the intervention of God. The Christian life is depicted as one long battle against evil that will only be fully consummated in the life to come. Sanctity has rarely been presented as cheap and easy; indeed, it has been reserved for the few; most of us manage at best to muddle through. Without the lavish mercy and loving-kindness of God we are doomed to death and disaster. Hence, one of the attractions of the Christian faith is precisely its radically authentic depiction of central features of human nature.

Because I have found this element in the Christian tradition very attractive, I have never been worried about the collapse of the popular or even vulgar version of original sin that was challenged in the nineteenth century. In fact, the church never canonized any specific doctrine of the fall or sin. Everybody in the faith accepted that human agents were sinful. In so far as there was a debate about how sin got started, there was a significant difference of opinion between the East and the West that got suppressed over time.[1] This was partly because of later divisions and partly because of the inevitable impact of Augustine on the West due to his sheer intellectual brilliance.

For the late Augustine, there was a fall to the bottom that was immediate and devastating for the future of the human race. Here is a splendid summary of the five elements in Augustine's doctrine of original sin.

> (1) The source of original sin is a *primal sin* in the Garden of Eden. (2) All human beings share in this sin because of our solidarity with Adam the progenitor of the race. (3) From birth, all human beings have *an inherited sin* (original sin itself), which comes in two forms: common guilt, and a constitutional fault of disordered desire and ignorance. (4) In addition, Augustine holds that the human race suffers a *penalty* of sin—human powers are weakened, and we will experience death. (5) Finally, Augustine speculates about how both sin and penalty are *transmitted* from generation to generation.[2]

Symeon the New Theologian took a very different line. We might summarize it graphically in this way. Adam and Eve were like immature teenagers. As soon as they got the keys to the car, the first thing they did was go out partying, get drunk, and then they had a spectacular crash on the way home. If only they had remembered the goodness and mercy of their parents, they would have come home, confessed to their stupidity and immaturity, and they could have started again. But they did not take that course. They gave in to their fears and their insecurities. They started lying, began making excuses, and multiplied their mistakes until they were in a hopeless mess. The effects of that mess then spread through the whole of creation and, in the end, we are in much the same boat that is depicted by Augustine.

Symeon's account of the response of creation to the sin of Adam is worth noting at this point.

> Therefore, indeed, when it saw him leave Paradise, all the created world which God had brought out of non-being into existence no longer wished to be subject to the transgressor. The sun did not want to shine by day, nor the moon by night, nor the stars to be seen by him. The springs or water did not want to well up for

---

[1] For a polemical but still useful treatment of the division see John S. Romanides, *The Ancestral Sin* (Ridgewood, NJ: Zephyr, 1998). For a very different account of the early tradition see Paula Fredriksen, *Sin: The Early History of an Idea* (Princeton, NJ: Princeton University Press, 2012). Chapter 3 provides a fascinating account of the differences between Origen and Augustine. For the longer background story see Gary A. Anderson, *Sin: A History* (New Haven, CT: Yale University Press, 2009).

[2] Jesse Couenhoven, "St. Augustine's Doctrine of Original Sin," *Augustinian Studies* 36 (2005), 359–96.

him, nor the rivers flow. The very air itself thought about contracting itself and not providing breath for the rebel. The wild beasts and all the animals of the earth saw him stripped of his former glory and, despising him, immediately turned savagely against him. The sky was moving as if to fall justly down on him, and the very earth would not endure bearing him upon its back.[3]

These classical accounts of the origin of sin represent exceptionally creative forms of Christian midrash on Genesis 3 that speak in a deep way to the human imagination. By midrash I mean here a reading that relocates the text in relation to other texts of Scripture and to life in order to expound a theological interpretation that serves symbolic and homiletical application.[4] They have survived in part because efforts at replacement are either commentary on them, and thus presuppose their content, or because such efforts fail to speak to the depths of human evil by focusing on this or that network of sins, say, violence or oppression, rather than on the reality of sin as embedded in the human condition.

Even so, the classical accounts have been subject to serious objections on various grounds. Thus, like literal readings of Genesis 1, they have been challenged on exegetical and historical grounds.[5] They have also involved theological interpretations of the nature of physical human death that do not fit our natural understanding of it as a constitutive element of human existence.[6] In addition, the standard account derived from Augustine involves claims about the transmission of sin and guilt from Adam and Eve that imply severe biological and moral difficulties. The bigger problem here is that Augustine and his disciples have tried to develop a detailed causal story of the origin of sin in Adam and Eve that would operate as quasi-historical and quasi-scientific explanations of evil. Once the classical accounts are re-read as creative Christian midrash, they can be shorn of the

---

[3] Symeon the New Theologian, *On the Mystical Life, The Ethical Discourses, Vol. 1: The Church and the Last Things* (Crestwood, NY: St. Vladimir's Seminary Press, 1995), 29. Emphasis as in the original.

[4] In reality it is a form of eisegesis rather than exegesis; however, such a reading practice is by no means arbitrary because it is a vehicle of significant and carefully pondered theological reflection. Clear witness of this is found in the extraordinary preaching one often finds in African-American churches.

[5] F. R. Tennant, *The Sources of the Doctrines of the Fall and Original Sin* (New York: Schocken Books, 1903) remains a classic treatment of some of the central issues involved.

[6] Theodore of Mopsuestia, a very important leader in the school of Antioch, rejected the common view that physical death was due to the sin of Adam. See Tennant, *The Sources of the Doctrines of the Fall and Original Sin*, 327. Paul's treatment of sin in Romans 5:12–21, where death is seen as the result of Adam's sin, represents a brilliant ad hominem argument where he and his readers assume a standard Jewish speculation about the meaning of the haggada involved. See Tennant, *The Sources of the Doctrines of the Fall and Original Sin*, 250–1. I have found that this text is pivotal in efforts to retain the view that physical death among humans is the result of the fall.

element of pseudo-history and pseudo-science and be received as deeply suggestive and even illuminating.[7]

In our current situation, we need to move beyond the classical accounts and immerse ourselves afresh in the extraordinary realism of the tradition, develop a really thick description of sin and evil, and articulate an ad hoc network of commentary that will give purchase to the need for salvation. This is the agenda I shall now attempt to execute in summary fashion.

Let me begin with a series of general platitudes.

First, in the explosion of theorizing about human nature we can readily detect the terrain on which we need to locate our doctrine of sin. A vision of sin is simply an attempt to diagnose what has gone wrong in the world. Indeed, the major visions of human nature that have surfaced across the centuries and exploded in the modern period consist broadly of the following elements. We have background beliefs about creation, a description of what is unique to being human, a diagnosis of what has gone wrong, a prescription for putting things right, a vision of the future, and a vision of ethics that fits all these elements when taken together.[8] What we have are competing theological and atheological narratives. Our doctrine of sin is simply the diagnostic element in each of these narratives. Of course, not everyone will speak of sin; but that is irrelevant. The critical issue is that we can readily identify the functional equivalent of sin when we plot the various options with care.

Consider the following list of options laid out in graphic summaries.

Think of three high-brow accounts. What does Freud suggest? Human agents are essentially a trinity of psychic energy systems: the ego, id, and superego. The real problem is sex and potty-training. An improper balance has developed between these energy systems due to early childhood development; the cure is psychoanalysis. What does Marx propose? Human agents are essentially workers. The problem with the world is unequal distribution of the means of production in capitalism; the solution is revolution. What about the claims of scientific humanism? Human agents are essentially rational animals with extraordinary intellectual capacities and ingenuity. The problem is ignorance; the solution is science, sociology, politics, and education.

---

[7] Thus, it is entirely appropriate to explore how far the notion of hereditary guilt makes sense given that human agents naturally belong in social units like nations or tribes that cannot be reduced to a collection of individuals. Equally interesting, it would be fruitful to explore how morally evil thoughts and dispositions might become inscribed in the brain, given the way in which mental activity can change the biochemistry of the brain. Thus, the plasticity of the brain opens up fascinating avenues of inquiry. However, these efforts must be supported by relevant warrants that genuinely secure the claims involved.

[8] I have adopted this schema from Leslie Stevenson, *Seven Theories of Human Nature* (Oxford: Oxford University Press, 1988). The latest edition of this text now has thirteen theories of human nature.

Now think of three low-brow accounts proposed by some popular television preachers. In the first, the picture of the human agent is that of an American who lives in Southern California. The problem is low self-esteem; the solution is pious, amateurish psychotherapy. Alternatively, the vision of human agents is that of an American who lives in Dallas at a time of economic depression. The fundamental problem is debt, shortage of money, sickness, and despair; the solution is God's guarantee of health and wealth. Alternatively, the picture of the human agent is that of an American overwhelmed by anxiety and spiritual emptiness. The critical need is to find daily inspiration to lead a purposeful life; the solution is to find a way in Jesus to find a better you. We need thirty thoughts for victorious living.

The point is obvious. Formally a doctrine of sin is initially an effort to chart what has gone wrong with the world. This is the intellectual domain that is in play.

Second, these doctrines are not scientific in any serious sense of that word. Here we shift to the epistemological. Theories of human nature are not provable in any obvious sense of the term.[9] Of course their adherents often claim scientific backing but this is an illusion. What we have are metanarratives of creation, freedom, fall, and redemption, or their functional, secular equivalents. In so far as there is evidence, the theory is radically underdetermined by the evidence. Most of the time we find ourselves drawn now to this or that way of locating what has gone wrong; we operate implicitly and informally. Those who have proposed fully scientific accounts as in the case, say, of Marx have turned out to be disastrous with millions of people ruined and killed. Indeed, the prevailing intellectual temptation is so to overreact to metanarratives that we deny that there is such a thing as human nature or a self.[10] Human agents are more like novels in which we invent ourselves as best we can. Perhaps we are really more like computer programs that are downloaded into the brain and that are enacted through various phases of our lives over time. But this is just one more metanarrative. It is one more vision of the human condition that in time will have to disclose the other elements of its wider narrative. The problem with modernity and postmodernity is that their

---

[9] We have gotten ourselves into a lot of trouble at this point by looking for kinds of explanations that are simply not available to us in this domain. Human action is not subject to the kind of scientific explanations that have been so successful at other levels of reality. Many a nasty revolution has been sold on the grounds that it embodies the rigors of natural science.

[10] One deep problem here is epistemological. The emotional fuel was the disappointment brought on by the failure of the epistemological perfectionism of many Enlightenment figures in their quest for genuine knowledge. The standard was set so high (geometry initially, and then Newtonian science, was often the paradigm) that, when other forms of knowledge did not meet this, then relativism became a live option. For a witty treatment of this and other related issues see David Stove, "Cole Porter and Karl Popper: The Jazz Age in the Philosophy of Science", in *Against the Idols of the Age*, ed. Roger Kimball (New Brunswick, NJ: Transaction Publishers, 1999), 3–32.

proponents have an inflated view of what kind of evidence is available. Modernity wanted scientific proof; no such proof is available; so postmodernists came along, became disillusioned modernists, and opted for a nihilistic, or a trivializing relativism, or updated versions of Marxism.

Third, the evidence for evil is all around us. Moral relativism is dead in the water after the terrorist attacks in New York that killed thousands of innocent people.[11] Even before that tragic incident, we were bombarded with catalogues of good and evil. We may disagree on the lists, but our public life drips with moralistic absolutes; and there is a price to pay if you disagree. In fact, all we need to get a vision of sin off the ground is to draw attention to common features of our daily lives. Women are brutally raped; children are abused; business leaders fiddle the books; sports stars resist drug tests; politicians buy their way into public office; clergy take advantage of vulnerable parishioners; terrorists deck themselves out in self-righteous moralism; police take bribes; mobsters take over communities; universities become party to intellectual vice. Consider the little things we do: we lock our doors at night; we take precautions in the evening in parking lots; we invent virus scanners; we carefully check the credentials of job applications even for theologians because they may have lied in their applications; we warn our children about talking to strangers. A doctrine of sin and the fall is a serious attempt to come to terms with such phenomena. The initial evidence for sin is all around us and within us. The challenge is to provide appropriate description and commentary.

Let me have a first shot at this target.

The tradition was right to turn to the early chapters of Genesis. This was a theological decision more than an exegetical decision, as the history of Jewish and modern Christian exegesis shows.[12] Theologians were trawling for helpful material that would fit the narrative of creation, freedom, fall, and redemption that was emerging in the creedal tradition. Clearly the early chapters of Genesis were a godsend. Indeed, the whole sweep of Genesis with its neat division between chapters 1–11 and 12–50 provided a splendid pattern of problem and solution that dovetailed with the quest for a vision of sin.

Genesis 1 provides the backdrop: God has created a good world with human agents as both the temporal and axial climax of God's handiwork. Chapter 2

---

[11] For a searing account of the moral outrage evoked by the attack on the Twin Towers see Tamer Elnoury and Kevin Maurer, *American Radical: Inside the World of an Undercover Muslim FBI Agent* (New York: Dutton, 2017).

[12] I find it interesting that the Jewish tradition—and indeed the Eastern Christian tradition—tend overall to develop a much more substantial account of human agency than has been common in Western Christianity, where doctrines of divine determinism constantly threaten to undermine this crucial feature of human existence. It is clear that this threat is in turn driven by worries about doctrines of grace that find it difficult to allow for a genuine human response to grace without falling into doctrines of merit that are unacceptable. This deeper worry will be taken up later in our work.

recapitulates in a new idiom the crucial place of human agents in the grand scheme of creation. It ends by posing a dramatic set of questions. How will these wonderful creatures (Adam and Eve) relate to God, to each other, and to the creation round about them? Chapter 3 reposes this question in terms of an alien agent (the serpent) who poses the dilemma in even starker terms. The dilemma is posed in an ascending progression of suspicion and innuendo. "Did God really say, 'You can't eat from any tree in the Garden'?" Clearly God may be something of a cosmic dictator setting up trivial tests that betray deeper and sinister intentions. Eve responds by exaggerating the command, adding the prohibition of touching to that of eating. Maybe God really is a cosmic spoilsport. The serpent seizes the opening. "No! You will not die." So God is a liar or he is incompetent. Do you really want to remain positively related to this kind of deity? And then the final blow: "In fact God knows that when you eat of it your eyes will be opened and you will be like God, knowing good and evil." The appeal now is positive. Disobeying God will lead to life not death; it will lead to immortality rather than mortality; it will take you out of this creaturely status and make you divine; it will take you out of ignorance into a knowledge of good and evil. It is not enough to trust God and obey God when he insists that a certain action is forbidden; we must have first-hand knowledge of good and evil. In the end, as Eve expresses the matter, disobedience and independence from God will bring true wisdom.

The ensuing material that runs from chapter 3 to the end of chapter 11 depicts a situation where things go from bad to worse, but where God's grace continues to operate in the midst of severe judgment. Von Rad's analysis is especially illuminating.

> The story of the Tower of Babel is therefore to be regarded as the end of the road upon which Israel stepped out with the Fall, and which led to more and more serious outbreaks of sin. The Fall, Cain, the Sons of Lamech, the marriages of the angels, the building of the Tower—these are the steps by which the Jahwist marked out the growth of sin. God punished these outbreaks of sin with increasingly severe judgments. Nevertheless there is also seen, mysteriously associated with this punishment, a saving and sustaining activity on the part of God which accompanied man.[13]

So, Adam and Eve are clothed; Cain is banished but protected; and the Flood was not the final end for there was a new beginning with Noah.

> Thus, along with acts of judgment, there always at the same time appeared a saving will of God—as sin waxed, grace waxed the more. At one point, however, this gracious protection, God's staying with those whom he punished, is absent: the story of the Tower of Babel ends without grace, and therefore, [as we have

---

[13] Gerhard von Rad, *Old Testament Theology, Volume I: The Theology of Israel's Traditions* (Louisville, KY: Westminster John Knox Press, 2001), 163.

already said] the main question which the primeval history raises for the reader is that of the further relationship of God to the nations. Is it now completely broken, and is God's grace finally exhausted? The primeval history gives no answer to this question (and how could it of itself have done so?). The answer to this most universal of all theological questions is given with the beginning of the saving history, the call of Abraham and Jahweh's plan for history indicated therein to bless "all the families of the earth through Abraham."[14]

Theologians, of course, have focused on the material in Genesis 3 as especially illuminating; and rightly so; they are engaging in a wider conversation than the one to which biblical theologians restrict themselves. Clearly the material in Genesis 3 is an extraordinary dialogue that explores certain fundamental features of the genesis of sin expressed in economical and figurative form. It is much too simple to say that sin arises because of a straightforward exercise of human freedom. So, we are often told that the meaning of the text is that we are given a choice between good and evil and it so happened that we just choose evil. This is much too superficial an account of the mystery of sin. The etiology of evil in human history begins with the entertaining of half-truths, with a hermeneutic of suspicion; it grows into radical falsehood and untruth; it morphs into distrust; it reaches a climax in disobedience. The pattern is simple: we are lured by half-truths and falsehoods about God, about ourselves, and about disobedience to God. This is the root of distrust. The fruit of distrust is disobedience and rebellion. This in turn leads to further denial, to illusion, to self-deception. We develop schemes of autonomy and self-justification that function as fig leaves to cover our guilt and our nakedness. Or we explore schemes of helplessness and victimhood that rob us our personhood and agency. These schemes lead us deeper and deeper into bondage, death, and destruction.

Aware of God, we resist relating to God because we think God is a cosmic spoilsport, a cop out to get us, or a dentist ready to drill before we get any anesthetic. We swing from thinking too highly of ourselves in pride to thinking too lowly of ourselves in false humility. The fundamental issue is theological: we yield to false views of God. We challenge the Word of God and consider the source as unreliable. This distorts our relationship with ourselves; we become inwardly disordered. We develop false views of ourselves. We see ourselves as autonomous little gods, rather than noble, dependent creatures. Or we see ourselves as pawns and victims thrown around by political or cosmic forces. These visions distort our relationships with others: the bonds of intimacy and trust are broken. Others are there to be used for our schemes and purposes; or others are seen as oppressors ready to tramp on us at every turn.

---

[14] Ibid., 163–4.

These visions in turn disrupt community, and they distort our relationship with nature and creation.

Now that we have gone that far, we develop a false view of sin. We think that sin will serve our welfare. We do not see sin as essentially destructive and deadly. We see it as something good for us; or we see it as something others do to us little poor innocents. We think that if we do not give in to sin, we will be missing out on "the good life"; or in despair we see no way out of the bondage inflicted on us by others. The judgment of sin is that we get further caught in sin. We become what we do. We become agents who turn in on ourselves and become slaves to our own choices and actions. These choices and actions lead to a whole round of characteristic vices, to a whole catalogue of sins with their own peculiar grammar.

We now have before us one way of exploring the nature of sin, that is, by means of a rich narrative of the origin of sin in human history and in our own lives as depicted in the saga of Adam and Eve. Consider quickly four ways of exploring sin that supplement this foundational strategy. First, we can explore sin by means of the many concepts that capture various dimensions of it. Here are a few: missing the mark, wandering from the path, straying from the fold, breaking the law of God, rejecting the covenant, and disrupting the harmony of creation. Sin is blindness to God, a hard heart, a stiff neck, hatred of the neighbor, transgression, moral folly, a disease of the soul, the destruction of shalom, the enemy of community, addiction to evil, and the breakdown of union with God. Sin is the war of the flesh against the spirit, the war of the passions against the mind, and the war of the demons against the good. Sin is weakness of will, the gap that exists between what we know to be right and what we actually do. Sin is a disfigurement of our nature; sin is not the way it is supposed to be.

Second, we can explore sin by drawing up lists of the manifestations of sin. The classical list of sins is to be found in the seven deadly sins: pride over against humility; greed over against generosity; envy over against love; anger over against kindness; lust over against self-control; gluttony over against temperance; sloth over against zeal. Nowadays we tend to gravitate towards lists of social, as opposed to personal sins: sexism, racism, injustice, exploitation, discrimination, bigotry, and intolerance. It would be helpful to have a list and analysis of, say, the seven deadly social sins.

Third, we can explore sin by trying to develop a hierarchy of sins where we identify paradigmatic sins and seek to subsume other sins under a single category. So, we can think of sin as pride, or as disordered desire, or as idolatry, or as the perversion of love, or as the murderous killing of character, or as selfishness, or as ingratitude. Hence we might develop an interrelated cluster of sins that provide a taxonomy of the sinful life.

Fourth, we can explore the nature of sin by way of the morphology of temptation developed in the ascetic and pietistic traditions of the church. John

Climacus in *The Ladder of Divine Ascent* gives the following anatomy of temptation.[15] Stage one is *provocation*: a quick thought to do a particular evil crosses the mind like lightning. Stage two is *coupling*: a conversation with the thought. Stage three is *assent*: agreement to act on the nudging or attraction that comes from the thought. Stage four is *captivity*: the thought becomes a mood that is frequently present in the mind, waiting for any opportunity for expression. Stage five is *passion* or addictive habit: the action becomes second nature, done now without premeditation. So, we move from thought, to recurrent entertainment, to determination to act, to act, to a series of acts, to a settled feature of one's character. Subsequently sin spreads like a virus. Think of the way hostility or gossip can become embedded in a community. Communities develop cultures; cultures develop into systems; and systems harden into regimes that are virtually impossible to eradicate. Clearly imitation and peer pressure play a part; but there is also an ineradicable element of freedom and a fatal bondage that readily becomes radical forms of corruption.

What might we say more formally at this point?

First, sin on this analysis is a redescription of human evil, so that human evil is cast in theological terms as ongoing disobedience to God originating in a pattern of intellectual suspicion and ending in a second nature of rebellion and blindness. The core originating cause of sin is distrust and unfaith. In speaking in this way, sin is not an explanation for evil; it is really a reconfiguration of evil within a much thicker description and analysis of human nature. Hence our proposal is decidedly deflationary compared to what was developed in traditional doctrines of original sin, say, in Augustine and its denial in Pelagius. We need to transcend this debate and reach for a richer and less restricted network of ideas. What we lose by way of explanation we gain by way of comprehensiveness and depth.

Second, sin is a radically contingent element in creation. It is not essential to the created order but arises as a contingent development that could have been otherwise. Sin need not be a permanent reality. Sin can be overcome; the disease can be cured. Third, sin is not just a collection of distinct sins but an underlying reality that is manifest in a multitude of various sins. Human agents do not simply commit sins; they become sinners. There is a dynamic process that has to be acknowledged and articulated. We develop a sinful nature. Fourth, sin is not a force set over against God ontologically. Sin is predicated of created agents who owe their existence, original and ongoing, to God. It is a secondary development that is permitted by God. Sin is not a reality found in its own right; it shows up in God's creatures that have been given genuine space by God to stand over against God; it involves the rejection

---

[15] John Climacus, *The Ladder of Divine Ascent* (Mahwah, NJ: Paulist Press, 1982).

of the good and therefore would not exist outside the existence of God's good creation.[16]

Fifth, sin does not undermine the fundamental goodness of the created order. Sin is nasty, destructive, pervasive, and deep; yet it cannot destroy the goodness of the human order that is built into creation and sustained by God. Humans in sinning become neither demons nor beasts; they retain their most fundamental nature as ontologically good creatures made in the image of God. Sixth, sin evokes the radical opposition of God in wrath and judgment. God is radically opposed to sin. God in judgment hands us over to our own passions and desires. This is not some fit of temper where God lashes out at us for what we have done. God's judgment is simply the full and unsullied expression of God's opposition to evil. A world without divine judgment would be a sorry place. If there is no divine judgment, then we will all have hell to pay for evil. The judgment of God over sin limits hell to those who systematically and resolutely refuse the goodness and kindness of God. This is often captured in the claim that we lose the likeness of God but not the image of God, where the theologian is taking a distinction without a difference and making money out of it theologically.

Seventh, while many of these sins are readily identified outside of faith, we know them best only through grace and divine revelation. We only know the depth of our predicament through inward grace and publicly transmitted divine revelation. Part of our predicament is our blindness, our ideological blinkers, and our self-deception. It is only grace and revelation that can expose the depths of sin and evil. It is revelation that shows not just the depths of sin but the breadth of sin. All of us have recapitulated the story of the fall. All of us have become what we do. Hence, all of us stand in the need of light, mercy, truth, forgiveness, and spiritual power. The reversal of this process is as complex as its genesis and development. The cure for sin depends on exposure to divine revelation, on repentance, on the rebuilding of trust, and on reunion with God. This is exactly the story of Genesis 12–50, beginning with Abram and working its way through the ancient patriarchs and on through the history of Israel. The full expression of this pattern is expressed in the coming of the full and final revelation of God in his Son. It is explored with great dexterity in varied contexts throughout the New Testament, and it is systematically but implicitly embodied in the catechetical practices of early Christianity.

It is common to accuse anyone who does not accept the standard Augustinian account of original sin of being soft on sin.[17] The standard line is that

---

[16] Here I come within striking distance of the doctrine of evil as the privation of the good but refuse to embrace it. For a fine treatment of this vision of evil see Kenneth R. Seeskin, "The Reality of Radical Evil," *Judaism* 28 (1980), 440–53.

[17] Even then, once one probes this objection, one finds that crucial elements in the Augustinian tradition have been quietly dropped. Thus, one rarely hears mention of his views on the transmission of sin through concupiscence and thus through sexual intercourse in which desire

one has become Pelagian or semi-Pelagian. Informed readers may have already whispered this to themselves as a way to outsource their theological investigation to a revered figure from the past. My aim, however, is to get beyond these hackneyed options and find a better way to think of the depths of human evil. I have resolutely insisted that we need a thick description of human sin, one that will be matched by the need for radical divine intervention on the part of the Son and the Holy Spirit. On that ground alone, I think my alternative account has much to commend it. In comparison with earlier accounts it is decidedly deflationary; but it is most certainly not thin or superficial.

However, the deepest objection to much traditional treatments of sin is that they do not go deep enough. They fail to come to terms with the reality of the demonic in treatments of human evil. This is a strange omission, given that the activity of Satan is all too readily and anachronistically read into the story of the fall in Genesis 3. To put this issue sharply, the standard doctrines of sin do not go all the way to the bottom; they do not reckon with the place of the demonic in accounts of the human predicament. The bottom is represented by the reality of demon possession.

In contrast to this, the canonical heritage of the church has a strange treasure hidden in its basement that is a severe embarrassment to the contemporary theologian, namely a robust commitment to the reality of the demonic.[18] This commitment shows up in straightforward acknowledgment to the devil and all his legions, in belief in the reality of powers and principalities, and in reference to the activity of fallen angels. It also shows up in the explicit practice of exorcism. There are various strategies for coping with this phenomenon. We can dismiss it straight off as superstition. We can treat it as an understandable part of a mythological or mytho-poetic worldview. We can treat specific instances of talk of the demonic as misdescriptions of phenomena that we would now treat as forms of mental illness. In most of these moves we can continue to speak of the demonic but recognize its rhetorical or metaphorical force. On this analysis, we continue to speak of the demonic but it is really a graphic way of driving home the pervasiveness and depth of evil in the world.

We need language of the demonic in cases of horrendous evil. Consider the following example, picked at random from a host that could be cited. In the

---

is directed at pleasure rather than God, or, his views on inherited guilt. Moreover, Augustine's views involve views of predestination that have proven to be morally otiose. I suspect that much belief in the modern period stemmed from problems in the details of Augustine's account of sin. For a famous case of rejection see John Rawls, *A Brief Inquiry into the Meaning of Sin and Faith, with "On Religion"*, ed. Thomas Nagel (Cambridge, MA: Harvard University Press, 2009).

[18] I shall take up this topic ontologically in greater depth in volume IV. For an interim treatment of this topic see my "Hope with a small 'h'," in Ingolf U. Dalferth and Marlene A. Block, eds., *Hope* (Tübingen: Mohr Siebeck, 2016), 331–45.

early 1980s Charles Ng and Leonard Lake became good friends and teamed up to live a life of brutal violence.[19] They would kidnap women, rape them, and keep them sealed in a little room in Wilysville, California. A series of hidden rooms were in fact built into the cabin system. Restraints were fixed to the walls, and the inner cell was wired for sound and fitted with a one-way mirror so they could observe at will. They videotaped some of their horrendous acts for their own records. Altogether, the bodies of seven men, three women, two baby boys, and forty-five pounds of bone fragments were recovered from in and around the cabin site. When they were finally finished with their captives, they would execute and bury them in shallow graves. The killings only came to an end through chance. Having broken the vice that they were using as a torture device, Lake and Ng drove into town to get a replacement. The clerk at the lumberyard spotted Ng trying to shoplift the vice and called the police. When they arrived, Ng had flown, but a trace on the car registration raised alarm, and a search of the trunk or boot of his car revealed an illegally silenced gun. Leonard Lake managed to commit suicide by cyanide pill while in police custody but Ng escaped to Canada where he shot a security guard and ended up in prison there in 1985. After much legal fighting and threats from the United States to Canada, he was finally deported on August 26, 1991 to stand trial. The legal bill to get him out of Canada was over 6.6 million dollars. Ng was a particularly cruel captor, preferring to beat women instead of rape them. He was sentenced to death, a verdict he continues to appeal. He is currently on death row in San Quentin State Prison. It is in cases like this that we readily reach for the language of the demonic. We can readily extend the terrain to cover instances of horrendous social or political evil.

However, we have to go deeper than this. There are manifestations of evil captured in the tradition and practice of the church that can no longer be swept aside as superstition or misdescriptions of natural phenomena. We need to speak directly and literally of the demonic, rather than simply treating such language as a metaphor for horrendous human evil. The phenomena are well documented. They recur across cultures. They do not fit our standard psychological and psychiatric taxonomies of mental illness or cognitive malfunction. They do fit paradigm cases of exorcism in the gospel records. They are inescapable if we move out of our parochial Western world and take seriously current developments in World Christianity. A number of significant psychiatrists, like Scott Peck, are prepared to take the demonic with radical seriousness.[20] And above all they are "curable" by the ministry of exorcism. For too long we have been captive to conventional naturalistic assumptions that

---

[19] There are several websites that tell the story that follows that are readily available on the Internet.

[20] M. Scott Peck, *Glimpses of the Devil: A Psychiatrist's Personal Account of Possession, Exorcism, and Redemption* (New York: Free Press, 2005).

exclude not just the demonic but other critical elements of Christian theology, including the very idea of divine agency. For too long we have done our theology in our armchairs and refused to explore the evidence that has emerged. For too long we have left this whole terrain to the Protestant underworld to sort out and exploit. My own considered judgment is that there are levels and agencies of evil that are genuinely demonic. It is right and proper that the Vatican now provides theological instruction and pastoral training in this terrain; this is a gift to the whole church of Christ.[21]

I understand the fear that this sort of talk evokes. We are sane, reasonable people. Being a robust theist, it will be said, is hard enough without having to take on board this kind of extra baggage. We have an appalling track record of mistakes where people have been misdiagnosed, ostracized, and even killed. We have next to no collaborative inquiry of the kind that will be needed to come to terms with what is at stake ontologically, theologically, or pastorally. There are ardent polemicists, Conservative and Liberal, who are ready to excoriate anyone who does not share their dogmatic convictions on the issue. However, our intellectual life cannot be governed by our fears. Moreover, at the heart of the Gospel is a victory over evil that knows no boundaries. We should explore the truth relentlessly; and there are times when the truth turns out to be far more complex and mysterious than we thought it was. Such is exactly my judgment in the case of the demonic. Agree or disagree, but let the evidence fall where it will.

Wherever we end up, we need a rich and robust vision of sin and evil. The comforting and plausible illusions of modernity are gone. The crowbar of terrorism has undone postmodernity, even though postmodernity will linger in the air indefinitely until the current generation gets bored with slogans and begins to do some serious philosophical reflection on what is at stake. We need a more robust vision of sin and evil for the times that lie ahead of us. Happily, there are more than enough resources in the Gospel to tackle any and every eventuality.

Ironically encountering the demonic provides its own measure of evidence for the truth of the Gospel. I mentioned at the outset the place of evil in bringing some to faith; it is fitting to take up this topic as I finish this chapter. Consider the remarkable comment of Lt.-Gen. Roméo Dallaire after his tour of duty with the United Nations Forces in Rwanda. Between April 1994 and July 1995 between half a million and a million Tutsi were massacred by members of the Hutu-led majority government. There were in the region of two million refugees as a result of the violence; many households were led by orphaned children. Many of the killings were carried out in churches; some Catholic nuns and priests were complicit in and took part in the preparation and

---

[21] For a historical overview see Francis Young, *A History of Exorcism in Catholic Christianity* (London: Palgrave Macmillan, 2015).

execution of the genocide. Dallaire was sent to intervene and save lives but failed to get the authorization from above that he needed. Thus, he was helpless in the face of the butchery that he witnessed. He wrote afterwards:

> After one of my many presentations following my return from Rwanda, a Canadian Forces padre asked me how, after what I had seen and experienced, I could still believe in God. I answered that I know there is a God because in Rwanda I shook hands with the devil. I have seen him, I have smelled him, and I have touched him. I know that the devil exists, and therefore I know there is a God. Peux ce que veux. Allons-y.[22]

We have here a remarkable argument for the existence of God that does not make it into the standard textbooks. However, our aim here is to engage in systematic theology; for the most part we can leave this little detour for further work in the epistemology of theology.

[22] Lt.-Gen. Roméo Dallaire, *Shake Hands with the Devil* (New York: Carroll and Graf, 2004), xxv.

13

The Church

Images, Origins, and Identity

> So then you are no longer strangers and aliens, but you are citizens with
> the saints and also members of the household of God, built upon the
> foundation of the apostles and prophets, with Christ Jesus himself as the
> chief cornerstone.
>
> Ephesians 2:19–20.

Contemporary Christians have come to look upon the church in a wide variety
of ways. Five images come to mind as competing snapshots of what the church
really is. Some see the church as a country club. It is a nice place to visit
regularly. It has a loyal band of officers; on occasion, it does laudable charitable
work; it provides a network for meeting important people in the community; it
has beautiful facilities in which to meet; and sometimes the music is excellent.
Others see the church as a kind of Noah's ark. The world outside is stormy and
difficult. Hence the church is a place to which one can escape for shelter. It
provides a protected space to shield one from the harsh realities of the world.
When the church itself becomes harsh and corrupt, you remind yourself of the
old aphorism: "We can endure the smells inside the church because we know
the floods outside are always worse." So, we grin and bear it. Yet others see the
church as a waterbed. Here the church is seen as a warm, fuzzy, therapeutic
community that provides rest and acts as a support group. It is not a place of
service or challenge; it is a place to relax, unwind, and lie down and receive
psychic and spiritual massage. Still others see the church as a loose confeder-
ation of states. In the political arena, each state has its laws, principles,
customs, ethos, ethnic makeup, and the like. The task of leadership is to foster
tolerance, hold the ring in disputes, and work for as pluralistic and inclusive a
community as possible. Likewise in the church. Others see the church as a
department of the state. Its role is to provide moral and spiritual resources for
the nation. In times of war, the task of its leaders is to provide warrant for the
actions of the state; in times of peace, the task is to ensure a robust vision of the
common good that keeps criticism and anarchy at bay.

Now, to be sure, these images are overdrawn, and they need not be taken in a wholly negative manner. Moreover, even in recent centuries much more positive images have surfaced as we can see in the naming of new Christian communities or denominations. Consider, for example, the church as the Society of Friends. This is a very positive spin to the church as country club. Or, consider the church as the Salvation Army. This is a sharp contrast to the church as Noah's ark or even the church as the ark of salvation. Or, consider the church as the Vineyard of the Lord. In this case, we envisage the church as an orchard bearing grapes to be made into wine to enliven our spirits. This is close to the therapeutic image of a waterbed, but one where the image is bent in a positive direction.

I begin this chapter in this way for two reasons. First, it illustrates a useful and long established way to focus our thinking about the church. It is very fitting and relatively easy to think in terms of images of the church. This is extremely popular in the biblical traditions, and we will return to these very briefly later. Second, the first set of images deployed here (country club, Noah's ark, waterbed, loose federation of states, a department of state) pose an immediate challenge that should be addressed at the outset. How do we relate this rather grim picture of the church and her life to the gospel of the kingdom and to the work of the Holy Spirit in inaugurating the kingdom of God on earth? Let's take this question as our initial order of business.

Alfred Loisy in a witty aside provides a useful point of entry to our topic. He said, "Jesus foretold the kingdom and it was the church that came."[1] The great merit of this aphorism is that it insists on a clear distinction between the kingdom and the church. Its negative side is that it is an expression at best of disappointment, at worst of cynicism. The church is not the rule or reign of God, but it is surely intimately connected to the rule of God. Just how this is to be worked out is a delicate theological issue.

The presence and action of the Holy Spirit provides the clue to solving the riddle of the relation between the church and the kingdom of God. Where the Holy Spirit reigns or rules, there God rules, there is the kingdom of God. Where the kingdom comes, there is the creation of a new community, the community of the Holy Spirit. Constitutive of the activity of the Holy Spirit is the creation of the church. So, constitutive of the coming of the kingdom is the creation of new people; within the kingdom of God the Holy Spirit creates a people. The rule of God subsists in but is not reducible to the life and work of the church. The church is a glorious treasure contained in the rule of God in history.

The Holy Spirit, however, does not work in a historical vacuum; nor is the activity of the Holy Spirit generic, abstract, and unspecified. These two points

---

[1] Alfred Loisy, *The Gospel and the Church* (Philadelphia, PA: Fortress Press, 1976), 166.

are intimately connected. Consider the intimate connection between the life and work of Jesus and the activity of the Holy Spirit. It was the action of the Holy Spirit that enabled Jesus to do what he did in his mighty acts of redemption and salvation. When this was achieved once and for all, part of the ongoing work of the Holy Spirit is to bear witness to Jesus and to create in us the very life that was manifest in the life of Jesus. Hence a community created by the Holy Spirit is one which will see who Jesus is and give him his rightful place as Lord and Head of the church. So, the church rightly ordered will acknowledge, welcome, and celebrate the Lordship of Jesus Christ, risen and coming again. This is a trademark of the activity of the Holy Spirit.

Another way to express this is to say that in creating the Holy Spirit does not bypass Jesus and the apostles whom he has trained and taught. The Holy Spirit acts at Pentecost in fulfillment of the promise to the disciples. The continuity between the work of Jesus and the activity of the early church is to be located in the ongoing action of the Holy Spirit. So, the Holy Spirit gathers up what has already been done in Jesus Christ and carries it over into a New Day in the history of the people of God. The Holy Spirit works in and through the apostles and other disciples already gathered around Jesus. From the outset, the church gathered as a group around the apostles and other disciples of Jesus, including his brothers and his mother. There are real live people who had customs, memories, insight, prejudices, and everything else a creature of history possesses. These, that is, Jesus and those first disciples, are necessary conditions for the emergence of the church as known after Pentecost. If there had been no Jesus and no apostles, there would not have been a church. However, these were not sufficient conditions. The Holy Spirit works in and through them to create the church. This is the crux of the issue theologically.

With the issue of the relation between church and kingdom resolved we now turn to a second question. Given that the kingdom has resulted in the creation of the church, how do we identify the church? Returning to our opening comments, we can also pose this question more precisely by means of the following questions. What is the referent for the images of the church noted above? How do we pick out that community that is the church? How do we distinguish the true church from spurious churches? Is there one true church to which disciples of Jesus Christ belong or should belong? Clearly dealing with these challenges is of pivotal significance given the intimate relation between the church and the kingdom which I have just sketched.

I propose that the problem of references be solved by noting a primary and secondary way of securing relevant reference. The primary referent is captured by the distinction between the visible and invisible church. The true church on this analysis is the invisible church, that is, all true believers across the face of the earth who are known to God and to God alone. We can also include in this those who have already died and now constitute the church triumphant in heaven. And we can extend it into the future to include those already foreknown by God as future believers. Some think of this body as the church universal; bodies of local true believers represent a unit in this church universal. On this analysis, we can think of big "C" Church as the Church Universal and small "c" church as either local congregations or as denominations and ecclesial bodies made up of local congregations. The great merit of this distinction is that it allows for there to be wheat and tares in the kingdom; applied to the church it recognizes that not all members of the church on earth are true believers. In addition, it takes seriously the long-standing tradition of speaking of the church triumphant in heaven and of the church that stretches all the way back into the Jewish tradition.

However, we also need to speak of a secondary referent, namely, the assembly of believers gathered in local congregations and assemblies. These can, of course, come together in wider networks of synods, conferences, national assemblies, and the like; so, this usage can be extended beyond the local congregation to include such configurations. Thus, we can speak of The Church of England, The Methodist Church, The Baptist Church, and so on. This usage of "church" as referring to local congregations and their embedment in larger units is so settled and widespread that efforts to eradicate it are ultimately futile. To be sure, there are deep disputes as to the criteria for inclusion. Does, for example, the Salvation Army which does not have sacraments, count as a church? Do theologically wayward bodies, say, those that deny the Trinity, count as a church? It is enough for now that we can identify paradigm cases of this secondary use; there is simply no solution to the problematic cases simply because there are no agreed criteria of inclusion and exclusion at this point. We have to live with a concept that has very fuzzy boundaries. I shall explain in a moment how we should deal with this fuzziness.

It is very natural, given this difficulty, that a very different answer to the problem of reference is to be found by claiming that one particular network of churches constitutes the one true church on earth to which all true believers should in good conscience belong. One relevant warrant for this move involves a historical narrative of development that begins with Jesus, moves through the apostles, and preserves a continuity of order and sacrament from the time of the apostles to the present day. A crucial lynchpin of this vision is the doctrine of apostolic succession. Christ bestows the Holy Spirit to the apostles for the transmission of grace, who in turn transmit the relevant grace through the laying on of hands to chosen successors, who in turn ordain deacons and priests to provide believers with the fullness of grace. In the Roman Catholic version, the apostle Peter operated as the leader of the apostles and his office is thereafter transmitted to the Bishop of Rome. Within a complex hierarchy of layers of authority, the Bishop of Rome is given the charism of infallibility to state and preserve the faith once and for all given to the apostles. Those outside communion with the Bishop of Rome lack, therefore, crucial spiritual and intellectual resources available in no other body of Christians but to those in communion with the Bishop of Rome. In the Eastern Orthodox version of this broadly hierarchical vision of the one true church, infallibility is predicated of the whole church in its canonical councils; thus, there is a robust rejection of the epistemic status of the Bishop of Rome. However, those outside communion with the Orthodox Church are clearly spiritually and intellectually impoverished, even though it is best to be agnostic about their status before God. A similar position is developed by High Anglicans who insist that they have preserved the historic episcopate, even as they have sought to eliminate those elements in the Roman Catholic Church which they deem to be unwarranted additions if not corruptions of the faith after the first four ecumenical councils.

In reaction against the claims of Rome in the West, Magisterial Protestants who trace their heritage to the great figures of the Reformation (Lutherans, Presbyterians, Congregationalists, Baptists, and the like) tend to identify the true church in terms of crucial practices. So, the church is to be found where the pure Word of God is preached and the sacraments duly administered. Later Protestants, taking their cue from the emphasis on the authority of the Word of God, identify the church with the restoration of the "biblical" conception of the church. Thus, the church had to be created anew either by the radical reformation of existing Protestant bodies or by creating the church from the bottom up with a blueprint derived from a proper reading of Scripture.

It would take longer than a haircut to provide a fair evaluation of these competing accounts of the identity of the one true church. There is a deep reason for this, namely, that the concept of the church is an essentially contested concept.[2] An essentially contested concept is a concept where protagonists in the debate cannot agree on the criteria for the identity of the concept deployed, yet they all have to recognize that the competing criteria of application and the conclusions related to them that they reject have merit. There is no decisive disproof of the opposing positions; yet every protagonist should stay at the table because the ensuing debate brings to light critical insights to the topic in hand that would otherwise not emerge. This is exactly our predicament with respect to efforts to secure agreement on the identity of the one true church.[3] To outsiders the whole affair looks like a hopeless dead-end where no resolution is possible. In reality, the intense disagreements, if properly handled, will yield all sorts of fruitful insights. This can readily be

---

[2] See W. B. Gallie, "Essentially Contested Concepts," in *Philosophy and the Historical Understanding* (London: Chatto & Windus, 1964), 157–91.

[3] I argue this case in my *Christian Philosophical Theology*, eds. Charles Taliaferro and Chad Meister (Cambridge: Cambridge University Press, 2010), 170–82.

shown by following the amazing progress made on debates about the unity of the church in the ecumenical movement of the twentieth century.

What this means is that what follows is to be read and pondered for what it is, namely, an effort to clarify some of the crucial issues at stake and make my own modest contribution to the debate. I shall provide a series of telegrams rather than comprehensive suggestions. My suggestions are in turn methodological, theological, historical, aspirational, and pastoral.

Methodologically, I propose that we shift from a linear to a prototypical account of the history of the church. In a linear account, we move forward from the apostles down through history to the present. Catholics and Orthodox will work with a vision of episcopal succession as mandatory; Magisterial Protestants will look to reform the existing developments this way or that. In a prototypical account, we think of the ancient church up to and including Pentecost as a pivotal development in the history of the church, and then allow for the prototype to be reinstantiated, if need be from the bottom up in new missionary situations.[4] Thus, we might think of the primitive church in the aftermath of Pentecost as the prototype and be prepared to acknowledge the recreation of that prototype through the working of the Holy Spirit across space and time. This will in turn require a hermeneutic of generosity in our relations with Christian communities different from our own. So, we work off the aphorism that where the church is there is the Holy Spirit; we begin from a default position where we take the claims of others to be the church or part of the church seriously and look for the work of the Holy Spirit present in their midst.

Moving to the theological suggestion, we begin with the proposition that where the Holy Spirit is, there is the church and the fullness of grace.[5] Thus, where we see the working of the Holy Spirit, say, in bringing folk into genuine fellowship with the Son and the Father, we operate from a position that recognizes their participation in the life and work of the church. This rules out the claim that they first have to read Scripture in the original languages in order to implement some kind of biblical blueprint here and now. It also rules out the claim that the first question to address to Christians in a different Christian community is whether the proper episcopal hands have been used to transmit the grace of the Holy Spirit. When we pose that question, the assumption in play is that, without episcopal ordination and apostolic succession, we are dealing with mere ecclesial bodies or merely voluntary associations of Christians. The default position, by contrast, is one of generosity driven by the aphorism that where the Holy Spirit is, there is the church.

---

[4] For a fuller exposition of this way of thinking about the history of the church see my "Method in Ecumenism," in Geoffrey Wainwright and Paul McPartlan, eds., *The Oxford Handbook of Ecumenical Studies* (Oxford: Oxford University Press, forthcoming).

[5] I am deliberately drawing here on Irenaeus' famous observation: "Where the Church is, there is the Holy Spirit; and where the Holy Spirit is, there is the Church and the fullness of grace."

Perhaps we might go so far as to say that the most important theological claim to advance about the identity of the church is that the church is first and foremost the creation of the Holy Spirit.

At this point it is tempting to identify the birth of the church with the event of Pentecost. Tempting as this is, it is a mistake. Both Jesus and the apostles were Jews; the very first expression of the church after Pentecost was the development of what we might call "Messianic Judaism," a version of Judaism that was Torah-observant.[6] We can also make this point by noting that the Jews already constituted the People of God, a People that stretches all the way back to Abraham and that has a long history served by prophets, poets, priests, and sages. Hence we must track the birth of the church back into the Israel of God reaching back into the lives of the Jewish patriarchs and their biological descendants.[7]

We now have a whole new concept that is logically prior to that of the church, namely, the concept of Israel. Our concept of the church is a derivative concept. The church is the *ekklesia*. The Greek means an assembly of the sovereign people in a city, a general congregation of all regular citizens. Hence it denotes in secular language both the People and the City. But it carries Hebrew overtones, for it translates also the Hebrew term (Quahal) for the chosen People, the People of God construed as a whole. The church is the Israel of God, the People of God, a new People grafted together by God into "a chosen race, a royal priesthood, a holy nation, God's own people."[8] But the Israel of God does not start with Jesus, the apostles, and the first disciples; it starts with Abraham. Moreover, the first phase of the church after Pentecost is not Roman Catholicism, or Eastern Orthodoxy, or Magisterial Protestantism, or a Restorationist "Church of Christ" and its cousins, but "Messianic Judaism." Furthermore, the most significant event in the history of the church since the Reformation is the reappearance of "Messianic Judaism" as a living expression of the Christian faith today. Put theologically, the first work of the Spirit after Pentecost as far as the church is concerned is the creation of "Messianic Judaism." And this group is properly identified as an integral, constitutive part of Israel.

Given this historical reality, it is no surprise that the first truly great crisis to face the church in the first century was the incorporation of Gentile believers into the Israel of God. The struggle was resolved in the end by an amazing generosity of spirit argued from the meaning of the covenant of Abraham by Paul[9] and from the reality of the outpouring of the Holy Spirit on Gentile

---

[6] For a rigorous defense of this see David J. Rudolph, *A Jew to the Jews* (Tübingen: Mohr Siebeck, 2011).

[7] Given the doctrine of the Trinity this whole history from Abraham onwards will be interpreted retrospectively as the work of the Holy Spirit.

[8] 1 Peter 2:4.   [9] Most notably in Galatians.

converts on hearing the Gospel.[10] Gentiles were given freedom to be Israel without becoming biological or "ethnic" Jews. Hence we have the development of a bilateral ecclesiology with genuine diversity, following out the promise to Abraham that the blessings of Israel were to be shared with all nations.[11] Over time, the growth of the Gentile church led to a reversal of the generosity shown by its Jewish older brother in the faith. The Jewish church was virtually eliminated and the Gentile church adopted a position of radical hostility to Jews and Judaism. Now that we have in our midst a reappearance of the Jewish church, it is not surprising that the relation between Christianity and Judaism is back as a pivotal topic of theological reflection.

The problems on this front are well known, given the long history of anti-Semitism within Christianity. However, the current exchanges give great grounds for hope and bear witness to the extraordinary grace of God in beginning the healing of the brutal and broken relations between Jews and Christians. To be sure, the relationships across the centuries between Protestants and Catholics have also been unbelievably brutal; and they live on in secularized form in places like Northern Ireland with no end in sight. Yet the treatment of Jews stands apart in its persistence and brutality. In the light of this the prayer of Pope John XXIII is breathtaking in its depth and simplicity.

> We realize now that many, many centuries of blindness have dimmed our eyes, so that we no longer see the beauty of Thy Chosen People and no longer recognize in their faces the features of our firstborn brother. We realize that our brows are branded with the mark of Cain. Centuries long has Abel lain in blood and tears, because we have forgotten Thy love. Forgive us the curse we unjustly laid on the name of the Jews. Forgive us that, with our curse, we crucified Thee a second time.[12]

Our interest here is limited to the ecclesiological significance of these extraordinary developments in the work of the Spirit in contemporary history, not least in the recent emergence of "Messianic Judaism."[13] It is not too much to say that theologians are scrambling to figure out what to say now about the identity of the church. The old bets are off, if we take this development seriously. All standard claims to be the original and therefore true church of God have been *prima facie* undermined. We can surely retain the theological claim that where the Holy Spirit is, there is the church; so, there can be no truck with disenfranchising "Messianic Judaism" by dismissing it as another

---

[10] Most notably by Peter in Acts 15.

[11] I borrow the term "bilateral ecclesiology" from Mark S. Kinzer. See his *Post-Missionary Messianic Judaism: Redefining Christian Engagement with the Jewish People* (Grand Rapids, MI: Brazos Press, 2005).

[12] Reported in "Our Eyes have been Cloaked," *Catholic Herald*, May 14, 1965.

[13] There are a host of theological issues to be pursued, not least the treatment of law and Gospel and the Lutheran tendency to play these off against one another.

religion or as one more sectarian variation on evangelical Protestantism. The issue is simple: just as the Jewish Christians had to come to terms with the work of the Holy Spirit among Gentiles, Gentile Christians and churches have now to come to terms with the work of the Holy Spirit among Jews. We are going to need lots of patience in the years ahead to deal with this challenge.

In the meantime, we should keep our nerve and keep alive our aspirational hopes and dreams. The church is one of the most important social institutions given to us; it is much more important than our military, educational, and medical institutions. We dare not abandon it in a fit of adolescent radicalism or in a moment of despair given the new challenges we face. It may help to keep the following in mind as we proceed. First, we need to come to terms with a more complicated narrative of the divisions within the church. These begin with the split within Judaism between those who became "Messianic Jews" and those who picked up and developed the tradition of Rabbinic Judaism. Only when that division is eventually healed will we be able to speak responsibly of the unity of the People of God. We also have to reckon with the split between the Jewish church and the Gentile church which became so pronounced in the fourth century and which took horrendous forms in the opposition to Jews in the medieval period. We all know the horrors of what happened in the twentieth century and, if we are alert, we know the dangers that currently beset the Jews in Israel. In contemporary terms this means that the current Jewish church or "Messianic Judaism" cannot be seen as a mere variation on the later splits between Orthodoxy and Catholicism, between Catholics and Protestants, and between one Protestant group and another. We have become deeply sensitized to the latter divisions in the twentieth century; and rightly so. Our failures to reach unity even between Orthodoxy and Catholicism reveal just how staggering the problem will be when we realize that resolving this division is but a foretaste of resolving the earlier divisions that have now come to light over the last generation. Our aspirational hopes now have become higher and more complicated.

Second, these hopes will only become real if we recover a vision of the church as first and foremost the work of the Holy Spirit all the way back to Abraham and all the way forward to the Eschaton. If unity is truly a gift of the Holy Spirit, then we must look afresh to a new Pentecost in the life of the church to overcome the obstacles that are now before us. This does not mean that we treat the Holy Spirit as a labor-saving device. It means that we must beware of those who would use the quest for unity and the various instruments for pursuing unity as the basis for their own agendas and power-plays. Sadly, this is one reason for the failure of the recent phase of ecumenism over the last half-century. It should be no surprise that the very word "ecumenical" has become a weapon to use against other Christians or a word to be dropped from our ecclesial lexicon. Happily, we have entered a new phase of ecumenical work that is coming to terms with this untoward but not unexpected development. Only the Holy Spirit can bring about that which in human terms is utterly impossible.

Third, in speaking of unity I have deliberately picked out one of the four marks of the church that shows up in the Nicene Creed. How should we handle the famous creedal marks of the church? "I believe in one holy, catholic, and apostolic church." How should we read this avowal? Think of the matter this way. This is not a definition but a verbal confession or witness. It is an attempt to describe four crucial aspects of a living historical reality, that concrete network of communities that emanated from Jesus and the apostles in history. So, the church is *holy*; it is "set apart," called out to be different, that is, to serve the purposes of God. It is *catholic*; it operates according to the sense and judgment of the whole; it is not parochial or partial in its commitments. It is *apostolic*; it stems from the apostles; it is not a departure from the apostles, even though it grows, develops, and even changes. Moreover, it shares the faith of the apostles and carries out the missionary work of the apostles. Then, finally, there is *one* church. There are not many churches or denominations or chosen peoples; there is one people, who reach back into the Jewish tradition back to Abraham and who have descended in succession from its Jewish foundation in the apostles and prophets.

More specifically, we should think of these marks of the church which are given in the indicative mood as disguised promises. They indicate what the church can be as she is fully open to the working of the Holy Spirit in her midst. To be sure, if we take the period after Pentecost as our guide there will be significant diversity. However, the diversity will be a reconciled diversity, as it was initially, embedded in unity where we share "one faith, one Lord, one baptism, and one God and Father of all, who is above all and through all and in all."[14] Likewise for the other marks of holiness, catholicity, and apostolicity. As one people, we will be set apart to embody the holiness of God; as one people, we will seek to make decisions according to the whole rather than insist on our own parochial agendas; as apostolic, we shall seek to carry out the mission of the apostles to make disciples of all nations. Yet none of these marks are mere human achievements; they can only come through radical openness and dependence on the work of the Holy Spirit. This will not happen without human effort, ingenuity, humility, and wisdom. Yet this too must be inspired by the creative energies of the Holy Spirit. It is the latter which alone can quicken hope when we face the formidable challenges that lie ahead, not least the challenge to come to terms with the initial division in the Israel of God in the first century.

No doubt much of this may sound like standard theological boilerplate. This is true, but these platitudes matter if we are to make progress in becoming

---

[14] Ephesians 4:5–7.

what God intended his church to be. The issues become less platitudinous and more contested when one begins to spell out the practical implications. However, these too matter, for they are essential to provoking new insights and options. So, let me lay my own cards on the table.

First, we must find a way to relativize our varied epistemological commitments. The biggest challenge here will be our handling of the doctrines of *sola scriptura* and papal infallibility. Neither of these claims should be canonical for the whole church, no more so than empiricism, rationalism, fideism, postmodernism, or the other host of proposals that crop up in epistemology. These, unlike the content of the Creed, are not canonical. They are efforts to secure an epistemology for Christian truth claims that are radically secondary in the economy of the church. This is in no way a call to be diffident about such matters; in their time and place they are interesting and even important. They should not, however, be canonical; indeed, making them canonical has been one of the chief sources of division among Christians.[15] We make the church captive to this or that epistemology of theology; and the quest for unity becomes absolutely impossible for there will be no unity in this domain. Nowhere is this captivity to epistemology more visible than in the reduction of the canonical heritage of the church to Scripture and in the transformation of the Scriptures away from a magnificent means of grace into a criterion of truth, warrant, justification, and knowledge.[16]

Second, we cannot dechristianize those communities that have been created by the Holy Spirit either in the wake of the division between East and West, or in the wake of the Protestant Reformation, or currently in the wake of the extraordinary growth of Pentecostalism. The old claim that all we have here is heresy or mere enthusiasm will not stand the light of historical or theological scrutiny. Nor will it do to claim that we know where the church is, but we do not know where it is not; as if we can be agnostic about the work of the Holy Spirit in, say, Methodism and the rest of the Protestant underworld. We must reckon with the genuine working of the Holy Spirit wherever we find it, and such working involves not just individual conversions, but the creation of radically diverse Christian communities. Anything less than this is a failure of love and logic.

Third, every effort needs to be made on all sides to recover and reappropriate the full canonical heritage of the church of the first millennium before the split between East and West. Paradoxically, the East in this process may itself

---

[15] One option worthy of consideration is the possibility of permitting claims about papal infallibility without the whole church endorsing them. This was the position of Newman prior to Vatican I; he believed in papal infallibility but did not think that the church as a whole should formally accept it. I doubt if Rome will welcome this olive branch, but if she did, then the possibilities for the reunion of East and West would be greatly enhanced.

[16] I have argued this case at length in my *Canon and Criterion in Christian Theology: From the Fathers to Feminism* (Oxford: Clarendon Press, 1998).

be provoked to make full use of its own canonical traditions; it may rediscover the significance of its treasures by observing the plundering of its resources by friendly aliens in the West. Beyond that, it is vital that we enter into a long-haul engagement with the resources developed in Rabbinic Judaism after the initial split between Messianic and non-Messianic Jews. In this regard the contribution of contemporary Messianic Jews to our understanding of the faith of the church is absolutely indispensable.

Fourth, we must reckon with the real possibility of divine judgment on all of us for our sins. Maybe our situation is analogous to Israel after the monarchy when God handed his People over to the full consequences of their rebellion.[17] God maintained his faithfulness to the covenant despite the lust for monarchy; indeed, God continued to work in and through the flawed institutions of his People. He continued his ministry of mercy and healing to the world despite rebellion and sin. There is here an analogy for understanding God's relation to the divisions among Christians. While maintaining continuity in history and preserving the canonical treasures of the church, God has scattered his People and driven them into exile so that they may come to terms with their sin. While remaining faithful to his covenant and continuing to pour out his Holy Spirit, God has withdrawn the fullness of his blessing, waiting patiently until we repent of our manifold sins and disorders. In a real sense we are entering a new wilderness, most especially within so-called mainline Protestantism which is dividing over issues related to sexual morality and marriage.

Fifth, as we repent and turn to the future, then we can surely see our way forward, for the future lies in a fresh Pentecost in the life of the children of God. If the one, holy, catholic, and apostolic church is the fruit of the working of the Holy Spirit, then it is here in the working of the Holy Spirit where we must relocate ourselves afresh today. As I have already noted, applying this insight to the references in the Creed (one, holy, catholic, apostolic), these descriptions are more normative descriptions than they are simply straight, historical descriptions. They are promises of what the church can be in the power of the Holy Spirit. Consequently, we may not really know the fullness of the marks of the church anew until we all repent and seek the fullness of the presence of the Holy Spirit. In our current Christian communities, scattered near or far from the original fountain, we only partially know the full treasures the Holy Spirit has in store for us. These lie in the future. The Holy Spirit may yet gather up her scattered treasures and join them all in one visible community which stands in historic continuity with the church of the holy apostles.

Construing the church as a community brought into being by the Holy Spirit undercuts all forms of triumphalism and arrogance. We possess nothing we have not received; and the preservation of what we have received must ever

---

[17] This theme is pursued with rare sensitivity in Ephraim Radner, *The End of the Church: A Pneumatology of Christian Division in the West* (Grand Rapids, MI: Eerdmans, 1998).

be an act of gratitude rather than a weapon to discredit the work of the Holy Spirit in others or a mechanism to exalt ourselves. This is pivotal in securing the genuine freedom of the Holy Spirit and in fostering a minimum of ecclesial civility.

As we make this journey into the fullness of the life of the church, we can surely redeploy the rich imagery applied to the church in the New Testament. Think of five of the many images available in the New Testament. There is the image of the church as the *Body of Christ*. There is the image of the church as the *Branches of the Vine*. There is the image of the church as the *Holy City*. There is the image of the church as a *Royal Priesthood*. There is the image of the church as the *Light of the World*. How shall we read these metaphorical descriptions of the church? Like the normative adjectives given in the Creed, I propose that we read them as veiled promises. What is at issue is not that we might take them literally. The greater danger is that we will take them flat-footedly and apply them to ourselves as we are and thus reduce them to what we find in our communities. What these images do is evoke a picture of what we can be when we allow the Holy Spirit fully to act among us. They display features of the church as it is meant to be in the power of the Holy Spirit. Hence they are an amazing treasury of hope and a charter of new creation. That we fall short of such descriptions is to be expected, but this is no warrant for despair, depression, or pessimism about the church. These images should summon us to a deeper repentance and to a firmer reliance on the work of the Holy Spirit.

So, we do not give up if our church is now a country club, a Noah's ark, or a giant waterbed. These were not what it was meant to be or what it is called to be. We are called and empowered to be the salt of the earth, a letter from Christ, the vineyard of the Lord, the bride of Christ, exiles in a foreign land, the Israel of God, the holy temple in which the living God dwells, a remnant chosen by grace, the slaves of Christ, a light to the world, a royal priesthood, the Holy City, the branches of the true vine, and the very body of Christ. Each of these metaphors provides a glimpse of the true greatness God has in store for the church today.

This is all well and good, it will be said, but where are we to find the one, true church that is so often invoked in discussions about the church? We come finally to the promise of pastoral commentary that I mentioned earlier. Let's dwell on this question for a moment. I propose that this is one of those recurring questions that have to be abandoned and reworked in the light of what I have presented here. Recall, what I have been assuming all along, namely, that systematic theology belongs beyond conversion and catechesis, so it only arises for those already initiated into the church. Readers not in this position need to step back and start with the Gospel of the kingdom and then move on to baptism and Christian initiation. So, I am assuming that the question only becomes a real one if one is entertaining doubts about one's current ecclesial location. Or it only becomes a pressing issue if one has been confronted, or maybe even bullied, with claims to be the one, true church of Christ. Once we identify this context then such anxious souls need to consider the following.

First, if they are looking for the church that was first, the one truly original church of Christ after Pentecost, then they should become Messianic Jews. This was the first and oldest expression of the church after Pentecost. However, if they are Gentiles, then they are expressly forbidden by Paul to join this church.[18] He insists as a matter of policy that the Jew should stay a Jew and the Gentile should stay a Gentile. As I have already noted, Gentile converts were shepherded into Gentile congregations and permitted to retain relevant elements in their cultural background. They did not have to become circumcised and join biological Israel. What this means is that the standard way of answering our question in terms of, say, Rome, or Constantinople, or Canterbury, or the local congregation of the Plymouth Brethren, is immediately off the table. If Jerusalem alone does not work, then neither will Rome alone, or Constantinople alone, or Plymouth alone, work. So, our standard question must be abandoned; its presuppositions have been falsified by historical investigation.

Second, we must get over the anxiety that often fuels the quest for the one true church. This question is now obsolete once we come to terms with the history of division within the People of God. Even if it lingers on like a bad cold, the concept of "church" is essentially contested; this means there is no proof available that cannot and will not be contested by rival efforts to secure the one true church. Adopting this or that option will always be met by rival alternatives whose adherents are all too ready to contest our decision. We need to grow up and deal with the long-standing reality of division and diversity.

It has been common at this point to rail against private judgment as opposed to the corporate judgment of the community. However, in the current context this is a bogus distinction. We can agree that if left to our own to work out everything "privately" from scratch, then the result would be disastrous. As Edmund Burke noted in another context, "We are afraid to put men to live and trade on his own private stock of reason; because we suspect that this stock in each man is small, and that the individuals would do better to avail themselves of the general bank and capital of nations and of ages."[19] However, we surely recognize that we have to exercise judgment on where the relevant spiritual capital is to be found; and we cannot outsource that decision to the first big general bank that comes along with all sorts of promises in hand. Moreover, this is not some kind of abstract point, for there are rival proposals on offer, say, between Rome and Constantinople. We can pretend

---

[18] See 1 Corinthians 7:18.
[19] Isaac Kramnick, ed., *The Portable Burke* (New York: Penguin, 1999), 451.

otherwise, but there is no escaping making up our own minds about the rival alternatives.

Third, the obvious solution to the anxiety is to stay where we are, give thanks for what the Holy Spirit has already given us in the Gospel, and pray that our humble abode will be open to the full working of the Holy Spirit wherever that may be found. Alternatively, if we are still trying to live off the capital of our own little bank, we need to abandon our individualism and use the best lights we have and become a functioning member of a local congregation. We cannot have Jesus without his body; we cannot have the kingdom and refuse the gift of the church that is embedded within it. So, we should repent of our individualism and make haste to the local congregation to which the Holy Spirit leads us. We cannot survive without the treasures to be found in the church; and we cannot flourish without the ministry of the church. It is both a duty and a privilege to act as mature adults and reach out for all that the Holy Spirit has in store for us in salvation.

14

The Church

Work, Ministry, and Sacraments

And now I know that none of you, among whom I have gone about proclaiming the kingdom of God, will ever see my face again. Therefore I declare to you this day that I am not responsible for the blood of any of you, for I did not shrink from declaring to you the whole purpose of God. Keep watch over all the flock, of which the Holy Spirit has made you overseers, to shepherd the church of God that he obtained with the blood of his own Son. I know that after I have gone, savage wolves will come in among you, not sparing the flock.

Acts 20:25–9.

The Church of England, it is sometimes said, is "a peculiar institution."[1] Given that the English are indeed peculiar, this should not surprise us. However, it is not clear whether this assertion is a compliment or a prosaic description. Set against standard theological descriptions of the church, say, as the Body of Christ, this description is certainly deflationary in content. It is also deeply ambivalent. Is it simply a neutral sociological description of the church? Or is it incipiently negative in that it suggests that the church like any other institution is subject to inevitable dysfunction, if not corruption? If we pursue the latter interpretation, we are faced with a further disquieting question: What should we do when the church fails, when savage wolves show up and ravage the flock? Put more dramatically, what does God do when the church fails?

We can, of course, avoid these questions by appealing to the holiness of the church. Given the holiness of the church as rooted in the action of the Triune God, we insist that the church cannot fail. Its members may fail, it is said, but not the church in its essence. We can only resolve the problem in this way if we

---

[1] See, for example, David Stove, *Cricket versus Republicanism and Other Essays*, ed. James R. Franklin and R.J. Stove (Sydney: Quaker Hill Press, 1995).

accept a very particular vision of the holiness of the church, that is, holiness as an empirical description of the church. On my analysis, holiness is not an empirical description of the church; it is a promise presented by means of an indicative sentence. It signals what the church can be when it is truly open to the full working of the Holy Spirit. So, clearly this way to solve our problem will not work.

There are, of course, those who seize upon the very idea of the church as an institution as the obvious cause of failure and corruption. It is precisely because the church became an institution, it is said, that is the root of its dysfunction. The story of a fall away from its original identity into an institution is at the heart of the problem. The only question is where and when this happened. Did it happen with the second generation, or with the developments that show up in the second century, or did it happen when Christianity became the established church after Constantine in the fourth century? This is no more acceptable as a solution to the challenge of failure as the claim that in essence the church is holy; it is merely its sinful members who fail. Once we trace the history of the church back into the history of Israel and forward from the training of twelve apostles and the leaders they appointed, this solution collapses immediately. It is nonsensical to deny that from the beginning the People of God took institutional shape as it moved across time and space. This whole line of thinking fades as quickly as dew exposed to the Texas sun in the middle of the summer.

I assume then that the church willy-nilly takes on institutional forms and practices. Indeed, I think that the church is the most important institution on the face of the earth, compared to, say, medical or educational institutions. This follows readily from my account of the nature and identity of the church developed in the last chapter. Thus, the church is created by the Holy Spirit, and this goes right back to her origins in Israel. The church is embedded in the kingdom of God; these can be distinguished in thought but they cannot be separated in reality. Moreover, without the church there would be no Body of Christ, no Vineyard of the Lord, no People of God, no Royal Priesthood, and the like. Moreover, following the language of Edmund Burke, it would be disastrous if we were spiritually left to work off our own little bank of theology and spirituality; we need the general bank of rich resources that are preserved in the church across the ages. To change the metaphor, we cannot capture a Mozart opera on a tin whistle, no matter how good we are at tin-whistling in our bathtub.

In this chapter I want to take up and pursue three further issues. I want to explore: the work and mission of the church; the varied ministries of the church, giving special attention to the ordained ministers of the church; and the sacraments and means of grace in the life and work of the church. Beyond that I will return to the problem of the failure of the church, drawing on the remarkable proposals of Symeon the New Theologian.

Before we speak of the varied ministries of the church it is important to stand back and reflect more generally on the mission or work of the church as a whole. Sometimes it has been said that the mission or work of the church is fundamentally to continue the work of Christ in the world. Two closely related theological themes have been used to undergird this suggestion. First, the claim has been made that the church is the body of Christ; and this has been pressed to undergird this conception of the church's work. Here the stress is on seeing the church as the ongoing extension of Jesus and his work. Secondly, it has often been claimed that the church is an extension of the incarnation. Hence what God did in Jesus Christ continues in the church. The incarnation, on this view, is not exclusively tied to the person and work of Jesus Christ but carried over fully and permanently into the life of the church.

This line of reasoning is both ill-founded and misleading. Its chief defect is that it fails to reckon with the uniqueness and ontological fullness of the work of God in Jesus Christ. There is a deep sense in which what God does and works in Jesus does not apply to the work God does in and through the church. In Jesus of Nazareth, God forgives, saves, atones, and liberates in a network of contingent actions in history. On the human side these acts are done through Jesus as a unique historical individual and person. Jesus saved us from our sins; he gave his life as a ransom; he made atonement. These were once for all historical acts. The church, in and of herself, does not forgive; she does not make atonement; she is not the Lamb of God that takes away the sin of the world.

This distinction is crucial. Without it we shall fall into despair. More importantly, without it we shall attribute to the church actions and attributes that truly and rightly only belong to Jesus Christ. Surely we must acknowledge the sin, the brokenness, the rebellion, and the evil of the church across the generations? Surely we must sympathize with those who love and even worship Jesus Christ but who have been beaten, scourged, rejected, and even killed by the church? Surely, we can identify with and hear even now the legitimate complaints of those who are glad followers of Christ but reject the church because of her disobedience and failure? Once we grant this dysfunction, then we cannot construe the church as an extension of the incarnation, *simpliciter*; nor can we see the church as doing what Jesus Christ has done uniquely for the salvation of the world. If we do not acknowledge this distinction, we shall be tempted to glamorize and idealize the church. This will pave the way for a new round of sectarianism where folk flee the church and pin their hopes on starting again from scratch. The current temptation, as represented by the influential George Barna, is to seek refuge in our own house church.[2]

---

[2] See Frank Viola and George Barna, *Pagan Christianity? Exploring the Roots of Our Church Practices* (Carol Stream, IL: Tyndale House, 2008).

This does not entail that there is not an intimate connection between the mission of the church and the work of Jesus Christ. We can capture this intimacy by saying that there are three closely related dimensions of the work of the church.

The first task of the church is to worship. This is the first work of the church, logically speaking. The People of God are to gather on the first day of the week, the day of resurrection; they are to break forth into songs of thanksgiving, praise, and joy; they are to relax before God, and they are to enter into the courts of heaven with thanksgiving; they are to lay aside all their earthly cares and acknowledge the mercy and grace of God which has been poured out on all creation in Jesus Christ. They are to join in communion with all who have gone before and to join in communion with angels and arch-angels and all the company of heaven in unrestrained celebration, thanksgiving, and praise.

If warrant were needed for this observation on the first task of the church, then I suggest two lines of argument. First, the church over time after Pentecost canonized a network of liturgies which refused to leave the work of the people in worship to happenstance. There were right and wrong ways to put God at the center of her life week in and week out, year in and year out. The church looked to its liturgical developments to carry the great treasures of the Gospel and the Scriptures. Second, reaching back into the life of Israel, it is astonishing that so much attention is given to the building of the tabernacle after the deliverance from bondage in Egypt. Indeed, the climax of the book of Exodus is the presence of the glory of God symbolized in the presence of a cloud.[3] It is clear that this was not one mere episode; the tabernacle and its successor buildings, like the temple, were to be a regular location for the presence of the glory of God. The theocentrism involved overshadows the moral success and failures of the People represented by the giving of the Law and by the acts of apostasy which are in the literary neighborhood of building of the tabernacle. This in no way excludes the place of personal and informal devotion ably represented by the Psalter. In fact, even this material is gathered up into the public worship of the People.

Closely related to this is a second dimension of the church's mission, namely waiting before God and inviting God's rule and kingdom to come here and now in every aspect of her life. Expressed simply, a basic call of the church is to wait quietly before God and invite God to rule and reign in her midst. This entails quietness, stillness, attentiveness, listening, and deep de-termination to seek the face and glory of God in the face of Jesus Christ. It is surely no accident that the great breakthrough of Pentecost required time set

---

[3] Exodus 40:34–5.

apart to wait upon God in the Upper Room and the prayers no doubt offered up to the Risen Lord.

This waiting should happen first and foremost in the church's worship, in her divine services. The place where we first pray, "Thy kingdom come, thy will be done on earth as it is in heaven" is in the church, and in the church on the Lord's Day. If the church cannot let God rule for one short hour on a Sunday morning, it is unlikely that she shall be able or willing to let God rule the rest of the week. Expressed rhetorically, if we cannot let God's kingdom come in worship, what hope is there that we will let God's kingdom come in our work, in our moral reflection, in our politics, in our personal relationships, or even in the rest of the church's ministries? So, the second work of the church is to wait, to pause, and to invite God to rule over her. Her task is to allow Jesus truly to be Lord, to let the Holy Spirit act fully and comprehensively, to let the Risen Lord work in and through all the members of the body.

The third task of the church fits neatly with the first two, namely the church is called to bear witness to Jesus Christ. "But you shall receive power when the Holy Spirit has come upon you; and you shall be my witnesses in Jerusalem, and in all Judea and Samaria, and to the end of the earth."[4] Note several aspects of witness. The church's witness is not to herself or to her acts but to Jesus Christ, crucified, risen, and coming again. It is done not in her own strength but in the power of the Holy Spirit. Moreover, it is carried, not simply out of duty or obligation, but out of compassion, mercy, and love; and that compassion, mercy, and love is both a deep human struggle and a gift of the Holy Spirit. Furthermore, this witness, in all its forms, will be costly and demanding. It will mean sharing the offense and suffering promised by Christ. It will involve being disliked and hated, being scorned and persecuted, being used and rejected. To think otherwise is to ignore the cross and to inhabit a fantasy world far removed from the real world we inhabit.

The form of the witness is at least twofold. It is in word. The church joyfully announces the good news to the ends of the earth. She heralds and gossips the news of the arrival and coming of the kingdom of God. She proclaims to the ends of the earth the Gospel of Jesus and the kingdom. She offers Christ in the proclaimed word. This is one form of her witness. Ancillary to this is the incorporation of those who positively respond into the reign of God. By baptizing and teaching, the church helps complete the word of witness. She fulfills the great commission and thereby increases the joy of heaven itself. As a byproduct, she plants new Christian communities across the face of the earth and multiplies her witness.[5]

---

[4] Acts 1:8.

[5] It is interesting that Matthew insists on making disciples the lynchpin of the mission of the church (Matthew 28:18–20). However, this is the climax of two summaries of the ministry of Jesus in Matthew that center on teaching, preaching, healing, and exorcism (Matthew 4:23–5,

Another form of witness is witness in deed. Corporately and through the life of its members, the church seeks to embody the rule of God in every facet of existence in creation and history. This will be expressed in a host of ways: in care for the environment, in the healing of the sick, in standing up to and removing injustice, in feeding the hungry, in welcoming the stranger, in clothing the naked, in helping those in prison, in entering into the world of politics with flair, and the like.

Since the emergence of Pentecostalism, the question of the more "supernatural" dimensions of the work of the church has come back on the table. Thus, we see the emergence of healing services, exorcisms, words of prophecy, and the like. Given the long years of skepticism that developed from the work of David Hume, Immanuel Kant, and others onwards, this is an astonishing development that has caught many by surprise and left a lot of church leaders bewildered. To be sure, this dimension of the church's work has never died out; it has been maintained in Eastern Orthodoxy and Catholicism; and it has had a vibrant underground life within revivalism and its offspring. Even so, where there has been talk of divine action it has focused on divine action in the sacraments and in the inner life of the believer in regeneration, justification, sanctification, and the like.

We might capture the theological challenge in this way. Much of Western Christianity has been obsessed with the doctrine of divine grace and its relation to human action and response. The current flurry of interest in the five-hundredth anniversary of the Reformation has brought all this back to our attention. Indeed, for Lutherans the only divine action that has seemed to matter is that of justification. The issue of divine power has been restricted to sanctification, so that grace has been construed as expressed in divine favor in forgiveness and divine energy in the Christian life.

Read in its canonical order from Matthew through Acts, the New Testament provides a very different picture. Even a cursory reading, say, of Matthew, reveals that the first manifestation of the kingdom is visible in Christ's miracles and exorcism; given that these are welcomed by the riff-raff, the issue of divine grace then becomes an acute one. So, the order is reversed.[6] Rather than first experiencing grace and then worrying about how to speak of divine power, we begin with the aggressive manifestation of comprehensive divine power over sickness, the demonic, nature, and death, and then find ourselves confronted with the reach of Christ to those who are normally excluded by the religious establishment. Even the disciples of John did not quite know what to

9:35–8) which are clearly picked up by the early church in the ministry of the apostles. So, I do not see Matthew and Luke as at odds with each other here.

[6] Matthew 8–9, unlike the treatment of similar material in Mark, intersperses his ordering of events with telling accounts of the response to the miracles of Jesus.

do, given their worries about the irregular piety of Jesus and his disciples.[7] It will take decades for the church to come to terms with this ordering of the inner logic of the Gospel. This ordering was a puzzle in the first century; it is an even greater puzzle in the twenty-first century for Christians uneasy about healing and exorcism. It will be a massive headache for those still burdened by the contraceptive pills of Hume and Kant who killed in the womb of conception any hope of direct divine action in nature and history in their epistemological and metaphysical operating theatres.

What is ultimately at issue is the very meaning of the Gospel itself. Once we recover a proper vision of the Gospel as first and foremost the inauguration of the kingdom of God, then we cannot evade the critical place of "signs" and "wonders" as integral to the works of God carried out in and through the church. These divine acts certainly have apologetic value, for they raise the question in the observer as to their source which requires coming to terms with the reality of God and his work here and now. More importantly, they make clear that the Gospel is not merely about some private transaction between the individual and God but also opens up a vision of radical trans-formation that will ultimately be fulfilled in the final realization of the king-dom of God on earth. The arrival of the kingdom means ultimately the end of disease, death, and the demonic; it will eventually embrace the very physics and chemistry of the universe when God's rule will refashion and recreate even the very physical universe itself.

We can sum up the whole of this unit in this way. The church's task or mission is to worship God, to wait before God and invite God to rule all over heaven and earth, and to witness across the earth in word and deed. The church that *worships* but does not wait and does not witness will be joyful, but it will be isolated and barren. The church that *waits on God* but does not worship and witness will be formally sensitive, but it will be passive and unfruitful. The church that *witnesses* but does not worship and does not wait will be activistic and moral, but it will be egocentric and judgmental. The church that *worships* and *witnesses* but does not wait will be joyful and activist, but it will be misled and misdirected. The church that *waits* and *witnesses* but does not worship will be moral and full of service, but it will be pharisaical and lacking in joy. Better then by far for the church to worship the Triune God, to wait before God and invite God's rule to come, and to witness in word and deed.

In order to carry out her mission and work the church is equipped with various ministries. Note the order here. It is not that the church has ministries

---

[7] See, for example, the material in Matthew 8–9 where we have a literary interchange which moves from "supernatural" divine action in miracle and exorcism to the varied responses these actions evoke. Paul's own ministry was thoroughly "supernatural" but this was overshadowed in his writings with the challenge of grace and other issues.

and then these ministries have a mission. The church has a mission and to carry out this mission the Holy Spirit gives gifts and ministries.[8]

We begin sorting through the issues initially by noting that from the beginning with Abraham the church has had designated leaders who handed over the faith and its practices from one generation to another. This becomes especially visible when Israel becomes a nation after the deliverance from Egypt and Moses is advised by his foreign father-in-law to appoint leaders to whom he delegates various responsibilities. This is followed up by the appointment of priests with designated responsibilities for the spiritual welfare of the people as a whole. With Jesus, we see the appointment of the twelve apostles who in turn appoint shepherds to take care of those who are initiated into the kingdom of God and into the church by baptism. Clearly, the Jewish church follows initially the patterns of leadership that existed in the first century. The appointment of deacons was developed on the hoof in that a division of labor was essential if the works of evangelism were to get the attention they required. The initial developments in the Gentile churches are murky initially, although we can clearly see the adaptation of the earlier Jewish model with the appointment of presbyters or overseers and deacons. By the second century, we can see the development of a threefold order of deacon, presbyter, and bishop.

At this point, the quest for the "historical church" and her ministry becomes as contested as the quest for the "historical" Jesus. Just as there is no theologically neutral account of the life and work of Jesus, there is no theologically neutral description of what emerged. We can surely agree that the appointment of leaders and various orders of ministry was not simply an exercise in secular wisdom; the Holy Spirit guided the church in her deliberations. This observation applies whatever story we tell of the developments in the early church in the aftermath of Pentecost. The great temptation, of course, is to insist on one particular development as exclusively the work of the Holy Spirit. Given that there was diversity both before and after Pentecost, the right way to approach the gift of orders in ministry is with a spirit of generosity. Expressed sharply, the default position should be one where we allow for the work of the Holy Spirit in the calling, evaluation, and ordination of those who are set apart for life-time service in the work of the church. Nor should we shy from calling ministries of order and succession charismatic; these are good gifts of the Holy Spirit given to take care of obvious functions and needs in the life of the church.

---

[8] We can, following the important work of Nicholas Afanasiev, make a parallel move in the development of ministry: there are practices, like offering thanksgiving, to be carried out and for these the church appoints various ministers. See his *The Church of the Holy Spirit* (Notre Dame, IN: University of Notre Dame Press, 2007), chapter 6.

We face at this point a very interesting internal struggle and discussion in the church. For centuries, we have conceived of the church as divided into two groups, the laity and the ministers or clergy. In everyday language in much of the English-speaking world, to enter the ministry of the church is to be ordained to the ranks of the clergy. Ministry in this perspective belongs exclusively to those set apart and ordained to the profession. The only real dispute, once this division was accepted, is over how to conceive of the various forms or ranks or orders of the ordained ministry. The divisions on this score run very deep indeed and are of historic proportions. Should we have a twofold ministerial order of elders and deacons, with one elder especially set apart as a teaching elder (the classic Presbyterian order)? Should we have a threefold ministerial order of deacon, presbyter, and bishop (the classic patristic order)? History is littered with variations on these patterns. In one way or another they have assumed a demarcation between laity and ministers that has increasingly come under criticism.

Some have attacked this distinction on the grounds of the priesthood of all believers. This line of argument is strikingly invalid. The priesthood of all believers has little or nothing to do with orders of ministry. It addresses primarily the issue of whether all Christians have direct access to God through Christ. Plainly they do. But this claim does not settle one way or the other the issue of a separate type of ministry or order of ministry in the church.

We need to express our correctives carefully. Our key problem has been that we have failed to acknowledge the generosity of the Holy Spirit in the church. The Holy Spirit is ingenious and generous, scattering gifts to every member. The treasures of the Holy Spirit are numerous; the Holy Spirit equips the whole church for the work of ministry. This is done sovereignly and individually. Every member therefore gets to participate in the ministry of the Holy Spirit in the church for the common good.

This amazing and generous gifting of the Spirit needs to be recognized, acknowledged, and owned in Christian initiation. As we enter the kingdom of God, we get commissioned in baptism to be agents of the kingdom, equipped in diverse ministries to serve God and the neighbor. At this point the quality of our catechesis and initial formation in the faith is crucial. The gifts imparted to the whole body are tremendously diverse; no normative list has ever been given, nor is one needed. All we need is a loose set of lists such as we have in Romans 12, 1 Corinthians 12–14, and Ephesians 4. These provide a synchronic snapshot of the ministries of the church as generally perceived at a single moment of time.

However, we also need a diachronic perspective on the ministries of the church. The church exists through time as well as in time. She is not just a collection of individuals bound together in the short term; the church is the People of God called to mission from generation to generation. Hence it was both sociologically essential and historically inevitable that within the total ministries of the church some ministries would focus on continuity, transmission, order, and discipline across the generations. This is recognized in the later Pastoral Epistles of the New Testament. Historically, these needs and their resolution evolved and developed as the need arose. As already noted, in the end the Gentile church in the earliest centuries developed a threefold order of deacon, presbyter, and bishop. This was entirely intelligible, as there were no precise orders of ministry delineated in Scripture. These orders of ministry should be seen as charismatic gifts in the church. In other words, the Holy Spirit provided for order, continuity, and succession across the generations.

Hence it was and is appropriate that the church should set apart and ordain deacons, presbyters, and bishops. Aside from their own ministries bestowed in initiation, these offices take explicit responsibility for the transmission of the Gospel and corporate faithfulness thereto across the generations. These orders in their own way are set apart and ordained for four purposes: to enable all to find their ministry of service in the body; to preach and teach the canonical commitments of the church, most especially its chief canon, the Scriptures, the Word of God; to administer and rightly order the worship of the church, most especially the sacraments which embody the Gospel in a special way; and to hand over the treasures of the church including the treasure of the publicly set apart or ordained orders of the church across the generations in new acts of ordination.

I stress again that these are charismatic realities in the church. They are gifts of the Holy Spirit and our decisions about training, procedures, and ordination must be approached in this light. It spells disaster when these particular ministries are "professionalized" and secularized. We are bound by this conception of these ministries to wrestle with issues of call and discernment. These matters require spiritual discernment in the body and cannot merely be approached in terms of skills, training, and election. It also spells disaster when we reduce all ministry to these ministries setting up unholy boundaries between the "ministers" and laity. The solution to this problem is not to do away with ordination or to get rid of the publicly ordained ministries by ordaining everybody. What we need is a deeper vision of all the gifts of the Holy Spirit for the mission of the church; a more precise vision of the particular ministries of those who are set apart to be deacons, presbyters, and bishops; and a steady resolution to let the Holy Spirit truly rule in our midst and create the fullness of the body of Christ.

From the preceding it is clear that those who are publicly ordained or set apart have a fourfold set of responsibilities. Within this set of responsibilities, it is also clear that one special responsibility is the responsibility of rightly administering the sacraments. The celebration of the sacraments will invariably fall into disrepair if discipline and accountability are not in place and exercised. The sacramental life of the church can very easily degenerate into a casual service where crucial elements of the service are omitted; where anything (including Coke and chips) is substituted for bread and wine; and where appropriate preparation is set aside because of sentimentality or carelessness. We can be sure that Murphy's Law will operate: If things can go wrong, they will go wrong. One way to prevent such degeneration is to establish a system of accountability wherein the elders or presbyters and bishops are given the publicly authorized and personally accepted responsibility of ensuring the proper ordering of the sacraments.

One very good reason for insisting that only, say, elders and deacons administer the sacraments is simply that of doing all things decently and in order. Given the human propensity for distortion and corruption, it is vital that the church protect herself against impostors and vagabonds. The great enemy here is laziness and carelessness, coupled with spurious arguments from the priesthood of all believers.

However, we have to cut deeper in our thinking; there are theological and not just pragmatic reasons for restricting our practice in the conventional manner. The Church possesses in her sacraments precious treasures that in the Holy Spirit mediate the very presence of Christ. We are not dealing here with empty signs and psychological memorials. In preaching, we are dealing with the Word of God in verbal proclamation through the action of the Holy Spirit. In the Eucharist, we are dealing with the body and blood of Christ given in the bread and wine through the action of the Holy Spirit. In baptism, we are not just dedicating folk to God but invoking the promise of God to work in and through the water we use and looking in faith for the Holy Spirit to make a real difference in the life of those baptized. We dare not trivialize these practices and materials; we are stupid and ignorant if we hand them over in the church without proper training and oversight; hence, it is entirely proper that they be placed under oversight and administration, and that they be restricted to those who are set apart for precisely that end in the life of the church as a whole.[9] In calling on the Holy Spirit in ordination to make this precious work possible we are expressing a deep intuition about the presence of the Triune God in our midst who comes to us in concrete, specific ways that bring genuine salvation from sin here and now. Our sacramental practice will reveal our theological presuppositions on this matter. For sacramental symbolists, it does not really matter in the end what we do and who does it. For sacramental realists, it really does matter what we do and who does it. We pay our theological money, and we get exactly the practice we pay for. Cheap and symbolist theologies give us cheap and minimalist practice; robust and realistic theologies give us robust and restricted practices. We should stand firmly on the side of robust and realistic theologies of the sacraments at

---

[9] I am not here restricting the training to the standard academic training common in the West; some of this training is so inept intellectually and theologically that it would be ludicrous to do so, aside from the fact that it is a recent development in the history of the church.

this point. The invocation of the Holy Spirit is no empty ritual; it is a serious invitation to the Holy Spirit to come and work in, with, and through the relevant practices.

What are we asking the Holy Spirit to do? In preaching, we are inviting the Holy Spirit to accompany the spoken word with an inward Word that will bring home the truth and significance of what is said to the mind and heart of the congregation. In baptism, taking adult baptism as the paradigm, we are inviting the Holy Spirit to come upon and indwell the baptized so that they are knitted into the Body of Christ and endowed with relevant gifts for the ministry in the church as a whole. In the case of infants, we are asking the Holy Spirit to come upon them and within them in a way appropriate to their status as infants so that in the future they may enter into the fullness of the working of the Holy Spirit in their lives. In the Eucharist, we are asking the Holy Spirit to work through the elements of bread and wine in such a way that we are spiritually nourished by the hidden life of the Risen Lord to live a life of faith, hope, and love.

Of course, it is the specific identification of the action of the Holy Spirit in the Eucharist that has been the source of intense discussion across the centuries. We can detect two kinds of inquiry, one so recent that it is scarcely discussed theologically in the literature, the other ancient and medieval but still very much alive today. On the more recent front, we have learned that the ancient practice was essentially a real meal which across the years became more and more formalized to the point where one can genuinely worry about the continuity between the earliest practice and the later developments.[10] One detects in the earliest practice a significant continuity with the Jewish practices of meals which were a powerful expression of fellowship, prayer, thanksgiving, and communion with the Risen Lord.[11] The difference between this and later developments can be graphically captured by the fact that one could go home literally drunk from the service. This more informal vision of the earliest practice dovetails with a wider informality where all the members were expected to participate by sharing in the manifold gifts of the Spirit present in their midst.

In the later developments, it is clear that the practices related to the Eucharist became more and more streamlined with all sorts of cultural additions introduced, additions which reflected, for example, the ceremonial conventions of Byzantine political practices and the symbolism they embodied.[12]

---

[10] For a brief but tendentious, biblicist narrating of this development see Ben Witherington III, *Making a Meal of It: Rethinking the Theology of the Lord's Supper* (Waco, TX: Baylor University Press, 2007).

[11] The potential forerunner for the Lord's Supper is that of the *chabûrah* meal shared by friends gathered for religious purposes.

[12] It is obvious that the church added other practices to baptism, most notably anointing with oil and the laying on of hands, that were not part of the original rite. This is a good reason to be skeptical of making much of baptism and Eucharist as sacraments authorized by Jesus. Too

To be sure, the core practices remained intact, but with the loss of the varied ministries of the members, there was an inevitable tendency to protect the practice from the everyday participants by developing theories of priesthood and sacrifice that in turn were wedded to elaborate metaphysical accounts of causation that focused on how the bread and the wine became the body and blood of Christ. This reached a climax in the West in Aquinas' elaborate attempt to describe what was going on in terms of transubstantiation, that is, in terms of the sacramental transformation of water into wine, of wine into the blood of Christ, and of bread into the body of Christ, including his muscles. These miracles in turn were enriched by a doctrine of concomitance in which it was held that once you had in hand the body and blood of Christ then you also had present the divinity of Christ. Not surprisingly, appropriate devotions were developed in order to reflect this understanding of divine physical presence.[13]

It is easy to get lost in the highways and byways of metaphysical speculations about sacramental causation at this point. There is a place for this in the work of the theologian. However, we should make haste slowly at this point.[14] We know what the basic options are. We can have a purely symbolic account that highlights a doctrine of divine absence and makes much of human action in remembrance and reflection. We can have a maximalist account which revives a doctrine of divine impanation where in an action parallel to the incarnation Christ indwells the bread and wine.[15] In between, we can have transubstantiation, consubstantiation, mysterious divine presence, deeming, and transfiguration.[16] Even those who insist on the canonical teaching of the Western Catholic tradition identified in terms of transubstantiation are often quick to say that this simply represents one way to capture the mystery involved. We should not get lost in this thicket of options at the cost of losing our fundamental bearings.[17]

much of our historical work in this arena is driven by epistemic anxiety about the transmission of grace and by exclusive claims to ownership by this or that church.

[13] I provide an extended account of Aquinas on divine action in the Eucharist in volume II chapter 8.

[14] I shall explore some of the more arcane issues involved in an examination of the fascinating proposals put forward by Michael Dummett as an alternative to what he thinks is a degenerative form of Aristotelian metaphysics adopted by Thomas Aquinas. See Michael Dummett, "The Intelligibility of Eucharistic Doctrine," in William J. Abraham and Steve W. Holzer, eds., *The Rationality of Religious Belief: Essays in Honour of Basil Mitchell* (Oxford: Clarendon Press, 1987), 231–62.

[15] This is the line taken by Marilyn McCord Adams, *Christ and Horrors: The Coherence of Christology* (Cambridge: Cambridge University Press, 2006).

[16] I shall take up the meaning of these options in my treatment of Dummett.

[17] Those who want to bet the store on Eucharistic practice as the cure for the major ills of the church are well advised to take a longer look at the history of those churches who did precisely that. Eucharistic fundamentalism is no more successful than biblical fundamentalism.

As we move forward, consider the following as basic. First, we need to take seriously the new historical information about the nature of Eucharistic practice in the early period and experiment with the celebration of the Lord's Supper in our homes. Where the doctrine of ministry allows it, we should authorize deacons to preside in order that things be done decently and in order. If this is greeted with consternation, then I encourage those who feel this way to examine the consternation that arose when presbyters rather than bishops were authorized to preside at the Eucharist in the fourth century.[18] Moreover, Gentile churches should enter into serious conversation with Jewish churches in order to think through the intellectual and practical issues involved.

C. K. Barrett, the distinguished New Testament scholar, provides a dramatic rendering of what might be possible given a vivid updating of what was going on in Corinth in the wake of Paul's missionary work there. Preaching at a service of Holy Communion in his own tradition, he notes that the Lord's Supper was likely held after work on a Saturday evening when church members gathered together to eat a common meal and to incorporate within it the mandate of the Lord to take bread and wine and eat in remembrance of what he had done for them. Noting that he had been exaggerating a tad when he described the meal initially as a kind of fish supper, he continued:

what I have just been saying is as good New Testament scholarship as I am capable of. This is what the Lord's Supper was like in Corinth, and in many places where Christianity began. We are having a simple sort of service today, but even so we shall not be doing what I should really like to do. I should like to have been able to say, 'on July 25 we shall meet not at 10.30 but at 12.30, and we shall have the Sunday roast beef and Yorkshire pudding on the premises. And we shall talk together about our joys and our problems as Christians and our church members, and how we say our prayers, and how we can possibly pay for the roof. Then a dozen people will give us bits of Christian truth, and we will pray together. Then I or some better person will say, 'Do you remember what Jesus did?' We'll do it in remembrance of him—remembrance that means faith, and loyalty, and service and obedience. It isn't only the Yorkshire pudding; I couldn't have produced that. And if I had, perhaps you would never forgive me. Perhaps now that we have only one service on Sunday, we could do it some Sunday evening, and if there are a few who would like, in thoroughly Methodist fashion, to share our understanding of Christian faith and life, not to mention our failures to understand Christian faith and life, they could do so. But that is not for me to say.'[19]

---

[18] See John Zizioulas, *Eucharist, Bishop, Church: The Unity of the Church in the Divine Eucharist and the Bishop in the First Three Centuries* (Brookline, MA: Holy Cross Orthodox Press, 2001).

[19] Ben Witherington III, ed., *Luminescence: The Sermons of C. K. Barrett and Fred Barrett* (Eugene, OR: Cascade Books, 2017), vol. II, 115.

Second, we should recognize, of course, that the practice of the Lord's Supper is mandated by the Lord and that it has been integral to the life of the church from the beginning. However, above and beyond all this, it is the recurring experience of the faithful that in this practice we do really come to be nourished by the bread and the wine, by the body and blood of Christ himself. This experience is much too deep and widespread to be ignored; it is a strong warrant not just for weekly practice of Eucharistic celebration but for insisting on a realistic as opposed to merely symbolic interpretation of divine presence and action. God does indeed meet us at the Lord's table and ministers to each in ways that are diverse and profoundly person-relative.

Third, in terms of divine action, we might well construe the relevant divine action along occasionalist lines. The formula is a simple one: the performing of certain human actions (the taking of bread and wine, the divine invocation in the epiclesis, the eating of bread, and the drinking of wine) become the recurring occasion in which God promises to meet with us according to our manifold spiritual and physical needs. Just as signing a check becomes the occasion for the exchange of goods, or the recurrence of a birthday becomes the occasion for the giving of diverse gifts, likewise, the practices related to the Eucharist become the occasion when God really does meet with us and feeds our souls with grace that makes effective our salvation. Given the promises and reliability of God, we can agree wholeheartedly with the long-standing conviction that the action of God is not dependent on the moral standing of those who preside. We look to the promises of God not to the virtues or vices of those who preside or participate.

Mention of potential vices of those who preside brings us in conclusion to an acute problem that was flagged out the outset, namely, the problem of failure within the leadership of the church. Paul warns us of this possibility when he speaks of potential savage wolves who will readily destroy the flock.[20] Jesus provides similar warnings when he speaks of the dangers of false prophets who appear in sheep's clothing but inwardly are ravenous wolves.[21] Symeon the New Theologian wrestles with this problem in his epistles; there have been many who understandably have raised eyebrows if not clenched fists about his orthodoxy.[22] He goes so far as to claim that the authority to perform sacred rites and to bind and loose can be removed from, say, unworthy bishops and presbyters, and given to worthy monks who thereby through the work of the Holy Spirit exercise a genuinely apostolic ministry.[23] It is no surprise that his life and work has been buried from sight across the centuries, for he advocates a charismatic account of ministry as opposed to a

---

[20] Acts 20:29.   [21] Matthew 7:15.

[22] See H. J. M. Turner, ed., *The Epistles of St Symeon the New Theologian* (Oxford: Oxford University Press, 2009).

[23] Ibid., 55.

purely juridical one that has been treated as manifest heresy. However, he stands as one of the canonical theologians of the church, so, though his work may be marginalized and buried, it can no longer be ignored.[24]

I share Symeon's profound if complex response to the problem of systematic corruption in the leadership of the church. The record of failure is there for all to see historically. The spiritual consequences of failure are at times devastating for the spiritual welfare of church members. The long-standing debates about the nature of reformation and renewal bear witness to the depth of the problem. Two considerations are enough to secure the position of Symeon, broadly conceived. First, it is unthinkable that God will abandon his project of establishing his kingdom here and now in the future. If he keeps his promise to the biological descendants of Abraham across centuries of failure and persecution, even more so can we be sure God will keep his promises to establish his kingdom and its communities to the end of time. If God's People fail, he will raise up stones to cry out in proclamation; he can even raise up stones as children of Abraham. Second, it is obvious to anyone not in the grip of some exclusivist, ideological vision of the church that God has again and again raised up all sorts of groups to carry the banner of the Gospel when the standing institutions of the church are abused and misused by the ravenous wolves who show up from time to time. By their fruits we shall know them. The big ecclesiastical battalions, the great churches of Christendom, will no doubt ensure that the work of God in their midst is noted and defended. It is the little platoons who have always needed to be defended from the hostile evaluations of the bigger battalions. Even so, the little platoons despite their vices and failings will be vindicated by God himself where necessary. For my part, I am content to serve as a door-keeper among one of the least of the tribes of Israel.

---

[24] I deal with the claims of Symeon in this arena in chapter 7 of volume II.

15

Salvation

Predestination, Grace, and Conceptual Orientation

> Jesus answered, 'Very truly, I tell you, no one can enter the kingdom of God without being born of water and Spirit. What is born of the flesh is flesh, and what is born of the Spirit is spirit. Do not be astonished that I said to you, "You must be born from above."'
>
> John 3:5–7.

At the outset, we need to clear the decks by resolving two central challenges that get in the way of a robust account of the Christian life in the kingdom of God. I have in mind the problem of predestination and the problem of freedom and grace. The first of these, the challenge of predestination, addresses the issue of God's design plan for salvation; the second of these, the challenge of grace and freedom, addresses the question of the relation between divine action and human action in salvation. For the moment, I shall leave the notion of salvation undetermined, that is, I shall take it as a generic, inclusive concept that refers to the reordering of human existence in the kingdom of God. So initially and provisionally I will use it to cover such concepts as justification and sanctification.

Predestination matters because it takes us deep into the divine decision to establish the kingdom of God here and in the life to come. It is God and God alone who decides to inaugurate his kingdom; and it is God and God alone who decides, say, the policies related to its membership. These matters are not worked out, say, by committees of experts, or by ecclesiastical commissions, or by an order of learned theologians. This surely is a relief, given what we already know about human sin and its effects. Yet the best-known vision of divine predestination has had the opposite effect; it has cast a deep shadow over the Christian tradition in the West; so much so that it has become virtually a taboo subject, like sex was to the Victorians; or like death is to many contemporary Americans. It has posited a vision in which God determines from all eternity that a certain number—Anselm thought the number matched the number of fallen angels—will be saved by the grace of God and a certain number will be damned forever because they fail to be given the requisite measure of grace. Moreover, even though they could have been saved if God had given them the appropriate amount of grace, they remain responsible for their damnation because they freely chose the way of rebellion and sin.

We see immediately that predestination spills over into the problem of grace and freedom. Calvin's doctrine of predestination is motivated by an intense desire to safeguard the doctrine of grace. The problem of grace and freedom is in essence a very simple one. It arises because of two convictions which are deeply embedded in the tradition. On the one side, Christians have maintained that salvation is a matter of grace. We do not save ourselves; God saves us; hence God deserves all the credit; we do not. On the other side, Christians have insisted that we are saved or redeemed as free agents. God does not save robots or automatons; God's salvation comes to genuine human beings who are in a real sense free. At the very least they can say "no" to God. Hence human beings cannot be saved without their cooperation. But once you allow cooperation, then this allows us to take credit, and salvation is no longer fully a matter of grace. Double, unconditional predestination is lurking in the wings like a lion ready to pounce and devour us. The situation is so hazardous, that any other notion of predestination will be dismissed as a pale imitation of the real thing.

Classical Protestant theologians have readily sacrificed the second half of the dilemma represented by the tension between grace and freedom. Put simply, they hold on to the claim that salvation is a matter of grace and jettison, if necessary, the insistence on freedom. The pressure to make this move is enormous. It is not difficult to see why the Reformers were pulled in this direction. Here is a sampling of the considerations that weighed with them. They lived under the shadow of the Augustinian–Pelagian debate, and there was no doubt that Augustine was on the side of the angels. In addition, the Reformers lived at a time when they could see the disastrous consequences of any doctrine of merit; these consequences were both spiritual and pastoral. Doctrines of merit had caused enormous psychological damage; and they had undercut the heart of the Gospel. Hence, they were convinced that whatever the Gospel was, it was a gospel of grace. Furthermore, human beings were liberated by God and not by themselves. Human beings, they felt, were deeply corrupt, they were in bondage; indeed, the will was subject to bondage; hence salvation had to be all of God, or there could be no salvation at all. This analysis was also supported by experience. Many of them had been dragged against their will into the kingdom of God. Augustine was a splendid example of this phenomenon; there were many others. So, any idea of sitting down dispassionately and making a decision for or against the claims of the Gospel was a fantasy that did not fit the facts.

All these factors made it difficult to keep the freedom side of the dilemma or dialectic intact. Some, like Martin Luther, dropped it entirely. Human beings are in bondage; they are free not to do good but to sin. Others, like Calvin, attempted to work out a doctrine where you have a kind of human freedom but where everything is ultimately determined by divine predestination.[1] Calvin has a kind of double-agency theory. God determines everything. However, when humans sin, the predestination of God works in such a way that the cause and occasion lies within us, and, therefore, we are free and justly judged by God. John Wesley tried a third way to solve it by pressing the significance of prevenient grace, that is, the grace which comes before justifying and sanctifying grace.[2] Such grace is given universally; it enables everyone to say "yes" to God's saving grace. Hence God restores a measure of freedom to everyone. Wesley, in fact, did not believe in free will; he believed rather in free grace.

We cannot solve this problem by some kind of parceling out of proportions. It is not as if we can attribute, say, ninety percent to divine agency and ten percent to human agency. It only exacerbates the problem to have a cake-cutting exercise. In fact, it plays right into the hands of Augustine and Calvin, for they rightly point out that this opens the door to a doctrine of works and merit with a vengeance. We can, they will say, take credit for the ten percent that is our part. If we are to solve this issue, we have to stand back and look at the terms in which it is expressed. Here we can get genuine help from modern discussions in analytical philosophy on the nature of explanation.[3]

Consider for a moment what happens when we try to explain why events happen. Causal explanations are really fascinating when you examine them carefully. Why did my car break down? What caused the fire in my study? What causes people to grow? What caused Hitler to go to war? We develop intricate theories and narratives when we try to explain why events happen. This is precisely the territory we are on when we are dealing with the grace and freedom problem. We are seeking to ascertain the cause of our salvation. Do we save ourselves? Or does God save us? We are trespassing on the terrain of causality.

When we use causal language, we can take it in two radically different directions. If we confuse these two directions, we will land in deep confusion. In one kind of causal explanation we are looking for the complete causal conditions. In this case, if you know the causes, you know the outcome. You have a classic case of deterministic causation. You are looking for the complete specification of the antecedent, necessary and sufficient conditions of the event. Suppose you are an auto-engineer and you want to explain how a car

---

[1] I provide an extended review of Calvin's position in volume II, chapter 10.

[2] For a fine exposition see Randy Maddox, *Responsible Grace* (Nashville, TN: Kingswood Books, 1994).

[3] See J. R. Lucas, "Freedom and Grace," in *Freedom and Grace* (London: SPCK, 1976). I provide an exposition and defense of Lucas' position in *An Introduction to the Philosophy of Religion* (Englewood Cliffs, NJ: Prentice Hall, 1985), chapter 12.

works. You will provide a comprehensive account of what is going on in terms of the laws governing engine combustion, the various forces at work in the environment, the laws of gravity, and so on. With this in hand you can predict and you can design cars. We deploy a complete causal explanation.

However, there is another kind of causal explanation. Here what we do is pick out the most significant causal factor at work in the situation. Suppose my house burns down. We ask: why? Reports from the fire department show that the cause of the fire was the fact that a student fire-bombed my house because of the low grade in the mid-term exam. This is intelligible. We tell all our friends about it. Why did my house burn down? It was fire-bombed by an upset student. This is not a complete causal explanation. To have that we need to know that the house was made of combustible materials, that the weather conditions were right, that the fire alarm failed, and so on. What interests us in this case is the ascription of responsibility and accountability. In this case, although we speak of a sole cause or agent, this is a locution which does not preclude the role of other agents and causes.

The whole debate about freedom and grace has hinged on ignoring this kind of causal discourse. The language of grace is our way of ascribing responsibility for salvation to God. We are picking out the crucially significant causal factor in salvation. This does not entail determinism; it does not rule out that humans have to respond and in a real sense act. What has happened is that this kind of causal ascription has been read as a full and complete account of all the antecedent conditions. This has led straight to a particular doctrine of divine foreordination and predestination; and in turn this has not permitted us to speak of a genuine human freedom in response to God.

Once you put the language of grace in its proper causal context, there is no need either to deny human action or freedom, or to ascribe merit or credit to humans for those actions they perform in their relation to God. This in turn frees us up to work through a really beautiful account of predestination, one which sees it as undergirding the extraordinary mercy of God. God has decided in eternity that those who respond in simple faith and repentance to his Word will be saved; those who do not, will not be saved. God will have mercy on whom he will have mercy; if a Gentile comes in simple faith to Jesus Christ in repentance and baptism, then he or she will be saved. This is God's decision; all sorts of folk may object for a host of reasons; this is an exercise in total futility; it has been predestined by God and God will not change his mind because we want to set up works of the law or various exercises in virtue as the condition for acceptance in his kingdom. To speak of gaining merit or taking credit is simply ludicrous in this case; it means we have failed to understand the lengths to which divine love and mercy has gone to rescue us from sin and evil. This is the first and final element that needs to be asserted without prevarication in thinking about divine predestination; it underwrites the extraordinary mercy of God. One of the great tragedies of Christian theology has been precisely that the doctrine has become a cover for its opposite, namely, a massive reduction in our vision of divine mercy and grace.

Any challenge to provide a novel resolution to the problem of grace and freedom will, no doubt, be greeted with skepticism. Some will go so far as to declare the problem a mystery on a par with the mystery of the inner life of the Trinity or the mystery of the divine and human in Christ. Thus, it will be immediately objected that faith in Christ, the crucial condition for salvation, is itself a gift of God; so even if we allow for human action as suggested here we are not out of the woods. As it happens, I shall insist in due course that human action is essential to salvation, so it looks as if I am setting myself up for massive failure. One way to frame this worry is to say that it is not enough to have the capacity, say, to repent or to take up our cross and follow Christ; we must also exercise that capacity and actually repent and take up our crosses. There is a gap between the capacity to perform an action and the actual exercise of that capacity. Hence, critics will readily seize on this as the Achilles' heel of my position. We need, it is said, divine action—often identified in terms of the action of divine concurrence—to bridge the gap.

There is at present a significant consensus across the board that some theory of double-agency is the only serious way out of the dilemma. So, my repenting of my sins is both a human act and a divine act. Somehow we are dealing with a very special kind of causality, a divine causality that can do the wonderful work, it is said, of bringing it about that I freely repent of my sins. To deploy the conception of causality I am working with here is to confuse divine causality and human causality, as if God were simply a bigger and better version of human agents. Really harsh critics will lift up the banner of idolatry at this point and walk away in triumph. Happily, such critics are no longer allowed to stone us, as in days of yore. Nor should they be allowed to transpose a difference in the semantics of causality into a full-scale spiritual attack on their opponents.

We are already knee deep in the metaphysics of agency and causality, so I will not presume to provide any kind of immediate rebuttal of the objections in play. However, suffice it to say three things in defense. First, my position involves a straightforward analogical use of the language of causality; so, I am not at all moved by an appeal to some kind of transcendent causality that has been used as an alternative. In fact, at best, this kind of move simply begs the question before us; at worst, it is entirely ad hoc. Secondly, I also think that the critic is playing fast and loose with the idea of a capacity. To have a capacity to perform an action is precisely to be able to perform that action; this is what any genuine capacity gives us. To be sure, we can be helped in exercising a capacity; but who will deny that we have the assistance of the Holy Spirit in coming to faith. However, assisting someone to do something is a far cry from bridging the gap between having a capacity and exercising that capacity. Finally, I defy anyone to say with a straight face that when I repent of my sins, God is also repenting of my sins; or that when I attend the means of grace, God is also attending the means of grace. Once we get back to the rough ground of looking at specific human and divine actions and eschew high-octane generalities about double-agency, the whole enterprise ceases to make coherent sense. Or at least this is how it appears to me. Hence, I recommend the complete reframing of the problem of grace and freedom as the way forward.

With these preliminary moves in place we can now move explicitly to thinking about the concept of salvation. I noted at the outset that I was using this concept in a conventional way to cover the concepts of justification and sanctification. As often happens in theology, even this way into our topic displays a mental cramp that will need to be relieved if we are to understand what is at stake. To get the relief we need, we need to step back and see the bigger picture. We need a framework for locating our discourse about justification and sanctification. That fundamental framework will be determined by two factors: by our account of the divine–human relation; and by our account of sin. This means that our doctrine of salvation will be rooted in a divine–human interpersonal relationship; more particularly, in the repair and restoration of the divine–human relationship. So, the fundamental framework is relational. This basic framework provides a map on which to plot the rich imagery used to explore what God does to save us and what happens to us as we respond to the action of God in our lives. Our language at this level is profoundly analogical or metaphorical. We deploy a rich range of concepts, and each of these has a range of suggestive possibilities which are almost inexhaustible.

The primary framework, I repeat, is relational, but relational understood, not in a narrow pietistic sense that sees God as our cosmic chum, but in a robust sense that takes into account the transcendence and holiness of God. We are to think of a variety of ways in which the relationship with God has been broken, how it is restored by divine action, resulting in a change in the human agent. All of this is to be seen within the horizon of the arrival of the kingdom of God and experienced in and through the life and ministry of the church. Initially I shall focus on the divine action, leaving the identity of the relevant human actions to later. While what follows may look like a dry exposition of lifeless concepts, in reality the various alternatives represent a rich tapestry of human experience.

Consider the concept of salvation. I have thus far treated it as an inclusive concept covering justification and sanctification; in its origin, it was tied to the idea of deliverance in battle. Thus, it depicted human agents as defeated. They were weak, powerless, and morally impotent. Now through the action of the Son and the Spirit they have been delivered; the ensuing result is that there is a new power at work in their lives; they have been rescued from defeat and made strong and whole. While the image starts out and draws its meaning from a very particular experience of defeat and deliverance, one can readily see why it was picked up as an umbrella concept to cover all that is done to restore human agents to union with God. Hence, it can be depicted in terms of the past, present, and future tenses. One has been saved; one is being saved; and one will be saved.

Closely related in meaning is the concept of reconciliation. In this instance the originating description speaks of hostility to God, reflected in turn in hostility to others. As a result of what God has done in Christ and the Holy Spirit, we are now reconciled to God and have peace with God. This peace in turn gives energy to be reconciled to neighbors and enemies. In this context, we can also speak of being totally and utterly forgiven by God. Closely related to salvation in meaning is the concept of redemption. In this case, we start out as slaves, as those held in bondage to sin, to idolatry, and to our disordered desires. In redeeming us Christ has in his death paid the ransom to rescue us from slavery; the outcome is liberty and freedom.

A very different set of concepts is drawn from the law courts. Consider the concept of justification. Here we are depicted in the wrong, as guilty in the courts of the Lord. But now, through faith in the work of Christ and in the faithfulness of Christ on our behalf, we are acquitted, declared to be in the right before God because of our faith, and are set free to love and serve God and our neighbor. This is not a mere verbal proclamation; we are put in the right before God. As a follow-up to this, consider the idea of the witness of the Holy Spirit, whereby we cry "Abba, Father." Again, the setting is that of the law courts. However, in this instance, the problem is one of condemnation and lack of assurance. Given what we have done and what we have been, we cannot believe that God has shown favor towards us; that his grace and generosity extends to us. In order to remedy this situation, the Holy Spirit bears witness with our spirits that we really are the children of God. This is not a matter of a mere deductive argument—the witness of our own spirit that we have been turned around—it is a matter of the inner voice of God telling us that we are his children in a way analogous to a child addressing his or her father in terms that are daring in their boldness and intimacy.

In turn, the image of being children of God calls up two other powerful images, namely, that of new birth or regeneration and adoption. The language of new birth depicts us initially in the womb, unaware of our standing before God, blind to the goodness of God, and deaf to the good news of the Gospel. Through the Spirit, we are born again; we get to start all over again, mysteriously given life by water and the Spirit. Switching to the language of adoption, we are no longer orphans not knowing who we are, bereft of a family identity; now born again, we belong to the family of God with brothers and sisters all over the world, and possessing a magnificent inheritance through the Son. Indeed, our crying "Abba, Father" means that we are now in an analogous relation to that of the relation of the Son to the Father through the Spirit.

Consider now three images drawn from the terrain of liturgy, including the pagan liturgy or cult of the Roman Empire. So, we are baptized by the Son in the Spirit. Here the language is drawn from the practice of dipping or immersion. Before, we were perhaps only nominally Christian, or we have merely turned in conversion to Christ. The Son immerses us in the Spirit; as a result, we are filled with God, intoxicated or drunk in the Holy Spirit. Compare this image with that of the image of sanctification. The basic idea is that of being made holy. Something, it can be an item of furniture or a building, starts out as profane, entirely devoted to secular usage. It is then sanctified, set apart for the purposes of God. Having come to Christ, we are now set apart for divine purposes; we are no longer profane but holy. Compare this imagery with that of the image of divinization. This time, the concept is drawn from the political cult of the Roman world where we begin with a person being merely human and earthly; then his status is transformed or changed so that he is not just the emperor but has become divine. He participates in the divine nature. As it was often expressed: God became human that we might become divine.

In the modern period, many have deployed the concept of conversion as a crucial concept to depict a pivotal element in the Christian life. Others have made much of the concept of liberation. The former has received extended psychological attention; the latter extended political attention. In the former case, the analogy in play is essentially spatial; we are lost, headed in the wrong direction. God has intervened and called to us to change direction, so we are now no longer lost but are headed in the right direction. In the latter case, the emphasis has fallen on the reality of oppression due to wider social and political arrangements. The latter is then spelled out in various political categories, often Marxist or post-Marxist in orientation. For this reason, they have not become the common coin of the realm. However, the image of liberation draws attention to the material ways in which salvation has been depicted, for example, in the Old Testament. It thus provides a point of entry for exploring the social and political changes brought about by the inauguration of the kingdom of God in Christ. The other image that shows up in this arena is that of reconciliation; the tension between that and liberation has been a source of fruitful enrichment that should be borne in mind in the arena of any theology of politics.

Perceptive readers will have noted by now the large number of concepts that have been used: salvation, reconciliation, redemption, justification, witness of the Spirit, new birth, regeneration, adoption, conversion, baptism in the Holy Spirit, sanctification, divinization, conversion, and liberation. It is initially very important to deploy as many of these as possible. Too often our concept of salvation is thin and emaciated. We are constantly tempted to reduce and simplify. If we are to attend to the full canonical witness, we need to ponder all of these rich notions. Even to work with just two concepts, say, justification and sanctification, is inadequate. To deploy just two out of the thirteen or fourteen is a very poor batting average. There is far more to the Christian life than simply justification and sanctification. The whole tradition needs to be corrected at this point.

The obvious rejoinder to this proposal is to say that Scripture only focuses on, say, justification or on justification and sanctification. Therefore, the tradition, following Luther, or Wesley, has been right to focus on these concepts to the exclusion of others. The reply to this is surely simple. If we take this route we will end up with a canon within the canon, as Luther shows only too well. It may well be that we even misread the designated canon within the canon. At any rate, it is almost inevitable that we will end up with a narrow reading of Paul as the heart of the Christian message. This is just plainly inadequate.

It should also be pointed out that if we look for a single focus in the canon, neither justification nor sanctification satisfies this quest. If there is one focus—and I stress the "*if*" here—it is surely to be located in the acquisition of the Holy Spirit. This is how the gospels describe the whole point of Christ's work, that is, that he baptizes us in the Holy Spirit. This focus dovetails in a fascinating way with developments among Pentecostals who have looked on baptism in the Holy Spirit as the great missing lacuna of the contemporary church. While they do not use the exact same language, this is what some of the great saints, especially of the Eastern church, pick out as the pearl of great price in the Christian life. At this stage, we need to be very careful how we proceed. In stressing the acquisition of the Holy Spirit, the Eastern church tends to neglect the significance of justification. Thus, one misses the note of assurance that accompanies the doctrine of justification. In stressing baptism in the Holy Spirit, Pentecostals have tended to restrict the designated experience they have in mind to episodes in the Christian life marked by speaking in tongues. One suspects that this enterprise is sometimes driven by epistemic anxiety and even spiritual distress. What is needed is a comprehensive account of Christian initiation into the kingdom of God that reaches for all that the Holy Spirit does in salvation, broadly conceived. So, our best policy is to explore all the concepts at our disposal in the tradition. If we neglect any of them we can bet our Sunday lunch that some sect or group will catch us off guard by pressing the significance of a neglected dimension of salvation.

We can see this at present with the deep interest in the socio-political side of salvation expressed by the heavy emphasis on liberation. This is a crucial corrective to the Lutheran and pietistic focus on, say, justification or new birth. It provides a healthy if somewhat overdrawn reaction against an obsession with the vertical dimensions of the individual's relation to God. As noted above, it serves as one point of entry into the relation between the kingdom of God and the world of politics. Yet it is not the only point of entry. Moreover, the solution to reduction at one end of our theology is not to opt for a reduction at the other end of the spectrum. There is no need to repeat the formal error of Luther by simply substituting liberation for justification. The solution is to expand and enrich our vocabulary to include all the verbs of God's acts of salvation. It is only by some such move that we can avoid a fresh narrowing of the faith and retrieve a thoroughly comprehensive analysis of salvation.

One way forward at this point is to take up these matters in the field of ascetic theology. For Catholic theologians, this has tended to concentrate on the interpretation of mystical states and experiences; for Protestants, this has tended to focus on discussion of the *ordo salutis* or *via salutis*, that is, the temporal ordering of the appropriation of, say, justification, new birth, and sanctification. Happily, there is now a serious effort to work comprehensively across denominational lines. Thus, the work of Phoebe Palmer, a very important figure in the Holiness Movement that gave birth to Pentecostalism, has been helpfully compared to Teresa of Avila in her journey into the life of God.[4] The cross-fertilization of different interpretations of baptism in the Spirit in the Charismatic Movement has also proven to be a rich field of comparative investigation.[5] Sorting out the various concepts deployed and relating these in a critical way to the phenomenology of the spiritual life is a daunting task. Equally daunting is the correlation of these concepts with the sacramental and other liturgical practices of the church.

We can usefully illustrate the difficulties by returning to the concept of baptism in the Spirit. For the sake of argument, let's agree that this is indeed a crucial concept, not least because all of the gospels insist that the Son had come into the world not just to die but to baptize us in the Holy Spirit. Let's also agree to the following additional propositions. First, that this work of the Son was initially fulfilled at Pentecost. Second, that the core meaning of this concept is that of immersion or dipping. Third, that many Christians across the Christian world have found this concept invaluable in capturing various experiences in which they have come to encounter God, sometimes in extremely dramatic forms. Fourth, that baptism in the Spirit is a vital concept for delineating the moral and spiritual power that make manifest the kingdom of God here and now. Even with all that as a potential consensus on the table, we are hard-pressed to relate the concept of baptism in the Spirit to the phenomenology of spiritual experience and to the sacramental and liturgical practices of the church.

Rather than engage in a lengthy excursion into the pertinent literature, let me cut to the chase and provide a brief summary of my own reflection to date.

---

[4] See Elaine Heath, *Naked Faith: The Mystical Theology of Phoebe Palmer* (Edinburgh: James Clarke and Co., 2010).

[5] For a very fine study see Francis A. Sullivan, *Charisms and the Charismatic Renewal: A Biblical and Theological Study* (Eugene, OR: Wipf and Stock, 2004).

To begin, Pentecost was a unique event in salvation history that cannot be repeated. It was constituted by a sending of the Spirit in fullness that had not happened before; and it was a corporate rather than a person-relative experience with its own unique features. So, to look, for example, to speaking in tongues as its hallmark is to ignore other features of what happened and to look for a repetition of what is strictly unrepeatable. Second, the language of baptism builds on the analogy of immersion or dipping. Hence it is possible and even apt at times to use this language to apply to various person-relative experiences that have various psychological and external effects and that make a significant difference in the lives of those who have such experiences. Thus, it is a mistake to broaden the notion to cover the full working of the Holy Spirit across the lifetime of a believer. We need to keep the core of the analogy with baptism, namely, immersion; otherwise the language is idling and becomes more confusing than illuminating. We can also allow for other ways of speaking of such experiences in terms of, say, infilling, or release, or the welling up of fresh spiritual waters in the life of the believer. Third, these experiences are often experiences of deep ecstasy and joy analogous to being drunk. However, there are also profound experiences of the Spirit, akin to the Spirit sending our Lord into the wilderness, where the believer is tested and honed in their commitment to God. They may involve periods of drought and barrenness where one learns to trust not in reason or experience but entirely and exclusively in the Word of God. They may also involve experiences of suffering and skepticism which are crucial to the ministry given to this or that Christian in the church. Consider Mother Teresa's amazing identification with the darkness of the dying after a network of exceptionally powerful divine locutions; or consider a philosopher who is called to deal with intricate epistemological and metaphysical issues that require a penetrating skepticism of conventional wisdom in order to get to the bottom of the issues. We are much too ready to reach for the sensational and the positive.

Given this kind of diversity, it is very important to deal realistically with the full gamut of experiences of the Spirit and to come to terms with the complexity involved. We need a rich network of verbs to describe the manifold workings of the Spirit; and we need to deal both with the joy and the suffering that are inescapable in the life of faith. A corollary of this observation is that we need to be diligent in attending to those practices of the church which are the standing channels of grace and which are mandated in serious forms of Christian catechesis. Positive experiences will come and go; they are vital for providing energy and long-haul motivation in Christian discipleship. However, periods in the history of the church in which various subjective and spontaneous actions of the Holy Spirit are rediscovered are often followed by periods of disillusionment and disappointment. Individuals who have been promised all sorts of very precise experiences in the name of the Holy Spirit can readily find that efforts to streamline the wind of the Spirit are hazardous for their spiritual welfare. We dare not underestimate, belittle, or reject the more supernatural works of the living God; but they are no substitute for the hard work of loving our neighbors and working through to sound doctrine. The Spirit is also at work objectively in the practices of the church and in the life of the mind. We need primal religion with all its ragged edges; we also need tough discipline to contain its emotional excesses; and we need the guidance of the Holy Spirit to discern and articulate the deep truths involved.

Austin Farrer captures one of the pivotal issues involved in this fashion, namely, the combination of intellectual reflection and Pentecostal life.

> The heart of Pentecost is spontaneity. Pupils are always liable to be overshadowed by their tutor's wisdom, and what if the tutor is divine? The disciples of Jesus had their learning first; the moments were all too few and precious in which they could study the words and ways of a divine master. Then like the good master that he was, he saw that he could teach them no more by word and presence, so he turned to another business he had on hand; he went and died for them, having told them of an inward teacher who would finish their education by a different sort of instruction, by truth springing from the heart, not entering through the ear. The loss of their first teacher left them powerless, without direction or aim except to pray for the new teacher from heaven. And then when the day of Pentecost was fully come, their bodies and the air surrounding them trembled with spiritual thunder. A rushing wind sang in their ears, the fire ran out in tongues, their lips moved, and sound broke out by a power not their own. This was the new teaching from heaven, but what did it say? To what did it move? The Spirit would show in due time but meanwhile here was spontaneity, here was life.[6]

There is, no doubt, much unfinished business on hand in thinking through the full meaning of Pentecost and what it is to be baptized in the Spirit; however, whatever we do we must not lose the rediscovery of life that Farrer highlights here. Farrer would have also been the first to insist that we turn again and again to the objective transmission of divine grace and energy in the sacramental life of the church, or what we might more broadly call the means of grace. We are, he wittily remarks, "fish out of water." Speaking as a convinced Anglican he captures this complementary element in this way.

> Our communion in Christ is not a fountain where we sometimes come to bathe or to drink. It is fresh running water in which we swim, and out of which we never go, the element of the Christian life as the air is to the element of our physical being. Baptism plunges us into the water of life and therein to remain. Confirmation completes our baptism, and then we are in communion. Of course the

---

[6] Austin Farrer, "Pentecostal Fire," in *A Faith of Our Own* (New York: World Publishing Company, 1960), 117–18. Other Christians will spell out the practices in their own inimitable way, but the stress on the objective transmission of grace can be owned by all. Consider the revolution that would be possible if we took the epiclesis, the invocation of the Holy Spirit, in our communion services more seriously.

Christian communion in which we have our being is not continuously gathered at the altar; it is held together by prayer, companionship, and sheer faith in a bond invisible which Christ sustains, not we. Yet at regular times, anyhow at the Sunday Eucharist, it is visibly manifested and physically united. As St. Paul says. 'Because there is one loaf, we many individuals are one body, we all partake of one loaf.' Christ gave two sacraments as universally necessary for salvation, says our Anglican formula. There was the sacrament of initiation, the plunge into the pool— baptism, of which confirmation is the completion; and there is the sacrament of indwelling and perpetual abiding. It is no accident that the most precious words of Christ about his unbroken spiritual union with his disciples, recorded by St. John, have their setting at the Last Supper.[7]

Return for a moment to the debate about grace and freedom. Central to that discussion is an attempt to safeguard the primacy of God's action in salvation. This is surely correct. I have kept this by stressing the role of God's actions in the vast array of imagery deployed and in the specific action of baptism in the Spirit. I have said next to nothing about our actions in response to God's action and initiative. Farrer indirectly notes here that engaging in the practices of the church is something that requires human action and effort. We have to show up for baptism and the Eucharist; we have to consume the body and blood of our Lord. God does not get us out of bed on a Sunday morning; nor does he do our consuming of the Lord's precious gifts for us.

We need, therefore, to insist on genuine human response as essential to any restored divine–human relation. Human response is not an ephemeral shadow; it is genuine and substantial. As Paul puts it, we have to "work out our own salvation with fear and trembling, for God is at work in us, both to will and to work for God's good pleasure."[8] What are we to do to be saved, to be restored to a right relationship to God? Surely the actions to be performed are something like as follows: We are to relax and hear the Word of God. We are to struggle against evil and pursue the good at every level of existence. We are to repent, turn, be converted. We are to hear the promises of God and believe them. We are to take up our crosses daily and follow Christ. We are to wait upon God in all the means of God. We are to consecrate ourselves fully to the love of God and our neighbors. We are to meditate and reflect unceasingly on the goodness and mercy of God made known to us in Jesus Christ. We are to open ourselves fully and unreservedly to the diverse action of the Holy Spirit in our lives. Of course, God makes such action possible, but they are our actions and it is our responsibility, not God's, to perform them. It is high time we gave a proper and rightful place to genuine human action in our relation-ship to God. Our account of grace and freedom must do more than tolerate mention of these matters; it must accommodate and celebrate them.

---

[7] Austin Farrer, "Fish out of Water," in *A Faith of Our Own*, 139–40.
[8] Philippians 2:12–13.

Regrettably, all the fuss about merit and credit has inhibited the ministry of the church on this front. We should embrace the role of human action and response with enthusiasm and flair.

Even so this emphasis on human action cannot be the last word. Theologians have been right to insist that we begin, continue, and end the life of salvation by the grace of God and the wind of the Spirit. Few testimonies capture this better than that of Tatiana Goricheva, a student in Moscow whose life was one long litany of folly and sin that had turned into a torment of "incomprehensible, cold, hopeless anxieties."[9]

> But the wind of the Spirit 'blows where it wills'. It gives life and raises the dead. So what happened to me? I was born again. Yes, it was a second birth, my real one.
>   But all in due time.
>   I was doing my yoga exercise with the mantras wearily and without pleasure. I should point out that up to this point I had never said a prayer, nor did I know any. But in a yoga book a Christian prayer, the 'Our Father', was suggested as an exercise. The prayer that our Lord himself prayed. I began to say it as a mantra, automatically and without expression. I said it about six times, and then I was suddenly turned inside out. I understood—not with my ridiculous understanding, but with my whole being—that he exists. He the living, personal God, who loves me and all creatures, who has created the world, who became a human being out of love, the crucified and risen God.
>   At that moment I understood and grasped the 'mystery' of Christianity, the new, true life. This was real, genuine deliverance. At this moment everything in me changed. The old me died. I gave up not only my earlier values and ideals, but also my old habits.
>   Finally my heart was also opened. I began to love people. I could understand their suffering and also their lofty destiny; that they are in the image of God. Immediately after my conversion everyone simply seemed to me to be a miraculous inhabitant of heaven, and I could not wait to do good and to serve human beings and God.[10]

This testimony would have been music in the ears of John Wesley. He would also have been delighted to read: "The Holy Spirit certainly works in a person until he or she has reached perfection."[11] So let's turn to that topic in our treatment of salvation.

---

[9] Tatiana Goricheva, *Talking About God is Dangerous: The Diary of a Russian Dissident* (New York: Crossroad, 1986), 17.
[10] Ibid., 17–18.   [11] Ibid., 34.

16

Salvation

The Possibility of Conspicuous Sanctity

> And you who were once estranged and hostile in mind, doing evil deeds, he has now reconciled in his fleshly body through death, so as to present you holy and blameless and irreproachable before him—provided that you continue securely established and steadfast in the faith, without shifting from the hope promised by the gospel that you heard, which has been proclaimed to every creature under heaven.
>
> Colossians 1:21–3.

All systematic theologians run into embarrassing biblical texts. Here is one to ponder. "Everyone born of God does not commit sin. Because his seed remains in him; he is not able to sin, because he has been born of God."[1] The general sentiment among Christian theologians is that sin always has the upper hand over against grace in salvation. To err is human; to sin is human; so, sin is our lot on earth. When we get to heaven we will be able to avoid sin, but, in the meantime, let's not get our hopes up. While we are reluctant to admit it publicly, defeatism is the order of the day. We are content if we can have forgiveness; beyond that we are skeptics.

We might brutally summarize the various theological options in this manner. I speak here in terms of popular exposition in our churches rather than historical or theological exactitude. For the Lutheran tradition, we are and will remain *simul justus et peccator*; at one and the same time we are justified and sinful. For the Reformed tradition, we are so corrupt and mired in sin that it is best to be realistic about its power in our lives; the best we can hope for is to grin and bear it. As the good Presbyterians of Ireland are wont to say, we all need to "thole." What is it to "thole"? You are out walking into a stiff rain and wind; so, stop whining, put your head down, set a straight course, and make it through as best you can. So "thole"; grin and bear it. For the Methodist tradition, the best we can hope for is to get a bit better every day, making

---

[1] 1 John 3:9–10.

steady progress onward and upward; if you cannot be perfect, well at least you can feel good about yourself. For the Roman Catholic tradition, you might make it into the calendar of saints, but only if you are among the select few who refrain from sex, live in poverty, and obey your superiors. For modern contemporary evangelicalism, the best you can aim at is a purpose-driven life. In this case business analogies embedded in a reduced and moderate Calvinism become the privileged image of the Christian life.

Perhaps we should take another look at the deep sentiments buried in this overview of our situation under grace. These options certainly capture the significance of the cross and the sin that caused it, but I am not so sure they adequately capture the significance of the resurrection and of Pentecost and the grace that flows from them. So, in this chapter I intend to develop a rich vision of salvation. Ideally my strategy is to articulate the kind of narrative, thick description, and theological commentary that would more than match the downward spiral of sin and evil that I sketched in my chapter on sin. Difficult as it is, we must try to develop a theology of salvation that will equal our theology of sin in its depth and attraction. My intuition is a simple one: the ascent to victory over evil made available by grace through the work of the Holy Spirit in and through the canonical heritage of the church is more than a match for the descent into evil and sin that we all readily acknowledge.

Let's concede immediately that the prevailing options mentioned above all have merit in their own specific way. Justification brings a freedom from the guilt of sin, and this surely has a foundational role in the life of faith. This was the great rediscovery of Martin Luther. We will struggle to our dying day in a battle against sin and evil; we do well to learn to "thole" spiritually. Gradual progress in sanctity really is possible, and it is important to gain a sense, not of feeling good, but of dignity and assurance in our relationship with God. Moreover, there are real sacrifices with respect to sex, money, and submission that are inescapable in a life of holiness. And there is a place for explicit intentionality, for clarity of purpose about our lives, in our journey to and with God. Hence there is insight and merit in the prevailing views about salvation, so that any optimistic vision of grace in the work of salvation must be cautious and realistic.

But why be optimistic? There are several sources that feed it.

Before we get to these, however, consider a number of rhetorical questions. Is not our pessimism about grace and our overplaying of the power of sin much too self-serving a doctrine for the theologian to be entirely comfortable? Does the direction of our thought in privileging sin over grace not seem altogether too convenient, giving us an irresistible let-out clause in the battle against sin? Is it not this privileging of sin the kind of doctrine you would expect to be invented by sinners to provide excuses for sinning? Might not our pessimism be one of the noetic effects of sin rather than the truth of the matter?

Turning to reasons for quiet optimism, surely the whole thrust of the faith is towards a robust optimism of grace. Where sin abounds, grace abounds all the more; the last word has to be with grace rather than with sin. God is greater than Satan, goodness is stronger than evil, grace is more powerful than sin. Consider what God has done in the good news we recite in the Gospel. God has come in his Son and defeated the works of the devil. God has inaugurated his kingdom in human history in the life, death, and resurrection of Jesus, so that God's active rule has arrived here and now. At Pentecost, the Risen Lord sent the Holy Spirit who proceeds from the Father and who immerses us in the life of the Triune God. The whole thrust of the Gospel of the kingdom of God is to move us towards radical and genuine transformation. The Triune God is more than a match for the world, the flesh, and the devil. Surely we need to find a way to express this theologically.

Let's tackle the issue of optimism from another angle. Working from within the canonical heritage of the church it is surely staggering the network of resources that are available in the battle against sin. We have the great liturgies of the church to draw us into the presence of God and into the company of the saints. We have the sacraments that mediate at the deepest level of our being the energy of the Holy Spirit and the Real Presence of the Son of God. We have the Scriptures to cultivate wisdom and mediate the Word of God. We have the Creed to give us a map for our journey. We have the saints and martyrs whose lives inspire us in very effective ways and set our hearts on fire. We have the icons to kindle our imaginations. We have the wealth of teaching in the Fathers and the tradition to engage us intellectually and foster discernment. We have canon law and regulation to set appropriate boundaries for life in the church. We have bishops, pastors, and spiritual directors to correct us, guide us, and encourage us. We have a vast literature and tradition of spiritual direction in which to immerse ourselves. We have, in short, a vast network of practices, persons, and materials whose primary function in the Holy Spirit is to create in us the mind of Christ. Surely we can say that God has been wonderfully generous to us in providing such a means of grace to heal our souls. Can we not hope and expect and believe that these means are truly effective in the battle against evil and sin? Is God finally incompetent in the world? Are the resources he supplies ineffective and broken? Surely not.

Just as we can track the path of descent into sin by way of narrative so too can we track the ascent out of sin up into salvation by way of narrative. Here there is a wealth of material to draw from but surely the obvious place is back in Genesis in the story of Abram. The crucial blocks of material in Genesis 12, 15, and 22 follow a simple pattern. God confronts Abram and promises to bless the socks off him. God will make a great nation from Abram; he will make his name great; he will bless Abram; and through Abram he will bless the whole world. Abram responds in faith; his faith bears fruit in obedience; and the blessings of God come rattling along from one generation to another. The call of Genesis 12 is followed by the covenant of Genesis 15; and the response of faith and obedience is hammered out in terms of a dynamic of trust and distrust, of obedience and disobedience. The climax of the story occurs when Abram's faith, now renamed as Abraham's faith, is tested to the limit and God steps in to replace Isaac with the ram caught by its horns in the thicket. The theological pattern here remains secure. The skepticism of Genesis 3 is displaced by the divine revelation of call and covenant; the distrust is displaced by a costly, ultimate trust that hangs by the sheer Word of God alone; the obedience becomes steadier and deeper; the blessings keep coming. Thus, the downward spiral of evil is reversed by an upward ascent of revelation, trust, obedience, and blessing. The whole affair is immersed in grace, that is, in God's gratuitous unmerited, unconditional generosity, loving-kindness, and mercy.

The story of the New Covenant does not displace this pattern. The New Covenant in Christ fulfills the Old Covenant by taking it to its fullest expression in the coming of God's Son through the energy of the Holy Spirit. In extraordinary grace, God comes in his Son, providing the full and final revelation of his all-out commitment to the welfare of the world. The light and the truth of God have overcome the darkness. In the life, death, and resurrection of Jesus, a new Adam appears who in his death sacrifices himself for the sins of the world. The risen Lord sends the promised Holy Spirit to those who have gathered in faith, and the blessings of God made visible in Jesus Christ have been flowing ever since. Salvation is the term we use to cover the reception and outworking of these blessings of forgiveness and new life mediated now through the Gospel in the church. The same pattern holds: revelation, faith, obedience, and blessings galore. And the New Covenant too is marked by divine grace from beginning to end and from top to bottom. We are swimming in the immensity of God's grace, that is, in God's gratuitous, unmerited, unconditional generosity, loving-kindness, and mercy.

This remedy for sin is no mere afterthought in the divine mind. We have nothing less than the glorious predestination of God before the foundations of the world to back it up. Those who come in faith and repentance to Jesus Christ are given a whole new destiny. Where before their lives were subject to death and self-destruction, they are now on their way to a whole new life in the kingdom of God.

> Blessed be the God and Father of our Lord Jesus Christ, who has blessed us [those who have come to faith] with every spiritual blessing in the heavenly places, just as he chose us in Christ before the foundation of the world to be holy and blameless before him. He destined us for adoption as his children through Jesus Christ, according to the good pleasure of his will, to the praise of his glorious grace he freely bestowed on the beloved.[2]

---

[2] Ephesians 1:3–6.

The writer goes on to catalogue the benefits that come from being in Christ, from entering into God's kingdom. So now we have redemption, forgiveness of our sins, access to the astonishing wisdom manifest in God's planning, the great privilege of living a life for the praise of Christ, and the promised seal of the Holy Spirit. The full catalogue of benefits requires a process of coming to know more and more about Christ, not least "the immeasurable riches of his glorious inheritance among the saints."[3] It also involves coming to grips with the "immeasurable greatness of his power for us who believe, according to the working of his great power."[4] This power is as great as the power that raised Jesus from the dead and exalted him above all human authority. Moreover, this was not just pious talk; this was exactly the power that was at work on the converts in Ephesus, who were now raised with Christ to live a whole new life. And the gift of such power was a matter of divine grace and kindness; it was not a reward for good behavior or pious activity. Indeed, the outcome of divine energy at work within them was what God intended from the foundation of the world. "For we are what he has made us, created in Christ Jesus for good works, which God prepared beforehand to be our way of life."[5]

Think of the issue in this way. We go to the train station and there are two trains, one going east and one going west. One is headed for hell on earth and hereafter; and the other headed for heaven here and hereafter. Once you step on the second train then the journey is one of unfolding benefits and security. We can depend on God to take us all the way.

> For those whom he foreknew he also predestined to be confirmed to the image of his Son, in order that he might be the firstborn of many brethren. And for those whom he predestined he also called; and those whom he called he also justified; and those whom he justified he also glorified.[6]

The goal of our existence, now that we have come to Christ, is not something that we make up for ourselves; we are not to draw up some kind of moral or spiritual program for ourselves; the program has already been set for us. We are now destined by God to live the life that God intended for us from the foundation of the world, a life powered by the divine energy that raised Jesus from the dead.

We now have a narrative of salvation that reaches back beyond the founding father of the church to the very plans of God determined in eternity and not subject to alteration on our part. The narrative is foundational but a thick description of the new life made available in Christ is also important. At this point we depart radically from the modern tradition of reducing salvation, say, to justification, sanctification, or liberation. In no way do I want to jettison these notions, but they belong in a much wider array of ideas.

---

[3] Ephesians 1:18.   [4] Ephesians 1:19.   [5] Ephesians 2:10.
[6] Romans 8:29–30.

Consider the concepts that are customarily available to us in unpacking what God has made available in Christ through the working of the Holy Spirit in this life: justification, acquittal, freedom from guilt; regeneration, new birth, conversion, new creation, cleansing from sin; life in the Son, life in Christ, buried and raised with Christ, life in the Holy Spirit, holiness, sanctification, baptism or immersion in the Holy Spirit, deliverance from evil, Christian perfection, renewal of the image and likeness of God, transfiguration, theosis, deification, participation in the divine nature; having the law written on our hearts, purity of intention, a single eye, total submission to God. Note how weighted this representative list is towards a non-triumphalistic optimism of grace; the pessimism of sin has been blunted.

Consider the lists that have appeared in treatments of the new life brought to birth through the Gospel.

First, think of the beatitudes. Blessed are the poor in spirit, those who mourn, the gentle, those who hunger and thirst after righteousness, the merciful, the pure in heart, the peacemakers, and those who are persecuted for righteousness sake. Second, think of the fruit of the Spirit. There is love, joy, peace, patience, kindness, goodness, faith, gentleness, and self-control. Third, think of the cardinal and theological virtues: prudence, temperance, courage, and justice, and faith, hope, and love. A variation on this list shows up around 410 in Prudentius: humility versus pride, kindness versus envy, abstinence versus gluttony, chastity versus lust, patience versus anger, liberality versus greed, and diligence versus sloth. In the medieval period, catechists developed a list of seven corporeal works of mercy: feed the hungry, give drink to the thirsty, give shelter to strangers, clothe the naked, visit the sick, minister to prisoners, and bury the dead. Fourth, think of the summary of the Christian life delineated in the single command of Christ: You shall love the Lord your God with all your mind, soul, and strength, and your neighbor as yourself.[7]

Clearly these lists help us fill out what is involved in the life of salvation in a very rich and attractive manner. They provide a rich tapestry of dispositions, affections, passions, emotions, habits, actions, and activities, which are made possible by the Holy Spirit in salvation. Christ's coming into the world really does make a difference for the better; the pessimism of sin has been blunted and replaced by an optimism of grace.

Consider finally in this regard the important material from ascetic theology where we are given substantial insights into the deep morphology of conversion and growth in grace. For Bernard of Clairvaux we have a fascinating network of shifts. We move from loving oneself for one's own sake, to loving God for one's own sake, to loving God for God's sake, and finally to loving oneself only for God's sake. Alternatively, he speaks of loving God in three

---

[7] It would be interesting to track down a list of the religious affections as found, say, in Jonathan Edwards as one more way into a thick description of the Christian life.

ways: loving God out of fear (servile love), loving God for a reward (mercenary love), and loving God as God's child (filial love).[8] In John Climacus and Walter Horton we have the ladder of ascent to perfection (*scala perfectionis*). In Teresa of Avila we have the journey into the interior castle of God's presence. In John of the Cross we have the ascent of Mount Carmel. In John Wesley we have the journey from the door through the porch into the house of religion. We also have a journey from the natural person, to the legal person, to the evangelical person. The importance of these materials is simple: aside from giving us a rich account of the nature of the spiritual life, they provide a lively account of the dynamic reversal of sin by leading us step by step into the fullness of the life of grace. Thus they capture an active, vibrant, dynamic dimension to growth in faith and grace. We see the goal of faith brought near by tracking it back into our life before and after conversion.

What might we say more formally at this point? Consider the following discrete comments. First, the heart and soul of the Christian life is to come to love God with all our heart, soul, mind, and strength, and to love our neighbors as ourselves. Everything else that we do or become is subordinate to love for God and neighbor. The goal of the Gospel is to enable us to love.

Second, Jesus Christ is the perfect expression of God's love. Hence imitation of Jesus Christ crucified is another way to articulate the heart of the Christian life. We are formed in the end in the image and likeness of that which we worship. To worship Jesus Christ in time involves internalizing what he enacted and lived. Compare those who worship sports stars, film stars, or pop stars. In time, they internalize the ways of life represented by these idols. Parents rightly worry about their teenagers when they become too attached to such figures precisely because they shape and transform them in ways that are unhealthy and even corrupting.

Third, love for the neighbor is grounded and rooted in God's love for us. Thus, the love of God is primary; we love God because God first loves us. We love our neighbor because in our love for God we love what God loves, starting immediately with our neighbor. To grow in faith is to become intoxicated with and addicted to the divine love and thereby to the objects to which that divine love is directed. Think of the Irish hillbilly used to country and western music and reared on meat and potatoes. He falls in love with and marries a woman who loves Mozart and sophisticated Italian food. Before he dismissed Mozart as highbrow and inaccessible; Italian food was exotic and distasteful. Yet in time he comes to adore Mozart, and he cannot wait to try out the new Italian restaurant in town. He has come to love the objects of the love of the person he loves. We readily come to love the objects of the agents we love. This is surely

---

[8] There is a fine summary of Bernard's position in Bernard of Clairvaux, *On Loving God with an Analytical Commentary* (Kalamazoo, MI: Cistercian Publications Inc., 1995), ed. Emero Stiegman, 67.

at work in the way that the love for God transforms our love for the neighbor. Loving God leads us into a love for the objects of God's love.

Fourth, there is a very special, if not unique, place for exposure to the cross of Christ in coming to experience the love of God and thus in coming to know the love of God for ourselves. It is no accident that the prayer of the thief on the cross has a special place in the prayers of the believer. Noting his just deserts the thief says: "Jesus, remember me when You come into your kingdom." It is at the cross where we see the depths of our own sin. Sin killed God. Sin reached into the heart of God and crucified him. Sin shed the precious blood of Jesus and suffocated him. It is the cross that exposes us for what we are: sinners who deserve nothing less than total banishment from God. And it is at the cross that we discover the freedom of justification by faith, that is, where we realize that it is only by simple, radical trust in God's grace and mercy that we can move forward in our relationship with God. The whole idea of merit, or credit, of gaining access to God by good works of piety or mercy, of having any claim on God in which we might boast, is crucified once and for all. We hang on God's mercy, we cling to the Word of forgiveness, and we discover how much mercy there is for poor sinners such as we are. We wash away our sins in the blood of Christ, and we are released from the past to embrace a new future immersed in the Spirit. Not all visions of spirituality fully capture this insight in the same manner, but I suspect that it belongs in every robust vision of salvation and naturally shows up in the liturgies and hymns of our traditions.

Fifth, the power and energy to love comes from the life of the Triune God incarnate in Jesus Christ, manifest in his resurrection, and shed abroad within us by the power of the Holy Spirit. To speak of merit or credit is completely otiose and inept. Life in both creation and redemption is fueled by the energies of the Triune God. The old distinctions between different kinds of grace make a point, but they can all too readily serve to distract and confuse; they carve up the seamless transformation of nature by the grace of God in redemption. There is one energy of the Triune God in creation and redemption.

Sixth, increase in love brings increase in our awareness of sin.[9] The more we are drawn into the life of God, the more we become aware of our sin and our sins. It is tempting to construe this development as a very strange form of self-deception. After all, if we truly grow in holiness then it seems odd that we are not aware of this truth, so perhaps we are self-deceived about ourselves and our sin before God. However, it is surely sin that leads to

---

[9] Wesley very clearly missed this in his doctrine of entire sanctification. He was convinced that we could have assurance of "Christian Perfection." It is no small surprise that this element in his doctrine of assurance was quietly dropped from his theology when his followers appropriated it over time. See my "Christian Perfection," in William J. Abraham and James E. Kirby, eds., *The Oxford Handbook of Methodist Studies* (Oxford: Oxford University Press, 2009), 587–601.

blindness and self-deception; it is very hard to see how growth in holiness leads to self-deception.[10] Perhaps we are then tempted to construe this as a paradox, but on reflection we will not find the mark of a paradox, that is, a seeming contradiction, in the neighborhood. In fact, it is clear why the proposition before us is true. First, heightened sensitivity to the love and holiness of God clearly increases our sensitivity to the reality of sin in our lives. Second, union with God exposes us to the glory of God that in turn exposes our spiritual diseases. So then, we can see how increase in love and holiness brings increase in our awareness of sin.[11]

Seventh, increase in love of God and neighbor makes a host of sins not just abhorrent but impossible. Consider a human analogy. I had an aunt and uncle back in Ireland who loved each other dearly. My aunt used to say: "There were times when I could have killed him, but I would never have betrayed him." Because of her love certain kinds of behavior were simply out of the question; they were simply impossible. Of course, the modality here cannot be logical. We all know that betrayal is logically possible; it happens again and again. The impossibility is moral and spiritual. It is simply impossible that I would deliberately harm my daughter. This is not a moral option; the love goes too deep; it is now, as we would say, second nature. It is likewise in our love for God. As we grow in love for God, all sorts of things become morally and spiritually impossible. It becomes "not possible to sin"; there is a reversal of the "not possible not to sin" formula. This increase in love overrules in the human heart the option of sinning. This surely is at the heart of the formation of genuine sanctity. To be a saint in the strong sense of that term is to be so filled with the love of God that sin ceases to be a serious option.

Eighth, even so the life of sanctity is marked from beginning to end by submission, repentance, suffering, struggle with virtue, darkness, self-denial, inward reflection, remorse, and self-criticism. Paradoxically it is also constituted by a spiritual peace, contentment, and happiness that the world can neither give nor take away. Through these complex states there is always human action, but it is action inspired and sustained by the Holy Spirit. Hence there exists in one and the same person both a cordial reserve because of sin and an irrepressible exuberance stemming from the life-giving mercy and joy of God. There is both a submission to God that ultimately fosters a fierce independence from others—a feature all too often noted by totalizing politicians and leaders—and a liberty in God to serve the needs of others.

Ninth, permit a final brief commentary on two interesting psychological elements that one finds in the quest for holiness. For some converts, the initial problem they face is the problem of guilt. They find it extremely difficult to

---

[10] This becomes even more bizarre if one is attracted to the intellectual virtues as important in epistemology.

[11] The classical biblical text capturing what is at stake is Isaiah 6.

believe that God really does forgive them, that he has done all that is necessary in Christ to atone for their sins. They believe that they are just too bad for God to forgive them; there is grace for others but not for them. Hence conversion can be a really demanding struggle as they come under deep conviction of sin. When they eventually grasp what is at stake, there is great relief and often a sense that now anything is possible by way of sanctity. However, this is short lived; they discover now another problem, the challenge of victory over evil as compared to the problem of guilt for past wrong-doing. Hence, it takes time for them to realize that this problem, like the problem of guilt, can only be solved by grace through faith. They enter a whole new round of struggle and suffering until they discover the power that raised Jesus from the dead is the answer to their new dilemma.

The human element in play at this level can be described in this way. The convert begins to look to God to help them deal with particular sins and temptations. These may be as trivial as coping with a difficult mother-in-law or as serious as dealing with aggressive hostility at work for their faith. To their surprise they find that the promise of grace to gain victory over evil is real; they find that they can respond with genuine discernment and love. The process is one of decision and surrender with respect to this or that evil in their lives; they choose to be open to the inner energy of the Holy Spirit that raised Jesus from the dead. In time, they find that this is a good start but it is not enough. They face the fact that what is at stake is the deep orientation of their life before God; what is at issue is not this or that choice but a meta-choice about the Lordship of Christ over every aspect of their lives. Hence, their struggle at this point becomes even more intense, requiring radical surgery in their lives akin to crucifixion. They undergo a death that leads by the power of God to a whole new life of resurrection through the grace of God. Perhaps this is one way to capture one aspect of the phenomenology of conspicuous sanctity that shows up in genuine saints. I speak of saints here, not the mundane, Pauline sense of all who in conversion have been set apart for God, but in another sense of a deeper conversion in which believers die to their own desires and passions and are totally immersed in the Holy Spirit who makes them amazing channels of love to all.

This takes us to the role of the saints in the formation of sanctity. I mentioned earlier that the canonical heritage of the church gives us abundant resources for tackling the problem of sin in our lives. God, as it were, gives us a network of diverse resources that through the work of the Holy Spirit create within us the very mind that was in Christ Jesus. As we immerse ourselves over time, say, in the Scriptures, in the icons, in the liturgy, in the Creed, and in the great teachers and Fathers of the church, we are drawn into a world of beauty, holiness, and love that becomes the air that we breathe. As we internalize this world, we are changed, all the while aware how totally dependent we are on the energy and grace of God from beginning to end. The end result is sanctity, a life of holiness and love that is invisible to the agents who exhibit it, but all too visible to those with eyes to see and ears to hear. We become saints, but totally inconspicuous to ourselves. The lives of the saints become in turn a very special avenue of divine energy and inspiration. It is worth dwelling on this for a moment. How might we analyze the role of saints in the fostering of salvation and holiness? Think of it in these ways.

First, the lives of the saints make holiness and sanctity real. As we reflect on their lives the life of salvation is taken out of the realm of theological conceptuality and speculation and embodied in living, breathing human beings who are our brothers and sisters. They make sanctity a live option rather than a paper option; they bring holiness home and our homes bear its fragrance and attraction.

Second, the lives of the saints operate as agents and instruments of inspiration. They draw us towards holiness not just as something possible but also as eminently beautiful and desirable. The lives of the saints beckon us to imitate them as earthy exemplars of the life of Christ who shines through them and empowers us to follow him through them.

Third, the lives of the saints act as windows into the nature of holiness. They operate as unseen mentors who form us in discerning judgments; they teach us the detailed and subtle character of holiness. As we live in communion with them, we live not simply in a world of moral rules or virtues, but also in world of exacting spiritual detail that takes us into the highways and byways of obedience and love. Through their eyes we see things differently and more accurately.

Fourth, the icons of the saints become a physical place where we are drawn to pray for the Holy Spirit to come and work in our lives in the same way He has worked in their lives, or at least to the same degree and with the same intensity. Hence our desires for holiness are quickened and sustained; we yearn that the energy of God becomes a never-ending stream that fills our hearts and lives; we encounter physical sites of grace that renew our souls and remake us in the image and likeness of God.

All this may sound odd to some ears, but not if they attend to the practice of the proper veneration of the saints and the icons. There is no question here of worshipping saints and icons. Worship belongs alone and exclusively to God, Father, Son, and Holy Spirit. What is at issue is veneration: the giving of grateful, loving attention, and respect to those who have made visible to us the energy of God to sinners. No doubt some will press the issue further. Can we hope for or count on the intercession of the saints in our journey of faith? Can we pray for those who have gone on to glory and joined the communion of saints? Our thinking is stained at this point by memories of banks of credit and merit. We recall Luther's vehement protest against indulgences, and we revisit in our minds and imaginations the vulgar bazaars that were the scandal of Luther's day.

I once knew a brilliant lawyer and businessman who in his younger days as a Roman Catholic carefully calculated the shortest prayers that would give him maximum release from purgatory and acted accordingly. Protestants very naturally have hard memories of a network of practices that clearly undermine the wonder and beauty of the Gospel and that all too readily take us into a world of spiritual bondage and skullduggery. This farrago of spiritual nonsense casts its shadow on the whole idea of the possible intercession of the saints. We also have metaphysical and practical worries. How could the saints ever hear us? What form of causality is in operation in a case like this? How should we direct our requests for assistance? Thus, we worry that an excursus like this is the beginning of a very slippery slope.

I have found it helpful to ponder the following testimony. I once had a remarkable friend who is now deceased. He suffered attempted murder at the hands of the KGB in Georgia, in the old Soviet Union. He was taken to the morgue and left there until the time for the autopsy. As the pathologists began this work, his eyes opened, and they suddenly realized that he was not dead. In the twilight zone between life and death he was aware of the times when an aunt was thinking of him. When he told her afterwards that he was aware of her thinking of him, and when his reports matched her memory, she was so terrified that she refused to talk to him again. Divine and spiritual causality are as real and mysterious as our "ordinary" conceptions of causality. After Hume, the idea that we have a quick and easy grasp of "causality" is a chimera. There are events that happen and we have no idea how exactly the causality works; but the event has happened, so there is real causality in operation.

There is no slippery slope here, if we keep our wits about us. We have absolutely no problems requesting our friends on earth to pray for us here and now. Not for a moment do we see this as somehow impinging on role of Jesus Christ as our mediator between God and us. The communion and intercession of the saints is simply the extension of the prayer meeting beyond the bounds of space and time. It is the extension of love and affection; it is not the effort to build extra bridges outside of the work of the Son and the Spirit to connect us to God. In worship, when we enter into the kingdom of the Father, and the Son, and the Spirit, when on earth we enter heaven, then the payer meeting is extended to embrace the whole company of heaven. We enter mysteriously into the communion of the saints, sharing together with the angels and archangels in the worship of the Triune God.

> But you have come to Mount Zion, to the city of the living God, the heavenly Jerusalem, and to innumerable angels in festal gathering, and to the assembly of the firstborn who are enrolled in heaven, to God the judge of all, and to the spirits of righteous made perfect, and to Jesus the mediator of a new covenant, and to the sprinkled blood that speaks a better word than the blood of Abel.[12]

---

[12] Hebrews 12:22–4.

It is altogether fitting that in such circumstances we should pray for those who have gone before us and that they should pray for us.

I have said enough by way of digression. Let me return to the main road. I have sought to unpack the place of the saints in the journey of healing and salvation. Let me come back to earth with this prosaic comment. Just as sinners sin differently, so do the saints exhibit conspicuous sanctity in their own inimitable ways. They show that real victory over specific moral evil and sin is possible.[13] Let me confine myself to two radically different saints in the modern Russian tradition that I find especially inspiring. I could have picked a host of other pairs in a radically different culture, but the choice made here serves my purposes.

Mother Maria Skobtsova of Paris (1891–1945) was a smoking, beer-drinking nun who ran a home for Russian refugees in Paris before World War II. Twice divorced—the first civil, the second ecclesiastical—she was born in Riga and became an atheist at fourteen on the death of her devout father. She flirted with the Russian Revolution, was scheduled to be killed by Trotsky's thugs,[14] but argued her way past her killers by claiming to be a friend of Lenin's wife. By then she had returned to faith, but her faith truly caught fire after the excruciating death of her daughter, Nastia, from meningitis. She was so distraught that she could not leave the death room for a day and a half. Later she wrote that at the death of someone you love

> the gates have suddenly opened onto eternity, all natural life has trembled and collapsed, yesterday's laws have been abolished, desires have faded, meaning has become meaningless, and another incomprehensible Meaning has grown wings on their backs...Everything flies into the new black maw of the fresh grave: hopes, plans, calculations, and, above all, meaning, the meaning of a whole life. If this is so, then everything has to be reconsidered, everything rejected, seen in its corruptibility and falseness.[15]

Living in Paris at this time she became a nun without a monastery, serving the poor, destitute, mentally ill, and other broken-down icons of the incarnation, especially among the Russian diaspora. She was sent with her son to the Ravensbrück concentration camp for helping Jews to escape the terror of the Nazis. She died there on Holy Saturday, 1945, having served all those around about her with extraordinary tenacity and compassion. Despite her controversial views and despite her radically abnormal life as a nun on the run, so to speak, she was canonized by the Holy Synod of the Ecumenical Patriarchate

---

[13] I suspect that this was one of the deep driving forces behind John Wesley's doctrine of entire sanctification.

[14] The line used by Trotsky to dismiss the party to which she belonged was memorable: "Your role is played out. Go where you belong, into history's garbage can!" See the introduction by Jim Forest, in *Mother Maria Skobtsova: Essential Writings*, trans. Richard Pevear and Larissa Volokhonsky (Maryknoll, NY: Orbis, 2003).

[15] Quoted in ibid., 19–20.

on January 16, 2004.[16] Remembering and venerating such a life is surely to
encounter and internalize the life of Christ himself. Living into her memory
draws us into seeing everyone we meet as icons of the incarnation and acting
accordingly.

St. Seraphim of Sarov (1759–1833) could not be more different in outlook
and ministry. He was steeped in the piety of his church from childhood, and
he never showed any wavering from its practice and vision. He was one of
those fortunate souls who never knew a day when he did not love Christ.
Entering a monastery at eighteen, he immediately developed a life of asceti-
cism that was abnormal in its extremity. After becoming a monk in 1786 at
the age of twenty-seven, he spent virtually all his time in church. At that time,
he took the name "Seraphim," the Hebrew for "fiery" or "burning." He once
experienced a Christophany at Divine Liturgy and was unable to speak for
days thereafter. After 1793 he took to living in a hermitage, where he was once
so badly beaten by robbers that he was left for dead and remained hunched for
the rest of his life. He took to praying in the forest on a rock, praying for a
thousand days with his hands raised to heaven. Eventually, he threw open the
door of his cells, and thousands came to him for spiritual counsel. One his
favorite sayings was this: "Acquire the peace of the Holy Spirit and a thousand
will be converted in a day."[17] We might refer to St. Seraphim as a saint who
superseded Pentecostalism in his experience of the Holy Spirit.

A man called Motovilov once sought him out in order to get his take on the
meaning of the Christian life. St. Seraphim told him that the heart of the
Christian life was marked by the acquisition of the Holy Spirit. Motovilov
found the whole idea abstract and unintelligible. When words failed by way of
response and explanation, St. Seraphim took to praying where they were,
sitting on a log on a gloomy Thursday afternoon in snow that was eight inches
deep. He took Motovilov firmly by the shoulder and said: "We are both now,
my dear fellow, in the Holy Spirit." Motovilov saw that the face of St. Seraphim
was brighter than the sun. In his heart Motovilov felt joy and peace, in his
body he felt a warmth as if it were summer, and a fragrance began to spread
around them. Motovilov was terrified by the experience, especially by the face
in front of him shining like the sun. St. Seraphim spoke: "Do not fear, dear
fellow. You would not even be able to see me if you yourself were not in
the fullness of the Holy Spirit. Thank the Lord for His mercy toward us."[18]
St. Seraphim died kneeling in prayer in 1833. He was canonized in 1893; his
memory is celebrated each year on January 2. Living into his memory draws us

---

[16] Mother Maria provides a stunning overview of spirituality in her "Types of Religious
Lives," a document that only recently came to light. It is readily available on the Internet.

[17] This has led some to describe the form of evangelism involved as "passive evangelism."

[18] Taken from the material supplied by Bishop Alexander (Mileant) on the Internet. The whole
conversation with Motovilov is readily available at several sites on the Internet. The conversation
was found by accident in 1902, some seventy years after the event around 1832.

into a constant reminder of the generous availability of the Holy Spirit to do more for us than we can ever ask or think.

I ended my chapter on sin by exploring the topic of the demonic. In that case, we were contemplating that kind of radical evil where human agents are ravished by the demonic to the point of possession. It is surely appropriate to end this chapter with the antidote. If the limit case of evil is demon possession, then the limit case of sanctity is transfiguration in the Holy Spirit. If what I have presented in the lives of Mother Maria and St. Seraphim is true (and can anyone who has taken the trouble to look at the record really remain a skeptic for long?) then sin really has been defeated. It is time that we developed a vision of salvation that matches our vision of sin. We need a realism and optimism of grace that will be more than a match for our realism and pessimism of sin. Thanks be to God for the victory he has given us through our Lord Jesus Christ!

17

Eschatology

Life after Death

'What no eye has seen, nor ear heard, nor the human heart conceived, what God has prepared for those who love him'—these things God has revealed through the Spirit; for the Spirit teaches all things, even the depths of God.

1 Corinthians 2:9–10.

Hester Ann Rogers was one of the extraordinary women leaders in early British Methodism. She was an exceptionally effective spiritual midwife in the class meetings. She was important enough to be present at Wesley's death. She was married to James Rogers, one of Wesley's preachers; and they were much in love with each other. She died in childbirth at the age of thirty-eight on October 10, 1794. James was devastated by her death. He wrote a poem that became the epitaph on her gravestone.

> What says the happy dead?
>   She bids me bear my load,
> With silent steps proceed,
>   And follow her to God:
> Till life's uneasy dream
>   In rapture shall depart,
> She bids me give, like her,
>   To Christ my bleeding heart.

A year later in 1795, James Rogers lost his daughter Martha. Both were buried in the same grave in St. Mary's Chapel-Yard, Birmingham. He gives the following account of what had happened.

Underneath the same stone lie also the remains of Martha, my second daughter. She was a lovely child, the darling of her mother, and seemed to partake much of her sweet, open temper; which of course endeared her so much the more to me. She died of a consumption, the foundation of which was laid by the small-pox, which she took in the natural way about ten months before. During her tedious affliction, she suffered much; and although resigned in a good degree, yet she was considerably affected at the thoughts of death. She would often repeat her little hymns and prayers, particularly these words,

'Gentle Jesus, meek and mild,
Look upon a little child,
Pity my simplicity,
Suffer me to come to thee.'

The manner of her repeating these lines convinced me that she felt them; and I was led to request that the Lord would manifest to her infant mind, in a way he knew, such a degree of that glory to which I saw my child hastening, as would at once comfort her in her pain, and encourage my poor heart, the wounds of which were ready on this occasion to bleed afresh. The Lord graciously condescended. About two hours before her spirit got the signal for dismission, she was uncommonly restless, and would not be left for a moment. She was perfectly sensible to the last; talked about various things with a loud voice, distinct and clear. She then suddenly stopped; and, after a short pause, cried aloud, 'It is me he means; Sally, (calling the maid,) it is me he means: I say he calls for me. Come, Sally, be quick and bring me my white things. There they are: I must have them all on! O Sally, I am fine. How clear and beautiful I look, don't I! I am dressed all in white!' In one minute after this, she turned on her right side, and breathed no more!

O what a joyful reception would she meet from her darling mother, who would, no doubt be waiting to receive her happy spirit, and present it to her adorable Lord! and with what joy do they now both behold His face who purchased the crowns they wear.

It was on March 23, 1795, my child took her flight to paradise, aged four years, one month, and twenty-three days. Upon her gravestone are the following lines:

'Angels, rejoice, a child is borne
   Into your happy world above;
Let poor short-sighted mortals mourn,
   While on the wings of heavenly love,
An everlasting spirit flies,
To claim her kindred in the skies.'[1]

We are not too sure what to do with something like this in the contemporary world. Think of three sets of alternatives. Does it display a morbid and sentimental attitude to death that is inherently superstitious and unhealthy? Or, does it express a lively and realistic sense of the hope of immortality enshrined in the Scriptures and the creeds? Is it a hopelessly egocentric and individualistic conception of immortality that has been borrowed from Greek philosophy and superimposed on the early Christian conception of the last things? Or, is it a perfectly appropriate working out of the logic of personal salvation already experienced in this life through the work of the Holy Spirit within and without the practices of the church and promised to us in the faith

---

[1] This record is found in an appendix to Rev. Thomas Coke, *The Experience and Spiritual Letters of Mrs. Hester Ann Rogers* (London: T. Nelson and Sons, Paternoster Row, 1852), 253–5.

once delivered to the saints? Is it a classical piece of pious escapism where illusion and wishful thinking take over and sift out the harsh realities of life? Or, is it a brilliant depiction of that ultimate reality which is generally cast aside in our culture by our greed, by our materialism, by our soulless secularism, by our shallow unbelief, and by our hardness of heart?

It is very tempting to turn aside and deal with the epistemological worries that these alternatives provoke. And in response to those worries it is equally tempting to yield to our skepticism. After all, who can know what the future holds? We are cast upon a sea of speculation that might well distract us from the moral and spiritual demands that arise every day as soon as we get out of bed in the morning. Yet it would be a serious mistake to yield to these temptations at this stage. We need to keep our nerve and explore what the great tradition of the church has to say about the life to come. We can then come to terms with our skeptical worries.

James Rogers' account of the death of his beloved daughter is interesting in part because it is so positive in its tenor and content. Yet it merely lifts the corner of the veil as far as the future is concerned. It helps immediately if we distinguish between two kinds of hope that arise in the arena of eschatology. The first kind of hope is focused on what we can call personal eschatology. What should we anticipate as far as our own personal lives are concerned? The second kind of hope is nothing less than cosmic in scope so we can call it cosmic eschatology. What does the faith teach us about the future of the cosmos in the hands and purposes of God? In this chapter I shall deal with the first of these hopes; I shall take up the second in the next chapter. Let's begin with two preliminary tasks: summarizing what the canonical tradition asserts in the arena of eschatology and then getting clear on what the language of eschatology signifies.

The Nicene Creed captures this distinction between personal and cosmic eschatology when it speaks of the future first in relation to its claims about Christ and second in relation to the future of the individual. Thus, it asserts that Christ "will come again to judge the living and the dead and that his kingdom will have no end." Very naturally, it speaks of the future of the individual in terms of the first person singular and in terms not of mere belief but in terms of sober expectation: "I look for the resurrection of the body and the life of the world to come." We see immediately that eschatology holds firm to the central theme of the Gospel, namely, the final consummation of the kingdom of God brought about by the Son. So, in general terms we are dealing with God's rule, already inaugurated in the life of Christ and partially experienced in this life in our experiences of the Spirit. More specifically, we can see that the future of the individual is couched in terms of the resurrection of the body, taking us back in thought and time to the resurrection of Jesus. Beyond these claims we are confronted with Christ exercising judgment on the living and the dead. So, this is what lies before us: Christ will one day return again, raise those who are no longer on this earth from the dead, exercise judgment, and usher in an everlasting kingdom in a life of the world to come. Put abruptly, this is a very terse account that ties together our future prospects with an implied account of the future of the cosmos. We can also reverse the order of thought here: our claims about the future of the cosmos include an account of the future of the individual. Notice that either way there is no mention of an intermediate state for the individual between death and the final consummation of all things. It is not that the reality of an intermediate state is denied; rather, we are to fix our mind on the bigger picture that is centrally about Christ and his kingdom rather than on ourselves and our worries about what happens when we die.

With the central affirmations of the tradition in place, let's take the full measure of the language of eschatology. Eschatology literally means talk about the end. There is a happy double meaning that is shadowed in the Greek and explicit in English. There are overtones which carry it in the direction of the last things, that which comes at the end. There are overtones that carry it in the direction of the ultimate, of that which is the final end or purpose of all things, that is, of the destiny of the world. To speak of the last things or of eschatology is not just to speak of the future of the world; it is also to speak of the final purpose and destiny of the church and the world. It is to connect talk of the future with talk of purpose and fulfillment.

This is why eschatology is logically and properly connected with hope and anticipation. Christians look forward in hope in a unique kind of way. We do more than anticipate certain events and states of affairs. We look towards events that will bring to full expression the purposes of God for creation. Eschatology is not just looking forward, like looking forward to good weather or getting married. Eschatology is inextricably linked to creation, to the fulfillment of God's purposes for the world, to God's final end and destiny for God's creatures. So, the end of eschatology is new creation. Eschatology is the full expression of God's destiny for the world. The point of creation is eschatology. Creation reaches its fulfillment in the end when God is all in all.

Ponder what is at stake in this account of the language of eschatology. We need to hold firm not just to the initial summary of the claims of the Nicene Creed but to the wonderful sweep of promise and fulfillment enshrined in the return of Christ, the resurrection from the dead, judgment of the living and the dead, and the full and everlasting arrival of the kingdom of God. What is at issue is the vindication of everything that Christ stood for, the full experience of the life God has intended for us as creatures and for the cosmos as a whole, and the final victory of God over evil reflected in judgment and in the completion of his kingdom for all time and space. We fail to see the beauty and wonder of what is at stake if we fail to register the good news that this proclaims and entails. There is coming a day when we shall be all that God intended us to be, and when our present life as represented by death, sin, disease, self-destruction, and the demonic will be no more, because God will indeed gain victory over evil.

It is very easy to lose sight of the attraction of this vision of the future. When we review the topics generally covered under eschatology, the subject collapses into a catalogue of terrestrial and extra-terrestrial events and realities. The catalogue can get very long if we allow it. It covers such matters as the second coming of Christ, the immortality of the soul, the resurrection of the dead, the final judgment, and heaven and hell. In Roman Catholic thought it also includes purgatory, limbo, and the beatific vision. In some branches of modern Protestantism, it also includes the rapture, the millennium where the saints reign with Christ on earth, the great tribulation, the restoration of the land of Palestine to the Jews, the conversion of the Jews, the Antichrist, and the battle of Armageddon. If we try to sort through all of these themes all at once we will be prone to lose heart. The obvious solution to this temptation is to return to the heart of the matter. And the heart of the matter is this: Christ will return, raise the dead to life, exercise final judgment, and hand over the kingdom to God the Father who will be all in all.

When we express the issue in these terms then we all have a stake in the issue. We are not just being curious, or speculative, or sentimental, or morbid, or escapist. We are wrestling with a thoroughly sensible theological issue. To avoid it is to evade our intellectual responsibilities. To avoid it is also an evasion of existential realities. The existential reality is this: the purposes of God for creation are called into question by the crises of history and by the deeply personal crisis of death.

Consider the following. Our experience of God in Christ through the Holy Spirit is an experience, which however full, is incomplete. God has acted decisively in Christ through the Holy Spirit to bring salvation, to bring victory and lasting freedom. This is both experienced and promised in the Gospel, and it is in keeping with the great love and power of God displayed in creation. That is one pole of our experience. The other pole is the ongoing reality of upheaval and death. Little children die of starvation. Teenage girls are raped. The oceans are polluted. Governments lie and deceive. Tyrants torture their victims. Snakes poison innocent people. Universities kill the life of the mind. Eventually we die and return to the soil. Eventually the planet itself may be destroyed by poisons and weapons or it will very slowly slide into oblivion sixty-five billion years from now.

Within these polarities we face a deep moral, spiritual, and intellectual crisis. It is true that the eschatological claims of the Christian tradition have always appeared fanciful and bizarre not just to intellectuals but to ordinary folk. However, at no time has this crisis been so intense as in the twenty-first century. The crisis is expressed in the deep divide that runs through the modern church in the West on the subject of eschatology. This is a divide that has no real parallel in the early church, in the Middle Ages, or at the

Reformation. The intensification of the crisis is manifest on the one side by an amazing interest in millennial speculation. A whole new vocabulary of eschatological discourse has been minted out of bits and pieces of Ezekiel, Daniel, and the Book of Revelation, deployed to give exact predictions of various events. The Gulf War of 1991, for example, precipitated a new round of theological nonsense, financial exploitation, and evangelistic manipulation. Fear, a sense of panic, or a sense of cosmetic triumphalism—all emerged, as they do in any great historical crisis. Eschatological speculation runs riot in the West. It can just as readily run riot among Orthodox Christians in Ukraine and among Pentecostals in China.

However, this is only one side of the intensification of the crisis. The other side is the exactly opposite extreme, namely the overcoming, or transcending, or even rejection of any specific eschatological hope, especially with respect to the individual. For the first time in the history of Christian theology, it has become common for Christian theologians to be agnostic about personal immortality or to reject it entirely.[2]

The intellectual challenge before us is this: How can we begin to make Christian claims about the future even half-way attractive? Do we really want to walk into the envisaged future with enthusiasm? Few who have written on eschatology have given serious attention to this challenge; perhaps we are doomed to failure on this front. So, I make no promises at this stage. However, we can all agree that this is a pressing issue. Somehow, we need to find our way back into the extraordinary good news represented by Christian claims about the future. We need to pause, set aside our doubts, walk around what Christ has opened up and prepared for us, and find ways to take fresh delight in the great promises of God in the Gospel. This is one reason why I began this chapter with the delight of a little child eagerly welcoming the prospects of an immediate reception into an intermediate state where she would be received by the risen Lord and reunited with her mother.

Permit a recent example that will bring us into our contemporary world. Some years ago, I visited in a hospital a woman named Lottie Groppenbecker who lived in Ripley, Ohio. She was well up in years and had been a nominal believer in her local church; she came faithfully to church on Sundays but showed little serious interest in the faith. She fell and ended up in the hospital. I was astonished at what I found when I visited her. She was beaming from ear to ear; she told me immediately that she could not wait to tell what had happened. Clearly, she had been close to death and had been in considerable pain. Then, out of nowhere, she found herself surrounded by what she could only describe as angels who gathered her up in their arms to comfort her. She

---

[2] See, for example, Rosemary Radford Ruether, "Eschatology in Christian Feminist Perspective," in Jerry Walls, ed., *The Oxford Handbook of Eschatology* (New York: Oxford University Press, 2008), 339.

also found herself immersed in an experience of divine love that left her speechless. In time, she emerged from this experience without any fear of death; in fact, she could now look forward to her death with a calm assurance of the grace and mercy of God.

Clearly in both cases cited, we are dealing with instances of near-death experiences. I appeal to them not as evidence for life after death, but in order to highlight the sense of joy and delight that they convey. Perhaps, experiences like this should be kept in the bosom of the church; cast into the world they will appear like pearls before swine. Paul captures this in his reticence in speaking of certain experiences that befell him. He also rightly draws attention to the spiritual dangers that accompany such experiences and that clearly were a serious problem for new believers in Corinth.

> It is necessary to boast; nothing is to be gained by it, but I will go on to visions and revelations of the Lord. I know a person in Christ who fourteen years ago was caught up in the third heaven—whether in the body or out of the body I do not know; God knows. And I know that such a person—whether in the body or out of the body I do not know—God knows—was caught up into Paradise and heard things that are not told, that no mortal is permitted to repeat. On behalf of such I will boast, but on my own behalf I will not boast, except of my weaknesses. But if I wish to boast, I will not be a fool, for I will be speaking the truth. But I refrain from it, so that no one may think better of me than what is seen in me or heard from me, even considering the exceptional character of the revelations. Therefore, to keep me from being too elated, a thorn was given me in the flesh, a messenger of Satan to torment me, to keep me from being too elated. Three times I appealed to the Lord about this, that it would leave me, but he said to me, 'My grace is sufficient for you, for power is made perfect in weakness.' Therefore I am content with weaknesses, insults, hardships, persecutions, and calamities for the sake of Christ; for whenever I am weak, then I am strong.[3]

Paul highlights the rare character of experiences that speak to the reality of "Paradise"; he also dismantles the temptation to romantic expectations of a life without suffering; yet he also confirms the reality of person-relative revelation that brings home the potential delights of the world to come.

Elsewhere Paul makes abundantly clear that he looks forward to an intermediate state once this life is over.

> For to me, living is Christ and dying is gain. If I am to live in the flesh that means fruitful labor for me; and I do not know what I prefer. I am hard pressed between the two: my desire is to depart and be with Christ, for that is far better; but to remain in the flesh is more necessary for you.[4]

This commitment to the reality of an intermediate state is confirmed by other persuasive considerations which clearly undermine the competing claim that

---

[3] 2 Corinthians 12:1–10.   [4] Philippians 1:21–4.

when we die we enter some kind of soul-sleep until the day of resurrection. The cumulative argument in favor of a conscious intermediate state is nicely summarized by Henry Sheldon.

> Not to mention the pregnant declaration that God is the God of the living and not of the dead, the continuance of conscious existence is implied in the parable of the rich man and Lazarus, in the appearance of Moses and Elijah upon the mount of transfiguration, in the assurance to the dying thief that he should enter paradise on the day of crucifixion, in the prayer of the martyred Stephen that the Lord would receive his spirit, in the expectation of Paul that departure from this life would make him present with Christ, in the representation of Peter respecting Christ's preaching to the spirits in prison, and in John's vision of the souls of those who had been slain for the confession of Christ, and who appear to have been still waiting for the resurrection.[5]

We have begun to explore afresh the character of life after death, beginning with the intermediate state for those who have entered into the kingdom of God here and now. Suppose we extend our reflection beyond this to the resurrection of the body, the final judgment, and the final manifestation of God's kingdom. What can we legitimately say? One way into this arena is to look at the network of images that are available. Here are five.

First, there is the image of Paradise spelled out in terms of a beautiful garden. The language of Paradise originated in ancient Armenian and Sanskrit and denoted a garden or park like the kind that surrounded a Persian palace. Thus, it was used in Genesis to denote the Garden of Eden. Just as Adam and Eve were placed into a magnificent garden, so too the future will involve inhabiting an environment symbolized in terms of a garden that will be even more beautiful.[6] This garden will have within it the tree of life, the source of true happiness and human fulfillment.

Consider the image of Paradise from an entirely secular point of view. Here is how Dylan Thomas, the Welsh poet, once described an idyllic place to dwell in an invitation to a friend to come and visit.

> Up to now, we have been living in hotels and pensions: expensive and unsatis-factory. And the Riviera sea was too tidy. Now, on the hills above Florence, some five miles from the centre, we have found a lovely villa in the pinewoods: beautiful, nightingaled gardens, cypresses, pillared terraces, olive trees, deep wild woods, our own vineyard and swimming pool, very tasty. There is a big

---

[5] Henry C. Sheldon, *A System of Christian Doctrine* (Cincinnati, OH: Jennings and Graham, 1903), 552. Sheldon cites the following relevant texts: Matthew 22:32; Luke 16:19–31; Mark 9:4; Luke 23:43; Acts 7:59; 2 Corinthians 5:8; Philippians 1:21–3; 1 Peter 3:19; Revelation 6:9–11; 1 Thessalonians 5:20; 2 Peter 2:9. It is equally difficult to square the positive picture depicted in these materials with the doctrine of purgatory where purgatory is understood as a state of suffering undergone as a punishment for the venial sins after the guilt of mortal sins has been remitted.

[6] See Luke 23:43; 2 Corinthians 12:4; Revelation 2:7.

room waiting for you. The cellar is full of wine. We live on asparagus, artichokes, oranges, gorgonzola, olive oil, strawberries, and more red wine. We have the villa until the end of July. Can you one? We'd love it, so much.[7]

In time Thomas became sick and bored with the hills above Florence; presumably gardens and hills that constitute a genuine Paradise created by God would not so readily become the source of boredom.

Second, there is the image of a wedding feast.[8] In this case we are invited to consider a magnificent meal set in a beautiful building where the atmosphere is one of joy and celebration. The guests are all in a festive mood; the wine gladdens the palate and warms the heart; the children are all dressed up and innocently enjoying the attention directed to them; the bride and the groom look their best and eagerly look forward to the consummation of their love for each other; the music and dancing bring the whole evening to a wonderful pitch of mirth and joy; the chefs are dressed in their best uniforms and bring out the best of their culinary arts; even poor old uncle Bob and aunt Maggie have buried their differences for the day and are smiling for a change. Everyone goes home and the afterglow lingers in their memories for months to come. Likewise, the life to come will be one of festive celebration and of deep enjoyment that the guests share with each other and with those who are honored because of their conspicuous sanctity and suffering for Christ.

A third image is that of a city, the New Jerusalem, brought down to earth from heaven. In this case, imagine your favorite city that you cannot wait to revisit. Your own city is perhaps a toy city, one built to order with predictable malls and four lane highways slicing through it because its inhabitants cannot wait to get home to the suburbs. But the city you have come to love is full of surprises with different quarters housing different ethnic groups and bringing with them the treasures of their traditions. It has ancient squares, magnificent buildings, diverse restaurants, and sections set aside for pedestrians. It has a park with scores of different trees and flowers that bloom like clockwork throughout the year. It has a river walk with excellent Irish pubs; it has small open spaces where local musicians bring the place to life; there are local artists at street corners who paint funny portraits at reasonable prices; the place resounds with the conversation of friends at open-air dinner parties; even the pigeons and stray dogs add a touch of color to the place. Likewise, the life to come will be like living in a city that never ceases to surprise and delight.

A fourth image is that of a house with many mansions.[9] Imagine now a magnificent castle lovingly built by a team of architects and workmen who spare no effort to provide luxury at every turn in the corridors that take you from one room to another. It took them fifty years to get the job done to the

---

[7] Constantine Fitzgibbon, *Selected Letters of Dylan Thomas* (London: Dent, 1966), 306.
[8] Revelation 19:9.   [9] John 15:2.

perfection desired. The dining room is surrounded with wonderful paintings; the sitting rooms are built with warm fires that dazzle in the Christmas season; the kitchen has all the modern equipment that is the envy of the best cook in the neighborhood; the bedrooms have ceilings that bring solace to the mind at the end of the day; there is a game room to entertain unruly teenagers; there is a wet bar to satisfy the most delicate palate; there is a music room for evenings with Mozart and Merle Haggard. Likewise, the life to come will be like exploring the nooks and crannies of a house with many mansions that bring deep delight to the mind and soul.

Finally, and closely related there is the image of a temple.

> I saw no temple in the city, for its temple is the Lord God the Almighty and the Lamb. And the city has no need of sun or moon to shine on it, for the glory of God is its light, and its lamp is the lamb. The nations will walk by its light, and the kings of the earth will bring their glory into it. Its gates will never be shut by day— and there will be no night there. People will bring into it the glory and honor of the nations. But nothing unclean will enter it, nor anyone who practices abominations or falsehood, but only those who are written in the Lamb's book of life.[10]

I leave it to the reader to dwell on this image and then make the relevant adjustments to fit the description given here. No doubt, this will be a challenge for the author has paradoxically introduced the image of a temple only to undermine it by speaking of God himself being the temple. A similar move is made in the use of the very language of heaven itself, for this denotes the very dwelling of God; and we are called upon to think of being ushered into the full presence of God in a way that is virtually impossible to conceive much less imagine. Even Austin Farrer, a theologian and wordsmith of the highest order, fails when it comes to providing a compelling description of what is involved.[11] We are tempted, as he was, to take refuge in the Pauline claim that what lies in store for us is strictly inconceivable given our dependence on linguistic resources that are bound up with mundane, physical existence.[12] Farrer captures the challenge this way.

> O my God, eye hath not seen, ear hath not heard, neither hath there entered the heart of man the provision that you have made for the happiness of your lovers. And yet, as the same scripture declares, you have revealed your bounty to us, for you have given us your Spirit to teach us what you bestow on us.[13]

However, we should not exaggerate the Pauline constraints, for both Scripture and tradition, as I have sought to illustrate, do indeed deploy earth-bound

---

[10] Revelation 21:22–7.

[11] See the opening section of the chapter on the resurrection of the body in his *Lord I Believe: Suggestions for Turning the Creed into Prayer* (Cambridge, MA: Cowley Publications, 1989), 71–3.

[12] 1 Corinthians 2:9–10.   [13] Farrer, *Lord I Believe*, 73.

images to good effect if only we could unlock the network of images they have given us. Moreover, Farrer himself seeks to capture crucial elements in the life to come by taking our experience of salvation here and now and stretching it to cover our future prospects. He does this by creatively exploring on the concept of reconciliation.

The first reconciliation will take place when the kingdom of the world will become the kingdom of God and of his Christ. In this world, we inhabit a universe in which things perish and deadly sins are accepted as custom; we experience betrayals; we ostracize those who seek God's kingdom and its values for this world and sometimes put them to death. In God's kingdom, the familiar ways, sayings, and motives of people will express the innocent sweet nature implanted in us by God. We will inhabit a city with one law and one speech; we will dwell in a paradise where deep roots in our being will nourish its fruits and flowers. The second reconciliation will be that between ourselves and our neighbors. In this world, we look out for ourselves; we instinctively put self-love before the love of others. We are not able to reconcile sense with reason, or appetite with justice, or self-love with neighborly love. In God's kingdom, we will constantly feed off the divine perfection; we shall love others by no effort but by single-minded delight. Because we will be filled with all the glory that we can contain, we will be happy to be the instruments of divine love and kindness.

The third reconciliation is that of body and soul. We are torn within so that there is coldness in our virtues and bondage if we give in to our passions. In the world to come, the springs of our nature will be warmer and more copious; reason will make apt judgments and the spirit will support its highest flights without compulsion. The fourth reconciliation is that between the contrary forces of created nature. In this world, we are self-assertive; we acknowledge justice but pursue our own interests. Nothing moves but by the destruction of other things; and everything dies to make room for others. In heaven, we will become truly ourselves but this will arise as we minister to the exploration of divine love and execute the counsels of God. The physical world itself groans as it waits for the liberation it will share in the benefits of our adoption and the redemption of our bodies. Finally, we ourselves will be reconciled to God. Though now we constitute a colony of heaven, there remains sloth, lust, shame, disloyalty, and obstinate pride. Hereafter, " . . . how sweet to lose my will and to have yours in perfect liberty; to converse as a son with you, through the Spirit of your Son."[14]

Farrer is here ingeniously expanding the experience of grace here and now and stretching it to explore what life will be like in the world to come. We begin with the tokens of divine mercy and love already given to us and refigure

---

[14] Ibid., 77–8.

them in the light of our final destiny. In doing so he also reaches back into the deepest yearnings of the human soul and sees them fulfilled partially in present salvation and then fully in the life to come. He is implicitly deploying the adage that grace perfects nature. This too has been a common way to think through the beauty of what lies ahead in life eternal. The best-known instantiation of this is to be found in ruminations about the beatific vision. The strategy in this case is simple: we take a central feature of human existence and look for its fullest satisfaction beyond the grace. We name a specific aspiration and follow through the logic of its fulfillment. God does not give his Spirit by measure.[15] "A good measure, pressed down, shaken together, running over, will be put into your lap . . ."[16] "If you then, who are evil, know how to give good gifts to your children, how much more will your Father in heaven give good gifts to those who ask him!"[17]

In the case of the beatific vision the relevant aspiration is our desire to know, to exercise the life of the mind. This initially sounds like a heaven designed by and for eggheads. However, this is only the case if we have a restricted account of the life of the mind. Abbot Vonier exploits this neatly by including in the life of the mind all that is beautiful.[18] So, presumably, even as we will know God and his ways, even as we know ourselves and what it means to be created and redeemed by God, we will come to know all things beautiful that God has made. Perhaps, we could extend this line of thought to cover all the sanctified aspirations of the human agent, mind, body, and soul. How exactly this would be spelled out is at present beyond me, but we can put that on the table for future reflection.

Thus far I have dwelt entirely on the positive aspects of the life to come, beginning in the intermediate state and culminating in the final ushering in of the kingdom of God beyond the resurrection of the body and the final judgment. Does the mention of judgment mar this effort to provide an attractive vision of what God intends for us? *Prima facie*, it surely must do so. One obvious reason for this is that we fear death because we know that there will be no way to hide from the full truth that is to be revealed. However, this should not be the last word on the matter. First, we know the judge of all the earth will do right. Second, we also know that the judge that we face is none other than the one who himself was judged and in being subject to our judgment gave his life in love to save us. It is difficult to imagine a more apt judge. Third, there can be no fulfillment of our deepest desires without facing up to the full truth about ourselves. Facing reality is an indispensable step in coming to terms with authentic human existence. Fourth, those who have come to Christ have already come to terms with their guilt and their sin and in a real sense have been set free from condemnation; this is a critical dimension

---

[15] John 3:34.   [16] Luke 6:38.   [17] Matthew 7:11.

[18] Abbott Vonier, *The Life of the World to Come* (Bethesda, MD: Zacchaeus Press, 2010), 18–19.

of the doctrine of justification by faith in Christ. So, we have already begun to come to terms with what is needed in terms of conversion and repentance. Finally, moving from ourselves to the judgment of others, there can be no heaven without the vindication of those who have been abused at the hands of others. The thousands of innocent children who were murdered by the Nazis will be raised from the dead and vindicated in the courts of the Lord. Those responsible, many of whom have walked free in this life, will face the Judge of all the earth and justice will at last be done. A world devoid of divine judgment would be a terrible place. There can be no heaven without a proper reckoning of the appalling evils that have occurred on earth. Thus, in this, even as we stand in fear and trembling before God, there will be inescapable consolation.

Perceptive readers will note that at this point we have arrived at the subject of hell. I am content to speak on this theme by way of summary judgments. The patristic tradition of the church was divided on this topic. Thus, Origen and Gregory of Nazianzus were universalists; others decidedly were not.[19] Surely we should say that the believer who has not been at some stage attracted to universalism has not taken the full measure of the grace and mercy of God. Some contemporary theologians avoid the language of universalism by noting that there is a hell but that it is empty.[20] Others allow for final judgment of the wicked and their punishment but then propose that the wicked will be annihilated.[21]

My own judgment on this has several components. First, it is interesting that the doctrine of hell does not show up in the Nicene Creed; so canonically I deem the matter to be open in a way that the other elements I have explored are not. As with theories of the atonement, there is room for amicable disagreement as to what should or should not be canonical. Second, while it is appropriate to use the language of punishment as it relates to the last judgment, it does not really capture what is at stake. What is at stake is whether human agents can radically rebel against God and utter an everlasting no to his offer of grace and salvation. Some find this psychologically implausible if not impossible.[22] I find it neither implausible nor impossible. A life devoted to sin and evil means a life where at some point there is no way back. Our freedom is a radical freedom to say no to God. Thus, I am not persuaded by the assertion that the divine yes will always wear down our no to God. We are not like the teenagers who will eventually wise up; we are adults who are taken seriously by our Creator. Third, the ultimate judgment happily belongs

---

[19] For a fine overview of the patristic material see Brian Daley, "Eschatology in the Early Church Fathers," in Walls, ed., *The Oxford Handbook of Eschatology*, 91–109.

[20] See Geoffrey Wainwright, *Doxology: The Praise of God in Worship, Doctrine, and Life* (New York: Oxford University Press, 1980), 460.

[21] See Clark Pinnock, "Annihilationism," in Walls, ed., *The Oxford Handbook of Eschatology*, 462–75.

[22] See Wainwright, *Doxology*, 460.

to God alone. It is a relief to leave the judgment of others to God. In so far as we have revelation on the matter, I am persuaded that there is a hell and that it is not empty. Both Jesus and Paul mediate significant special revelation that is relevant. Consider the daring passage that speaks of the blasphemy against the Holy Spirit: " . . . whoever blasphemes against the Holy Spirit never has forgiveness."[23] I take this in context to mean that if we are confronted with God in the person of his Son and, using our full intellectual and spiritual faculties, we accuse him of being in league with the devil, then we have reached the point where we cannot recognize our sin and thus cannot turn in repentance and be forgiven. Paul is clearly emphatic:

> They (speaking of certain folk in Thessalonica) shall suffer the punishment of eternal destruction and exclusion from the presence of the Lord and from the glory of his might, when he comes on that day to be glorified in his saints, and to be marveled at in all who believe, because our testimony to you was believed.[24]

To be sure, we can always contest the interpretation of the relevant texts; but in the end one must follow the light one discerns in them; for my part I stand with the stream of the tradition that takes hell with radical seriousness. However, the first word in eschatology is not the judgment of the inveterate wicked but the extraordinary prospects of the final fulfillment of the will of God for the creatures made in his image and for the transformation of the cosmos to reflect in all its fullness the glory of the Triune God.

It is time to tackle the skepticism I highlighted earlier. Straightaway let me announce that from the outset, the Christian claims about the life to come and the end of the world were rightly grounded in divine revelation. The central eschatological claims of the tradition have depended crucially on the promises of God as expressed in the whole sweep of redemptive action. The inner logic of this is clear. God and only God knows the purpose and end of creation. We know only in so far as God has revealed these matters. In attempting to discern the content of divine revelation the normative traditions of the church have been both confident and cautious. The tradition has been confident that the work of judgment and salvation begun in Christ will reach its climax both for the individual and the cosmos. For the individual, Christ has broken the fear of death. Christ has trampled down death by death. Already judged and raised in Christ, we shall share in the resurrection of the body already achieved in Christ, and we shall inherit the fullness of eternal life. For the cosmos, it too will be recreated in the great and final Day of the Lord. The caution is beautifully expressed by Paul in a striking quotation from the prophet Isaiah: "What no eye has seen nor ear heard nor the heart conceived, what God has prepared for those who love him—these things God has revealed through the Spirit; for the Spirit searches all things, even the depths of God."[25]

---

[23] Mark 3:29.　　　[24] 2 Thessalonians 1:8–9.　　　[25] 1 Corinthians 2:9–10.

These are not a matter of reason or probabilistic experience or argument. These matters are spiritually discerned. They are fanciful, foolish, and folly outside of the context of the Gospel and outside participation in the life of the Holy Spirit. These are gifts bestowed by God and understood through the Holy Spirit. They are part of the secret and hidden wisdom of God, which God decreed before the ages for our glorification. We know them in so far as God has revealed it to us. Such revelation does not come to us by way of prediction but by way of promise, which we already see fulfilled here and now in a partial but real way. We have already entered into the End Times. We are already participating in the Last Days. We have already come to participate in the Age to Come. We have already been raised with Christ. The kingdom is already here. The kingdom will one day come in all its fullness.

Once the claims of divine revelation are in place, then we can indeed see how this fits with the kind of claims which when taken in isolation and independently of divine revelation yield next to nothing. So, we can claim that God would not give us longing for life beyond the grave and leave that longing unfulfilled; we can argue that it would be extremely odd for a God of love to make creatures in his own image and then simply allow our lives to vanish like grass from the fields. We can even be intellectually encouraged by well-tested reports of near-death experiences. At the very least, these can help undermine our initial intuitions about death represented by the observation that when we die, it looks as if all is over. Near-death experiences can bring us up short and challenge our native intellectual instincts as formed within the skepticism of our culture. Above all, the divine revelation as given in the promises of Christ is supported by his resurrection from the dead. In the early church, given that resurrection was clearly associated with the end of history and the final triumph of God's purposes of creation, it is no surprise that some of them expected that the end of history would happen in the near future. We have just crossed over into the second topic that has been central to eschatology, namely, the topic of the end of the world. To that, let us now turn.

18

Eschatology

The Final Consummation

Then I saw a new heaven and a new earth; for the first heaven and the first
earth had passed away, and the sea was no more.

Revelation 21:1.

The doctrine of the Second Coming of Jesus Christ is the capstone of any
serious Christian vision of the universe. For many it is a sharp stone in the
shoe. I propose that the Second Coming of Christ be seen as the best news
possible for the future of the universe. It is the Great Easter message for the
world. It promises a manifestation of the superabundant grace and love of God
for the universe as a whole. This was precisely how it was seen by the first
generation of Christians; retrieving it is not just the ultimate test of nerve for
those who take seriously the particularities of divine action in the Christian
tradition; it is also the platform for fresh engagement with the challenges and
crises of human history. In a moment, I shall cleanse the theological stables of
the debris that has bedeviled the discussion. I begin with an initial summary
statement of the central claims to be pursued.

The Nicene Creed is a marvel in terms of its modesty and economy: we are
to look for the resurrection of the dead and the life of the world to come.
However, let's flesh this out a little. Jesus of Nazareth is not a paper Jesus,
buried in a book in the past. He is risen from the dead as the eternal Son of
God and the secret Lord of history. He came first as the lamb of God to deal
decisively with human evil in the inauguration of the kingdom of God. He has
stood resolutely with his People, Israel, and launched them on a worldwide
mission to the whole Gentile world. He is present now through the working of
the Holy Spirit, within and without the church, whom he has sent to defeat the
powers of evil in our lives. He will come again as victorious Lord to gather up
all that God has done to date and secure the full realization of God's purposes
for the universe that was created out of nothing. Within this God will raise us
not to a ghostly life of disembodied spirits but to a resurrection of the body
that will fit the new environment planned by God. The agents and forces

ranged against him are already obsolete; in due course they will be utterly defeated. The universe itself will then know a transformation that will be glorious in scope and beauty. All this will be accomplished through the almighty power of divine love. Even now we dare to prepare in both church and society for that Great Day when God will be all in all. Bring out the bread and wine, hire a top-notch Mariachi band, and let the celebrations begin.

What is at issue here is the royal ministry of Christ in the future. Our unease stems not just from our native skepticism; it also stems from our failure to work through the extraordinary character of Christ's first advent.

> For the grace of God has appeared bringing salvation to all, training us to renounce impiety and worldly passions, and in the present age to live lives that are self-controlled, upright, and godly, while we wait for the blessed hope and the manifestation of the glory of our great God and Savior, Jesus Christ.[1]

In so far as we appreciate the beauty and grandeur of what Christ has done already, then it is natural to eagerly anticipate the final display of the victory over evil that is already manifest in conspicuous sanctity.

For my mother's generation in Ireland the full, royal ministry of Christ was essentially a fleeting apparition of the Christian tradition. She only had access to bits and pieces of a much richer narrative. Late in life she came to faith; but I remember my childhood as Protestant but effectively anti-Christian. In the home Jesus was a distant figure who interfered with life; he was certainly not someone you would invite to a party to cheer up the guests. My generation effectively left the faith. As I have noted earlier, what gripped me was the depth and pervasiveness of evil. Coming to faith opened up a whole new world centered in Jesus of Nazareth. That world was a world that was haunted by the real prospect of victory over evil. Even so, my natural intellectual disposition is a combination of both curiosity and skepticism; the journey of faith, like Abraham of old, has been one of five steps forward and three steps backward. Sorting out what to say about cosmic eschatology represents perhaps the deepest challenge of all in working one's way into the full contours of divine action.

On this front, the contribution of the Irish has been bad news and good news. The bad news is that John Nelson Darby, a lawyer turned evangelist-priest who suffered at the hands of his episcopal superiors in Dublin, has left a flawed theological legacy that permeates wide sectors of the church. Darby resolved a personal crisis, where he was forbidden to evangelize Roman Catholics for political and imperial reasons, by borrowing and developing a vision of history that was punctured by a string of historical crises which were brought to a dramatic climax by no less than two returns of Christ. The first rescued the church by a visit of Christ to the air in a snatch and grab operation;

---

[1] Titus 2:11–13.

the second would usher in a millennium of peace prior to the denouement of history at the far end of the ages.[2]

The good news is that it was another Irishman, Robert Henry Charles, who provided the antidote. He gave forty years of his life to sorting through the genre of eschatological and apocalyptic literature, providing the critical resources for taking seriously the amazing good news locked away in its Christian forms.[3] Charles mastered all the relevant languages (Hebrew, Aramaic, Greek, Latin, Syriac, Armenian, and Ethiopic) and opened up a train of inquiry that rightly continues in scholarly circles in our own day. I only hope I can capture the genius that his work involved and the startling note of joy and hope that it supplies for our understanding of divine action in the future.

I am for better or worse setting a high bar for success at this point. I know in my bones the many reasons why we hesitate, prevaricate, and run for intellectual cover when it comes to the topic of cosmic eschatology. So, let me dispose of these as we get down to work.

First, we now know that the future of the universe as understood empirically by science is *prima facie* at odds with the tenor and content of the Christian tradition. As far as the future is concerned, we are looking at sixty-five billion years when the world as we know it will come to an end with either a big freeze or a big crunch.[4] Over against this distant but grim scenario, the theologian who takes the specifics of divine action seriously asserts that Christ will return, raise us from the dead, finish off the forces of evil (human and demonic), and establish an abundant and glorious kingdom. Scientists will quibble over the details; however, they will and should carry on their work wherever the evidence leads them. If we look at what they say in the eye, the old chestnuts

---

[2] Dispensationalism, while it remains exceptionally popular in certain circles, is essentially an exhausted research agenda. Beginning with the proposals developed by Darby and disseminated in the Scofield Bible, it has the following elements: an exclusivist commitment to *sola scriptura*, a literalistic interpretation of Scripture as the default position in hermeneutics, a doctrine of the fall of the church, a systematic schema of dispensations that interprets history as a whole, and a complex network of future predictions usually beginning with the rapture at the onset of a seven-year period of tribulation and ending with heaven and hell. It presents itself as a rational explanation for reading Scripture as a whole with special emphasis on the interpretation of apocalyptic texts. Thus, it offers a raft of hermeneutical proposals that are to be verified or falsified, initially by exegetical study, and eventually by future historical and cosmic phenomena. Mastering it can be as complex as mastering the theology, say, of Thomas Aquinas or of Karl Barth.

[3] R. H. Charles, *Eschatology: The Doctrine of a Future Life in Israel, Judaism, and Christianity* (New York: Schocken Books, 1963). This work was first published in 1899. In the interest of full disclosure, I should report that R. H. Charles is a great-uncle by marriage. One finds at times in the secondary literature that like other Irish theologians he is stolen like our best soccer players by the English. Much of his work is now passé given more recent study but it represents a great pioneering work of scholarship in the English language.

[4] For a fine overview of the scientific options see George F. R. Ellis, ed., *The Far-Future Universe: Eschatology from a Cosmic Perspective* (Philadelphia, PA: Templeton Foundation Press, 2002).

about the conflict between science and the Christian doctrine of creation and providence seem at first sight mere difficulties that can be readily resolved. With respect to the doctrine of creation, we can rightly say that God works in, with, and through the natural order; if there is divine direction with or without unseen intervention from within, we can live with either option without due strain. With respect to cosmic eschatology, the situation is radically different. From the side of science, we are looking at long-haul developments that will work themselves out inexorably and naturally. From the theological side, we are looking at dramatic divine intervention, complete with the resurrection of our bodies, an ultimate judgment, and the utter transformation of the heavens and the earth.

However, the apparent contrast and disjunction is illusory. The crucial issue is epistemological.[5] Given the proper constraints and methods of cosmology, we look and see what the future holds by hearing what the cosmologists tell us; we should even marvel at what we hear. The warrant for theological claims is radically different: we look to divine revelation as mediated in the promises of God. This changes everything without in any way interfering with the intellectual pursuit of science. To be sure, if the scientist claims to know all there is to know about the future, then she will be brought up short by the claims of the theologian. However, at that point the scientist has become a philosopher of history, claiming to have the last word on the future of the universe; the wise scientist will get on with her mundane work. The theologian for her part will respect the results of science; however, she has her own resources and warrants for her claims and must learn to read those resources with integrity and flair.[6]

We can capture what is at stake by means of analogy. Scientific claims about the future involve mundane claims about what is up ahead for the universe as a whole. The theological claims are constituted by a cosmic drama that is neither a philosophy of history nor a cosmic myth of, say, progress or endless repetition. It is a drama of creation, freedom, fall, and ultimate redemption.

> The doctrine of the second coming teaches us that we do not and cannot know when the drama will end. The curtain may be rung down at any moment: say, before you finish reading this paragraph. This seems to some people intolerably frustrating. So many things would be interrupted. Perhaps you were going to get married next month, perhaps you are going to get a raise next month; you may be on the verge of a great scientific discovery; you may be maturing great social political reforms. Surely no good and wise God would be very unreasonable as to cut all this short? Not *now* of all moments!

[5] See my "Eschatology and Epistemology," in Jerry Walls, ed., *The Oxford Handbook of Eschatology* (New York: Oxford University Press, 2008), 581–95.

[6] For a fine treatment of the issues see David Wilkinson, *Christian Eschatology and the Physical Universe* (New York: T & T Clark, 2010).

But we think thus because we keep on assuming that we know the play. We do not know the play. We do not even know whether we are in Act I or Act IV. We do not know who are the major and who are the minor characters. The Author knows... That it [the play] has a meaning we are sure, but we cannot see it. When it is over, we may be told. We are led to expect that the Author will have something to say to each of us on the part that each of us has played. The playing it well is what matters infinitely.[7]

The use of an analogy drawn from literature takes us naturally to the second challenge that crops up for the unwary theologian, namely, the language used. Put simply, Christian discourse about the future readily deploys the language of apocalypse. This is as foreign to modern and postmodern readers as is the language of hagiography in describing the lives of the saints. It was the language of apocalypse rather than the language of hagiography that R. H. Charles cracked open with such astonishing results.

Let us pause for a moment with the language of hagiography. Josephine at a young age has joined a convent and has given her life to daily devotion to Sweet Jesus and his Blessed Mother. After several years, she becomes fed up being a holy Josephine. So, she decides to live it up in order to find out what real life really is. Like the lively daughter of a Pentecostal pastor, she has had enough of high-octane piety and decides to leave. She plans her exit carefully. At a set hour in the late afternoon, the pious nuns line up two by two and march into the dining hall. Right when they turn the corner to enter, she breaks away, slips out under the cover of the evening darkness, and heads for the bright lights of the city. For a while, she is delighted; but then, life turns sour. So, she swallows her pride and decides to go back to the convent. As it happens, she arrives just at the moment when the nuns are headed for their regular evening meal. She slips quietly into the exact spot with her old companion and heads into the refectory. To her astonishment, nobody says a word or bats an eyelid. A week later she discovers why. The Blessed Mother had taken her place on the day she ran away so her life on the run and the shame she experienced were entirely hidden from her community. She died in peace many years later and was welcomed by angels into the abode of the saints above.

We have difficulty with a story like this in part because our imaginations are trained to wince when we encounter it. The modes of thinking and the practices of the natural sciences (and of history) have understandably shaped our intellects and sensibilities. However, the problem runs deeper than this. The narrative turns our ideas about causality and epistemology inside out and upside down. We have no analogies or correlations to help us cope with the actions of the Blessed Mother. If we are Protestants, we are haunted by the

---

[7] C. S. Lewis, "The World's Last Night," in Lesley Walmsley, ed., *C. S. Lewis, Essay Collection: Faith, Christianity and the Church* (London: HarperCollins, 2000), 49.

hoary debates about saints with their well-stocked credit cards of merit. The story is laced with the kind of supernaturalism that strikes us as superstition on steroids. However, this simply shows how impoverished our hermeneutical resources are. The story is essentially an entertaining way to capture the sheer abundance of grace and mercy available to wayward believers. It undercuts our obsession with our shame and guilt by overwhelming us with supernatural intervention and mercy. So, it invites us to relax, come to terms with our miserable failures, and move on in the life of faith. Hagiography is written in a register to nourish our souls; it is not prosaic material to be taken in a literalistic sense.[8]

We face a similar dilemma in dealing with material that is identified generally as eschatological and apocalyptic.[9] This is not a mere sideshow in the biblical materials, as Charles so effectively showed in his pioneering work. The problem is that we will be driven to distraction if we read it like an editorial in *The Times* or the *Wall Street Journal*. We will be treating the authors involved as if they have minds as pedestrian as our own. It is not that the material does not convey relevant information about the future, for it does. It is rather that the information is conveyed in a register that turns our regular causal and epistemological modes of thinking upside down. My aim here is not to provide even the beginnings of a comprehensive reading of the relevant material. My aim is to undo the mental cramp and cut to the chase on what needs to be said in the deflationary form of systematic theology I am practising.

Consider the following material taken from the story of Pentecost in Acts. Peter is explaining what has just happened. He notes that the folk are not drunk and then he deploys a lengthy quotation taken from the prophet Joel.

> In the last days it will be, God declares, that I will pour out my Spirit upon all flesh, and your sons and daughters will prophesy, and your young men shall see visions, and your old men shall dream dreams. Even upon my slaves, both men and women, in those days I will pour out my Spirit; and they shall prophesy.[10]

So far so good; this sounds like an apt way to interpret what has just happened on the day of Pentecost. However, the quotation then continues.

> And I will show portents in the heaven above and signs on the earth below, blood, and fire, and smoky mist. The sun shall be turned to darkness and the moon to

---

[8] For a splendid treatment of the distinction between literal and literalistic see Iain Provan, *The Reformation and the Right Reading of Scripture* (Waco, TX: Baylor University Press, 2017), 81–106.

[9] By eschatology I mean that locus of doctrine that deals with the life to come; by apocalyptic I mean a particular genre of writing that seeks to describe future events. For a seminal treatment of the concept of eschatology see George B. Caird, "The Language of Eschatology," in his *The Language and Imagery of the Bible* (London: Duckworth, 1980), chapter 14.

[10] Acts 2:17–18.

blood, before the coming of the Lord's great and glorious day. Then everyone who calls on the name of the Lord will be saved.[11]

This latter material is a classic piece of apocalyptic writing drawn from the prophet Joel. Peter is not in the least embarrassed to use it to describe what is happening there and then on the day of Pentecost. Clearly, if we are mystified, the problem is on our end not on Peter's end. Read in a prosaic and literalistic manner, the passage makes absolutely no sense. So, something else is going on here.

It is not difficult to see what Peter is doing. Two elements are obvious. He is using language about the "coming of the Lord's great and glorious day" to describe what is happening here and now in the divine visitation of the Holy Spirit sent by the Risen Lord on the day of Pentecost. In other words, Peter is using language of the End of History to describe events happening now within history. What is happening now fits into the wider narrative of God's purposes for the rescue of the world from alienation and evil. Second, this use of apocalyptic language is deployed to bring home the urgency of immediate action. The hearer needs to call upon the name of the Lord and be saved, that is, begin now to participate in the divine project launched in human history by Jesus of Nazareth. We have an expressivist and prescriptivist use of theological discourse. By breaking the conventions of causal discourse, Peter through Joel is expressing how important the events just witnessed really are; at the same time, he is prescribing an urgent course of action for the hearer to get with the divine program for which Peter has become an ambassador and leader.

Perhaps we are shielded from this kind of discourse because we do not know the language of good country and western music. When the great and inimitable Willie Nelson loses his girlfriend to another drunken suitor, he reaches entirely naturally for apocalyptic language. So, he tells us that the stars have ceased to shine and that the moon no longer sheds her light at night. He has witnessed the End of the World; the earth has opened up and swallowed him whole. What has happened is so momentous that this is the only way he can express how terrible life is at the betrayal of his lover. And as we are entertained by the amazing riffs on his battered guitar, we are drawn into his experience and given a way to express our own experiences of loves lost and encouragement to pick up and move on, a theme that might well be taken up in the next song in the wonderful cycle of material.

For those not attuned to the wonders of country and western music, it is not difficult to find other examples. Thus, we speak of it being hell last year in our marriage; or we say that going to long faculty meetings is like purgatory; or that visiting the lake district of Fermanagh is like encountering heaven on earth; or that the tax policy of the Republicans signals the arrival of Armageddon for

[11] Acts 2:19–21.

the poor; or that experiencing firsthand the brutality of the Nazis is encountering the End of the World. Readers can furnish their own examples. Scholars who deal with recent Continental philosophers can supply a whole new raft of cases where eschatological language is used to speak of the drama of the loss of faith or whatever other cultural crisis of truth or authenticity has gripped their imagination. In the meantime, the impoverished analytic philosopher and theologian cannot make sense of what they are reading. Their semantic, causal, and epistemological hair has been set on fire and they are looking for the fire-extinguisher.

In the meantime, we come back down to earth and are drawn into the future plans that God has for his People and his creation up ahead. The standard claim that the early Christians expected the Great and Final Day of the Lord just around the corner is a gross exaggeration when we note how they used apocalyptic language. Apocalyptic language was their natural linguistic habitat; so, some could readily see the promised return of the Son of Man as fulfilled in the events related to the fall of Jerusalem.[12] This was the prophesy that was made by Jesus in his role as a prophet to Israel. Earlier prophets had warned about the fall of Jerusalem in an earlier generation; it was no surprise that Jesus as Messiah should also have a prophetic role in his unique ministry. No doubt some may have misconstrued what he prophesied and were tempted to take it as a warning about the Great and Final Day of the Lord at the end of history when God would at last fulfill his purposes for the world. However, this is not the most natural reading of his message to Israel. As we have seen, Peter can readily use apocalyptic language to describe what happened at Pentecost. We should expect no less from Jesus speaking as a prophet. Hence, we can lay aside the standard exaggerations about the immediate end of history that stem from a prosaic and literalistic reading of prophesy in the New Testament.

We also need to have a genuine feel for the aspirations of the first generation of Christians. Who can blame them given what they had been through if they wanted the Lord to come back immediately and clean up the mess that human existence is without God. They were doing their best to deal with a whole new phase in God's project to establish his kingdom on earth as it was in heaven. They had come to believe that God had raised Jesus from the dead, an event they associated with the final resurrection at the end of the world. Some friends and family members had naturally found the very idea of such an event to be an anomaly out of its proper sequence and therefore impossible. They could not fit it into their timetable just as Greeks could not fit the resurrection of Jesus into their worldview. For those who followed Jesus, the resurrection of Jesus had been followed up with the great event of Pentecost and the bestowal of the Spirit promised of old; they had come to experience

---

[12] Mark 13.

the powers of the age to come. So, it was small wonder that they were eager to enter the next phase of God's plans for the world.

Eager expectation is surely a phenomenon that very naturally arises because of intense religious experience and because of a longing to see the kingdom of God come at last and see God finish what he had begun in Jesus. Karl Barth provides a splendid reading of what is involved in his chapter on Christoph Blumhardt in *Protestant Theology in the Nineteenth Century: Its Background and History*. Blumhardt had experienced a fresh outpouring of the Holy Spirit in his ministry that included exorcisms and divine healing. He had seen Jesus take on the powers of darkness and win. Out of these experiences, he began to develop a theology of hope. He began to long for the final victory promised in the Gospel. Here is part of Barth's witty account of what emerged in Blumhardt's life.

> We have already heard how Blumhardt regarded the dawn of a historical period of grace preceding the *return of Christ* as being imminent, so definitely, that in old age, at the beginning of each year, he would say with increasing excitement: 'This year might . . .' There is a credible tradition that at Bad Boll a coach was kept ready, year in, year out, with all its equipment, ready to begin the journey to the Holy Land to meet the returning Christ if need be.[13]

It is easy to smile at the naïveté involved; perhaps the laugh is on us for our impoverished and skeptical appropriation of the promises of God related to the final transformation of the world.

Blumhardt clearly looked forward to God's final victory over evil and darkness that would occur with the return of Christ. In doing so, he is drawing on the wider narrative of the resurrection of the dead, the last judgment, and the recreation of the heavens and the earth. He is also clearly hinting here at a period before the return of Christ that would be a time of grace. In other words, he was invoking the language of a postmillennial outpouring of the Holy Spirit before the end of history. More generally, he is reaching for an account of the transition from this world and its history to the final reconfiguration of all things in Christ. We are now getting deeper into the details of eschatological reflection so let's take up this topic and see where it takes us.

We can pick up two sets of themes that deserve mention immediately. First, there is the material that focuses on such themes as the millennium and the Antichrist. While often taken idealistically, these are best seen as symbolic efforts to deal with the hopes and fears that readily crop up in the crises of human history. Thus, the language of the millennium speaks of what is possible were there to be a fresh Pentecost in human history where the Holy Spirit would usher in a time of conversion for the individual, comprehensive

---

[13] Karl Barth, *Protestant Theology in the Nineteenth Century: Its Background and History* (Valley Forge, NJ: Judson Press, 1973), 647.

renewal for the church, and justice and peace for society.[14] By contrast, the language of the Antichrist and related themes depicts the possibility of massive rebellion against God on a regional or even global scale led by a world leader hell-bent on destroying the work of God in Christ and the church. Second, there is the material that focuses on the conversion of the Jews and the return of the Jews to the land of Israel. These clearly refer to possible events in history and it is far from clear how they are to be warranted. In Paul, the conversion of the Jews is essentially an intuition that, given the pivotal place of ethnic or biological Israel in the purposes of God, one day Jews will come to see Christ as their Messiah.[15] As to the return of Jews to the land of Israel, this would seem to be more of a return to the pre-Christian promises of God to Abraham and his progeny, as opposed to a specific prophesy related to the founding of the state of Israel in 1948.[16] It could also be read as an act of providence related to the survival of the Jewish people after the horrendous events of the Holocaust.[17]

While there is intense interest in these themes in some circles, the whole enterprise is effectively cut short by the fact that Christ himself insisted he did not know the relevant information. "But about that day or hour no one knows, neither the angels in heaven, nor the Son, but only the Father. Beware, keep alert; for you do not know when the time will come."[18] Even if we did know, the likelihood of getting any of the details right are surely slim; think of how easy it was to miss the character of the first coming of Christ in Bethlehem. While Christ insists that his coming is a fulfillment of the ancient promises, there is a real sense in which what he says and does is part and parcel of what it is to understand those promises. Moreover, it is plausible to read Paul as wrestling over time with how best to think through the future actions of God in history and beyond, rather than supplying a take-it-or-leave-it account of how God's final victory over evil will be accomplished.[19] We can see similar developments in other themes in Scripture, not least in the way various claims and counter-claims about eschatology are advanced. This should not surprise us in the least given the contrasting ways in which the biblical authors handle, for example, the tension between divine blessing and suffering in the Old Testament, or between faith and works in the New Testament. This feature of Scripture, while incompatible with those standard views of Scripture that insist

---

[14] Charles provides a useful account of the origins of this language in 2 Enoch in *Eschatology*, 315.

[15] Romans 11:25–32.

[16] I plan to take a look at this topic as a test case for examining claims about divine action in contemporary history in volume IV.

[17] Contrary to popular opinion, it has nothing to do with the prophesies found in Dispensationalism where the return of the Jews to the land of Israel is predicted to happen *after* the rapture of believers in the air and *after* the seven-year period of tribulation.

[18] Mark 13:32–3.   [19] This can be confirmed by a chronological reading of Paul's letters.

on smoothing out its tensions into a consistent whole, should be welcomed rather than excoriated. The Bible is not a set of crossword puzzles with the answers to be worked out by precisionist, rational theologians; it is a diverse set of texts that operate as an indispensable means of grace.

Furthermore, set against the unfulfilled aspirations of many theologians in their quest for a detailed account of the future, the material in the Nicene Creed is wonderfully modest and to the point. We are to look for the resurrection of the dead and the life of the world to come. Earlier I spelled this out further in terms that sought to capture the note of victory over evil, the full realization of the purposes of God for creation, and a transformation of the universe that will be utterly glorious in scope and beauty. I also hinted that the deeper vision involved should spur us on to prepare for that Great Day when God will be all in all. Let me now explore this more modest agenda by means of theological commentary and brief ethical exhortation.

First, the themes of the resurrection of the dead and the transformation of the world belong naturally together. The life to come is to be a fully embodied life, where the goodness of embodiment will be recognized afresh as a wonderful gift from God. We can readily become engrossed at this point in debates about the exact nature of the envisaged body; however, this is where we touch on the transformation of created order with a new heavens and new earth. Whatever the nature of the body and however we sort out apt continuity, it will be a body properly fitted to the whole new environment which it will inhabit. Clearly resurrection in some sense entails some kind of spatial and temporal existence that will dovetail with the radical transformation of the heavens and the earth.

Second, when the hope of resurrection first arose in Israel this was as much a corporate matter as an individual matter; resurrection was tied to leaving the community of God on earth and joining the community beyond the grave. The resurrection of Christ gives us glimpses of what might be at stake but leaves us with as many questions as we have answers. So, life in the world to come involves not a selfish commitment to personal survival, a theme more apt in the case of a doctrine of the immortality of the soul, but to a life as citizens of a righteous kingdom. Within this future world we enter into communion with the saints of all ages. The blessings, including appropriate awards, will not be given apart from our brothers and sisters in the kingdom. So, we are to envisage a common life drawn from all nations and all ages, where individualism, not to speak of spiritual self-absorption, will be gone forever.

Third, the experience of divine judgment will be both sober and liberating. It will be sober because we will face our lives as seen by God rather than through our own distorted perspectives and delusions. The judge of all the earth will judge rightly. We rightly develop a sense of fear at this point. Here is one way to think of the kind of fear involved. It comes from Studdert

Kennedy, an Anglican priest well acquainted with the killing fields of World War I.

> I do not fear God. *He could not, and would not, do me any harm, anywhere, or at any time.* If I have any fear of him, it is a fear that is born of love, a fear of grieving Him, which love begets. He is, and always will be, pure, infinite, unmitigated Love. His justice cannot be separated from His Love—justice has no meaning apart from love. If He is Judge of the World, He is not in the least like a human judge, for a human judge administers those pains and penalties, which a chaotic and sinful community believe to be necessary in order that some measure of order and decency may be maintained; but in the nature of things, the man condemned must often be less of a sinner than the jury that condemns him. . . . With that sort of justice, God has nothing to do. He will never send anybody to hell—He could not, for to send a man to hell would be to drive him away from Himself; and whosoever cometh, either here or hereafter, He will not him cast out.[20]

There is a touch of Irish exaggeration here, for there are sadistic criminals who are a lot worse than the juries that condemn them. Moreover, it is a stretch to posit some sort of second chance in the life to come. However, Kennedy has captured an absolutely critical element of what is at stake in divine judgment. We can be sure that God "*could not, and would not, do me any harm, anywhere, or at any time.*" Our fear is a unique fear engendered by encounter with unsurpassed, holy love. Moreover, those who do end up in hell are not punished by God; they have determined their own future by their own choices and actions.[21] So, we rightly approach the experience of divine judgment with proper sobriety.

However, we should also think of future divine judgment as liberating. First, such judgment means that those who have suffered at the hands of godless tyrants will be exonerated. As I noted in the last chapter, all the innocent children who have been incinerated will be raised from the dead and vindicated before God. The righteous who sought to protect them will be honored. We need not here think of compensation, for taking that road will lead to the loss of our moral moorings in that nothing can make up for the suffering involved. Moreover, we can be sure that those who inflicted suffering on them will face a divine judge who can and will act with justice. We will behold that we live in a moral universe, even though exactly what that will look like can be left in the hands of God. Finally, such judgment as we ourselves will encounter will be liberating in the sense that we will come to terms with the full truth of our existence for good and ill. Thus, we will be able to move forward without the lingering debris of our darkened conscience and with full insight into the

---

[20] G. A. Studdert Kennedy, *The Wicket Gate* (London: Hodder & Stoughton, 1923), 58. Emphasis mine.

[21] The alternatives are obvious and need no extended commentary. First, conditional immortality after a period of retributive justice; and second, universal salvation after folk eventually come around and acknowledge the error of their ways.

depths of our moral and spiritual existence. Only then will we be able to enter into the full joys of personal eschatology.

Returning to our theological commentary, we look, fourth, at the radical transformation of the heavens and the earth. Our ancestors tended to think first and foremost in terms of doomsday scenarios. Either because of fear of God or because of a desire for vengeance on the wicked, the default position was one of cosmic annihilation. In some cases, they were misled by the blood-curdling language of apocalypse. This was and is a fatal mistake. It would be the functional equivalent of God annihilating his People after the apostasy of the golden calf and starting all over with Moses.[22] We can expect Moses and a host of others to protest against God's covenant with creation after the flood. What is at issue is not annihilation but radical transformation.

The really deep issue here takes us back to our doctrine of God and our doctrine of creation. On the one hand, taking the transformation of the world seriously requires a wholehearted sense of the almighty power of God. Nothing less than a God who is omnipotent, omnipresent, and omniscient has the capacity to transform the world from top to bottom, from the furthest worlds in space to the smallest atom and molecule. On the other hand, for God to annihilate his creation would be to undermine the claim that the world is a good world. It is not a perfect world; but it is indeed a good world. What is at issue, then, is a radical transformation that brings it to a fitting perfection. Nature will cease to groan as it enjoys a redemption similar to the redemption of our bodies. Jürgen Moltmann has made a daring suggestion at this point. He envisages history as "a universal information process with many strata and ramifications."[23] He then posits relevant change in this domain.

> The form of the old world was sin, death, and transience; the form of the new one will be righteousness and justice, eternal life and imperishability. The eschatological transformation of the universe embraces both continuity and discontinuity. All the information of this world remains in eternity, but is transformed.[24]

We are close at this point to the limits of intelligibility. The same observation applies to the daring suggestion that in the transformation of the world we will encounter nothing less than the deification of the universe.[25] Perhaps we should speak of transfiguration rather than deification, for with transfiguration we avoid breaching the Creator–creature distinction. We have a hint of what might be possible in the transfiguration of the Son in Mount Tabor and the transfiguration of the body of Christ in his resurrection. There is a pleasing

---

[22] Exodus 32:11–14.

[23] Jürgen Moltmann, "Cosmos and Theosis: Eschatological Perspectives on the Future of the Universe," in Ellis, ed., *The Far-Future Universe*, 258.

[24] Ibid., 257.

[25] An important source for this is Sergius Bulgakov, *The Bride of the Lamb* (Grand Rapids, MI: Eerdmans, 2002), 417–28.

indication here of the action of the Holy Spirit in that transfiguration reminds us plausibly of the work of the Spirit in making "the clothes of Christ shine, such dazzling white, such as no one on earth could bleach."[26] Paul draws attention to this latter line of thought when he says: "He [Christ] will transform the body of our humiliation that it may be transformed to the body of his glory, by the power that enables him to make all things subject to himself."[27] We are also reminded of Isaiah in his magnificent vision where "he saw the Lord, high and lofty . . . "[28] and the Seraphs "called one to another and said 'Holy, holy, holy, is the Lord of hosts; the whole earth is full of his glory.'"[29] Clearly, what is happening in thinking about the transfiguration of the universe is that the transfiguration of Christ is being extended to capture the potential transformation of the cosmos.

It brings us up short to think that the physical universe will be subject not just to the sustaining and providential activity of God but to the very saturation of the universe by the Holy Spirit. Yet we have traces of this even in this life in those exceptionally rare instances of transfiguration of the body in figures like Symeon the New Theologian and Saint Seraphim. We are dealing with an immersion in the energies of the Holy Spirit that transform the materiality of the body. We also get hints of this in those rare cases where the body of the deceased is not subject to the normal consequences of decay and corruption.

Consider in this regard the reports arising from the life of Archbishop Dmitri of Dallas. I knew Archbishop Dmitri intimately; he was one of the kindest souls I have ever met, full of peace, cheerfulness, intelligence, and unadulterated goodness. He was originally a Southern Baptist before converting to Orthodoxy; he taught Spanish for a time at Southern Methodist University; he was a brilliant cook and a friend of little children; later in life he looked like an old and cherished Russian monk in the streets of Dallas. He made visible what a true bishop of the church should be. At one time, he was in the running to become the Metropolitan of the Orthodox Church in America; the leaders of his church were not ready for such a bold move; so, he came back to Dallas to become a saint. After his death, his modest parish built a small chapel to contain his remains; when his casket was opened five years after his death, his body was not subject to decay. There is unimpeachable testimony to this effect. There is now a wonderful icon that is the first sign that one day he will be canonized by his church, and deservedly so. Nothing of great significance hangs on whether readers believe what I have just recounted. I am reaching for hints of the effects of the Holy Spirit on our fragile bodies in this life as a harbinger for the radical transformation of the universe in God's good time in the future.

We can legitimately set all this aside in our reflections on the resurrection of the body and the life of the world to come. We readily confess that what lies ahead is beyond conceiving, so great are the wonders and blessings that

---

[26] Mark 9:3.   [27] Philippians 3:21.   [28] Isaiah 6:1.   [29] Isaiah 6:3.

the final arrival of the kingdom of God will bring. What is not legitimate is to sit back and do nothing about the penultimate arrival of that kingdom here and now. Five factors have led to passivity at this point. First, we harbor doomsday scenarios that focus on a wrong conception of judgment. Second, we fear guilt by association from past pundits on eschatology. Third, we have an inadequate grasp of the power of God available to us in the aftermath of Pentecost. Fourth, we are all too ready to lose our nerve in the face of determined opposition and of ignorant interpretations of Christian eschatology on the part of our critics and enemies. And fifth, we have a long-standing skepticism and unease about the place of genuine human action in salvation and the inauguration of the kingdom of God by the Son through the working of the Holy Spirit.

If what we say about cosmic eschatology is true, then the proper response is obvious. We should prepare for that Great and Final Day of the Lord by fostering holiness across the face of the church; by cleaning up the environment; by building first rate universities where the life of the mind is valued and cultivated; by rendering all earthly tyrannies and political corruption as obsolete as horse-drawn carriages in the age of space travel; by entering the political arena with flair and understanding; and generally by spending our unworthy and brittle lives in the service of all our neighbors. It is the Triune God who has inaugurated his kingdom; it is the Triune God who sustains and provides it with the gifts and energies it needs; and it is the Triune God who will assuredly bring it to fulfillment in the world to come. This is the best possible news for the future of the universe. It is the great Easter Message for the Cosmos.

In the meantime, we exercise our God-given and redeemed agency in all aspects of life with enthusiasm and flair. And we assuredly keep in mind those dire warnings about the Antichrist, even as we constantly look back to the victory over sin already won.

> And sitting down they watched Him there,
> The soldiers did.
> There, while they played with dice,
> He made his sacrifice,
> And died upon the Cross to rid
> God's world of sin.
> He was a gambler too,
> My Christ,
> He took His life and threw
> It for a world redeemed,
> And e'er His agony was done,
> Before the westering sun went down,
> Crowning the day with its crimson crown
> He knew
> That He had won.[30]

[30] Studdert Kennedy, *The Wicket Gate*, 177.

Select Bibliography

Abraham, William J. *The Logic of Evangelism*. Grand Rapids, MI: Eerdmans, 1989.

Abraham, William J. *Canon and Criterion in Christian Theology: From the Fathers to Feminism*. Oxford: Clarendon Press, 1997.

Abraham, William J. *Crossing the Threshold of Divine Revelation*. Grand Rapids, MI: Eerdmans, 2006.

Abraham, William J. *Divine Agency and Divine Action, Volume I: Exploring and Evaluating the Debate*. Oxford: Oxford University Press, 2017.

Abraham, William J. *Divine Agency and Divine Action, Volume II: Soundings in the Christian Tradition*. Oxford: Oxford University Press, 2017.

Abraham, William J., and Frederick D. Aquino, eds. *The Oxford Handbook of the Epistemology of Theology*. Oxford: Oxford University Press, 2017.

Abraham, William J., Jason E. Vickers, and Natalie B. Van Kirk, eds. *Canonical Theism: A Proposal for Theology and Church*. Grand Rapids, MI: Eerdmans, 2008.

Afanasiev, Nicholas. *The Church of the Holy Spirit*. Notre Dame, IN: University of Notre Dame Press, 2007.

Alston, William P. "Functionalism and Theological Language," in Thomas Morris, ed., *The Concept of God*. Oxford: Oxford University Press, 1987.

Anderson, Gary A. *Sin: A History*. New Haven, CT: Yale University Press, 2009.

Arthur, William. *The Tongue of Fire, or, the Power of Christianity*. New York: Carlton and Porter, 1859.

Augustine, *On the Trinity*. Hyde Park, NY: New City Press, 2012.

Barr, James. *The Concept of Biblical Theology: An Old Testament Perspective*. Minneapolis, MN: Fortress Press, 1999.

Barth, Karl. *Protestant Theology in the Nineteenth Century: Its Background and History*. Valley Forge, NJ: Judson Press, 1973.

Beilby, James, and Paul P. Eddy, eds. *The Nature of Atonement: Four Views*. Downers Grove, IL: IVP Academic, 2006.

Bernard of Clairvaux, *On Loving God with an Analytical Commentary*, ed. Emero Stiegman. Kalamazoo, MI: Cistercian Publications Inc., 1995.

Bray, Gerald L., ed. *Ancient Christian Doctrine, I: We Believe in One God*. Downers Grove, IL: IVP Academic, 2009.

Brown, William P. *The Seven Pillars of the Universe: The Bible, Science, and the Wonder of Ecology*. New York: Oxford University Press, 2010.

Bulgakov, Sergius. *The Bride of the Lamb*. Grand Rapids, MI: Eerdmans, 2002.

Burleigh, Michael. *Earthly Powers: The Clash of Religion and Politics from the French Revolution to the Great War*. New York: HarperCollins, 2005.

Burleigh, Michael. *Sacred Causes: The Clash of Religion and Politics from the Great War to the War on Terrorism*. New York: HarperCollins, 2007.

Burleigh, Michael. *Blood and Rage: A Cultural History of Terrorism*. London: Harper Collins, 2008.

Burleigh, Michael. *Moral Combat: Good and Evil in World War II*. New York: HarperCollins, 2011.

Butterworth, G. W. *Origen On First Principles*. Gloucester, MA: Peter Smith, 1973.

Caird, George B. "The Language of Eschatology," in his *The Language and Imagery of the Bible*. London: Duckworth, 1980.

Catalamessa, Raniero. *The Mystery of Pentecost*. Collegeville, MN: Liturgical Press, 2001.

Charles, R. H. *Eschatology: The Doctrine of a Future Life in Israel, Judaism, and Christianity*. New York: Schocken Books, 1963.

Climacus, John. *The Ladder of Divine Ascent*. Mahwah, NJ: Paulist Press, 1982.

Coke, Thomas. *The Experience and Spiritual Letters of Mrs. Hester Ann Rogers*. London: T. Nelson and Sons, Paternoster Row, 1852.

Coleman, Robert E. *The Masterplan of Evangelism*. Grand Rapids, MI: Revell, 1993.

Cooper, John W. *Body, Soul and Life Everlasting*. Grand Rapids, MI: Eerdmans, 1989.

Couenhoven, Jesse. "St. Augustine's Doctrine of Original Sin," *Augustinian Studies* 36 (2005), 359–96.

Crisp, Oliver D., and Michael C. Rea, eds. *Analytic Theology: New Essays in the Philosophy of Theology*. Oxford: Oxford University Press, 2009.

Dallaire, Lt.-Gen. Romeo. *Shake Hands with the Devil*. New York: Carroll and Graf, 2004.

Davison, Scott A. "Divine Providence and Human Freedom," in Michael J. Murray, ed., *Reason for Hope Within*. Grand Rapids, MI: Eerdmans, 1999.

DeDuhn, Jason. *The First Testament: Marcion's Scriptural Canon*. Salem, OR: Polebridge Press, 2013.

Denzinger, Heinrich. *Compendium of Creeds, Definitions, and Declaration of Matters of Faith and Morals*. San Francisco: Ignatius Press, 2010. Forty-third edition, revised, enlarged, and in collaboration with Helmut Hoping, edited by Peter Hünermann in the bilingual edition.

Dummett, Michael. "The Intelligibility of Eucharistic Doctrine," in William J. Abraham and Steve W. Holzer, eds., *The Rationality of Religious Belief: Essays in Honour of Basil Mitchell*. Oxford: Clarendon Press, 1987.

Edwards, Jonathan. *The Religious Affections*. New Haven, CT: Yale University Press, 2009.

Ellis, George F. R., ed. *The Far-Future Universe: Eschatology from a Cosmic Perspective*. Philadelphia, PA: Templeton Foundation Press, 2002.

Elnoury, Tamer, and Kevin Maurer. *American Radical: Inside the World of an Undercover Muslim FBI Agent*. New York: Dutton, 2017.

Farrer, Austin. *A Faith of Our Own*. New York: World Publishing Company, 1960.

Farrer, Austin. *Lord I Believe: Suggestions for Turning the Creed into Prayer*. Cambridge, MA: Cowley Publications, 1989.

Farrer, Austin. *Reflective Faith: Essays in Philosophical Theology*. Eugene, OR: Wipf and Stock, 2012.

Farrer, Austin. *Words for Life*. Eugene, OR: Wipf and Stock, 2012.

Forsyth, P. T. *The Work of Christ*. London: Independent Press Ltd, 1938.

Fredriksen, Paula. *Sin: The Early History of an Idea*. Princeton, NJ: Princeton University Press, 2012.

Gallie, W. B. "Essentially Contested Concepts," in his *Philosophy and the Historical Understanding*. London: Chatto & Windus, 1964.

Goricheva, Tatiana. *Talking About God is Dangerous: The Diary of a Russian Dissident*. New York: Crossroad, 1987.

Gregory, Jane. *Fred Hoyle's Universe*. Oxford: Oxford University Press, 2005.

Gregory of Nazianzus. "On the Holy Spirit," in *The Nicene and Post-Nicene Fathers*. Grand Rapids, MI: Eerdmans, 1983, Vol. 7.

Hazony, Yoram. *The Philosophy of Hebrew Scripture*. Cambridge: Cambridge University Press, 2012.

Heath, Elaine. *Naked Faith: The Mystical Theology of Phoebe Palmer*. Edinburgh: James Clarke and Co., 2010.

Hicks, Stephen R. C. *Explaining Postmodernism: Skepticism and Secularism from Rousseau to Foucault*. Roscoe, IL: Ockham's Razor Publishing Company, 2017.

Julien, Maude. *The Only Girl in the World: A Memoir*. London: Oneworld, 2018.

Kelsey, David H. *Eccentric Existence: A Theological Anthropology*. Philadelphia, PA: Westminster John Knox Press, 2009, *Eccentric Existence: A Theological Anthropology*, 2 volumes.

Kierkegaard, Søren. *Training in Christianity*. New York: Vintage Books, 2004.

Kilby, Clyde, ed. *A Mind Awake: An Anthology of C. S. Lewis*. San Diego, CA: Harcourt, Inc., 1968.

Kinzer, Mark S. *Post-Missionary Messianic Judaism: Redefining Christian Engagement with the Jewish People*. Grand Rapids, MI: Brazos Press, 2005.

Kramnick, Isaac, ed. *The Portable Burke*. New York: Penguin, 1999.

Lampe, G. W. H. *God as Spirit*. Oxford: Oxford University Press, 1977.

Lewis, C. S. "The World's Last Night," in Lesley Walmsley, ed., *C. S. Lewis, Essay Collection: Faith, Christianity and the Church*. London: HarperCollins, 2000.

Loisy, Alfred. *The Gospel and the Church*. Philadelphia, PA: Fortress Press, 1976.

Lucas, J. R. "Freedom and Grace," in his *Freedom and Grace*. London: SPCK, 1976.

Luney, Robert. "The Lucan Text of the Lord's Prayer (Lk XI 2–4)," *Novum Testamentum* 1.2 (1956), 103–11.

McCord Adams, Marilyn. *Christ and Horrors: The Coherence of Christology*. Cambridge: Cambridge University Press, 2006.

McDonnell, Killian. *The Other Hand of God: The Holy Spirit as the Universal Touch and Goal*. Collegeville, MN: Liturgical Press, 2003.

MacKinnon, D. M. *The Church*. London: Dacre Press, 1940.

Maddox, Randy. *Responsible Grace*. Nashville, TN: Kingswood Books, 1994.

Min, Anselm Kyongsuk. "Solidarity with Others in the Power of the Holy Spirit," in Bradford E. Hinze and D. Lyle Dabney, eds., *Advents of the Spirit: An Introduction to the Current Study of Pneumatology*. Milwaukee, WI: Marquette University Press, 2001.

Neiman, Susan. *Evil in Modern Thought: An Alternative History of Modern Philosophy*. Princeton, NJ: Princeton University Press, 2004, 2015.

Ober, Josiah. *Demopolis: Democracy before Liberalism in Theory and Practice*. Cambridge: Cambridge University Press, 2017.

Ogden, Schubert M. "Prolegomena to Practical Theology," in his *On Theology*. Dallas, TX: Southern Methodist University Press, 1992.

O'Neill, Onora. *A Question of Trust: The BBC Reith Lectures, 2002*. Cambridge: Cambridge University Press, 2002.

Pais, Abraham. *Subtle is the Lord: The Science and Life of Albert Einstein*. Oxford: Oxford University Press, 1982.

Pannenberg, Wolfhart. *Systematic Theology Volume 2*. Grand Rapids, MI: Eerdmans, 1994.

Paul, Robert S. *The Atonement and the Sacraments*. Eugene, OR: Wipf and Stock, 2002.

Peck, M. Scott. *Glimpses of the Devil: A Psychiatrist's Personal Account of Possession, Exorcism, and Redemption*. New York: Free Press, 2005.

Plantinga, Alvin. *Warranted Christian Belief*. New York: Oxford University Press, 2000.

Plantinga, Alvin. *Where the Conflict Really Lies: Science, Religion, and Naturalism*. Oxford: Oxford University Press, 2011.

Procter-Smith, Marjorie. "Feminism and Spirituality," in Robin Mass and Gabriel O'Donnell, eds., *Spiritual Traditions for the Contemporary Church*. Nashville, TN: Abingdon, 1990.

Provan, Iain. *The Reformation and the Right Reading of Scripture*. Waco, TX: Baylor University Press, 2017.

Radner, Ephraim. *The End of the Church: A Pneumatology of Christian Division in the West*. Grand Rapids, MI: Eerdmans, 1998.

Rawls, John. *A Brief Inquiry into the Meaning of Sin and Faith, with 'On Religion'*, ed. Thomas Nagel. Cambridge, MA: Harvard University Press, 2009.

Romanides, John S. *The Ancestral Sin*. Ridgewood, NJ: Zephyr, 1998.

Rudolph, David J. *A Jew to the Jews*. Tübingen: Mohr Siebeck, 2011.

Sanneh, Lamin. *Whose Religion is Christianity?* Grand Rapids, MI: Eerdmans, 2003.

Schüssler Fiorenza, Francis, and John P. Galvin, eds. *Systematic Theology: Roman Catholic Perspectives*. Minneapolis, MN: Fortress Press, 1991, 2 vols.

Scruton, Roger. *Fools, Frauds, and Firebrands: Thinkers of the New Left*. London: Bloomsbury, 2015.

Seeskin, Kenneth R. *Thinking about Torah: A Philosopher Reads the Bible*. Lincoln, NE: University of Nebraska Press, 2016.

Sheldon, Henry. *System of Christian Doctrine*. Cincinnati, OH: Jennings and Graham, 1912.

Skobtsova, Maria. *Essential Writings*, trans. Richard Pevear and Larissa Volokhonsky. Maryknoll, NY: Orbis, 2003.

Soskice, Janet Martin. *Metaphor and Religious Language*. Oxford: Clarendon Press, 1985.

Stevenson, Leslie. *Seven Theories of Human Nature*. Oxford: Oxford University Press, 1988.

Stove, David. *Cricket versus Republicanism, and other Essays*, ed. James Franklin and R. J. Stove. Sydney: Quaker Hill Press, 1995.

Stove, David. "Cole Porter and Karl Popper: The Jazz Age in the Philosophy of Science," in Roger Kimball, ed., *Against the Idols of the Age*. New Brunswick, NJ: Transaction Publishers, 1999.

Studdert Kennedy, G. A. *The Wicket Gate*. London: Hodder & Stoughton, 1923.

Sullivan, Francis A. *Charisms and the Charismatic Renewal: A Biblical and Theological Study*. Eugene, OR: Wipf and Stock, 2004.

Swinburne, Richard. *The Existence of God*. Oxford: Clarendon Press, 1979.

Swinburne, Richard. *The Evolution of the Soul*. Oxford: Clarendon Press, 1986.

Swinburne, Richard. *Providence and Evil*. Oxford: Clarendon Press, 1988.

Symeon the New Theologian. *The Discourses*. Mahwah, NJ: Paulist Press, 1990.

Symeon the New Theologian. *On the Mystical Life, The Ethical Discourses, Vol. 1: The Church and the Last Things*. Crestwood, NY: St. Vladimir's Seminary Press, 1995.

Symeon the New Theologian. *Divine Eros*. Crestwood, NY: St. Vladimir's Seminary Press, 2010.

Tabbernee, William. "'Will the Real Paraclete Please Speak Forth!' The Catholic-Montanist Conflict over Pneumatology," in Bradford E. Hinze and D. Lyle Dabney, eds., *Advents of the Spirit: An Introduction to the Current Study of Pneumatology*. Milwaukee, WI: Marquette University Press, 2001.

Tennant, F. R. *The Sources of the Doctrines of the Fall and Original Sin*. New York: Schocken Books, 1903.

Tillett, Wilbur Fisk. *Providence, Prayer, and Power*. Nashville, TN: Cokesbury, 1926.

Turner, H. J. M., ed. *The Epistles of St Symeon the New Theologian*. Oxford: Oxford University Press, 2009.

Turretin, Francis. *Institutes of Elenctic Theology*, Volume I. ed. James T. Dennison, Jr. Phillipsburg, NJ: Presbyterian and Reformed Publishing Company, 1992.

Viola, Frank, and George Barna. *Pagan Christianity? Exploring the Roots of Our Church Practices*. Carol Stream, IL: Tyndale House, 2008.

von Rad, Gerhard. *Old Testament Theology, Volume I: The Theology of Israel's Traditions*. Louisville, KY: Westminster John Knox Press, 2001.

Vonier, Abbott. *The Life of the World to Come*. Bethesda, MD: Zacchaeus Press, 2010.

Wainwright, Geoffrey. *Doxology: The Praise of God in Worship, Doctrine, and Life*. New York: Oxford University Press, 1980.

Walls, Jerry, ed. *The Oxford Handbook of Eschatology*. New York: Oxford University Press, 2008.

Ware, Kallistos. *The Orthodox Way*. Crestwood, NY: St. Vladimir's Seminary Press, 2002.

Welker, Michael. *God the Spirit*. Minneapolis, MN: Fortress Press, 1994.

Wilkinson, David. *Christian Eschatology and the Physical Universe*. New York: T & T Clark, 2010.

Witherington III, Ben. *Making a Meal of It: Rethinking the Theology of the Lord's Supper*. Waco, TX: Baylor University Press, 2007.

Witherington III, Ben, ed. *Luminescence: The Sermons of C. K. Barrett and Fred Barrett*, Volume II. Eugene, OR: Cascade Books, 2017.

Yong, Amos. *Who is the Spirit? A Walk with the Apostles*. Brewster, MA: Paraclete Press, 2011.

Young, Francis. *A History of Exorcism in Catholic Christianity*. London: Palgrave Macmillan, 2015.

Zizioulas, John. *Eucharist, Bishop, Church: The Unity of the Church in the Divine Eucharist and the Bishop in the First Three Centuries*. Brookline, MA: Holy Cross Orthodox Press, 2001.

Index